Daniel Liderbach

Why Do W

New Ways ....ding

PAULIST PRESS
New York/Mahwah, N.J.

Library of Congress Cataloging-in-Publication Data

Liderbach, Daniel, 1941–
    Why do we suffer? : new ways of understanding / Daniel Liderbach.
      p.   cm.
    Includes bibliographical references and index.
    ISBN 0-8091-3319-9
    1. Suffering—Religious aspects—Christianity.   2. Theodicy.
  I. Title.
  BT732.7.153   1992
231'.8—dc20   92-12767
                                                                          CIP

Published by Paulist Press
997 Macarthur Boulevard
Mahwah, New Jersey 07430

Printed and bound in the
United States of America

Contents

iv

To those teachers who most formed me:
Jean Dezort,
Timothy Kelley,
Frank Houdek,
Frank Smith, and
Joseph Wulftange

Preface

This book is the result not only of my own research and writing. It is also the result of my living within conditions that were conducive to writing.

The first such condition was provided when Canisius College of Buffalo, New York released me to write for a year. I spent the year in Germany, where I was free to do research and write.

A second condition was my interaction with individuals who assisted me in my inquiry into the theology of suffering.

In the primary position stands the late William V. Trowbridge, M.D., whose manner of dealing with suffering became a foundation for my reflections.

There are also scholars who graciously assisted me in research: three from Germany—Peter Steinacker of Wuppertal, Friedrich Mildenberger of Erlangen, and Wolfhart Pannenberg of Munich; one from Switzerland, Klauspeter Blaser of Lausanne; and one from Austria, Raymund Schwager of Innsbruck.

A third condition was my interaction with two fellow members of the Society of Jesus—a theologian, Joseph A. Bracken, and a poet, Francis J. Smith. They very generously read and criticized the manuscript before it was published.

Introduction

I. THEOLOGICAL POSTURE

Human suffering oppresses not only those who endure its weight, but also those who claim to believe in a God who is good and powerful. I believe in such a God; I therefore acknowledge the oppressive problem posed by human suffering.

First of all, the enigma of suffering is manifest in the complexity of the problem of suffering. On the one hand, human suffering slams its victims against the solid wall of the problem of evil. On the other hand, human suffering has transformed some of its victims into the most beautiful of human persons.

The problem of suffering thus began quite early on in my research to appear to me to be a paradox. That tonal color of suffering I have kept in focus as I have formulated my understanding about how one can confront suffering and yet believe in God.

Secondly, those who have reflected upon paradox in human experience have expressed their reflections in the language of images. Such persons as Martin Luther, William Shakespeare, W.H. Auden, and John Updike come to mind. Those who are even distantly familiar with the writings of those men are aware that they relied upon their imaginations to present their reflections. Paradox summons forth the language of the imagination.

The paradox of human suffering has summoned me similarly to use the language of imagination in presenting my own reflections. Thus I have chosen to rely more upon the language of imagination than upon the language of reason and analysis.

II. TERMINOLOGY

There will appear in this book a word that I have used both because of its denotation and because of its connotation. This word not only indicates a meaning; it also suggests an attitude and a value that express my conclusions Thus, as we begin, there is value explicitly to define that term.

"Numinous" is a word that was coined by Rudolf Otto in his seminal book, *The Idea of the Holy*. Otto had need of a word to refer to those occurrences within human experience that cannot be attributed to any known cause. Thus he chose to fashion such a word. He selected the Latin word *numen*, which conventionally has been translated as "the divine." Otto used that Latin word to fashion his new adjective, "numinous."

This latter word, "numinous," he then used to refer to those occurrences within human experiences that cannot be attributed to known causes. Although his explicit intention was to use this word to denote those events with no known cause, he used the word to connote the divine presence active within human experiences.

III. THE FIGURE OF JOB

The figure of Job from the Old Testament book of Job emerges in five different discussions in the book. If the reader asks why Job recurs so often, then the function of Job in this book needs to be explained.

Job is the mirror image of each human. Like each of us, Job is confronted by an unexpected suffering, but is left without any comprehension about why he suffers. As for us, so for Job suffering and the God who stands behind suffering remain always incomprehensible.

Job's mirror image of human suffering shatters, however, in the story of Job's suffering as having significance in a cosmic drama acted out by God and the figure of Satan. The suffering of each human person cannot be resituated within such a context that renders our suffering somewhat significant.

On the other hand, Job had not learned anything about that cosmic drama. When the voice from the whirlwind addressed Job, it failed to explain anything about the wager with Satan. Instead it summoned Job not to understand his suffering, but to trust that God's superior wisdom was responsible. In this Job was being asked to respond in the manner that each human is asked to respond:

without comprehending why we suffer, we are asked to trust that there is a wisdom hidden within it.

This assessment of suffering is reinformed by Job in the power of his arguments against his four friends who insist that Job's suffering can be understood. Like us, Job was convinced that suffering cannot be reduced to a rational analysis.

Nor had Job's religious faith offered him any relief from his suffering. On the contrary, his faith, which was personified in the voice from the whirlwind, insisted that religion asked that the victim endure suffering in passive ignorance.

Job does illumine one facet of suffering for us: he insisted that suffering cannot be caused by sin. Thus, he summoned us to liberate ourselves from the self-induced guilt which assumes that we suffer because we have sinned.

IV. A SCHOLARLY CHAPTER

This book might be read by two distinct groups of individuals. Some might read the book out of their desire to answer questions concerning human suffering. Others might not only desire to answer such questions, but also hope to situate the contribution of this book within the scholarly dialogue concerning human suffering.

Those who have no interest in the scholarly dialogue might prefer to ignore the fifth chapter. There I have concentrated the effort to enter into the scholarly dialogue. I have written the other chapters in such a manner as to keep them generally free from such academic concerns.

Those who read not only to answer questions concerning suffering but also to situate the book within the scholarly dialogue will be satisfied in their second desire by attending not only to the chapters in which the question of suffering is addressed, but also to Chapter 5.

1

Evil as a Human Occurrence

Sensuous images abound in *La Dolce Vita,* Federico Fellini's 1960 film-probe of the decadent life of modern Rome. One of those sensuous images is still used in film ads today—Anita Ekberg, her magnificent shoulders completely bare, dances seductively in Rome's Tivoli Fountain. However, the image that has continuously remained in the forefront of my memory, even after thirty years, is not that, but a completely non-sensuous one.

The image is a scene in the late evening. A well-dressed man sits in the luxury of his Roman apartment. He rises from his chair and walks into the bedroom of his two little children. Walking to the bedside of the two sleeping children, he draws a pistol. Aiming carefully, he fires bullets into the heads of the two sleeping innocents.

Though the specific motive for those murders is no longer available in my memory, the general motive is clear—the father could not tolerate the thought that the evils of Roman decadence would smash into his beloved children. So he removed his children from life.

Suffering weighs upon the shoulders of every human. Each person is thus uniquely able to identify those at-hand events that have unraveled the order that one had vainly hoped to find in life. The experience of suffering has so weighted every shoulder that we find ourselves to be no longer agile; many are no longer able to direct life toward their authentically chosen goals.

There is no need here to identify for an individual those occurrences that that person has experienced as immediate and personal encounters with suffering: the failures in self and in others, the undeserved illnesses, the deaths that struck down persons who while alive had inspired hope, the betrayals of trust, the deceptions, and those other experiences that appear to erode the paths along which each had hoped to direct one's life. Each individual without any assistance can identify the specific evils that he or she has encountered in life.

Because each person bears one's own suffering upon one's own shoulders, each is the unique seer who alone can address the question of the meaning of that burden of suffering which he or she bears.

Nevertheless, there is an abundance of reflective, scholarly writing on the problem of evil. Those scholarly efforts to discern a resolution for that problem reveal to one who reads them that the problem of evil is a watershed. In formulating a response to evil, scholars fashion hypotheses on the meaning of human life. I too fashion my own hypothesis.

VARIOUS THEOLOGICAL WORLDVIEWS

More general approaches to the problem of evil are the theologies of monism and dualism.

Monism envisions the universe as a harmonious unity. Within that unity, monists situate evil as integrally bound up with the divine purposes for the universe. The starting point for monism is to fashion an interpretation of the world which acknowledges both the goodness and the power of God. Monism proposes a worldview that attempts to integrate belief in the one God with everything in the world, including the evil that is found within the universe.

The weakness of monism's interpretation is that it can appear so to domesticate evil within the divine plan that evil can no longer appear as forbidding. Thus, that which had been a problem to be solved can appear to be dissipated as it is integrated into the divine plan. Thus the analytical approach to evil by monism does not appear to be acceptable.

Dualism, on the other hand, insists that good and evil are utterly and irreconcilably opposed to one another. This radical tension will, according to the dualists, remain until either good overcomes evil or evil overcomes good.

Extreme dualists, such as Zoroaster (born c. 1000 B.C.E.), Mani (born c. 215 C.E.), and the Albigenses (twelfth and early thirteenth centuries C.E.) so interpreted dualism that the dualistic universe required two deities, one good and the other malevolent.

Moderate dualisms, e.g. Plato (c. 428 to c. 348) and John Stuart Mill (1806–1873), propose that there is a single, benevolent divine being who is not infinite, but finite in power. Thus the divinity is unable to prevent evils from marring the universe. This deity stands over against an independent realm of chaos and intractable matter.

The starting point for this form of dualism is that there can be no resolution of the tension between good and evil. That tension always remains; it therefore requires a dualistic interpretation of all that is.

In either case there is a problem with dualism's analysis of evil. Both forms of dualism conclude that God cannot be wholly and unqualifiedly good. This follows first from dualism's claims that God is good, that aside from God there is a source of evil in the world, and that God struggles with that source without being able to overcome it. Secondly, the problem follows from dualism's suggestion that the world results from the nature of God. The good God has made the world. However, then the problem arises— namely, the good God struggles against that part of the world that is evil. Thus, God is not entirely good: the evil as well as the good in the world has been created by the Godhead.

This book, as a result of my worldview, is located firmly in the school of monism. It begins with the belief that there is one God and that this God allows both good and evil to occur in the universe. The belief assumes that God's purposes and projects are being achieved as much in the negative occurrences within the world, such as suffering, as in the positive occurrences. It develops its understanding of the relationship between God and evil with both theological and phenomenal sensitivities. Thus it avoids the trap that generally catches monism: monists are often too cerebral, too removed from the anxiety of the human experience of evil.

Particular monistic approaches to the problem of evil are the theologies of Augustine of Hippo and Irenaeus of Lyons.

Augustine's fundamental interpretation of evil was that it is a privation of good stemming from misused freedom. This position had been the approach of the neo-Platonist Plotinus, whom Augustine had carefully studied and whose thinking he had faithfully integrated with his own.

The basic privation of good for Augustine was the moral evil which resulted from Adam's misuse of free will in primordial history. That evil had been inherited by each individual historical person.

There were, however, other evils according to Augustine's perspective. There were divine punishments for the misuse of free will; there were evils which were consequences of the various chosen manners of living. This variety of such choices that Augustine had acknowledged reveals that Augustine considered the universe, in spite of its evil, to be versatile, rich, and valuable.

Thus, according to Augustine, God sees all things, including evil and sin, as combining to form a wonderful harmony for the world. Consequently, evil detracts neither from the harmonious beauty of the world nor from the sovereignty of the good God.

However, Augustine's analysis of evil demonstrates the typical weakness of monistic approaches to the problem. In order to defend the goodness of God, Augustine's doctrine of "the privation of good" makes evil appear no longer to be evil. Monism often so suggests that evil is not the problem that every human finds that it is empirically. Nevertheless, Augustine had himself encountered empirically the power of evil to destroy; he had therefore sought to resolve that problem. Evil had not been for Augustine merely the absence of something else; it was a reality which had terrified him with its power.

Thus, there is a serious weakness in Augustine's analytical approach to the problem of evil.

Because Augustine lived at an early and more plastic stage in the development of the Christian tradition and the growth of the Christian mind and because his work was peerless in its time, his thinking had exercised and has continued to exercise a monumental influence upon the Christian tradition. Very few Christian thinkers in the west, even in the present, can claim with accuracy to be independent of Augustine's thought. His monistic interpretation of evil and suffering continues to influence the Christian tradition.

Irenaeus assumed an imaginative point of view. His perspective was more humane and compassionate.

Irenaeus was born approximately in 130 C.E. in Asia Minor, where he was a disciple of Polycarp of Smyrna, who had known the apostles of Jesus. Irenaeus died in approximately 202 C.E. in Gaul at Lyons, where he had been bishop. Thus Irenaeus had lived long before Augustine, i.e. before the era which had conventionalized its interpretation of the problem of evil, and as a result he had been able to fashion a creative theology without the restraints of tradition. Nonetheless he apparently used the works of Justin Martyr and Theophilus of Antioch.

The foundation of his theology was that all humans have been created as imperfect, immature creatures who need to undergo moral development and growth. They need to grow so as to become sensitive and responsive to the Spirit of God who is active within them. Then they can be brought to become the good humans that their maker intended them to become.

Thus the fall of Adam and its consequences were interpreted by Irenaeus not as utterly malignant and catastrophic events in the history of humanity. That would be the vision which Augustine would fabricate. For Irenaeus, the fall of Adam had not completely disrupted God's plan. Rather, Irenaeus envisioned the fall as human, i.e. as understandably and predictably the result of human weakness and immaturity.

Similarly, life's trials are not, as they would be for Augustine, divine punishments for sin. Rather, Irenaeus proposed that the troubles and anxieties of our world provide the divinely appointed environment in which humans can develop toward a responsiveness to Spirit that is the fulfillment of God's purpose for humans.[1]

This interpretation of the meaning of evil has provided a preview to the theology of suffering that I will eventually develop.

Long ago Clement of Alexandria (d. 220 C.E.), Methodius (d. 311 C.E.), and Gregory of Nazianzus (d. 389 C.E.) had based their theologies upon that of Irenaeus.

However, we need not rely upon the problem as it has been developed by one or other scholar in a manner that may appear distant and academic. Let me propose a particular, concrete experience to serve as a stimulant to reflect upon each one's experience of evil.

A man died.

That death was externally conventional. Death's blade fell, as it always does, without concern for the needs of those who depended upon death's victim. The man's wife lost her spouse. His young children powerlessly lost the protection of their father. These might have been told that the earth is not stable beneath anyone's feet; yet, people generally assume such stability. That family, like every family, had relied upon the stability and security that the father had provided. Death had destabilized them. There was no court of appeals; the man died.

At such times one of the overwhelming questions is not so much why this particular tragedy occurs, but why the survivors had been so foolish as to assume that the ground under them had been stable. That death had the effect of making that ground appear henceforth always unstable: life was thus situated within the context of the fragile.

Previously the family had assumed that their chosen goals were attainable, provided that they dedicated themselves to those goals with a generous degree of discipline, concentration, and self-sacrifice. Now, as death swept through the family, they discovered that every goal was fragilely contingent.

EUCLID AND EINSTEIN

Death and evil occur within the context of a physical world. The Greek mathematician Euclid had envisioned the context of the world by fantasizing a two-dimensional world in which all problems are soluble by means of reason and analysis. A Euclidean mind is a mind which has assumed that a rigid logic determines every occurrence. The Euclidean mind regards the evil events in the world and concludes from logical reasoning that a person cannot respond positively to a God who permits such evil to occur.[2]

However, the world is not two-dimensional; it is constituted by more dimensions than humans have as yet been able to imagine. Thus those individuals who allow themselves to regard the world from the Euclidean perspective are seeing through a pair of spectacles which distort the occurrences within the world.

Ivan Karamazov in Fyodor Dostoevski's *The Brothers Karamazov* can be considered to be a model of the Euclidean mind.

Ivan Karamazov, a man with broad experiences of the world, was visiting his brother Alyosha who had chosen to dedicate his innocent life to God. Ivan poignantly asked how Alyosha would resolve the problem of evil that he, Ivan, had encountered.

Children's suffering was the form of evil upon which Ivan

focused. He cited a specific instance of it. An eight year old serf boy had thrown a stone at a dog which belonged to a general. When the general learned that the boy had thrown a stone at his dog, he had his dogs tear the boy apart before the eyes of the boy's mother. That suffering of an innocent child enraged Ivan.

Then he analyzed the justice of that evil with his Euclidean mind; he deduced that the general should have been punished. Under no circumstances could Ivan's logical mind endorse the justice expressed by the mother of the slaughtered boy; she had praised God: "Thou art just, O Lord, for thy ways are revealed." Rather, logical order and clarity demanded that the general be tortured in a manner more vicious than that by which he had tortured the boy.

There are, indeed, many persons with such Euclidean minds; they perceive all of life's experiences with the clarity and logic of Ivan. That mind finds many such examples of injustice. That mind is often, therefore, enraged at the God who for any reason whatsoever has permitted the innocent to suffer.[3]

The image of a God who allows such suffering enrages every Euclidean mind. Such an image of God even now enrages those many persons who assume that life can be comprehended with the clarity of the Euclidean hypothesis: every event can be reduced to a neat, logical plane. Many assume that the solutions to all problems can be derived in that simple and solid certitude. Each of us shares to some extent Ivan's clean approach to justice: we demand that those who have either allowed or caused the innocent to suffer be forced to accept their logically appropriate punishment.

However, Euclid's fantasy needs to be corrected or at least balanced by an approach to life that is imaginative. The individual who hopes to comprehend life holistically needs always to address life with imagination as well as with analysis. Critical indeed is the need for a holistic worldview, i.e. a perspective which includes as many dimensions of the world as possible. Such a perspective may tend to be ambiguous and less than certain. However it is appropriate for the world in which we find ourselves.

Albert Einstein so addressed the physical universe. He acknowledged that in thus reflecting he was enabled to perceive not the universe of fantasy, but the world in which we live. He discovered the world to be a multi-dimensional complexity. In such an actual world, reason and analysis were no longer adequate. Thus, the Euclidean mind is inadequate for the complexities of the world. Einstein's mind used an intuitive imagination in order more adequately to comprehend that world. This mind, the Einsteinian mind, which is trustingly vulnerable to images, seeks to defend the goodness and wisdom of the world, even in the face of the destruction effected by evil.

Dostoevski's image of the mother's trust reveals that Dostoevski had such a vulnerable approach to life.

Similarly, Augustine of Hippo, a monist in his approach to evil, defended the goodness and wisdom of God. Augustine too had remained conscious that, to reflect about evil, he had to remain aware of many dimensions. He interpreted evil as the privation of a good. Thus evil was for him not something that diminished the goodness of the world, but simply an absence. He insisted that the goodness of God's creation remained inviolate. However, humans choose to turn away from good and to select that which lacks goodness; such choices destroy the goodness that God had created.

Moreover, because Augustine had so trusted in the goodness of all of God's creation, he had assumed that evil must be a necessary element in a universe which is wholly good. God alone is able to contemplate the aesthetic beauty of the entire universe. From the perspective which sees the world's beauty, so Augustine argued, every occurrence, even occurrences that appear evil to the human mind, contribute in different ways to the perfection of the universe as a whole. The evil occurrences, which are not evil in God's perspective, are integral for the beauty of the whole.

However, the human mind, confined in its contemplation of the universe to particular space and time, can regard occurrences only in limited contexts. In such contexts an occurrence can appear to be evil because its contribution to the whole of the universe cannot be observed.

More twentieth century thinkers have shared in Euclid's perspective than in Einstein's. With logical sensitivity they assume that that which appears to the senses is that which is so. Thus they have criticized the trusting, Einsteinian minds' defense of the present form of the world. Such trusting minds tend to prefer the present form of the world as appropriate. For example, in the present form of the world humans are able to choose; they are therefore able not only to offend, but also to love.

However, those who reflect with the Euclidean mind reject the value of a world which permits evil as a condition for love. They assess as categorically unacceptable any evil, even evil as a condition for loving or for turning from love.

So they desire to cut adrift the trusting, vulnerable minds by the following caricature of those who defend the goodness of creation: a good God would make the world to be a hedonistic paradise for humans. Euclidean minds envision God to be like a pet-keeper who should build cages for the pets so that they are safe from every insecurity. These minds then denounce the actual world because of the lack of security experienced by its creatures.

This is superficial scratching.

It ignores the profound vision of Irenaeus (120–202 C.E.). Irenaeus proposed that the purpose of the world is "soul-making." The world is a place for forming the higher potentialities of the human personality. This, he argued, would be impossible in a world that contained no pain or suffering. Without evil the more heroic human virtues would not be able to be formed within the world, but people would remain passive.

The trusting, Einsteinian mind cannot but acknowledge that these Euclidean thinkers have a problem with evil as a humanizing event. Euclideans naturally assume that there is no such effect; they cannot with Euclidean certitude discover specific positive effects in those specific human lives that have been shattered by evil's effects. The Einsteinian mind, however, will not assume that the multidimensional world has only those effects that the human mind can know with certitude.

Clearly, the Einsteinian trust in life and the Euclidean mind's logic about life are the classic approaches to the problem of evil. That problem can be stated as the demand by the powerless to know why the events of life are beyond human control. Alternatively, the problem is the futile effort to protect one's life and the lives of loved ones from tragedy. Or it is the vulnerable human insecurity before the random attacks of life's destructive forces.

The trusting response to the problem is to rely upon the goodness of God, while at the same time acknowledging the occurrences of evil in the world. The problem of evil results from the consequent tension: How could a good God be expressing divine love in the tragic destruction of human lives?

2

Reflecting Upon Evil

The humans who seek to comprehend the world must assume that there are occurrences within the world that are more complex than human understanding can grasp. As Albert Einstein had envisioned, the world's material events occur in a complexity of more than four dimensions. Thus, because humans seek to comprehend non-material events which are partially made up from material events, humans seek to comprehend events which occur in a complexity of more than four dimensions.[1] Yet human understanding is only capable of articulating itself in a language that expresses a four-dimensional worldview.

There is a value here to try to imagine that problem: How does one envision a material occurrence within the actual world? For example, Einstein envisioned triangles not in two dimensions, but upon the multi-dimensional globe. He discovered that triangles then have more than one hundred and eighty degrees. Thus the realistic, Einsteinian mind discovered that the world is quite different from that which it had been found to be by the logical, Euclidean mind.

So, too, Einstein then used his imagination to describe the path of an object traveling the shortest distance between two points in actual space. He discovered that the shortest distance between two points is not a straight line, but a geodesic. That is, the realistic, Einsteinian mind had again discovered that the world is quite different from the world which the logical, Euclidean mind had assumed it to be.

Einstein's general relativity has thus made humans aware that we live in a physical universe that is so complex and so far beyond the range of our mind's images that we must approach it with expectant wonder, rather than with the assumption that the world's occurrences are in a harmony of logic.

Nevertheless, the human intellect tends to proceed on the assumption that, because the human mind can grasp only four dimensions, there are only four dimensions. The intellect assumes that that which fits into the structural capacity of human logic is in itself so fitted.

Consequently, when humans conclude from evil occurrences that there is no God, they overlook a critical piece of data: there are a great many human persons who respond to evil events by rejecting the conventional wisdom that finds no value in evil. They judge that there is something, or someone, or a kind of presence within the world, even within evil events, that is not restricted to the world bound by sense data. There appears to be in their consciousness an ideal of a goodness that they have not observed within sense experience.

This consciousness of a non-empirical value within the world deserves to be introduced into the discussion of the problem of evil.

Even in the midst of evil occurrences, these persons appear to be conscious of a goodness in the world, of a world far better than that which they sensuously experience.

The Euclidean mind, however, finds in the world bound by sense data no evidence for God and thus balks at an acknowledgment that there is a non-sensuous goodness or such a non-empirical presence within the world.

A plausible explanation for the awareness of that presence is that the human consciousness is formed only partially by the experience of the senses, but partially by the numinous traces of a non-sensuous goodness.[2]

Those who have studied Karl Rahner's "supernatural existential" will have realized that many persons have indeed glimpsed such a non-empirical presence within their experiences. For example, some have discovered resolutions to their psychological tensions, though the occurrences within the world may suggest that there are no such resolutions. Others have rejected the inevitability of death and defended this by claiming that they were vaguely conscious that there is more to human life than they had experienced. Others have hoped in the midst of despair and defended this hope by claiming that they were vaguely conscious that there is more to human life than the surrounding gloom.

Nevertheless, the source of evil remains a most serious human question. Evil continues to appear and to confront humans.

THE BOOK OF JOB

The author of the book of Job confronted the problem of evil by directly acknowledging its incomprehensible questions.

The author of Job lived in the era of Persian dominance over Israel, i.e. the fifth to the fourth centuries B.C.E. Thus the poet was face-to-face with a severe tax that Persia had levied on Israel. That tax had been driving the poor of Israel into spiraling poverty. They had lost their farms, their wine presses, their homes, and eventually they lost access to any means of production. Some had thus sold their children into slavery in order to pay that tax.

The creditors for these poor were the aristocrats of Israel, those "lawless and godless" Jews who flourished as a result of their consuming the property of the poor.

The poet of the book of Job thus placed Job in a context similar to the actual context of the contemporary Jews. There the "lawless and godless" flourished, while Job, a righteous, generous, and pious man, had fallen precipitously into ruin.

Within that context the people of Israel had faced a "crisis of wisdom": they no longer knew who spoke for God. The authors of Israel's wisdom tradition had developed a theodicy, but had failed in that to explain how God was still being good to the Jews oppressed by the tax.

The long dialogue between the "friends," fashioned by the poet of the book of Job, imitated not the Jewish, but the Babylonian theodicy of Saggil-kinam-ubbib. The purpose of that dialogue was to probe for the justice of God in relation to the suffering of the righteous poor.

The poet concluded the book by asserting that the problems of the poor in his time could not be solved. There was no stopping the "lawless and godless" from prospering. Nor was there any halting of the poor and righteous from plummeting into ruin.

The poet went so far as to envision God as defending that situation (Job 38–41). His God argued that the human mind could not comprehend the wisdom that God was using to direct world events under the Persians.

Nonetheless the poet of the book of Job fashioned a brilliant work. He grounded the human dialogue of his book upon the questionable assumption that God is protecting from significant evil all those who deserve divine love. Job was one who deserved God's love. However, Job had encountered just the contrary.

THE STORY OF JOB

The poet imagined the story of Job to have begun at a session of the divine assembly. There God had called Satan's attention to Job's unequaled probity and piety. Satan had questioned the disinterested character of this piety and suggested that Job, bereft of his material blessings, would curse God to his face. This wager was accepted by God. God granted Satan permission to test Job by any means short of an assault on his person. Thus the trials of Job commenced.

All that Job had acquired was then taken away from him. A raiding party of Sabeans attacked his oxen and asses and carried them off; moreover, they slaughtered the servants who had been watching over Job's cattle. A bolt of lightning struck among Job's sheep, burned the sheep, and destroyed the shepherds. The Chaldeans raided and carried off Job's camels and slew the servants who had watched the camels. On a day on which all of Job's sons and daughters were assembled in the house of the eldest son, a great wind struck the house and brought the structure down upon those who were there. All were killed.

These tragedies occur at the very beginning of the book of Job. They focus the problem of evil: a good God had allowed a good person to suffer the loss of all that was most valued.

In the next thirty-seven chapters of the book a human dialogue is developed concerning the problem of evil. Job concludes that he must reject the conventional wisdom which understood suffering as the punishment for sin.

Then in chapter 38 the poet envisioned a voice from "out of the whirlwind" to address Job and the other dialogue partners. The voice cautioned Job, his friends, and us not to assume that God shares in the conventional wisdom—God is not limited by the law that requires the divine one to protect good persons from all harm, but punish only those who had sinned.

Nonetheless, so the voice argued, humans must not assume that suffering gives humans the license to question God's justice, as

Job had done. The divine voice refused to submit to questioning but rather criticized Job because he had challenged the divine power and providence. Thus the poet of the book presented no satisfactory, rational answer to the evil of suffering.

THE REQUIREMENT TO TRUST

Humans are thus thrown back not on wisdom, but on faith in the God who wills, faith in the God who refuses to submit to human questioning. Confronted by the actions of this God, humans have no defense. Moreover, any hope that a person might have put in anyone or anything other than this first and last divine one was vain. All relational or rational efforts to explain evil were futile. The only response to questions about suffering was trust in God, though that trust is not possible without moral struggle and spiritual agony.

This struggle and agony occur especially when devoted servants of God are oppressed by apparently random tragedies. Because even these devout humans cannot know how God works out the divine purpose, they are abandoned to a mental struggle and agony.

Furthermore, in a more radical statement the author of the book of Job denies that believing in a God who is good has any relationship with experiencing evil in human life. God is indeed envisioned by the poet as good; nonetheless, God's goodness is envisioned as beyond the range that the human intellect can comprehend. Thus, while the poet casts God in an aura of goodness, the poet also depicts that God as choosing to allow evil. The author of Job proposes that God acts for purposes and goals that only God can comprehend. The meaning of the evil and of the suffering that humans encounter remains within the unsearchable darkness.

SUFFERING AS A CRISIS FOR FAITH

However, because human minds have continued to search for meanings of such experiences, the doctrine taught by the author of Job has appeared to be unacceptable. Humans insist upon the right to know why they must encounter an experience which they would never choose. A God who hides the significance of the encounter with evil and suffering is so intolerable that many humans have decided to ignore such a divinity.

This rejection of the God who hides divine meanings has consequently led some also to insist that, if such a God did exist, then such a God could not be good.

TRUST IN SPITE OF EVIL

This lack of faith results largely from the shadow cast by the divine choice to hide the meaning of evil. Some humans suspect that such hiding by God implies that this God is embarrassed by divine powerlessness.

There is for some a measure of comfort in non-theistic, paradoxical theses that resolve human enigmas. The Buddhists, for example, resolve the problem of evil with the paradoxical doctrine that everything in life is illusion.

Evil and suffering within the world lead others to conclude that there is no god.

Alternately, the agnostic might conclude that God is treating humans as pawns in a divine strategy, perhaps as playthings for a divine duel with evil. Job's God, for example, is engaged in a courtly duel with Satan. This God appears to be far removed from personal concern for human anxieties. Thus that God consequently appears to be something other than a personal divinity.

This rational reflection might tend toward boredom: human reason spins irresolutely in reflecting upon the problem of evil.

NEED TO LOCATE GOD IN FOG

Consequently, when reasonable humans, even theists, address the problem of evil, they need initially to acknowledge that God is shrouded in fog.

3

Suffering: A Form of Evil

A fisherman can find that the line on his reel has become so knotted that he can do nothing else but cut the line. The problem of evil can appear to have become so complex that it resembles the impossible knot on the fishing reel. The problem is so impossibly complex because of its apparently haphazard dimensions: one dimension of pain, another of failure, a third of God's agency, yet another of cause, still another of lost purpose, and others that may be identified by students with different perspectives.

One of these dimensions, however, is the evil that is human suffering—every human person can identify particular experiences of suffering in his or her life. Thus, this third chapter narrows the focus to center upon suffering as an evil that has repeatedly driven persons to search for some meaning in the burdens of life. Each suffering person seeks to unravel the mysterious web that results when suffering entwines with the other experiences of life.

One such focus upon human suffering could be pain. Pain is a physical sensation.

The human experience of pain introduces suffering, which includes with pain a psychic anguish.

Classical suffering stands at a great distance from normal suffering. For example, the sufferings portrayed as experienced by Jesus and Job have been interpreted as suffering on an epic scale.

The suffering that normal human beings endure is far different from that. Human suffering is not generally experienced as epic in scale. This chapter distinguishes between the epic form of suffering, such as that of Jesus and Job, and the commonplace suffering of other persons. The commonplace victim encounters suffering while the world carries on its business: healthy persons continue with their engagements, pausing long enough to do little more than notice that one or other individual happens to be absent.

22

THE EPICS OF SUFFERING

However, the myth of the suffering of Jesus portrayed all human persons as reconciled with God because of Jesus' suffering. His suffering had epic significance. Because he suffered, all humans are able to hope to be with God in bliss forever.

Clearly, cosmic wheels had turned.

The epic myth of Jesus' suffering seeks to reassure humans that their suffering, which can be united with that of Jesus, has meaning.

The epic myth of Job is similar.

Job had lost all of his possessions, all of his children, his position within his community. Moreover, he was afflicted physically with piteous boils.

However, Job's most grievous suffering was that he found himself to be trapped within the proceedings of God's judgment without being able to understand why he had been trapped there.

Thus he pleaded to know why he had been indicted; he begged God to make some sense out of the torturous experiences that he had to suffer.

However, Job did not receive the satisfaction of having an indictment read against him; he had to suffer without knowing that there was a reason for his suffering.

That was the greater suffering of Job: he could not persuade the divine judge to reveal the indictment. When the voice from the whirlwind addressed Job in chapters 38 to 41, Job still did not learn the reason for his suffering. He still was unable to wrest from the divine judge whether there was a reason for his being indicted. The voice from the whirlwind was not a resolution of Job's problem. On the contrary, the voice confronted Job only with the right of God to remain eternally silent before the limited intellect of humans.

The author of the book of Job chooses to answer that question more modestly. The biblical author does not presume to know how God responds to those who are just, nor to those who are unjust. However, the author completely recasts the conventional Jewish mold: he resituates the problem within the context of trust. The person who strives to be just needs to trust God, although one may have no concept of why one ought to strive to be just and may seriously doubt that the effort to be just is a value.

The book of Job has proposed that the question cannot be

answered with rational analysis, as the Jewish wisdom had taught, but only with a trusting faith. Another manner of expressing that context is to say that the book of Job proposes that only those can resolve the problem who apply their imagination by trusting.

SUFFERING WITHOUT EPIC POETRY

However, to observe that people suffer without reason remains a cardinal torture for those who live in the twentieth century. Franz Kafka constructed his novel *The Trial* upon just that fundamental human anxiety.

Joseph K., whom Kafka envisions as suffering without reason, enters an empty cathedral, where he is addressed by a voice from the cathedral.

In contrast with the advice that the voice from the whirlwind offered to Job, the voice from the empty cathedral urged Joseph to use his reason to find the path that would lead him to a just resolution.

Thus, when two unidentified visitors later come to take K. away, he applies "the wisdom" learned from the voice. He assumes the position of a reasonable, autonomous human being and refuses to be arrested without knowing why.

The two visitors then murder Joseph K.

Franz Kafka has thus differed from the author of Job in his response to human suffering. Kafka has proposed that suffering is a mystery, that therefore reason provides no access to the enigma of suffering. In fact, when reason is so applied, it leads to disaster. In the case of Joseph K., the attempt to reduce the mystery of suffering to reason led to K.'s being murdered. Thus in the image of K.'s murder, suffering becomes even more of an enigma. Neither Joseph K. nor the reader knows why K. was murdered. Not only has Joseph K. been forced to suffer more as a consequence of his effort to use reason, but he has lost any hope of discovering why he had been indicted.

In the context of *The Trial*, that had been the acute suffering— K. had a psychological need to learn why he had been indicted. He dies without knowing whether there had been a reason for his arrest.

Kafka has thus insisted that reason cannot discover whether there is a reason for human suffering. Reason is in Kafka's vision unable to address the problem.

Thus Franz Kafka envisions the problem of suffering in this manner—the problem is so enigmatic that one cannot hope to find a resolution by using reason alone.

However, on another level, Franz Kafka and the author of the book of Job are in complete agreement. For both of them the acute pressure of the problem of suffering is not the pain. The pressure point is that one is forced into suffering without knowing whether or not there is any reason to have to suffer.[1]

Moreover, the earlier story of Job's effort to be open and good to all persons elicits from us an immediate sympathy; we identify him as a great human person who did not deserve to suffer. In Job's life there was nothing that deserved punishment.

Yet suffering closed its grip on him. Maybe he did not complain, did not curse God, did not blaspheme. However he did ask the human questions: Why me? Why now? What is God doing? Where is the justice that God is supposed to maintain in this world?[2]

The wisdom of ancient piety was unable to resolve Job's anguish. Job needed an answer appropriately tailored to the unique suffering that he bore.[3]

However, because Job's suffering was the result not of something appropriate to Job, but of a drama between God and Satan, because Job's suffering was caused not by himself, but by cosmic wheels, there was no answer appropriate to Job's suffering.[4]

Therefore Job was forced to wonder whether God had not made an error in administering his punishment. Yet the author portrayed Job as finally trusting that God makes no mistakes.

Indeed, the poet's "voice from the whirlwind" could offer Job no understanding appropriate to Job's unique experience of suffering nor to Job's questions. Hence Job was left to stumble through the confusion in which there was no clear path, no meaning.

As with Job, so with all who suffer, the victim feels deprived of the right to define oneself. Somehow the victim, like Job, has been abandoned to be thrashed by the whippings of the impersonal and anonymous power of suffering. Like Job, in his suffering the victim is left isolated. There is something terribly amiss in God's absence and silence.[5]

"The voice from the whirlwind" offered nothing that Job could interpret as an answer appropriate to his rage; he received no resolution for his fury at the world's injustice. Rather, the voice offered a piety and a worldview that appear to be naive.

Moreover, even though the poet imagined in the epilogue that God allowed Job to stand up again with the dignity that had been taken away and to live as he had previously, Job had not been allowed to receive any hint that might answer his intelligent questions about why he had suffered.[6]

Consequently, we have a right to be troubled by the poem, to object that Job had been too hasty in abdicating his right to comprehend his sufferings. Prior to his surrender to God in chapter 42, Job had appeared to be more like us. He was like us when he refused to be content to be cursed and stricken without knowing why. We are sorry to read that he had not continued uncompromisingly to insist that he would not accept his sufferings without an explanation. Would that he had continued to protest, to refuse the condescension shown by "the voice from the whirlwind." Or perhaps we could respect him if he had granted to the voice the right to deal with him as a master deals with a serf.

However, we do not respect Job's willingness to have allowed the voice to have destroyed his children for no known reason. We do not respect Job's assumption that his children would forgive the voice for their senseless murders.

However, Job submitted. The voice had so humbled Job that he accepted the whole of his suffering even without any comprehension of why he was accepting it.[7]

This was Elie Wiesel's interpretation of the suffering of Job as partially a model for our manner of enduring suffering and partially a model for how we ought not to respond to suffering.

However, though the solution to suffering offered by the author of the book of Job may be satisfying from the point of view of one who intends to defend the greatness of God, it overlooks the contemporary respect and reverence for the needs and the rights of the person.

After "the voice from the whirlwind" had humbled Job, there had been again in the supernal court a gathering of both the sons of God and those of Satan. God had then directed the attention of Satan to Job as a blameless and upright man who had continued to fear God even as he endured the loss of his possessions, his health, and his children. Job's suffering was woven into cosmic significance.

However, our human encounter with suffering appears to be far more irrelevant not only to the cosmos, but apparently to God, and certainly to the events that unfold beyond our sickbeds.

The corporation vice president who suffers a debilitating stroke soon becomes conscious that his business continues to function without his presence. His colleagues might have previously told him that he had been essential for the operation of the business. However, when suffering removes him from those operations, business continues to function without him.

Cosmic wheels fail to turn when this man suffers.

In our experiences of suffering the world goes right on with no more than a compassionate pause to note how sad it is that one or other person must suffer. Life goes on. Only in epic myths, such as the myths of Job or Jesus, do cosmic wheels turn as a consequence of a person's suffering. Moreover, those wheels turn in a poet's human imagination.

In our sufferings, on the contrary, no cosmic wheels turn because one of us has been yanked out of the processes of history. Suffering simply and indifferently pushes the afflicted person aside.

SUFFERING AS A CONSEQUENCE OF TORTURE

Humans suffered grievously in the concentration camps of the Third Reich. Viktor Frankl judged that one of the most grievous tortures there was the systematic dehumanization. Day in and day out humans were treated as chattel; thus they gradually lost any sense of individual dignity, lost the basic physical desires to maintain life, lost the dread of death. For example, the desires to satisfy hunger or to satisfy sexual drive evaporated. The prisoners became apathetic in defending themselves. They lost any sense of sympathy for others who suffered humiliations or beatings.[8]

Viktor Frankl survived years of imprisonment in four of those camps. In his capacity as a psychiatrist, he later analyzed the conditions that had enabled some prisoners to survive those camps. His conclusion was that those had been able to survive who had been

motivated to find a meaning in life, a meaning especially in the
dehumanization that was imposed within the camps.

The individual prisoners had searched for some concrete image
or symbol of meaning by which they could continue to motivate
themselves. Some prison inmates had found that meaning by imagining that some meaning clung to their then demeaned lives. Other
prisoners had imagined meanings based upon their memories; generally these had selected specific persons or projects that they desired
to retain as fixed centers for their lives.

A widower had fallen into depression because he had to face
life without his wife. Prior to her death the specific meaning that he
had discovered in the camp was a compassion for his wife. Because
she had died before him, he lost his meaning.

A mother was consumed with loathing for life's experiences
because her younger son, eleven years old, had died. Moreover her
older son was afflicted with infantile paralysis. She loathed the life
that had become her fate. The specific meaning that she discovered
was the image of herself in comparison with a woman who had had
no children and who thus faced an even greater emptiness.

Viktor Frankl himself had found that the specific image which
motivated him to stay alive was his desire to rewrite the scientific
manuscript that had been taken from him and destroyed when he
had first entered the concentration camp at Auschwitz.[9]

In each of these examples the meaning that the individuals had
discovered as motivating them to continue had been a sensible image which they could at any moment imaginatively bring to the
forefront of consciousness. These meanings were not vague hopes
that there might somewhere be a purpose for their staying alive. On
the contrary they were intuitive leaps of the imagination toward
specific visions.

Such suffering in the holocaust had inverted the Jewish meaning
of belief in God. The Jewish tradition of faith had developed a belief
that God works within the events of history. The Jewish Passover
feast of unleavened bread, the Seder meal, reinforces the belief that
God cares for "the chosen people" in every event of history.

However, the historical event of the holocaust had forced the
Jews to revise completely their interpretation of the meaning of that
belief.

Ignaz Maybaum, for instance, has reflected upon the holocaust in terms of the Hebrew word *churbam*, i.e. not divine care, but destruction in historical events.

The first such *churbam* occurred when the temple of Solomon was destroyed. Its effect was that the Jewish people became the people of the diaspora—a people with no land and no state.

The second such *churbam* occurred when the temple of Herod was destroyed. Its effect was that the Jewish people could no longer worship God with a prayer of sacrifice. After the destruction of the temple of Herod their prayer could no longer be acts, but rather words.

The third such *churbam* was the holocaust. Its effect is that the presence of God within historical events has come to be no longer a care, but a flaming and consuming divine wrath. God had used Hitler to change Jewish belief. Hitler had so orchestrated antisemitic hatred in Germany that "the Aryan race" would no longer permit the Jewish people to live among them.

Then Hitler had turned to other nations of the world to request that they adopt the Jewish people as refugees from Germany. Maybaum judged that, if God had been caring for "the chosen people" through the events of history, God would have moved some nation to adopt the Jewish refugees. However, no nation was so moved; each nation found that it was too occupied with its own problems to take in the Jews.

Consequently, Hitler settled upon "the final solution" for "the Jewish problem." Gradually the Jewish people began to realize the profound significance of that "final solution." Hitler had set about to exterminate the Jewish people from the face of Germany.

Meanwhile God failed to respond.

Thus, no longer could they believe that God cares for "the chosen people" through the events of history.

Many Jews then severed their relation with their previous belief. As a result of Hitler, God's herald, many Jews became secularized members of a secularized civilization. Many henceforth acknowledged their "holy land" as not a state on the coast of the Mediterranean, but as the future of humanity. There is nothing else that many Jews could any longer identify as sacred, no other future which such Jews could regard as their destiny. They could no longer confront the events of history with the confidence that God was there caring for them.

On the contrary, the event of the holocaust or "the day of the Lord," which Amos had foreseen, came not as light, but as darkness, judgment, and annihilation. Thus, the Jewish people may need to choose to step into that future which had been identified for them by the historical events of the holocaust. At least Maybaum found no other meaning for the traditional Jewish faith.[10]

Suffering in the holocaust had so inverted life for such Jews that they no longer hoped to find a meaning in a transcendent One.

A similar Jewish thinker who has reinterpreted the traditional Jewish faith since the holocaust is Elie Wiesel.

Born in Sighet, Hungary in 1928, Wiesel has in his books graphically narrated Germany's gradual tightening of the limits within which the Jews in Sighet were permitted to live. Eventually Germany had reestablished the old Jewish ghettos, which separated the Jews from others of the human community.

Then in 1942 the Hungarian secret police compelled the Jews of Sighet to abandon their ghetto and to surrender themselves to the police.

They were transported by train to a village which at that time was unknown to them: Auschwitz. There families and sexes were separated and imprisoned. Many of those Jews were not seen again. In the various cellblocks the Jews were deprived of food and forced to undergo physical and psychological tortures that civilized people of the 1980s find so unthinkable as to be unlikely.

Later that year Elie Wiesel, who was a strong boy of fourteen years, along with his father, mother, sister, aunts, uncles, neighbors and friends, were forced to make a death-march from Auschwitz to Buchenwald, a distance of more than a hundred miles.

Of all the members of his family and associates, only Elie survived. He had experienced the near annihilation of the Jewish people.[11]

Wiesel's question for Jewish belief has been how God was caring for "the chosen people" in the holocaust.

His questioning of God's ways is quite different from the conventional Jewish piety, which urged believers to trust that there is somewhere a vague purpose that God is accomplishing in all human experiences. Often this is expressed in such simple expressions as "This must be God's will."

CHRISTIAN JUSTIFICATION OF SUFFERING

That conventional Jewish theodicy has also been a Christian theodicy. The British Christian philosopher, Martin D'Arcy of Oxford, used that theodicy in his *Pain and the Providence of God*. D'Arcy proposed that Christians trust that the universe is a context in which life is worth living. This, he argued, is demonstrated by the millions of lives of those who have loved life. God has provided a desirable and worthwhile context for life. In that context the cost of so enjoying life is experiencing life's pains of growth. Those who grow have responded to events that create tensions within life. Without the pains of so struggling the enjoyment of human life appeared to D'Arcy to be impossible. Thus the world, as it is, even the world with evil, is the only world in which humans, as we know them to be, are fit to live. The defense of the goodness of God in that context is that God assists humans to enjoy that life by providing them with those natural occurrences with which they are made competent to respond to the tensions in life.

Human freedom is one such natural occurrence; humans are free to choose their attitude toward every event that they encounter, including the event of evil.

D'Arcy's criticism of that theodicy is his judgment that suffering is not simply a privation or an illusion. Conventional theodicy has claimed that suffering is a privation that can be solved by an attitude.

THE MORE GENERAL JUSTIFICATION FOR SUFFERING

However, such a theodicy is too far removed from the immediate concrete anguish of suffering. It seeks to resolve the immediacy of sensuous anguish by turning to the intellect; it ignores that the anguish of evil is endured by the sensuous spirit and body, not by the intellect.

Faced with the inadequacy of such an insensitive effort to resolve the problem, the reflective person needs to fashion a resolution for human suffering that is more sensitive experientially and psychologically.

Perhaps the resolution of Irenaeus of Lyons deserves to be cited again in this chapter. Irenaeus proposed that, in order to grow into the human persons that they can become, humans need to encounter the trials and sufferings of life. Those who respond to life's sufferings by growing in compassion, generosity, and self-giving have succeeded in growing into the likeness of God.[12]

This moral value of suffering can perhaps be appreciated by imagining humans in a world without human suffering. If there were no misery or anguish in the world, then one might find that there would be a correlative absence of those moral virtues that persons develop as they respond to suffering. Such a world might lack compassion, unselfishness, courage, and determination. Such a world might not be a world in which persons as we know them would choose to live.

Conversely, the world in which there is suffering has been the context in which some persons have become more humane as a consequence of their suffering; suffering can elicit human sensitivity.

Survivors of earthquakes have responded compassionately to those who had been victims. Similarly, survivors of war have sacrificed themselves with abandon to those who had been injured.

In Albert Camus' *The Plague*, Rieux was such a person. He appears in the book as a doctor who remembers a plague in which he had found himself, at Oran, a port city on the Mediterranean coast of Algeria. Residents in Oran are falling victim to the plague and dying. In his chronicle of the plague he recalls that, when the plague had struck, he was a citizen not of Oran, but of France. Consequently, he could have left Oran, returned to France, and preserved himself from the plague. He was also aware that, by staying in Oran, he would be able to do nothing significant enough to halt the plague.

Nonetheless, with his medical skills he was able to offer very modest, even if temporary, relief to victims of the plague.

Rieux chose to remain in Oran in order to do for the plague victims the very little that he was able to do. He chose to risk contracting the plague himself and to respond to the victims. He so chose not because of a reasonable hope of accomplishing anything significant or permanent, but because of an interior motivation to do that which he could for those in need. He chose to forego personal security and happiness. His wife he sent to a distant sanitarium, while he dedicated himself to compassionate work for those struck by the plague. He eventually judged that his efforts were having little effect. The plague's destruction of human life was too massive to be halted.

Yet he remained with the victims to do for them whatever he might be able to do.

Irenaeus envisioned such humans as Rieux to represent a value that there is in suffering. Because of suffering there appear persons of such moral fiber as Rieux; the human community is morally enriched by persons who have so encountered endowed suffering.

4

Theodicies of Suffering

The theodicy of Irenaeus argued that human individuals are unable to develop the moral strength that transforms them into better persons unless they encounter suffering. If they were so to live as never to suffer, then they would not have the accustomed stimulant to grow into human persons who can contribute to build the human community.

However, even the freshness of Irenaeus' approach to suffering has flaws.

First, it proposes that the resolution to suffering is moral development.

However, the person who acutely suffers may have lost, as a consequence of the pain experienced, the power of willing to direct his or her moral development. Suffering can so overwhelm the consciousness that the suffering one can lose the power both to focus conscious intentions and to respond.

Thus Irenaeus' intellectually oriented resolution of suffering fails to undo the web that can strangle those who suffer. There have been persons who have become mean, petty, angry, and resentful as a result of their suffering. In such persons Irenaeus' "soul-making" solution has not resolved the problem. For such victims of suffering, Irenaeus is able to offer no justification for the heavy weight of suffering.[1]

THE BIBLICAL JUSTIFICATION FOR SUFFERING

However, one can certainly propose an alternate approach to the problem of suffering. One can argue, in fact, that every human life is a mystery. In such an approach one needs to use not analysis, but imagination in reflecting upon life. Then there can be no rational resolution for suffering, other than to acknowledge that suffering is rationally incomprehensible.

The orientation of this wisdom is that God is able to observe all experience from the divine perspective, while humans cannot so holistically observe experience. Thus humans could not appreciate an explanation of how the whole of history fits together. Conversely, they could not appreciate an explanation of how evil fits into that whole.

That vision of wisdom is expressed quite powerfully in Isaiah 55:8-9:

> "My thoughts," says the Lord, "are not like yours, and my ways are different from yours. As high as the heavens are above the earth, so high are my ways and thoughts above yours. . . ."

This Judaeo-Christian folk wisdom insists that even if God's ways cannot be perceived or understood, nevertheless God acts decisively against evil. Consequently, God is the human hope in the face of evil.

Nevertheless, reflective believers have complained insistently that God still remains somehow responsible for the occurrences of evil.

The mystery becomes more dense.

The mystery is more dense in that the God who bears some responsibility for the occurrence of evil is also the God who acts decisively against evil. Because evil presents such a mystery, believers do not have the words appropriate to speak about either the causes or the meaning of evil.

An illustration of this fact of the mystery of evil is Matthew's portrayal of Jesus' refusal to tolerate evil. In Matthew 23 the evangelist portrays Jesus as vividly condemning the scribes and the Pharisees for their failure to relieve the burden of the Jewish law. Matthew's Jesus was there portrayed not as one who tolerated evil, but as one strenuously fighting against it.

Yet one can argue that the God of Jesus Christ had somehow been involved in every evil.

Thus suffering is enigmatic. Hence the human effort reasonably to comprehend suffering can only fail.

Some of those who are confronted by this mystery would be helped by myth, i.e. an imaginative addressing of experience. The imagination can approach suffering in such a manner that it resolves immediate anguish. Myth is not an approach that attempts to resolve suffering by intellectual complications.

Suffering persons sometimes find that many of those whom they confront during their suffering present themselves as knowing quite well how to deal with suffering. Yet the knowledge and skills of those persons tend to have little to do with the actual anxieties of the victim of suffering. That is, many of the persons who encounter the victim of suffering resemble the individuals who gathered around Job; they come to tell the victim that they comprehend why he or she is enduring suffering. Yet they have little capacity to be sensitive to the fears, anxieties, hopes, or needs of the afflicted person. As a result, the one who is suffering can experience himself or herself to be alienated from those persons.

There are other individuals who confront the suffering person from an entirely different perspective. Some insist upon regarding human suffering, even that which is caused by sin, as to some extent positive. Pierre Teilhard de Chardin so viewed the evil caused by sin.

TEILHARD'S ATTITUDE TOWARD SUFFERING

In Teilhard's worldview, as human persons become more human, the problem of sin becomes more acutely an obstacle for the process of human evolution. Just as the good effect of God's creating is the convergence of all matter in a great integration, so the evil effect of sin is the disintegration of matter in a random diffusion.

Nonetheless, there is a statistical need for sin in the process of evolution. This follows from the kind of process that evolution is: there is not a pre-determined path along which it proceeds; it needs to search out the various alternatives that may be suitable for human development. Humans use independence and freedom in contributing to this search for alternatives; they explore by means of "trial-and-error." Thus, sin, i.e. error, functions within the process of free human development. Only with the right to explore by means of "trial-and-error" can humans exercise their freedom.

Hence evil has become flesh. Evil has taken a functioning place within the evolution of human flesh.

However, God is able to use that evil of sin to achieve the good of evolutionary convergence to Omega point.[2]

However, that divine use of evil to achieve good was not the attitude of God toward the suffering that was portrayed in the gospel narratives. Jesus of Nazareth on the cross was portrayed by Mark and Matthew as apparently challenged to suffer alone. His only support was found in those very few friends who had stayed with him in his suffering. In the gospel of Matthew those few were Mary Magdalene, Mary the mother of James and Joseph, and the mother of the sons of Zebedee. The gospel of John includes among those at the foot of the cross the mother of Jesus, his mother's sister, Mary Clopas, and the beloved disciple. Only those beloved and loving persons were sensitive enough to remain with the suffering Jesus as he moved into death. However, there was no effort on the part of the evangelists to portray God as present to, nor as a comfort to, the dying Jesus.

In this Jesus represents the general pattern. Many of those who suffer must face their pain, anxieties, and fears alone.

However, those compassionate ones who remain with the suffering person and respect his or her competence as a human being suggest to the afflicted one that the experience of suffering, even the experience of moving toward death, is a human experience.

There have been persons who attempt to work out a worldview or explanation for those who suffer so that they can find meaning in their lives even after the devastation of suffering.

A classic example of this effort is the book *The Problem of Pain* by C.S. Lewis, who was a forty-two year old optimist.

IMAGINATION AND THE DISPOSITION TOWARD SUFFERING

The research that was done to prepare my book, however, belies that assumption. The person who reads that book by Lewis discovers an author who has made a grand assumption: every occurrence within human experience can be reasonably comprehended by a person who is willing to give sufficient concentration to the task of working out the rational relationships within experience. Based on that assumption, the author claimed to comprehend suffering within that intricate web of supports for human life that he had formulated with rational effort. The book is a rational masterpiece that had been fashioned by an optimist.

Nevertheless, C.S. Lewis drastically altered this assumption when he encountered acute personal suffering caused by the death of his beloved wife. Then the intricate web of supports for human life that Lewis had formulated with rational brilliance twelve years earlier came tumbling down. In its place there was nothing that could be identified as rational optimism.

This collapse into apparent nihilism is documented in Lewis' *A Grief Observed*, a collection of Lewis' reflections upon the utter mystery of suffering. He makes no reference in these later reflections to his earlier book, nor to his earlier assumption that every experience in life can be comprehended by reason if a person is willing to concentrate. However, in brilliant flashes of insight and in prickling images he sketches his glimpses of suffering as a mystery that he indeed could not comprehend.

There are many who share this vision of suffering with Lewis, i.e. many who are able to discover no rational meaning, but only mystery in the experience.

The purpose of this book is so to resituate the mystery of suffering within a context that will permit the mystery to remain indeed a mystery, but to be considered anew.

5

A Dialogic Introduction to Myth

A foundation for study of human suffering has been acknowledged to be human life; the broad problem of evil is the enveloping fog in which each individual passes his or her life.

Both the enigma of evil and that of suffering have frequently been approached along the path of reasoned analysis. However that path has been at least convoluted, if not also idealistic.

The study of human suffering might discover an appropriate line of approach in the reflections of more contemporary scholars. Thus, this study now turns its focus to the published works that provide the data for the scholarly work of the late twentieth century west.

This chapter will first turn to scholarly reflections upon the problem of evil, next to those upon the problem of suffering, and then to scholars' hypotheses concerning the method by which to approach those enigmas.

I. EVIL

A scholarly dialogue has focused upon the problem of evil. Not untypically, academic works have attempted to demonstrate that there is evil in the world.[1]

No such demonstration will be attempted in this manuscript. Each individual is presumed to be quite competent to point to his or her own experiences of evil.

A. *Mollification of Evil by Analysis.*

The personal conviction of the reality of evil can dialogue critically with the scholarly effort which mollifies evil by an intellectual analysis. For example it confronts the intellectual analysis by the neo-scholastic tradition.

At its high point neo-scholasticism identified with Thomas Aquinas' (1226–74 C.E.) analysis of evil—evil is the absence of that good which is natural and due to a thing.[2] Thomas further presumed that God had thereby achieved a greater good through the medium of the gradation of goodness that had been communicated to creation.[3]

That neo-scholastic tendency to mollify evil by analyzing its occurrence has continued even into the twentieth century.[4]

1. Apparent Values in Evil

Despite that apparently shallow analysis, that approach to evil has an unexpected depth, a surprising evaluation of life: humans in general find that the experienced world is a worthwhile place to live. Life is so worthwhile that humans generally resent death.

Perhaps human life becomes zestful as a result of its struggle against such natural dynamics as fear, sloth, and cheap love, i.e. against the dynamics correlative with evil. That is the only world that humans know as suitable for them to inhabit. Conversely, a world without evil might be so unsuitable for human habitation that humanity might there lose hope.[5]

Two reflections might here be made.

The neo-scholastic analysis has directed its concern less to the enigma and more to its own presumptions.

However, there might be an unexpected value in the mollification of evil.

For example, one evolutionary hypothesis has identified evil as a catalyst for transformation within the world.[6]

Furthermore artists have directed attention to the positive tones within the shadow of evil. Their myths value the experience of evil as enabling humans to develop.

The Greek myths of Oedipus, Ajax, and the Bacchae, William Shakespeare's *Macbeth*, and Fyodor Dostoevski's *The Brothers Karamazov* are imaginative expressions of human development effected by evil.

The artists' reassessment of the value of evil has been taken over by some scholars to resolve the problem of evil within their disciplines. The biblical myths of divine violence (the books of Numbers and Genesis include divine vengeance because of blood) and redemption (John's gospel claims salvation because of the murder of Jesus) were encounters with evil that effected positive development of the human community.[7]

Third, there is a trace of evil in generous self-surrender to another person in love. Yet that is more positive than negative.[8]

Thus there appears to be value in the enigma of evil. However there has emerged as yet only one manner in which one can so address that enigma that one discovers such value: one needs to be imaginative in situating oneself in relation to evil.

2. Evil's Inherent Value

Nevertheless, the interpretation of evil as having positive effects is not readily accepted.

A major objection is that it diverts attention from the actual effects of evil, which are humanly unacceptable. Those confronted by evil demand that the evil be removed.

There have moreover been radically negative conclusions drawn from the effects of evil.

David Hume concluded from the effects of evil that either God does not intend that humans be happy or the supposed architect of the world planned the world with nothing that can be compared with goodness or wisdom. The best that might be said of the God who permits evil to exist in the world is that God is entirely indifferent to all worldly occurrences.[9]

Albert Camus drew a different conclusion which is no less radical: one who refuses to accept the continued oppression of the human family cannot but shout a defiant "no" to the conditions that oppress humanity. Thus, Camus' Rebel defies the chaos, abuse and the God that human persons are forced to endure.[10]

Fyodor Dostoevsky's Ivan Karamazov is such a rebel, who had not denied the existence of God, but had summoned God to appear before the human court of moral virtue.

The flaw in the approach to evil taken by Camus and Ivan Karamazov is the assumption that human reason is capable of so analyzing evil that it can select the appropriate response to that enigma. However, the repeated failure by philosophical minds to analyze evil adequately suggests that evil is a mystery that cannot be analyzed.

Yet, there is color in Camus' human responsibility to remove evil, when it is compared with Friedrich Schleiermacher's contented analysis of evil. In the nineteenth century Schleiermacher concluded that there is evil in the world because human beings choose to structure their lives with behaviors that result in evil.[11]

That analysis of the evil in the world has been identified with the evil in the Old Testament. For example, the evil suffered by King David was the consequence of his adultery and murder in the Bathsheba–Uriah event (1 Kgs 1:6; 2:24).[12]

From a pastoral perspective the evil of suffering is a moral challenge to its victim: Is God present even within the experience of evil?[13]

The crux for belief in the face of evil is the passionate claim by some that evil demonstrates the non-goodness or even the non-existence of the Judeo-Christian God.[14] Others, however, claim that evil demonstrates human freedom. These urge humans to trust in the God hidden behind evil.[15]

B. A Tangent from the Problem of Evil

Moreover, the evil in the world renders the world more habitable for humans as they now are.[16] Yet the victim of evil has little interest in such hypotheses, but seeks to be relieved of evil.

Moreover human reflections on evil can never penetrate to God's inner counsels. That observation is most suitable in this chapter, which is surveying the scholarly analyses of evil. Evil will remain at least a paradox, at most a mystery.[17] The approach that humans might use to address evil is therefore not by way of reason, but by imagination.

C. Evil Not Reducible to Analysis

The rational comprehension of evil is based upon a specific assumption—namely, there is a harmony between the logical structure of the human mind and the actual occurrences within the world. Though the wonders of contemporary physics suggest that there is such a harmony, the universal human experience of intellectual frustration suggests the contrary: evil remains incomprehensibly beyond the range of intellectual analysis.[18] Thus, the human community has fashioned myths to identify the source of evil.[19]

That respect for the mystery of evil is seen in the anti-wisdom of the book of Job. That book urges humans to respect the mystery of evil. Neither poet nor philosopher is able to comprehend evil.[20]

Nonetheless there continue to be philosophical efforts to analyze the problem of evil. In the twentieth century there has been a "transcendental," intellectual analysis of enigmas such as evil.[21] Those who have read that analysis cannot but wonder why that analyst had so greatly reverenced Albert Einstein, but had not followed Einstein's example of approaching enigma not intellectually, but imaginatively.

Teilhard de Chardin erred in assuming that evil has a derivative value in stimulating human evolution.[22]

The critically reflective person might assume a position contrary to that. One might assume that the cloud of mystery casts its shadow across much of human experience and that therefore there is no manner in which logically to comprehend such shrouded experience. Consequently one cannot presume to grasp the purpose either for each occurrence or for the goals toward which experience is leading.

That orientation toward life as incomprehensible appears both in the gospel of Matthew and in an ancient Chinese folk tale.

Matthew envisioned life as mysterious:

> But now I tell you, do not take revenge on someone who does you wrong. If someone slaps you on the right cheek, let him slap you on the left cheek too (Mt 5:39).

The inverted meaning of this text suggests that rationally motivated behavior is out of place within the kingdom of God. In the kingdom one is to presume that the purposes and goals of existence can be grasped only by responsive behavior, not by analysis.

A similar respect for life's mystery is found in the old Chinese folk tale.

> A horse disappears. The owner of the horse is upset. There is a wise man who does not know that there is any reason to be upset. The horse returns, leading many horses into the corral of its owner. The owner rejoices; the wise man does not know that there is any reason to rejoice. A boy begins to entertain himself

by riding the horses and breaks his leg. His neighbors are upset; the wise man does not know that there is any reason to be upset. A war breaks out; all young men are drafted. However, the young man is still limping because of his broken leg and, therefore, does not have to go to war.

The folk tale envisions evil as a mystery that cannot be judged. The far-seeing person is the one who is able to discern that which is good and that which is bad—only God can so judge. Humans cannot comprehend the value of evil, neither the evil of being slapped on the face (Matthew's gospel) nor the evil of fleeing horses nor that of a broken leg (the Chinese tale).[23]

Evil needs to be acknowledged as a mystery.

Yet that evil is not to be tolerated while one observes that it threatens other persons. Thus Matthew's sermon on the Mount counsels:

> You have heard that people were told in the past, "Do not commit murder; anyone who does will be brought to trial." But now I tell you, whoever is angry with his brother will be brought to trial, whoever calls his brother "You good-for-nothing!" will be brought before the council, and whoever calls his brother a worthless fool will be in danger of going to the fire of hell (Mt 5:21–22).

Similarly the myth of Jesus having driven the money-changers out of the temple counsels that one is not to tolerate but to fight against the evil that threatens others.

Nonetheless, even one who fights evil cannot hope to comprehend its meaning and purpose.[24]

That is the only acceptable worldview for those who believe that they are encountered by God in every occurrence and every moment. The believer is challenged by that worldview both to endure personal evil and to resist the evil that threatens others. However because he or she believes that God weaves love into all of life and that love itself is a mystery, the believer cannot presume to be able to comprehend the meaning and purpose of the mysterious events of life.

The larger context of life for the believer is that God is encountering the person with love in every experience. Therefore the faithful ones leave themselves open to the mysterious occurrences of evil that encounter them in life, though these encounters cannot be comprehended, only imaged.[25]

II. SUFFERING

Thus far the chapter has introduced the scholarly dialogue concerning evil. Next it introduces the scholarly dialogue concerning human suffering.

A. Absence of Meaning in Suffering

An acute source of anxiety for the victim of suffering is the awareness that the creator God has failed to provide an evident meaning for suffering for those who must endure it. The creator can appear to be indifferent to the human need for meaning.[26]

Victims of the concentration camps of the Third Reich were aware of that anxiety. They might identify with Franz Kafka's portrayal of Joseph K. in *The Trial* and with the portrayal of Job in the book of Job; those are mirrors of contemporary victims of suffering. Like actual victims, those mythical victims had to endure problems and trials that appeared to them to be random accidents that had unjustly fallen upon innocent bystanders.[27]

Victims of suffering often so interpret their ordeals to be random accidents rather than justified punishments. Victims often perceive themselves to be violently pushed aside by the seemingly indifferent swipe of the force of evil. A malevolence interferes with their lives, disrupts the values that they had held, and exacts personal anxiety from them, who had been innocent spectators of life. Such suffering is entirely different from "the absence of being" that had been neo-scholasticism's definition of evil.[28]

Victims of suffering are conscious not of that metaphysical absence of being, but of a moral crisis. They find themselves confronted with a demand that they fashion a response to their suffering.

For example, Boethius (ca. 475–524 C.E.), the Roman statesman and philosopher, had found himself confronted by that demand. His imminent execution challenged him to find a disposition that might make his suffering more tolerable. It is less significant to know the attitude that he adopted, more important to recognize that suffering for him was a moral crisis, a demand that he assume a moral attitude.

The victims of suffering most often are confronted not by the metaphysical question of the meaning of being, but by the moral question of how to discover some meaning in the critical moments of suffering.[29]

However, that moral crisis is at times so sharpened that victims conclude that their anguish cannot possibly be the responsibility of a good God.[30]

The Old Testament hypothesis for suffering was that it is a consequence of sin. The suffering of King David was caused by his sins. The logical connection appears to be firmly argued in 2 Samuel 12:9–12. However, David, the victim, did not find that his suffering was any more tolerable because of its moral justice (2 Sam 12:16–18).

Similarly the victims of suffering in the books of Job and Jeremiah do not conclude from moral justice that a positive attitude toward their suffering is therefore available. They find the bite of suffering to be intolerable, even when they learn that the bite is a consequence of their own actions.[31]

B. Vain Search for the Purpose of Suffering

Nor does suffering as redemption appear to render suffering to be tolerable. The grinding crucifixion of Jesus of Nazareth was interpreted by his followers to have been God's action of redeeming the entire human community. Nonetheless, the linkage between the execution of Jesus and human redemption has always remained thin. Moreover, even those who endorse that linkage have not therefore been less repulsed by the crucifixion.[32]

In the same vein, suffering as a vehicle of God's purposes has not on that account appeared to be acceptable. Believers have not adjusted well to the demand that they suffer because of the mystery of God's will, i.e. of God's choice to achieve the divine purpose at the cost of human suffering.[33] That effort to justify the cost is far too removed from the payment; it expects the victim to evaluate himself or herself as nearly insignificant.

Yet there have been believers who have demonstrated an extraordinary degree of faith when they were encountered by suffering. One of these was Jakob Boehme, a German mystic in the early seventeenth century. Believing in the God who hides in the cross, he believed in the divine Spirit who conceals the divine self within such ambiguous occurrences as suffering. That Spirit was for Boehme both "the firm ground," i.e. the cause of all that is, and "the swamp ground," i.e. the source of negative experience. Boehme was no less confident of "the swamp ground" than of "the firm ground." God encounters the believer in both equally.[34]

So to believe in the God who reveals and who hides demands that the believer allow himself or herself to be not only open to God, but also vulnerable to the God of surprises. Boehme was a model of such belief.

Nevertheless, such open and vulnerable belief requires the disciple to risk an hazardous adventure in traveling without the security of one's free autonomy. On the other hand, that journey can be expected to end with the disciple's having become not an analytic rationalist, but a moral person of belief.[35]

C. Suffering an Enigma

Regardless of the manner in which victims of suffering respond to their anxiety, they acknowledge that the experience of suffering remains beyond the grasp of human comprehension. As far back as the sixth century B.C.E., when the book of Job was composed, the poet of that book was convinced that the encounter with suffering could not be understood (Job 28–41).

In harmony with that poet, Jakob Boehme had concluded from the experience of suffering that mystery shrouded not only the God who allows suffering, but the divine purposes, and even the experience of suffering itself.[36]

III. METHOD—THE ENLIGHTENMENT OR THE VISION

Thus far this chapter has surveyed a sampling of the scholarly dialogue concerning evil and suffering. There is as well a dialogue among scholars concerning the method by which to reflect upon the evil of suffering. That dialogue has brought into the focal center two methods that are inversions of one another: reasoned analysis and myth. The rest of this chapter surveys a sampling of that dialogue.

A. The Dismissal of Myth by the Enlightenment

The context in which to situate the search for a method by which to reflect upon suffering is the enlightenment. That major cultural adjustment had identified reason as the power that is adequate to comprehend and explain every human experience. On the reverse side of that coin which endorsed reason is the side that dismissed myth as a method of explaining experience.

Perhaps the pristine champion of the power of reasoned analysis was Immanuel Kant (1724–1804). He insisted that humans can anchor themselves within the objective world only by using their reason. On the other hand, he insisted that the use of myth resulted in situating the self not in the objective, but in the "noumenal" or fanciful world.

Auguste Comte (1798–1857) then proposed his doctrine of positivism: only that statement has meaning which can be verified in sense experience. Therefore the myths of religion are among the most primitive forms of seeking meaning. Rational persons have been liberated from such fictionalized, religious consciousness. They have discovered the freedom of rational, empirical criticism; they have become liberated from the fiction of myth and myth's religions.

The dismissal of myth in favor of analysis was championed by Max Weber (1864–1920). He set out to demystify each understanding of the world. i.e. to comprehend each occurrence by strict rationality. To do so, he intended to strip power from any interpretation that was not rational. Weber intended to demonstrate that poems, values, or beliefs that had been used to understand experience were no more than devices that had been fashioned to substitute for objective reasonings. With the enlightenment all such myths were to be relegated to the nursery; reasonable adults fashioned analyses to explain.

Within the context structured by the enlightenment, the demystification program of Rudolf Bultmann (1884–1976) made sense. Bultmann interpreted the biblical worldview to be that of the pre-scientific age in which the biblical authors lived.

The critical question that Bultmann posed was how humans in the era of empirical science could comprehend the New Testament. In Bultmann's judgment, the New Testament articulated a primitive, three-tiered universe: above, heaven; here, earth; below, the underworld. However, twentieth century believers have a rationalist, Descartian worldview, i.e. they confront the world as an empirical object "over against them," not as a mythical object described for primitive cultures. In Bultmann's opinion they therefore judge the biblical myths to be fantasy. Consequently, modern biblical theology is challenged to demythologize the Bible, i.e. to interpret the meaning of the Bible by removing the myths that are there.

However there are scholars who have interpreted demythologization as an effort to erode the foundation not only of religion, but of history, allegory, symbol, poetry, psychology and philosophy as well. For such scholars myths need to be maintained, though they do need properly to be interpreted. Myths are not to be interpreted literally, but with the awareness that they are imaginative expressions of occurrences.[37]

Not only those academic disciplines but reflection upon the problem of suffering can be approached only by way of myth. The evil of suffering must be situated within a mythical context if one has any hope of interrelating that evil with the enigma of God's goodness.[38]

If the scholar does not so situate the interrelation of suffering and God, then one is presuming that one can comprehend the interior life of God. The interior dynamics of God are beyond that grasp of the human intellect. Consequently, the only method by which to address that interrelationship is to use the imagination, as was done in the book of Job.[39]

B. The Turn to Myth as Necessary

There has been an inversion of that attitude toward enigma that the enlightenment endorsed. For example, during the enlightenment two renowned German poets, Friedrich Schiller (1759–1805) and Johann Goethe (1749–1832), turned against the demands of their age, the age of reason. They judged myth to be more valid than reason, more accurate than fact. In their judgment, myth provides humankind with a mirror of life.

Contemporary theologians, even some in the forefront of theology, have similarly reinterpreted the value of demythologizing. Many have acknowledged myth to have a unique value: it heightens the consciousness to the acts of the spirit within human history. It also recognizes the foundation upon which culture has been established. For example the Jewish culture had been based upon the consciousness of Yahweh's activity within history; the Christian culture, upon Christ Jesus as the Son of God. Both of these visions can be presented to their cultures only by means of myth.[40]

Even theologians in the Thomistic tradition have made the turn to myth. Some of these judge that theology can have access to genuine spiritual enigmas not by way of reason, but by way of the imagination. Thus, some of these argue for the need to turn to mythic language in such discussions.[41]

Others claim for myth at least as prominent a value as has been claimed for reason. Myth has a distinctive place in western consciousness and culture.[42]

Still others argue that theology can no longer be evangelical; modern culture has little interest in scriptural arguments. Theology needs to fashion images and myths about how God might be encountered not in the scriptures, but within the experiences of western, secular culture. There is a need for myths if believers are to address the seemingly absent God who nonetheless acts in environments of suffering.[43] Modern believers find it difficult to use reason to approach God when their culture's use of reason suggests that the God of reason must be a God of determinism and certitude.

Yet the vision of Schiller and Goethe needs to be refocused. Believers in the twentieth century need to rediscover the mythic symbols that already function as mirrors of the world for the surrounding culture.

At least one of the more secular disciplines, relativity physics, has so recognized its need to make the turn to myth. The enigma of sub-atomic interactions baffled physics until it began to attempt to explain the quantum world in myth. Thus physics now explains that world not only in terms of such images as "quarks" and "gluons," but "spins" as well.

As natural physics now uses myth, so too history, so too must belief.

C. *The Turn to Myth in Reflecting upon Suffering*

The repeated effort to address the problem of suffering needs as well to acknowledge that neither analysis nor reason, but myth has shown itself to be the adequate manner of addressing such a befogged world. For example, the poet of the book of Job is widely considered to have taken one of the best approaches to that enigma. Yet that poet's method is mythical.[44]

That paradigm of reflecting upon suffering deserves to be copied. Then suffering can be appreciated within the context of the victim's autonomy. Yet reason concludes that suffering severely limits autonomy. Thus theology can acknowledge the autonomy of the victim only if it structures its discussion in mythic images.[45]

The apostle Paul so situated the problem of suffering. When he discussed his own trials (2 Cor 11:24–28; 12:7; Gal 4:13, 15; 6:11), he mythically situated his sufferings not within the context of logic and analysis, but within that of the cross and resurrection. He repeatedly portrayed the destiny of the disciple to be a share in the suffering, death, and resurrection of Christ Jesus.

Thus a contemporary reassessing of the problem of suffering might wisely choose to use myth in order to situate human trials within a larger context. The method of situating an event within a non-experiential context, such as within the context of a transcendent God, is to use myth.[46] There appears to be no other manner in which to locate a sensuous event in relation to a non-sensuous, numinous Spirit. That Spirit transcends not only sense experience, but also reason and logical systems. Thus one can reflect upon the Spirit only by means of images.

The function of myth is to project into temporal, sensuous experience an awareness of an atemporal, non-sensuous Spirit. That is the purpose of the myths of the exodus, the incarnation, the resurrection, the conversion of Paul, etc. These situate their audiences not within historical occurrences, but within numinous events in experience.[47]

The intelligent believer can, if he or she uses myth, do reverence to the mystery within the experience of suffering. Conversely, without myth one can interrelate neither with that numinous mystery nor with the other Christian mysteries. Nor could one be aware of a transcendent God, nor of the presently reigning Christ, nor of victory over death, nor of the God who is constantly present. Any reflection upon any meaning requires that one leap away from the data to images that explain that data.[48]

The Christian concepts of "the cross" and "the paschal mystery" can so be interpreted. They are images of the non-sensuous manner in which believers are in union with a non-sensuous, transcendent Lord.[49]

So too the Old Testament had used images to reflect upon Yahweh, who is transcendent, not sensuous. Old Testament myths do not articulate a primitive worldview, but an expanded view of how immanent individuals might interrelate with a transcendent Lord.

Thus, when Bultmann redirected the scriptural discussion to empirical experience, he severely limited the breadth of vision of the biblical authors. Consequently, demythologization was a failure. Christianity needs to accept the vision that was fashioned in myth.[50]

For example, there are visions of the mythic Christ in Paul's letters to the Colossians and to the Philippians. In the first Paul envisions the Christ as having been the model whom God used to create and to redeem the world (Col 1:15–20). In the second Paul envisions the Christ as having surrendered his divine prerogatives in order to save all humans (Phil 2:6–11). In order to express those visions, Paul needed to articulate myths. If the Bultmannians choose to remove those myths, then they strip the New Testament of its vision of who Christ is and reduce the identity of Christ to immanent concepts.[51]

D. Myth, Meaning and Value

That very brief sketch of the reassessment of demythologization serves to prepare the reader to be open to both a "remythologization" of the New Testament and the need for myth in reflecting upon suffering. Current biblical reflection has been acknowledging myth as having a critical function—namely, to mediate explanations of the natural, the social, and the spiritual environment. Hence, rather than removing the myths from the New Testament, much biblical criticism has been probing to discover the worldview that had been presented by those myths.[52]

That reversal of Rudolf Bultmann's orientation is not a rejection of Bultmann, but a recognition of that recently discovered valuation of myth which Bultmann could not have known. He had understood myth to be no more than an imaginative expression— thus, a trip into fantasy. Consequently he judged that the only intelligent approach to the myth in scripture was to "demythologize" it, i.e. to strip it away in order to arrive at the authentic self-revelation of God.[53]

However, those illumined by the contemporary reassessment of myth are aware of other dynamics operating within myth. Myth is not only an imaginative expression, but myth expresses an occurrence. Those who fashioned myths did so because they judged myth to be the appropriate expression for the occurrences being expressed.

Those who take myth seriously, however, need to remain conscious that myth is indeed imaginative expression. Martin Luther had failed to do that. He adopted the inverse of Bultmann's approach to myth and judged that the occurrence was not only expressed by myth, but was also described by myth. Thus Luther interpreted the myths of the Bible in a fashion that is very nearly literal. He misinterpreted the New Testament. He took Paul's mythic statement on good works literally: no good work that a person performs has any effect on salvation.[54]

That fails to acknowledge myth as expressing mystery. Luther judged that myth addressed not a numinous mystery, but an analytic problem—namely, how practically to receive the gift of salvation.

Contemporary evangelical theology often repeats Martin Luther's analytic approach. It often uses scriptural myths as though they address salvation not as a mystery, but as an analytic problem. They presume therefore to be able to judge that only Christ Jesus could make to God the satisfaction due for sin. Only the suffering of Jesus, not that of humans, has any value for salvation. The analysis of the words of the New Testament leads inevitably to that logical proposition; there is no mystery there.[55]

E. The Vestibule to the Myth on Suffering

However, the "remythologization" of the New Testament is reorienting believers to the mystery of the Jesus event.

Moreover the reassessment of the profound value of myth equips reflective individuals to evaluate a myth on suffering as a value. The following chapter fashions the Lewis-Chesterton myth in order to explain suffering mythically. That is no more fantasy than are the myths of the Greeks or the myths of the New Testament. Like all myths, the myth on suffering is the imaginative expression of an occurrence.

6

Mystery in Myth

The context for a theology of suffering has been constructed in the prior chapters. That is, before one can fashion a meaning for suffering, one must be aware of the contours that consciousness assumes as a consequence of the problem of suffering. Every human person eventually makes allowances for those contours as he or she encounters suffering.

This chapter is seminal; it builds within that foundational context. The building takes shape from the importance of myth as a vehicle for cultural understanding.

This importance appears when one surveys human efforts to make sense of actual but enigmatic human occurrences. Mystery is such an occurrence—humans have attempted to make sense of mysterious occurrences, such as death, by myth, e.g., the myth of the after-life.

When suffering is addressed without myth, the mystery of suffering stands forbiddingly distant from comprehension.

The brief reflections of the previous chapters have documented that analytical attempts to approach that mystery by means of reason have been wide of the mark.

On the other hand, some artists in the western culture have recognized that there is a manner in which humans are able to approach mystery: the path of the human imagination is the path by which artists approach enigma.

However, the rationally oriented human is very likely to balk at the suggestion that there are mysteries. The rationalist tends to smile condescendingly when he or she reads that "mystery" is an enigma for which there is no solution. Rationalists are committed to the power of human reason to resolve every problem, to sort through every enigma. Thus the rationalist tends not to agree that there are enigmas which human reason cannot solve.

In order to assess the validity of the commitment of the rationalist to reason as absolute, we might reflect upon some of the enigmas which western artists have chosen to approach by using their imagination.

Mature, educated westerners can so easily assume that the significance of human life can be grasped only to the extent that one judges on the basis of factual, empirical, and historical data. They can assume, on the other hand, that, to the extent that their awareness is influenced by myth, to that extent they cannot grasp the significance of occurrences.

However, such a rationalist might learn from Albert Einstein's explanation of how he grasped and expressed the meaning of nature's general relativity. "An intuitive leap of the imagination" was his explanation for how he had formulated his physical theory.

If the meaning of an event is not superficial, but profound, such as general relativity, that meaning has often been expressed only to the extent that it has been formulated imaginatively.

Thus artists use their imagination. The objects of art vary greatly. There are a great many enigmas that artists have chosen to present in myth rather than in other genres.

An enigma was addressed by Albert Camus in his novel *The Plague*.

The mystery that Camus had there approached is that an individual may be motivated interiorly to sacrifice self for others, though there may be no reward, but only penalty for such self-giving. Measured by the criteria of reason, such self-sacrifice appears to be foolish. Thus Camus addressed this enigma not by way of a rational essay, though he was expert in writing such essays, but by way of a myth.

Rieux, the doctor in the plague, chose to sacrifice himself for others without any hope of reward for that sacrifice. On the contrary, his expectation was that he would himself become a victim of the plague and die.

Enigmas are genuine occurrences within human experience; however, they are such that they had not appeared to be suitably reducible to rational analysis.

This consideration provides the basis for a definition of myth.

Myth is the imaginative expression of an occurrence.

A particular occurrence is imaginatively expressed because its significance cannot be captured by a purely objective description. On the contrary, because the occurrence is significant as well as enigmatic, its meaning is expressed imaginatively.

Such an occurrence may have an historical grounding: the occurrences in the New Testament gospel narratives had historical groundings. However, those occurrences needed to be expressed imaginatively.

Thus myth or imaginative expression has been used to express such occurrences in order to capture their significance. Those meanings might otherwise appear to be incomprehensible, i.e. if one were to address them with no more than rational analysis.

However, there have been serious misunderstandings of myth by those who have not properly understood that with myth they were confronting imaginative expressions of occurrences.

The later New Testament writers, for example, apparently had not comprehended that they were dealing with myth.

The occurrence of Jesus' suffering and death was a great enigma. Thus, the earliest Christian preachers formulated myths about that enigma. The myth of the paschal mystery is an imaginative expression of the enigmatic occurrence of Christ Jesus' victory over death.

However, some later New Testament writers interpreted the early preachers' myths about Jesus' paschal mystery as though they were dealing with an historical, rational problem, not with a mystery.

Thus, with rather too great a facility some of them interpreted the myth in analytical propositions. For example, they analyzed that the death of Jesus meant that all humankind has been reconciled with God.[1]

The cardinal value of myth has been identified as bringing persons to an awareness of the presence within the world of that which is actual, though non-empirical, e.g. the transcendent Spirit.

Myth frequently emerges from the pristine traditions of a people. Such traditions report not historical but actual occurrences. These may indeed lie outside history and be beyond the range of common human experience; they were nonetheless actual occurrences for specific persons.

The experience of suffering is one of those occurrences that humans have chosen to approach by way of myth.

Consequently, our reflection upon the problem of suffering now begins its ascent toward an answer by way of a myth that I have fashioned. The myth begins with the death of a man.

7

The Lewis–Chesterton Myth

When Clive Staples Lewis (C.S. Lewis) died, he found himself moving away from his inert, dead body; he moved toward the Light that was invitingly drawing him to itself. Because his body held no more interest for him, he looked ahead to the dark tunnel through which he was moving, as he traveled toward the light.

From the shadows on the side of the tunnel a figure stepped forward, obviously intending to intercept him.

The figure spoke: "Excuse me. You will not recognize my appearance. However, you created me in your Space Trilogy. My name is Ransom."

Lewis was immediately relieved to find that he was not going to be alone here—relieved, moreover, that he had apparently been expected.

Ransom continued, "May I call you 'Jack,' as your friends address you?"

"Of course," responded Lewis. "Since you are a creation of my imagination, you are closer to me than those who know me only in the lodges of England. Call me 'Jack.' "

"Well, Jack, I've come to meet you, in order to let you know that, as far as I can tell, you are going to have a serious problem here.

"You had been someone of whom everyone here was so proud. Your books had argued so persuasively that there is a great value in Christian belief, that God is to be trusted, that human life is an adventure in which persons can trust.

"Your early book, *The Problem of Pain*, argued convincingly that God is to be praised even in the face of the tragedy of human suffering. Everyone was so proud of you.

"However, the notes which you wrote after the death of your wife are a different matter altogether. Those notes present a completely different attitude toward a life of faith, toward God, and toward human life.

"Moreover, they are being published in a book, *A Grief Observed*. The many people who have grown to reverence your writing are going to be greatly influenced by the vision of God that you have presented in that book.

"Unfortunately, you are going to influence those many people to form a very negative attitude toward God. Jack, why did you have to do a complete reversal from the hopeful attitude in your *The Problem of Pain?*

"You turned from praising God as the support of humans to, in the later book, identifying God as the cosmic sadist who struck Beethoven deaf.

"You rejected God because you accuse the divine One as freely experimenting with our experiences, our beliefs, and our love.

"Thus, you even called God 'the cosmic sadist,' 'God the vivisector.'

"You claimed that God frustrates us by depriving us of our bowl of soup, then gives us another bowl of the same soup."

At that point Lewis interrupted.

"If you remember, Ransom, I also wrote there that God had made us human, not angelic. Because we are no more than human, we have extraordinary difficulty in accepting God's abuse of our spirits."

Ransom gave no heed to this interruption. Rather, he went on.

"You challenged God's goodness. You proposed that if God is good in the tragedies that humans must endure, then not only are human tragedies good, but lies are also good.

"You dared to argue that in the only life that we know the sufferings that God sends are greater than our gravest fears and expectations. Since God has so treated us during our lives, you conclude, why should we expect the divine manner of dealing with us to be different after death?[1]

"Jack, I'm afraid that you are going to be held responsible for those attitudes. Because of the influence that you have on so many people, you are going to be judged as more answerable for such self-expressions than are those people who simply mumble them in private.

"Jack, every individual has to undergo suffering, even as Joy did, though very few comprehend any meaning inhering in the experience. Yet one has to trust that one will find, as Joan did find, that the experience of suffering teaches one to be more human.

"One has to have such trust even though the divine purpose may not appear to exist. Though one may not be able to grasp such a purpose while one lives, one may later discover that it had been unobservably worked out within one's life."

"Wait," Lewis shouted, interrupting Ransom's lesson. "You have been interpreting the experience of suffering on a plane that is strictly rational, only human. You have cited the value of suffering as being a lesson that leads the victim to be more compassionate, more present, more respectful of others, less judgmental, and so on.

"However, as elevating as such virtues might be, as human as the experience might lead the victim to become, I refuse to endorse the experience of suffering—unless I can perceive that suffering leads its victims to a much more grand dimension of being than that which reason offers."

At that moment a second character emerged from the shadows of the passage. With the gait of a heavy man and spectacles on his round, happy face, he came forward as one intent upon a purpose.

"Jack, have a good laugh at yourself," was his self-introduction. "You've been someone that I've greatly admired. You've been giving yourself to the exciting occupation that I used to practice. I used to write mystery stories about Father Peter Brown."

At that, Lewis knew that the heavy man was Gilbert Keith Chesterton. In his fascinating detective stories about "Father Brown" he had used his imagination to explore various paths that reason could travel in resolving intricate crimes or enigmas.[2]

However, he had focused not upon the value of the imagination, but upon the power of reason. Moreover, he knew that his readers could become readily tired of the stories that were no more than explorations of reason's powers.

Thus he could acknowledge the superior value of Lewis' stories, which explored the various imaginative possibilities for imagining human life. For example, Lewis' three books, which are identified as the space trilogy, imagine human life in a manner that is extraordinary.

"By abandoning yourself to your imagination, you had been able to fashion the kind of narrations that people found to be fascinating," Chesterton continued.

"My suspicion had been that you, therefore, had recognized that every human person, yourself included, must be slow to put a great deal of importance on rational, non-imagined expressions of human thought. After all, every thought has been imagined.

"However, Jack, you have now taken your own rational thoughts far too seriously. Your collection of notes, which Ransom cited as *A Grief Observed*, is no more than a collection of analytical ideas. Why are you taking them so seriously? Jack, have a good laugh at your own foolishness in being so serious about your ideas.

"They are not the ideas that have been imagined by some great epic poet, i.e., not by Homer, or Dante. Rather, they are the results of a handicapped, frustrated, and angry reason.

"Then take a more careful look at your assumption that you can comprehend the divine purpose. Look at how you have assessed the importance of your own mind. When you presume to comprehend the mind of God, you have presumed that your mind is the measure of the divine mind. Of course, when I put the situation before you in that manner, you immediately acknowledge that you had adopted your own assumptions as valid without having first criticized them. You will also acknowledge that you cannot hope to comprehend the divine purposes with either the criteria of reason or the analysis of causes.

"Ransom, you had praised our friend, Jack, here for his earlier book on suffering, *The Problem of Pain*. However, in that book Jack had made just the presumption that now appears to be foolish—he presumed that he was able to comprehend the purposes, methods, and goals of the divine mind. He had, therefore, presumed that his mind was the measure of the divine mind.

"Thus, Ransom, I disagree with you concerning *A Grief Observed*. That latter book is much more the kind of a book that one would expect a believer to write. In that book Jack acknowledged that the human mind is able to comprehend nothing of the purposes, methods, and goals of God.

"On the contrary, the human mind finds God's choice of the mystery of suffering to be totally incomprehensible. There is nothing in that experience which can be identified as having a specific or concrete value.

"Furthermore, Jack, you are certainly aware, now that you have lost your beloved wife and have pondered the significance of the god who had allowed Beethoven to go deaf, that God cannot be comprehended, that God is mystery.

"There are individuals, some of whom you know, who would have concluded from the disasters in their lives that there is no God. However, your response to the disaster in your life was, rather, to demand an explanation from the God who had acted without explaining the divine purpose. You remained faithful to your belief in God, though you refused to endorse the divine act that appeared to you to be sadistic.

"However, God is not the 'cosmic sadist' that you had imagined—or, perhaps I should say, that you had failed properly to imagine.

"No, Jack, you need to move your thinking onto a completely different plane. The God who is beyond the grasp of the human intellect must not be reduced to the criteria of human judgment. If God were no more than human judgment could grasp, then, indeed, God would be the cosmic sadist, as you had claimed. However, we need always to assume that God is somehow more.

"Of course, you will respond to that by demanding to know what 'more' can mean in this case. Unless one can identify in some manner the meaning of this 'more,' then one can judge that one is being treated with the same divine condescension with which Job was treated.

"So, let's begin with a literary search for that 'more' within human experience.

"There have been a number of literary figures who have expressed that they were conscious of a mysterious presence within human life. For example, John Steinbeck in his *The Log from the Sea of Cortez* narrated a sea expedition in search of marine life. Steinbeck was accompanying Ed Ricketts, a most unusual man and a friend, on a cruise through the Gulf of California in 1940.

"The expedition's ship, *The Western Flyer*, approached Estero de la Lune, which Steinbeck described as 'a bad place' that caused the men on ship to have 'bad feelings, bad dreams, and little accidents. The look and feel of it were bad.'

"Just at that time the men on the ship became aware of an enigmatic presence—'We had a curious feeling that a stranger was aboard, some presence not seen but felt, a dark-cloaked person who was with us.'[3]

"Steinbeck and the others on the ship had become conscious that there is 'more' to human life than the persons and things that surround us.

"However, Jack, you might be more at home if we turn to a literary figure that is closer to you in time and culture.

"So, let's consider a contemporary and colleague of yours, Thomas Stearns Eliot. Like you, Eliot chose to be known by his initials, T.S.

"Eliot had been alert to anything that suggested that there was present within human experience something 'more,' i.e., anything that suggested that human life offers to us more than material wealth, more than health, certainly more than suffering.

"Eliot had read the account of Shackleton's Antarctic expedition. That party of explorers, at the extremities of their resources, had the constant perception that there was one more member in their party than could actually be counted. He used this extraordinary account in the 'What the Thunder Said' section of *The Waste Land*.

> Who is the third,
> who walks always beside you?
> When I count
> there are only you and I together—
> but when I look up the white road
> there is always another one walking beside you
> gliding,
> wrapt in a brown mantle,
> hooded—
> I do not know whether a man or a woman
> . . . but who is that on the other side of you?

"Eliot continued with yet another image which suggests that there is 'more' present to us within our experience than we can comprehend. He cites a fable from the *Brihadaranyaka–Upanishad* on the meaning of Thunder.

What is that sound high in the air
Murmur of maternal lamentation
Who are those hooded hordes swarming
Over endless plains, stumbling in cracked earth
Ringed by the flat horizon only.

"Finally he cites Dante's *Inferno*, XXXIII, 46:

> I have heard the key
> Turn in the door once and turn once only
> We think of the key, each in his prison
> Thinking of the key, each confirms a prison
> Only at nightfall, aethereal rumours
> Revive for a moment a broken Coriolanus.

"Dante was evidently aware of slight hints within his consciousness that the sensuous evidences within life did not exhaust the occurrences available to the human spirit. Thus Dante cited Coriolanus, the main figure in Shakespeare's tragedy *Coriolanus*. That man had been destroyed by the people of Rome. Dante perceived some suggestions that Coriolanus, although ruined as far as we know from Shakespeare, has somehow been revived—there are 'more' occurrences available to human consciousness than we can grasp sensuously.

"However, in your present anger, you can't be expected to be inspired by the presence of a vague 'more' that Steinbeck, Eliot, Dante, or anyone else might have glimpsed.

"Jack, the 'more' which will be of much more interest to you is that which you have unwittingly perceived and made the focus of your reflections in *A Grief Observed*.

"Apparently you are unaware of that which you had there acknowledged.

"Your grief because of your wife's death was not a response to the death that Joy had suffered; you knew that she suffered the very same fate that every human person meets.

"No, you responded to an interior summons from your spirit."

Lewis was too honest to remain quiet. "Just a minute. I was not responding to a spirit; I was genuinely in a rage against being deprived of the only person who had taught me to enjoy being alive."

"Yes, you were in revolt, Jack," Chesterton retorted. "However, you were in revolt against the experience of your life. You had judged with utter certitude that your wife had been taken from you; yet you revolted against that obvious and certain fact of your experience.

"Apparently, you were in revolt against your experience because you were responding to something else; you were responding to something that was not identical with your exterior experience. My analysis of that revolt is that you were rejecting the data of your experience in favor of the summons of an interior movement that pushed you toward affirming that you could expect 'more' than you found in experience.

"Jack, you were evidently aware of an internal summons from a vague 'someone' who had invited you to imagine that there is more to human life than can be grasped by means of sight, touch, hearing, and so on.

"Moreover, you responded positively to that summons, though you seem not to be aware that your response was positive.

"You are a man of good judgment. You are certainly aware that normal humans die. You are perhaps acutely aware that very few humans avoid personal tragedy.

"Yet you raged both at Beethoven's having gone deaf and at your wife's death. You did this even though you were fully aware that Beethoven, a human being, had to expect suffering in his life. You raged at your wife's death even though you were fully aware that no human avoids death.

"When you lost Joy, you judged that you had lost more than your life could tolerate. You were coming undone.

"Yet you were also aware that within you there was a something or someone who whispered to your consciousness that you could demand that life be grasped not as defined in measurable quantities or even qualities, i.e., not as defined by suffering and death. No, the interior summons urged you to envision life in a manner so grand that it was a vision of hope. This hushed voice urged you to understand yourself neither in terms of successes and failures, nor of wealth and poverty, nor of health and sickness, not even of life and death.

"No, the whisper urged you to expect far more.

"Jack, you obviously chose to respond to that interior summons—you wrote *A Grief Observed*. There you insisted that life must be more than that which it appears to be; life cannot simply be an event bound by walls that move ever closer together. No, you there demanded that life had to nurture human individuals in a manner far different from that which you had actually experienced.

"You chose to judge as false the implications of your empirical data. These data led you to conclude that life can be comprehended in quantities or even in sensual qualities.

"You demanded the 'more' of life. You confronted the empirical data by insisting that life must be more grand than they had suggested. That is, life had to be more grand than a game played in a ring. Life could not be for you simply a sport in which, not bulls, but humans were no more than objects of play to entertain the bored gods.

"Jack, you were imaginatively responding to your spirit, even if you did not realize that.

"However, you did realize that you expected 'more' from being human than the patterns that you have observed. You demanded that life had to signify more than death and burial, though that had been the fate not only of Joy, but of everyone who has been human. You were aware of a non-sensuous 'more.' You had a sense that there was 'something' that you judge to be yours by an inherent right. You have that sense even though you knew that no human had escaped from the tragedy and death at which you railed.

"You had testified in your *A Grief Observed* that you were acutely aware of a numinous, non-sensuous 'more' that was available to humans apart from sensuous experience.

"Jack, that's why I had asked you to laugh at yourself. You've not separated your experience of rage from the grand vision of life that you discovered in your suffering. You had come through that pain to see that life is far more grand than your health or Joy's death. Life is more grand than the successful developing of a more human community. You envisioned life as more grand than humans have the capacity to grasp either by the senses, or by reason, or even by imagination.

"Moreover, as a believer in Christ Jesus, you had prayed. Indeed, even in your time of desolation you had been faithful in giving yourself to prayer. You then had no evidence that there was anyone who was hearing your prayer; yet you faithfully continued. Evidently you were then vaguely aware that there was 'more' to human experience than the psychological comfort that some seek in prayer. You found no such comfort.

"You were willing to trust that an imperceptible Someone heard your prayer, even though you received no confirmation of that. You trusted in that Someone who is 'more.'

"Furthermore, you have known people who stand out in relief from others because of just such hope as you then experienced. These are those who maintain their optimism even when they find themselves surrounded by a darkness which offers no hint that they have a basis for hope.

"These people were able to hope in such a condition because they were aware that there is 'more' as a basis for hope than that which can be identified by the senses. They were able to trust that a better condition for them would emerge, not from the darkness that surrounded them, but from the Someone in whom they had hoped as the 'more.' This Someone is for them the foundation for hope at all times.

"The identification of such experiences as the human awarenesses of the numinous One within human experience has been done for those still living by Karl Rahner.[4]

"However, Jack, no doubt you wonder how this reflection upon the 'more' relates to your unique experience of suffering.

"Well, an animal can be afflicted with pain; it then responds sensuously. For example, a dog which receives a nasty cut on its paw might respond by a brief whine prompted by its pain. Then the dog will lick the wound. The wound heals. The dog goes on with its life. There is no longing for a better way of life. There is no raging that such painful occurrences befall animals.

"Conversely, there is an entirely different response when a human is afflicted with pain. Of course the human seeks sensuous relief, seeks to be healed, hopes to resume the previous patterns of living, and generally seeks to avoid such misfortunes in the future.

"However, the human also longs for something 'more.' Humans long not only for a more stable physical condition, but also for personal comfort; more significantly, they long for the psychological reassurance that everything in life is consequently going to be good.

"The human victim of suffering hopes to find that subsequent life will be a value that is beyond physical pain, even beyond physical health or physical wealth. The human individual insists upon hoping that there is greater value that satisfies one's every desire, not only those that can be identified."

"Just a minute," Lewis interjected. "You are asking me to lay aside my rational approach to life and to address the experiences of life as though I were living in a fantasy."

"Jack," responded Chesterton, "you have given abundant evidence in your writings that you are much more comfortable with an imaginative approach to life than with a reasonable approach. Think for a moment of your so-called science fiction trilogy. You there assumed the need to approach human experience not reasonably, but imaginatively; you demonstrated there that in so approaching our experiences we can grasp more of the subtle dynamics of consciousness than we can grasp reasonably.

"Moreover, you would have strongly objected if anyone had accused you, in presenting the adventures of our friend Ransom here, of addressing life as though it were fantasy.

"No, you had there demonstrated that by using the imagination to approach experience, we can grasp far more than we could grasp if we were to use only reason."

Chesterton went on: "Ransom, that is my reason for being ambivalent about Jack's *The Problem of Pain;* the author of that book tried to approach the mystery of human suffering by way of reason, rather than by imagination.

"Jack, you have been much more than one who would be identified as 'a reasonable man.' That's part of the problem now—you now are insisting upon your right to take a reasonable approach to the problem of suffering. Meanwhile you are ignoring your instinctive response—namely, to approach the problem imaginatively. Moreover, you are refusing to acknowledge the value of that imaginative approach, though most of your own writings had taken just such an approach.

"Finally, you need to laugh at yourself. You appear foolish because you are ignoring the vision that you had expressed in *A Grief Observed.* You there gave evidence that you had responded to a Someone who cannot be identified with sensuous experience.

"Jack, don't you see what you've done? First you've envisioned

life as made up not only of the human community, but also of a
Someone who cannot be sensed, a Someone who might be identified only as a mysterious presence among us.

"Then you've envisioned life as supported by hope. You have
insisted that life cannot be simply that which it appears to be. No,
you insist that life must be much more grand than our evidence
suggests. You envisioned life as something far more than we might
conclude from our senses, from our reason, or even from our imagination. You envisioned the human response to life to be a disposition that can only be described as hope.

"Yet you are carrying on as though you had no more than a
collection of facts with which to think about life."

Confused and embarrassed, Lewis had the self-assurance to
acknowledge the validity of those criticisms. So Lewis responded,
"You've sounded a chord that has set off a harmony within me. I
have always tried to respond to tones that are put together from
life's more subtle music. We need to approach life with a sensitivity
for those tones; life is too slippery to be approached with nothing
more than a sensitivity to reason. No, we have more of a chance to
grasp the more important dynamics occurring around us if we approach life imaginatively.

"Furthermore, I agree that I had ignored my own imaginative
approach; I had focused only upon my rational approach to the
experience of Joy's death. You've correctly pointed out that I had
been uncharacteristically rationalistic. I need to review my own
attitudes.

"However, your image of the 'more' that we can hope to discover in life gives me pause. I perceive in that image how difficult
the human mind can sometimes find the imaginative worldview.

"For example, your image of the 'more' is most difficult for us.
That 'more,' which you insist is active within the experience of
suffering, is not a neutral dynamic, like an x-ray, but a Someone
who acts with love and power in our interior lives. However, when
we look at the victims of suffering, we certainly have trouble believing that in their interior there is such a Someone loving and caring
for them. On the contrary, they appear to be vulnerably besieged
by a force that is unopposed as it attacks them.

"You insist that we have such trouble because we are not being
sufficiently imaginative.

"You insist that in the experience of suffering there is a danger in using only reason. Only imagination might allow us to be aware of suffering's subtle dynamic, i.e., more aware of your 'more,' in spite of the negative attack that controls and oppresses the individuals who suffer."

Chesterton could see that the discussion had reached a critical point. "The question that you must now face, Jack, is what your imagination permits you to observe in your own experience of losing Joy. If our evaluation of the relative values of reason and imagination is not applied to your experience of suffering, then it remains no more than a theoretical notion that belongs on a shelf."

Lewis was silent as he absorbed this thrust that his colleague had directed to his effort to control his life. He could discuss the value of imaginatively perceiving the experience of suffering. However, it would be quite another task so to apply that discussion to himself as to alter his emotional response to suffering, especially to his suffering as a result of the death of his wife.

He stared for some time through Chesterton's spectacles. That moment of quietly absorbing this challenge lengthened into several seconds, even minutes. Perhaps in no prior conversation had he been so silent when he might have spoken.

Finally he glimpsed a path along which he might travel and still respect his pain at being separated from Joy; he resumed the conversation. "Yes, you have indeed uncovered within my rage a trace of hope. In my refusal to accept the enforced separation between Joy and myself there has been an unexplainable demand that life can be better than it is.

"The critical issue that you force me to confront is that I am incapable of explaining that demand. I am fully aware that every human individual can expect to encounter tragedy and to die. Yet I have steadfastly refused to accept the tragedy and the death that have disrupted my life. Apparently I do perceive within my consciousness a vague awareness that human life can be better than the only life that any of us has experienced. Apparently I do nurture the hope that life can be much more than a series of joys, followed by a series of tragedies, and terminated by the vacuum of death.

"Our sensuous experience, however, suggests no such hope. We observe with our senses that almost all of us suffer grievously. We observe with our senses that with no exceptions we die.

"Yet, as you have pointed out, I do find within my conscious-ness the hope that life can be better—no, the demand that life must be better.

"My mind buckles, however, when it asks where that hope might have arisen. It could not have arisen within sensuous experi-ence.

"You urge that a numinous Someone has planted that hope within my consciousness so as to give me, during my experience of suffering, a glimpse of a 'more.' This faint glimpse of a 'more,' which was given to me in my pain, suggests that there is in our lives more than the pain that we endure, more than our joy, more than our work.

"My broad-faced, bespectacled friend, you have pushed open a gate that I had not even seen. You have directed me to acknowledge a meaning in human suffering that I had grasped without even noting that I had something within my hand. You have opened my eyes to see that in the experience of suffering I received an experi-ence that made me aware of life as more rich and more beautiful than it had been before I suffered."

Finally Ransom spoke after his long silence: "This has been quite a remarkable experience for me. I had always assumed that you men of letters had exhausted the full range of human wisdom. After all, you, Mr. Lewis, had created me."

"Wait, Ransom," interrupted Lewis, "You're calling me 'Jack.' "

"All right, Jack, I was sure that you knew everything. Yet I've just found myself alongside you as we both were instructed by Mr. Chesterton here.

"However, the real wonder of this for me has been that I have learned to be conscious of human experience as something far more deep than I had assumed. I've observed that you, Jack, have also become so conscious.

"For example, there appears to be active, even within the expe-rience of suffering, an Uncontrollable One who leads the suffering individual to be conscious that human life is far more grand than either suffering or material wealth.

"Apparently this Numinous One is beckoning the individual who suffers to love that which lies within this expanding horizon of human experience, even as it expands to include suffering. This Numinous One urges humans to commit themselves to their experiences even to this extent: they surrender the search for security; they risk venturing onto whatever paths this Uncontrollable One opens to them.

"Apparently, the one who suffers is offered a worldview that is based upon a profound trust. However, this is not a trust that the victim will escape from suffering, but rather that life without material securities, even without the material security of health, can be an experience of hope and confidence. The experience of suffering, thus, can be a passage into a new dimension of living. Life can then be an event of far greater depth and far more personal satisfaction than health or . . ."

Lewis interrupted: "Let me break in here. As I listened to you, Ransom, I agreed with you. We have learned that the experience of suffering can lead the victim to perceive life as having greater depth and greater satisfaction than the victim might have perceived before the experience of suffering.

"However, let's not be vague. What actually is that 'depth'? In concrete terms how is one able to be more confident about life?"

Chesterton took up that challenge. "Jack, you've lost your orientation already. You had just caught a glimpse of the depths of life; you had just perceived how personally satisfying life could be. Have you already lost sight of that?

"Let's return to the vision that T.S. Eliot had fashioned in *The Waste Land*. He offered the vision that there is always Someone Else there, especially during moments when life is extremely vulnerable. During the most extreme dangers of their Antarctic expedition, the explorers were conscious that there was one more Someone among them than they were able to count.

"There is in suffering a greater depth and a more personal satisfaction than the one experiencing suffering perceives: the Numinous One is always present.

"The suffering one perceives that the Numinous One is not only present with us in every experience, but is loving and supporting us in every moment. Thus the victim of suffering finds self to be oriented toward a non-sensuous source of hope, toward a reservoir of power that resolves human anxieties. However, there has never been an empirical sensing of that source. No one has ever comprehended its mystery. Nonetheless, that source is ever near and accessible."

The voice of Ransom then brought this mythical meeting to a

conclusion. "Jack, you now can walk through the night with a light that had not previously illumined your way.

"Look at the difference that this assessment of experience makes in your own encounter with suffering.

"Look at the difference that it makes in the great problem of evil that weighs not only upon you, but upon every individual.

"Look at the difference that it makes in your self-understanding, especially as you attempt to understand how to make some sense of your life.

"Look at the difference that human imagination has made for those individuals who will be imaginative as they seek answers for the problems of evil and suffering."

Again, Lewis uncharacteristically paused as his two visitors waited.

Finally he spoke. "In my writing I'd used my imagination for others; my imagination functioned to create stories that entertain.

"Now I perceive that I can use my imagination not only for others, but for myself in my own effort to comprehend the meaning of my experiences.

"The crucial events of my younger life had been those which I could approach imaginatively. If I use my imagination to approach the suffering of my latter years, then I might envision that life's most crucial events are personal encounters, not only with others, but with a Numinous Other."

The myth ends.

THE LEWIS–CHESTERTON MYTH AND THE CHRISTIAN VISION

The myth has been presented here in order to formulate a response to the forbidding problem of suffering.

The myth enlightens with that vision of the human person which the evangelists had learned from Jesus of Nazareth.

However, Jesus had presented his vision in a form quite different from that used in the myth above. Thus one may have the right to object that the Lewis–Chesterton myth has not been derived from the vision of Jesus. Before one could identify the vision of the myth with the vision of Jesus, one would need to find an explanation of the vision of Jesus that is similar to the vision of the myth.

Jesus identified his vision as signifying that "the kingdom of God is in your midst." Thus an explanation of the vision of the myth needs to converge with Jesus' vision of the "kingdom of God."

There have been a number of efforts to explain Jesus' meaning of the kingdom. All agree that the fundamental meaning of the kingdom is that God is present everywhere and active as king within the human community. Some, e.g. Norman Perrin, go on to interpret this divine activity as incomprehensible to the human mind. Perrin cites, as evidence to support that interpretation, Jesus' parables that cannot be interpreted according to human meanings, e.g. "Let the dead bury their dead" (Lk 9:60).

Fortunately, there is at least one effort to describe the presence and activity of God, i.e. the kingdom of God, as the incomprehensible event that Jesus proclaimed. Moreover, this description is remarkably similar to Chesterton's interpretation of *A Grief Observed.* However, neither in Lewis' work nor in the works to which I am referring are the words "kingdom of God" used. Conversely, the words used by both sources to identify the fundamental human experience appear to be forbidding. Nonetheless, one can argue convincingly that Karl Rahner was describing the kingdom of God in his description of the supernatural existential.

In his supernatural existential Rahner identified characteristics in modern individuals which suggest the activity of the Spirit. Rahner was there modifying the characteristics that Jesus in his parables of the kingdom had identified as indications of individuals who live in God's presence. He interpreted human persons as being fundamentally responsible to be aware of the interior summons that invites them to live in the spirit.

To live in the spirit signified for Jesus something much different from what many people appear to have assumed.

The foundation for living in the spirit is that God is present absolutely everywhere, in every possible human experience. Another manner of expressing this would be to say that the spirit of God is present and active within every experience. The individuals who are sensitive and responsive to their spirits, therefore, are sensitive and responsive to God or to the kingdom of God. This is quite a different sensitivity and responsibility from being conventionally religious. One can here recall that the leaders of the Jewish religion had judged that Jesus was too opposed to some of the conventions of the Jewish religion, e.g. the extremisms of venerating the sabbath. Therefore they decided to execute him. Yet Judaism is a good religion.

Rahner reformulated that foundational Christian perspective as his "supernatural existential." He creatively reexpressed the New Testament's perspective, that the kingdom of God is to be found in absolutely every experience. There are suggestions in every individual's conscious experience that there are dynamics which reveal a non-material something or someone operating in every occurrence.

The manner in which one can approach the meaning of being conscious of this something, or someone, or spirit is to ask what kind of awareness or what kind of an experience the evangelists understood to be the summons by the spirit.

Rahner interpreted the summons to live in the spirit not as a pious feeling; nor is it a feeling of expansiveness during a religious feast; nor is it a gentle consolation. It is quite a different kind of experience; it is an experience that many claim to be beyond the range of living humans' consciousness.

Yet he cited many such human experiences.

For example, one individual may choose to be generous to another, though the other takes for granted the generosity and makes no effort to repay.

Another may choose to obey only because of an interior, incomprehensible summons.

Another makes an effort to love God, though no response is forthcoming, other than a total silence, an emptiness, or a void.

This last example suggests the experience that C.S. Lewis had acknowledged after his wife died. He had turned to God for an answer; he received no response other than a total silence.

Thus at this point the "Lewis–Chesterton" myth borrows from Karl Rahner the perspective which he had identified as the supernatural existential. That Rahnerian perspective on human experience makes good sense of the vision of life that Lewis formulated in *A Grief Observed*.

Those who are free enough to acknowledge the experiences

that Lewis had acknowledged in *A Grief Observed* have chosen to respond to the spirit that Rahner identified. Thus, they have chosen to live in the spirit.

They may not be conscious that they have responded to a supernatural summons; Lewis certainly had not been so conscious until Chesterton enlightened him. They may remain thoroughly engaged in the concerns of secular life.

Yet they have acknowledged within themselves an awareness that they are oriented to that which is more than a natural convention. Thus, as Karl Rahner has argued, they have therefore chosen to live, perhaps without being so aware, before the presence of God within human life.[5]

KARL RAHNER'S VISION AND SUFFERING

The words more often used to identify such a description of the presence and activity of God in the human community are the theology of the Holy Spirit. In his final and integrative book, *Grundkurs des Glaubens*, Karl Rahner has little more than this to say about the Holy Spirit:

> The context in which Jesus Christ is to be grasped is Jesus' presence to and relationship with his spirit. Jesus' situation within that context was the grace of the spirit that had been given to him. In a similar manner the context in which every individual is situated is that the same spirit works as grace in them; the same spirit is everywhere, works in all, and influences every event.
>
> As a consequence, God's intentions can be understood to be active within not only the incarnation and the cross, but within all events in all humans' lives. This does not mean that God had intended that every event occurs precisely as it is experienced; it does, however, mean that God participates in every event.
>
> Moreover, it means that God intends that every event, not only the incarnation and the cross, work toward the same final goal—namely, final union with God. This is not an abstract intention. On the contrary, through the activity of the spirit within every event, God participates in every event within the world.[6]

That is the whole of Rahner's explicit treatment of the Holy Spirit. One can interpret that treatment as being basically the basic lines of the supernatural existential. In both the one and the other, God is understood to be actively participating within the life of the individual. In both God seeks to influence the individual to be aware that the dimensions of the world are much more broad than sense experience suggests.

However, concerning the kingdom of God Rahner had nothing to say in his final book.

Nevertheless, his theology of the supernatural existential deserves to be identified as his effort to build an argument that defends God's universal presence and activity in the midst of the human community. Moreover, that is the same argument that Jesus had mounted in proclaiming the kingdom of God.

For Jesus the human awareness of self is that human life is a unity which is the consequence both of the earth and of something else.

Human life is certainly integrated radically with the earth; it is a product of the earth.

However, human life has developed; it is now different from the earth because of a dynamic that is non-secular. This dynamic, which works within the interior of every human, is integrally related with matter. However, only humans appear to be conscious that their lives are not restricted to earthly matter. Only humans appear to be conscious that their lives are becomings. They can interpret their becoming to extend beyond their earthly boundaries and to reach beyond life to a perfection greater than life.

This perfection has been understood by Rahner to signify that humans are capable of experiencing a non-material presence. Thus they are capable of experiencing a presence that is not mortal.

The experience of such a non-material, non-mortal presence is the interior experience of spirit.

Those human individuals who are responsive to the spirit are conscious of themselves as spirit-oriented individuals.

This spirit tends to look beyond the earth to a receding horizon. It looks beyond matter to the fullness of life, to the full power of life, to a goal that is a sovereign, free, and undeserved gift.

Rahner proposed that the consciousness of these interior movements and of this heightened self-consciousness are the self's awareness of the personal self-revelation of God. This self-revelation may not take the form of objective data, such as the dogmas that come from the offices of the church. This divine revelation, rather, takes the form of that interior ground upon which one can build a radically free and autonomous self-awareness.[7]

This proposal that an individual's self-awareness is the personal self-revelation of God might, however, appear to be radical. Nevertheless, conventional Christian doctrine has traditionally taught that the word of God arises within the individual, not from a material source outside of the individual, i.e., neither from the church, nor from preaching, nor even from the words of the Bible.

PRAYER AND SUFFERING

The persistent teaching of Christianity has been that the word of God comes to the individual from the person's interior life. Each person finds in the interior dynamics of one's spirit the self-revelation of God.

This individualized self-understanding, which has here been interpreted to be the self-communication of God, may not appear to the individual explicitly to be the divine revelation.

In the Lewis–Chesterton myth, C.S. Lewis had not explicitly recognized that his radically free, autonomous self-awareness after his wife's death had been his interior summons to live in the Spirit. He certainly had not explicitly identified an interior experience as having been a summons to hope.

Transcending over material concerns needs to be made more explicit.

It can be made more explicit for those who are sensitive to their interior dynamics. Persons are interiorly summoned to reflect upon more than their immediate surroundings. They are aware of their capacity to ask questions about their lives. They can propose various possibilities for the future. They can be conscious that they live within a horizon that appears to recede even asymptotically.

At the same time, they are aware of their radical limitation, e.g. C.S. Lewis had to confront the death of his beloved. However, humans such as Lewis can look beyond their limitations. Then they experience themselves no longer as limited by the surrounding world, but as transcending the material world.

God's pervasive goodness is significant in our reflections upon the rage against God that C.S. Lewis expressed in *A Grief Observed*. Unable to discover God's pervasive goodness, he was rejecting as evil the God whom he had always believed to be good. However, because Lewis remained conscious that he always remained a creature, his actions remained always bound into the goodness of God; God's providence continued to evolve even through the apparently evil choices that Lewis made. Consequently, as Chesterton pointed out to Lewis in the myth, even in the choice to strike out against God, Lewis was affirming his trust in God's good providence, which is always in the process of evolving a better world.

In so experiencing one's self, one insists that one is free to trust not in the immediate environment, but in the unknown, in something more than material, certainly in the future possibilities toward which one moves.

Of course, one can choose to restrict oneself to one's material surroundings and to allow that which is other than matter to have no influence upon one's life.

However, the individual can choose to trust in one's interior dynamics. Karl Rahner understood that self as a process, as a dynamic who moves forward into an uncertain future. Then one finds oneself to be confronted by the choice, how to respond to the interior summons to move forward.[8]

That is the experience of being summoned to a self-transcendence, the primordial experience. It is the more authentic self.

The self-transcending individual must decide to what extent one will respond to the spirit's summons which sets one in relief from one's sense experiences and orients oneself to a transcendence.[9]

The self-awareness that emerges from one's spirit is more likely to be recognized as the revelation of one's unique manner of being human. When one responds freely to one's spirit, then one responds to God's self-revelation in one's experience of being free.

Some experiences might be more appropriate to enable the individual so to be aware of this radical freedom.

For example, the individual may have the experience of being invited by one's spirit to give oneself to attempt to arrange for better medical treatment for AIDS victims.

Or one may choose to respond to someone with an obedience that is not necessary. Conversely, one may choose to abandon a life of obedience.

Another may radically and freely protest against that which one finds intolerable.

Still others may allow themselves to be spontaneously generous.

Finally one may refuse to accept a death.[10]

However, the more important issue here is Karl Rahner's proposal that God communicates the divine self to individuals in the self's more intimate experiences. This doctrine rests upon the awareness of the transcendence of every individual's spirit. The awareness of this transcendence of one's spirit is the foundation for God's self-revelation of God to the individual.

One's spirit may reveal the self's transcendence not only during experiences of religious behaviors, such as during times of prayer or worship. One needs to reverence one's spirit not only then, but also during experiences that are not at all religious. Experiences within the profane dimension of life could be cited:

• the spirit may summon one to transcendence during behaviors in one's workplace;

• in one's interpersonal relationships, especially in one's moments of loving someone who cannot respond or who will respond only weakly;

• in one's social responsibilities, but perhaps most especially in one's response to an experience of death.

In all of these sense experiences one needs to learn to reverence one's spirit, especially within those experiences that move the self toward an awareness that there is mystery within life.

Lewis in his *A Grief Observed* was certainly responding to his spirit in a manner that departed from the conventions of the theology of the church. Thus Lewis' notes appear to be anything but a divine revelation.

However Lewis had there discovered that his spirit was radically free and able to move toward its own freely chosen goals. That was an experience of transcendence.

C.S. Lewis had experienced this radical freedom in the form of a choice to withdraw from the God who appeared to him to be forbidding. Lewis had indicted that God as the "cosmic sadist."

However Lewis had thereby experienced himself as transcendental insofar as he had been aware that he could be radically free from the conventions of those around him and transcendently free enough to leave aside the conventions of the church, while abandoning himself to his spirit.

This freedom in the case of C.S. Lewis and in the case of many can seem to be something quite different from the self-revelation of God. Certainly in the myth neither Lewis nor Ransom, but only Chesterton had been able to recognize this radically free spirit for who it was.

However, even though the meaning of this freedom had not been recognized, it still moved Lewis away from his previously heteronomous immanence within conventions and toward an autonomous transcendence. That is the experience of a transcendent grace received from God.

However one does need to reverence not only one's own interior mystery, as Lewis did, but also the intimacy to which one is invited by one's interior life.

Then the self discovers that one is an autonomous subject, not a model that follows pre-arranged and predictable behaviors. Then one discovers, as Karl Rahner has proposed, the interior movement that directs one to be aware that the transcendent God has become intimate within the interior of the self.[11]

This identification by Karl Rahner of the supernatural existential interprets quite well C.S. Lewis's self-awareness as he wrote his *A Grief Observed*. There he had acknowledged within his self a radical freedom that revolted against the death of his wife. Lewis was in that self-awareness responding to his spirit to move away from the conventions of the surrounding religious life and toward a mystery. The mystery in this case was the revolt against human death, even though Lewis was fully conscious that no human has escaped death.

CHESTERTON'S AND RAHNER'S VISION

Conscious that he was a creature who was dependent upon an absolute who supports every creature, he was also conscious of the self as being free and responsible. That is, he experienced himself as being challenged to formulate his own attitude toward the experiences of his life, e.g. toward the death of his wife. Conversely, he had judged that he was not simply the consequence of material causes or prior events. On the contrary, he was aware of his freedom to develop in a manner that was unique to himself, even when so to develop might lead him to confront the supposed plan of the absolute one who was supporting him.

Lewis, as a creature, was conscious not only of the absolute One who was his support, but also of his freedom to criticize the plan of the absolute One. Thus he was affirming in an inverted manner his human relationship both to the absolute One and to the world; he was conscious of being responsible to both. As Chesterton had remarked, in *A Grief Observed* Lewis had expressed, perhaps in an extraordinary manner, the attitudes that are appropriate for a human creature.[12]

Thus he was experiencing the self-communication of the transcendent God.

Chesterton had been able in the myth to identify that self-awareness for what it was: the encounter between Lewis and the Numinous One; the discovery within the experience of suffering that one was not alone—a Someone, a mysterious Person was always there.

Moreover, Chesterton had recognized Lewis' choice in his movement toward the mystery of life to live with hope.

The goal of so having correlated the supernatural existential of Karl Rahner and the experiences of C.S. Lewis in *A Grief Observed* has been to suggest that there was purpose in Lewis' suffering. The wider goal has been to suggest that there is meaning in the suffering of every person. That meaning is that the victim responds to the summons of the spirit within the enigmatic and forbidding problem of suffering.

The major purpose, however, has been to present that the seemingly obvious rejection of Lewis by God, and the rejection of God by C.S. Lewis, needed to be reinterpreted. In *A Grief Observed* Lewis had encountered the Numinous One within the experience of his suffering. Moreover, he had responded in a radical freedom to that One's invitation to move into a transcendent mystery and, thus, to live in hope.

8

Myth Illumines a Path
Through the Fog

The value of the myth concerning suffering can easily be over-looked by the mature, educated adult.

Those individuals in the twentieth century tend to seek solutions for their problems not in myths, but in empirical data, or in carefully reasoned arguments.

Thus, their initial response to the Lewis–Chesterton myth on suffering may be to smile at its childishness.

Thus, the individual who has assessed myth quite simply as fantasy might do well to resituate myth. Myth has value in relation to the enigma that it attempts to unravel.

ACKNOWLEDGED NEED FOR MYTH

Many occurrences within the world, even within the physical world, have not been able to be described. Quantum physics, for example, acknowledges that it cannot and does not even hope to be able to describe such physical occurrences in the micro-world as tunneling, or the pairing of particles separated by immense distances.

On the other hand, myths have been found by many peoples to be the appropriate medium of articulation for enigmatic occurrences in history, tragedy, philosophy, morality, poetry, ideology, and theology.

However, the twentieth century, which is still influenced by the enlightenment's reverence for reason, has inherited a problem, because peoples continue to use myth as an expression of occurrences.

MYTH EXPLAINS

In my effort to address the problem of suffering, I have used myth. I have done so in order to draw the readers into the context of suffering and to orient the attitudes of those readers.

Those goals render the use of myth as the appropriate means of addressing the enigma of suffering: myth is able to make more sense of the available data of enigma.

The physical sciences can serve for us as a model upon which to build a revaluation of myth.

Physical science intends to describe. Myth intends to explain. In order to appreciate that relativity of an interpretation to its intended purpose, we turn again to the importance of relativity in the physical sciences.

There, interpretations can have value in relation to one set of data, e.g. classical physics in relation to motions at relatively slow speeds. However, the interpretations of classical physics have no value in relation to another set of data, e.g. in relation to motions at dramatically increased speeds.

On the one hand, according to the criteria of Isaac Newton's classical physics of determinism, the measurement either of extension or of time is independent of the motion of the person who may be doing the measuring.

Newton's criteria were used by observers who move at relatively slow speeds.

On the other hand, however, according to the criteria of Einstein's theory of special relativity, the measurement of an object is necessarily a relationship between that object and the motion of the person who is doing the measuring.

His hypothesis of general relativity interrelated all speed both to light and to the warp of the surrounding adjacent space.

There are other such dramatic examples of interpretations which have values that are restricted by a relativity.

We might consider Albert Einstein's method: every scientific theory is formulated by an intuitive leap of the imagination.

Of course, the scientist who formulates an intuitive leap of his imagination into a hypothesis is expected to ground that hypothesis in empirically verifiable data. However, that hypothesis had first emerged from an intuitive insight, from a certain leap of imagination, i.e. from a certain myth. The scientist who formulates such a hypothesis is acutely conscious that he had been able to organize data in a manner that they had not previously been organized only because he had imaginatively leapt away from the data to a myth.

To the extent that such imagined hypotheses have been verified, to that extent science has developed—science is imaginative subjectivity.

This has been an argument to answer the question about how humans had discovered that their knowledge is relative.

Thus, in an effort to persuade, I formulated the mythical dialogue between C.S. Lewis, G.K. Chesterton, and Ransom together with concrete symbols of a conversation.

The myth is a value relative to at least six criteria.

First of all, it relates to the comprehension of suffering. It was not intended to verify a hypothesis in sense data, nor to persuade with rational arguments. However, it was fashioned so as to provide a satisfactory explanation of the meaning of suffering.

Secondly it orients the readers. The myth disposes the readers to recall or to learn certain values.

THE MYTHICAL EXPLANATION OF SUFFERING

If the images and symbols used in a myth are harmonious with life as an individual experiences it, then the individual will value that myth as confirming one's comprehension of experience. Conversely, the individual will remain indifferent to a myth whose images and symbols are dissonant with one's own experience.

The relativity of myth, like the relativity of science, art, or any event in public life, consists in the value of the expression relative to a persuasive expression.

It needs to persuade. When poetry, science, music, or public life uses persuasive symbols, then the image-maker and the myth enter the circle of public discussion. Then a myth's imaginative expression of an occurrence is endorsed.

Thus the persuasive expression of the enigma of suffering is the measure of the Lewis–Chesterton myth. The enigma of suffering certainly lies outside of the range of those data that human reason has been able to understand. Thus, in order to address the enigma, individuals might well attend to myths about it.

The imagination fashioned the Lewis–Chesterton myth in order both to address the enigma of suffering and to respect that enigma. It has not intended to describe, but to explain the experience of suffering.

Even if the human encounter with suffering has not here been described, there still may be value in this imaginative expression that explains suffering.

RATIONAL HESITATION TO ACCEPT MYTH

In the Lewis–Chesterton myth Ransom had reacted to Lewis' response to suffering in *A Grief Observed* with a stereotypical convention: he withdrew in shock from Lewis' rejection of God's manner of dealing with those who suffer.

However, Chesterton was responsible enough to respond authentically. He proposed an inverted meaning for Lewis' expression of grief. He proposed the need for all believers in God to reverence the new perspective of God's ways that his inversion envisioned. Thus he proposed that, with that new perspective, believers would evaluate Lewis' genuine expression of grief quite differently.

That is the approach that a responsible self needs always to take—to perceive occurrences from the perspective available to one's inner self. Only then is one liberated from being restricted to passive reactions and enabled to choose actively to respond in a manner that is one's own.

Within the myth C.S. Lewis is acknowledged by Chesterton to have been responsible, first in owning his own perspective on his suffering, then in fashioning his own appropriate manner of responding.

The myth challenges those who suffer to own similarly their own perspective on their suffering and then to fashion an action appropriate as their own response.

The perspective of the Lewis–Chesterton myth lays hold of a directive for the human encounter with suffering; namely, the need to use imagination or symbols, rather than to use reason to make sense of that encounter.

The myth is properly assessed if it is so comprehended.

9

The Possibility of Response to This Myth

This is possible, however, only to the extent that the victims allow their spirits to lead them to perceive themselves as freed from the limitations of their immediately surrounding world. They can hope in a world that cannot be sensed only if they interpret themselves to be part of a process that is evolving a better, even if unseen, world.

Then the victims of suffering have responded to their spirits. Then they have entered the domain that transcends the senses in a uniquely human manner.

The victims may still revolt against the limitations of the sensible world. Lewis certainly found himself to be in revolt against the loss of his wife.

Nonetheless, they can so orient themselves toward such unknown and uncertain goals only if they have become radically free from the human tendency to satisfy themselves sensually.

So to orient themselves is too much to ask individuals to achieve by strength of their own wills. However, it is not too much to ask of people who are able to trust not in their own wills, but in their spirits.

Those who so respond to their spirits are those who have in some manner learned to be conscious of the non-sensuous dynamics within the world. When a victim of suffering, or any individual, has learned so to become aware, then she or he has discovered a source of value that is to a certain extent unlimited. It is unlimited insofar as it is a dynamic that is not bound by the limitations of the senses.

Then the victims of suffering have opened themselves to a future that is being fashioned by the absolute One.

There are other values in the Lewis–Chesterton myth. The symbols of that myth are values insofar as they provide access to that which actually occurs in the experience of suffering, i.e. to that which occurs in the consciousness of those who suffer.

THE PRESENCE OF THE NUMINOUS ONE

The myth proposes a symbol of the Numinous One as present within the experience of suffering.

Thus the question that needs to be asked and answered is whether the myth gives access to an awareness that, within their suffering, victims had perceived, however faintly, a summons from the Numinous One. The myth identifies such an awareness in Lewis' conscious demand that human life should be free of suffering.

Those familiar with Karl Rahner's transcendental anthropology have learned to value such inversion from another perspective. Karl Rahner interpreted the kind of perception that Lewis had experienced to be the awareness of oneself as transcendent or spirit-oriented. According to Rahner, human self-awareness includes moments in which the individual is conscious of being summoned to rely not upon one's material limitations, thus not to concentrate upon one's material experience of suffering, but to rely upon a dimension that is available to human awareness by way of the voice of one's spirit.

Then the individual is summoned to be aware of one's ability to live outside of the limitations of one's material life and to move toward the mysterious center from which the summons appears to come.

Fourth, the symbols of the myth are values insofar as they elicit trust from those who encounter them. The symbols of the myth can make no claim to authority apart from their effectiveness.

The suffering myth does envision for those who suffer a perspective of trust. The myth proposes that there is human value within the experience of suffering. It proposes that this value can be appropriated by those who respond to their suffering, as the myth envisions Lewis to have responded to his suffering. If the myth fails to communicate that trust, then it has no genuine value.

THE INVERSION OF MEANINGS

The New Testament myths have been widely recognized as the appropriate imaginative expressions of God's presence and activity in the world.

The purpose of the Lewis–Chesterton myth was that it might be recognized as an appropriate image of the Numinous One's summons to those who suffer.

The New Testament proposes the image of the kingdom of God. That vision fabricates the perspective that God is actively present in every human experience, including suffering. Thus every experience is transformed to be a profoundly elevating event.

An example of the transforming trust that the New Testament proposed in order to situate God within the worldview of its readers is found in the Letter to the Hebrews.

> During his life on earth, he offered up prayer and entreaty, aloud and in silent tears, to the one who had the power to save him out of death, and he submitted so humbly that his prayer was heard. Although he was Son, he learnt to obey through suffering; but having been made perfect, he became for all who obey him the source of eternal salvation and was acclaimed by God with the title of high priest of the order of Melchisedech" (Heb 5:7–10).

The passage refers to an event in Jesus' life—"he offered up prayer and entreaty . . . so humbly that his prayer was heard." That event was the apparent silence of God as Jesus was murdered.

However, that apparent silence is mythically transformed by the worldview of the kingdom of God: God, present in every experience, thus indeed did hear the prayer of Jesus. God then transformed the murder of Jesus into a total victory. Consequently, through his death Jesus achieved universal, eternal salvation for all humans and gained the status of becoming the eternal high priest.

This vision of Jesus' glorification in being crucified might initiate a debate on whether and how he could have been glorified in capital punishment.

However, there are believers who assume the worldview that God was so present and active in the death of Jesus. They respond to the vision of Jesus' glorification not by debating, but by hoping that God is similarly present and active within all the experiences of their lives, within their experiences of suffering as well.

The Lewis–Chesterton myth on suffering similarly proposes a transforming worldview.

Insofar as one assumes the conventional perspective that sense experience exhausts the content of life's experiences, then one might very well look at life with at least skepticism, if not cynicism or even dread.

However, one might rather assume the perspective of the suffering myth. The myth proposes that the Numinous One is present with the one who suffers and is revealing to that person that the life of suffering is being transformed. Then the victim of suffering is enabled to look at life with hope, trust, and passionate love.

Moreover, the symbols of the myth are values insofar as they are repeated with some frequency. Persons who frequently repeat a myth have been persuaded to live with the worldview that is fashioned in the myth.

The Lewis–Chesterton myth is a value to those persons who repeatedly trust that the experience of suffering is an event in which the victim can hear the Numinous One summon one to live in hope.

Such victims hope as well that suffering not be a part of human life. The victims hope that life is more than suffering, more than health, more even than matter.

RESPONSE TO THE NON-EMPIRICAL WITHIN THE WORLD

There is need, however, for the hoping victims to recall frequently that the occurrences described by the myth are not identifiable with empirical data. Rather, they are occurrences that have been imaginatively narrated—the occurrence of suffering appeared to be suitable for myth because it is enigmatic and elusive.

There are many events that elude perception by the senses. For example, the responses of some individuals to the beauty of a person or to a calming scene are such occurrences.

These imaginative expressions are generally found in works of art, e.g. painting, sculpture, music, dance, or myth.

Furthermore, the symbols of the myth are values insofar as they propose a satisfying worldview. The Lewis–Chesterton myth intends to lead persons away from the worldview of the conventional explanation of suffering as a punishment and to reorient them toward a worldview that is markedly unusual. It provides a directive; it illustrates an appropriate path that victims of suffering might suitably choose to travel.

The myth symbolizes a life in which one is aware of being invited to trust that humans are constantly supported by the embrace of the Numinous One.

THE RESPONSE TO THE MYSTERY OF SUFFERING

Thus those who have suffered are invited by the myth to imagine that this One is building a relationship through the experience of suffering. Life is becoming a process that is more personally fulfilling than it would be without the constant care of this One. This presence is building life to be an experience that suggests more hope than humans could otherwise expect.

This chapter has been explaining the value of the Lewis–Chesterton myth. The purpose of this has been to indicate that this myth has neither more nor less value than the symbolic hypotheses fashioned by artists, scholars, or scientists. Any hypothesis has a value insofar as it had accomplished that for which it was fashioned.

A hypothesis in physics is fashioned so as to describe the available physical data. A hypothesis in art history, to describe the influences that have formed artistic expressions. Those in history, to describe the interconnection of actual, past events.

The hypotheses of these areas of specialization can be assessed as valuable insofar as they succeed in accomplishing that for which they were fashioned. If they were fashioned in order to provide a description, then they are valuable only if they describe. If they were fashioned in order to provide an explanation, then they are valuable only if they explain.

The Lewis–Chesterton myth of suffering was fashioned in order to explain. It was intended to explain the meaning of suffering for those who suffer. It has explained this meaning as a consequence of a Numinous Presence who communicates to the victim of suffering.

Certainly, every attempt to address the meaning of suffering has left the experience wrapped in mystery.

The Lewis–Chesterton myth intends, nonetheless, to explain that most incomprehensible experience of bearing pain. Indeed, those who have borne pain, whether that pain has been physical or psychological or both, are acutely aware that in itself that experience offers to its victims no positive significance. Suffering offers, rather, a blank wall of hard steel into which the suffering person blindly slams.

The Lewis–Chesterton myth provides a meaning for those who so crash. It attempts first to peel back for those individuals the layers of scar-tissue that have hidden the significance of their experiences of suffering and then to lay bare the significance that those victims of suffering had perhaps unconsciously glimpsed.

10

The Presence Encounters Those Who Suffer

The worldview proposed by the Lewis–Chesterton myth permits the individual to assume that three paths lead out from the dense fog of suffering.

First, one perceives that in the experience of suffering the victim is summoned to focus not on self, but upon a mystery that situates the self beyond pain. One of the assumptions that therefore needs to be put aside by the victim is that life would be more human if the victim could only continue the patterns of life that had been available before suffering entered one's life.

The victim needs to open one's self to an entirely new self-interpretation. The Lewis–Chesterton myth envisions C.S. Lewis as one who had opened himself to a new interpretation of self because of his encounter with suffering. In *A Grief Observed* he had dimly perceived that his prior assumptions, and thus his prior patterns of living, had as a result of his encounter with suffering become anachronistic.

In his academic career he had pursued comprehensible goals, such as to fashion entertaining stories, to persuade more people to believe in God, to attract better students, and to pursue academic prestige both in England and abroad.

Then, as a result of the death of his wife, he found himself to be tumbling into an abyss. Consequently, he recognized that he needed to change his assumptions about the goals for his time and energy. No longer did he hope to write entertaining stories, to achieve greater influence, to attract better students, or to gain more prestige.

The new worldview that his suffering had offered to him placed him in this perspective; the goal of human life was to rise above the plane of secular pursuits and to reorient oneself to the mystery within life.

From his new point of view he perceived that he could interrelate with the newly perceived mystery of being alive. He could trustingly interrelate with an interior, numinous voice that summoned him into that mystery.

Chesterton had further disclosed the mystery that had opened before Lewis by identifying that numinous voice as a person.

Moreover, from that new point of view Lewis, as a result of reorienting himself to this mystery, was more able trustingly to interrelate with his fellow humans.

A NEW, MYTHICAL WORLDVIEW

The experience of suffering had made available to Lewis a dramatically new worldview.

This worldview first of all allowed Lewis, as well as other victims, to assume a new perspective. He was invited by the interior voice to become faintly aware of human life as mysterious.

From the perspective of that new point of view, those who suffer may be asked to fashion novel patterns in response to life's mystery.

Secondly, the new worldview includes the perception that the mystery encountered in the experience of suffering can be identified in one manner only: the mystery is a personal presence.

One of the devastating pains endured by the one who suffers is that the experience of suffering has left the victim of suffering isolated. The new perspective is that in the experience of suffering one may discover that one is constantly attended by a personal presence. The victim may find that suffering is not the impersonal isolation that it often appears to be. Furthermore, the encountered presence can somehow appear to be the master of every human experience. It can appear, however vaguely, to be master not only of the experience of suffering, but also of the life experiences of those who are healthy. Consequently, the experience of suffering can appear to introduce a new and extensive value-system for the victim.

Of course some victims of suffering choose to be content analytically to identify that interior voice as an illusion of a futile hope fabricated as an antidote to suffering's mindless fury. However, others choose to trust imaginatively to identify it as a person who is somehow leading the victim toward an unseen goal.

These victims may perceive this numinous person to urge them to trust not only while they suffer, but in every life experience.

Moreover, the victim is able to imagine being in a relationship with this presence. Although this presence cannot be perceived with the senses, it can be dimly imagined.

Furthermore, even the painful life of the victim is a preferable life, because one can be in a relationship with this personal presence. This relationship can appear to offer to the victim an abiding love, a greater interior freedom, and a confidence that every human experience, even that of suffering, is mysteriously personal.

THE VALUE OF THE MYTHICAL WORLDVIEW

A great value of such a perception of life is that it can resolve not only the profound anxieties of suffering, but also the anxieties caused by many of life's compulsive insecurities. Those who encounter acute suffering can be aware that they are not less secure than every individual: every individual can live only insecurely.

Nonetheless, they may be able to perceive the presence of the Numinous One as engaged with their anxieties and insecurities. In such a case, if they rely upon this Numinous One, they will appear to have a greater certitude and security than if they relied upon exterior values.

The Lewis–Chesterton myth offers this worldview: as long as one can use one's imagination, no experiences can lay siege to one's life.

Those who share the perspective of that myth are conscious of living within a mystery that is trustworthy. Moreover, those who share the perspective of that new worldview are able to approach every experience, even that which can appear to cause anxiety or insecurity, as a new opportunity to remain open to the mystery that is life.

That is certainly a more social and human manner of responding to anxieties than to withdraw into the isolation of self-pity, anger, or defeat. Yet the one who pursues only perceptible values may be tempted so to withdraw. The perspective of the Lewis–Chesterton myth invites one, even the one who is tempted to withdraw, so to respond to every experience that one hopes and trusts. One may so respond even though one may not be able to perceive sensuously that such hope or trust will be fulfilled.

THE NEED TO LIFT ONE'S VISION

Of course, such victims of suffering continue to live in the shadow cast by their pain, insecurity, loneliness, and anxiety. However, they can also live in hope. They might even be adventurous enough to hope that life can somehow become more satisfying, exciting, even thrilling. They can hope that life will be less static, more adventuresome, even while it may continue to be a source of insecurity and anxiety.

That mythic perspective is capable of raising the eyes of those who suffer above life's recesses. That perspective allows them to focus instead upon the expansive horizon.

That is the horizon that is available to the person who accepts the myth as a value.

Thus the one who encounters the enigmatic experience of suffering is challenged. The challenge is to avoid the temptation to analyze suffering, but to turn to myth in order to fashion a value for suffering and to recognize that all meaning has been fashioned in myth. Thus if the victim of suffering situates himself or herself within myth, he or she can discover a meaning for suffering that is positive, not negative.

Otherwise, without myth one would encounter only something like the senseless flow that had been experienced by the blind, deaf, and ignorant Helen Keller. However, when she discovered myth, i.e. discovered that there is a universal system of symbols, then she discovered the human access to meaning in life.

Nonetheless, the person who chooses so to encounter suffering will still be troubled. That person may still find that in several ways the experience of suffering destroys the powers of life, erodes the ground underfoot, and too easily eliminates those sparks of light which had allowed one previously to hope.

However, one will be able to negotiate through those waters
with imagination. One will thus be able to encounter suffering and
to find that one's self has come to a new assurance. As a result of the
myth one lives in the assuring presence of the Numinous One,
discovered in the myth.

THE BIBLE'S MYTHICAL VIEW OF SUFFERING

At this point the discussion turns to the profile of suffering
that was fashioned by the authors of the Christian New Testament. Those writers needed to fashion myths about the meaning
of suffering.

The person who occupies the focal point of their books had
suffered a terrible death as a criminal in a case of capital punishment. Thereafter the authors reflected upon that disaster and imaginatively fashioned a myth with which to express the meaning of
Jesus' suffering.

The meaning of their myths has been summarized thus—his
suffering was the only path that could have led to the divine victory
planned by God for the entire human community.

The evangelist Luke fashioned this into his myth of the charm-
ing dialogue between two of Jesus' disciples and the Risen One on
the journey to Emmaus. Luke put into the mouth of the Risen One
the meaning of the suffering that the crucified Jesus had had to face:

> "Was it not necessary that the Christ should suffer these things
> and enter into his glory?" And beginning with Moses and all the
> prophets, he interpreted to them in all the scriptures the things
> concerning himself (Lk 24:26).

"The things concerning himself" that Luke may have imaged
the Risen One as having interpreted could very well have been the
experiences in Jesus' life that recalled the images from the myth of
the Suffering Servant of Isaiah 53. The early Christian community
often used that myth to formulate its image of the crucified Lord.
With that myth Jesus could be interpreted as having vicariously
suffered for all people.

Isaiah had imagined his Suffering Servant as one marred so
totally that he could no longer be identified, as a man of sorrows, as

one despised and rejected. The meaning which Isaiah had imaginatively fashioned for this victim of suffering and the myth which Luke's Risen One may have applied to himself was that the Servant (in Isaiah) and Jesus (in Luke) had born the griefs and sorrows that were due to all human beings. In so bearing the suffering that is actually due to all humans, the Servant and the Crucified One were imagined to have healed and made whole all humans (Is 53:4–5).

That was the kind of victory that the evangelists portrayed God as having planned for Jesus of Nazareth. That was such a victory, however, that was possible only if Jesus was willing to pass through the mystery that surrounds suffering.

Luke and the other evangelists had not claimed that Isaiah's myth of the Suffering Servant could be extended from Jesus' sufferings to interpret others' suffering. However, they have implied that persons who suffer encounter therein a positive, not a negative human experience. Those who suffer receive in that experience the opportunity that Jesus had received—namely, to give themselves wholly to the mystery and to the Numinous One who is present in the mystery.

In the suffering that Jesus had endured, Jesus had the opportunity so to give himself.

This inverts the conventional approach to suffering. The senses perceive suffering to lead to a defeat; it is therefore to be shunned at all costs. The New Testament challenges believers trustingly to perceive that suffering can be accepted with trust.

Perhaps those who suffer may not know how their suffering could be a victory. In fact, some New Testament scholars argue that even Jesus may not have known how his suffering might have been anything other than a total defeat. Yet both in the evangelists' myth about Jesus' experience of suffering and in the Lewis–Chesterton myth, the one who suffers is challenged to trust that in the mystery of suffering one encounters not a futile experience, but somehow a more grand project.

THIS WORLDVIEW REQUIRES HOPE

Thus the one who suffers can trust that victory comes to those who hope. Such extraordinary confidence in the individual who suffers is possible not because one trusts the mystery to be satisfy-ing or attractive, but because one trusts the Numinous One. To the victim that One will most likely not be present to the senses; yet the victim can trust. The individual can imitate Lewis' imaging, even motivated as it was by rage.

Apparently in the experiences which C.S. Lewis cited in his *A Grief Observed*, he had only a very dim vision of a presence within his grief. He had neither sensed nor understood that presence. How-ever, he had responded to something in his grief that he could not sense.

This trust in that vague something was critical. It enabled him to enter into the unknown dimension of his future.

Without such a trusting worldview, one is likely to perceive little else than that one has been unwillingly separated from the life that the healthy enjoy.

However, before one can assume such a trust, one needs to ask how one might be able to adopt such a perspective.

This question appears to be founded upon prior questions—namely, whether one trusts that the Numinous One can be present in every experience and whether one is willing to form a relation-ship with that One.

In the New Testament Jesus was portrayed as suffering ex-treme anxiety (Gethsemane) and violence (Golgotha). Yet in the midst of that suffering he was portrayed as having trusted in the Numinous One ("My God, my God, why have you . . ."—Psalm 22). He was imagined as trusting that his experiences, although apparently destructive, were ultimately good.

HOPE IS GROUNDED IN THE "ABBA" EXPERIENCE

This trust was portrayed as grounded in Jesus' perception of his relationship with the Numinous One, whom Chesterton identi-fied in Lewis' rage and whom Jesus identified as "Abba." Jesus was envisioned as having considered that his relationship with the myste-rious "Abba" (and, hence, with mystery) was the fundamental event in his life. All other experiences, even his suffering, were imagined to be understood by him to belong within his Abba-experience.

Every experience was imagined as having been perceived by Jesus as offered to him by the loving Abba. Nonetheless, some of those experiences led him into situations that he could not comprehend. Still, he was portrayed as trusting that the Numinous One had invited him so to orient himself toward mystery. Thus Jesus was portrayed as needing to imagine that there was something more in those mysterious situations than he was able to grasp with his senses, his reason, or his analytical powers.

Consequently, his experiences of severe anxiety in Gethsemane and of violence on Golgotha were portrayed by the New Testament as his responding to the Numinous One, not simply as his experiencing anxiety or suffering. Jesus was portrayed as having trusted that not only the more conventional events of his life, but even those apparently destroying events had been lovingly offered to him by Abba ("My God, my God, why have you . . ."—Psalm 22).

Because that relationship was the primordial event in his life, suffering was, consequently, a positive opportunity to nurture that relationship.

Jesus, before being arrested, was portrayed as having gone to the Mount of Olives, i.e. to the garden of Gethsemane, to pray. There the evangelists Matthew, Mark, and Luke portrayed him as having entered into a dialogue with the Numinous One—his Abba. They portrayed Jesus as having struggled to trust that Abba was with him even as the events of his life moved toward his desperate execution.

This interpretation of the hidden purpose of Abba in choosing that Jesus suffer suggests a perspective for those who suffer and who frustratingly ask the purpose of suffering. As the purpose of Jesus' suffering was hidden from him, so the purpose of every person's suffering remains similarly hidden.

The evangelists also portray Jesus as still trusting that his Abba was with him even as death was erasing his life.

Matthew and Mark portray him as praying the first line of Psalm 22 in his last moments of life, "*Eli, Eli, lama sabachthani?*" (Mt 27:46). That was not a cry, but the opening line from Psalm 22, a prayer of trust in the midst of suffering. Thus, even as he endured the torture of death, Jesus was envisioned as having trusted that the Numinous One, his Abba, was with him and was offering that death to him.

The evangelists had fashioned a Christian ideal—namely, those who suffer can trust that God has a purpose in having chosen that particular individual to suffer. Therefore, they have a basis for hope that their suffering has a significance. They are urged to imagine that there is more to suffering than the pain and destruction that overwhelm its victims.

NOT HOPE, BUT ALIENATION

Yet how can those who suffer envision in an honest manner that a personal God is present within the experience of suffering: those who suffer are acutely conscious not of being accompanied, but of being isolated. How can they honestly envision that the Numinous One is summoning them from within the mystery of suffering? What could be the basis for such faith? What evidence has been offered to those persons to invite them so to trust in a personal presence? Might this trust in a presence not be only a wish, a projection of one's fantasy, or even a frantic escape from the dread that one is completely isolated? Might the choice to trust in a presence, therefore, be nothing more than a fantacized escape from the hard-headed perception that is actually available to those who suffer? Might this trust be no more than a vain hope that, while the human community goes on with the business of living, those who suffer are not as useless as they appear? Perhaps this trust is but the evangelists' blindly leaping in the dark in the hope that the Father-God accompanied Jesus in his sufferings.

THE SUMMONS BY THE INTERIOR VOICE

In an effort to argue against such attitudes, I presented the Lewis–Chesterton myth. There Chesterton interpreted *A Grief Observed* not as a fantasized hope, but as a genuine human response to an actual human experience. Chesterton focused upon the evidence in Lewis' suffering that had been the outline of Lewis' human experience of being summoned.

Chesterton had supported Lewis by citing "What the Thunder Said" in *The Waste Land* by T.S. Eliot. There Eliot had acknowledged the additional Someone who was present with Shackleton's Antarctic expedition during those times when the possibility of staying alive appeared to be lost.

The vision offered by Chesterton is that, during such times of extreme human need, especially during times of physical suffering, the victim glimpses somewhere within that he or she is not alone. There is an additional Someone who is accompanying the victim.

Some might quite easily dismiss this as a futile hope that arises from the desperation of being alone. However, the vision available to the imagination is that this Someone has been repeatedly glimpsed.

That presence had been vaguely glimpsed by the Shackleton expedition.

The Steinbeck voyage through the Gulf of California had also been conscious of being accompanied by such a presence.

The myth identifies that presence as having appeared to Lewis as he composed *A Grief Observed*.

This Numinous One appears with such frequency among human persons that it can indeed induce a pause in one's reflection. Among humans, this experience of the presence of an extra Someone in moments of human extremities is so widespread that one might be very reluctant casually to dismiss it.

This might prompt one to question whether humans rage at suffering rather than accept it because they dimly perceive something that other animals have not perceived? Have humans heard a summons during experiences of suffering from a Someone who encourages them to aspire to a superior form a life? Do those who suffer receive, as C.S. Lewis received, an invitation to demand that life be not destroyed by suffering? Does a Someone urge humans to envision life as too great to be destroyed by suffering? Does this One urge them to insist that life be always led along paths that lead, if not to joy, then at least to hope?

Because that interior summons is heard by almost every individual human who suffers, it appears to be universal. Thus it needs to be taken seriously. The interior summons has been interpreted to come from a Someone.

Moreover, because this summons is a universal experience among those who suffer, it therefore appears to be more than a wish. It perhaps arises from a Someone who is more than a wish.

Some of those who have chosen to respect this interior movement have identified it as the spirit.

That individual is more human who reverences the spirit that moves in one's interior life.

Conversely, to the extent that one ignores that spirit, to that extent one is closing one's self off from one's authentic, interior, and human dynamics.

Jesus of Nazareth had urged his hearers to take that interior dynamic very seriously. He taught that the Abba–God communicates with humans through such movements of the spirit.

They are to respond to the spirit with more fidelity than they respond to the demands of reason. They are to perceive that the journey toward greater humanity lies not along the intellectually alluring path of logical systems, but along the vaporous path of spirit.

This, if while discussing the spirit, they were to attend only to the demands of reason, then they would be dismissing the spirit as an empty wish. There are persons who refuse so to dismiss the spirit. They trust that in such interior summonses the spirit is inviting them, even in their suffering, to trust that there is a mystery into which the victims are invited to enter. They have chosen to put more weight upon the subtle, non-sensuous, incomprehensible, and fleeting movements of their interior spirits than in the more socially valuable results of logic, reason, politics, and economics. They have, moreover, chosen to live by the values that are found within the enigmatic contours of mystery.

BEING HUMAN IS MYSTERY

This is part of the mystery of being human! An example of one who was conscious of this mystery is Robert Bolt. He projected his awareness of mystery onto his characterization of Sir Thomas More's response to the Oath of Allegiance.

King Henry VIII had pleaded with More to take the Oath recognizing Henry to be the head of the church in England.

More refused. He consequently was deprived not only of his office as Henry's Chancellor of the Realm, but also of his wealth and his freedom. Henry imprisoned More in the Tower of London in order to force him to swear to the Oath.

Robert Bolt's portrayal of More in prison is Bolt's imaginative expression of his own response to a non-rational, interior movement.

The context in which to situate this imagined portrayal is Bolt's self-confession in the introduction to the play: "But I am not a Catholic, nor even in the meaningful sense of the word a Christian."

Though not motivated by the demands or the doctrines of the Christian faith, Bolt had still discovered that a person can attain to an acute sense of self. He evidently concluded that those who have a sense of their own interior self-worth discover a mysterious interior movement that may be mysterious, but that appears to be superior to all other values. Bolt had created the character of Thomas More as one such human person.

> Thomas More, as I wrote about him, became for me a man with an adamantine sense of his own self.
>
> This account of him developed as I wrote: what first attracted me was a person who could not be accused of any incapacity for life, who indeed seized life in great variety and almost greedy quantities, who nevertheless *found something in himself without which life was valueless* and when that was denied him was able to grasp his death [italics mine].
>
> Anyway, the above must serve as my explanation and apology for treating Thomas More, a Christian saint, as a hero of selfhood.[1]

The point to be emphasized here is that Robert Bolt, while not subscribing to the Christian doctrine of the presence of God within the individual, expressed his own vision of the peerless value of an interior presence. He expressed this by creating the character of Thomas More, who "seized life in great variety and almost greedy quantities." Before being imprisoned, More had lived a materially satisfying life.

However, as Bolt continued in the introduction to the play, Thomas More "nevertheless found something in himself without which life was valueless." Bolt envisioned the person More as discovering that the enigmatic, interior movements of the spirit were of more value than the materially satisfying life that was More's to seize if he but ignored his spirit.

Thus Bolt created the dialogue within the play between More, his daughter Margaret, and his wife Alice:

> Margaret: But in reason! Haven't you done as much as God can reasonably want?
> More: Well . . . finally . . . it isn't a matter of reason; finally it's a matter of love.
> Alice: You're content, then, to be shut up here with mice and rats when you might be home with us!
> More: (flinching) Content? If they open a crack that wide (between finger and thumb) I'd be through it.[2]

Robert Bolt's Thomas More portrays the tension that the individual experiences when one chooses to place one's value in one's spirit, although one knows that one's value appears to be more securely placed in one's material satisfactions.

If Thomas More had taken the Oath, as a great many of the prelates and priests of his England had done, he would have resumed his power and wealth as Henry's Chancellor of the Realm. However, Bolt imagined that Thomas More, or any individual, could respond to the spirit's invitations rather than to pressure or to the power and wealth that an individual might otherwise seize.

Bolt's Thomas More responded to an interior movement that summoned him to say nothing, though he therefore was to remain in prison and, eventually, to lose his life. Bolt was expressing his own awareness of the presence of a Numinous One. Though not a believer, Bolt was affirming a presence who so relates to the individual that one can choose to pay any price in order to respond to that presence.

Each one of us knows such persons. They are genuine human puzzles. They have chosen to base their values not upon reason, or power, or acquisitions, but upon a reverence for the interior movements of their spirits.

They are the ones who go so far as to trust, even in suffering, to respond to their spirit's summons to enter mystery. They do not calculate the cost of so responding.

They have responded to the summons to live with the confidence that life is better, not to the extent that they acquire more, but to the extent that they embrace life as they encounter it.

This is a hope based not upon that which can be sensed, but upon a spirit that can be no more than vaguely glimpsed.

However, the mystery of life is seen not only in such people. The mystery of life is seen by all individuals in the experience of the interior non-sensuous spirit. All can be aware of the interior mystery in the form of the presence of One who summons. All can be aware of the interior invitation to enter into mystery and, thus, to respond to life in a manner that is at odds with conventional manners of responding.

THE SPIRIT—WITNESS TO MYSTERY

All individuals, including the victims of suffering, can acknowledge this presence, this non-sensuous spirit. Who could have the power to gain access to human consciousness, even to those painful moments when the individual is constantly being distracted by the experience of suffering? One cannot help but hypothesize that the One who could have such power is the One identified by believers as God.

God is believed to have created the world and, thus, to have control over everything, even, to an extent, over human consciousness.

Thus the victim of suffering can imagine that one's interior voice is that of the transcendent God, summoning the victim to believe that God continues to fashion the world even in the experience of mystery. God is believed always to be expanding the horizon within which humans live and in which they discover their future. In experiences of suffering, God is believed to be carefully pruning the human branches.

The evangelist John had envisioned the God of Jesus Christ as the vinedresser who cuts away every branch that bears no fruit and who prunes every branch that does bear fruit so that it bears even more (Jn 15:1–2).

This vision of God's incomprehensible, mysterious activity in the midst of the human community is similar to the vision of the Lewis–Chesterton myth: the victim of suffering needs to trust that the interior movement is God, who uses human suffering to nurture creation. Sometimes that God judges that creation can be better nurtured by the suffering of pruning than by a word of comfort.

HOPE FOR THAT WHICH CANNOT BE SEEN

Thus, first of all the one who suffers is called, even from within the midst of pain, to believe that, in encountering painful and seemingly unjustified experiences, one is being led toward something better. Nonetheless, this something better may most probably remain shrouded. Therefore, one can permit one's self so to be led only to the extent that one chooses to proceed with trust and hope. One can so let go of the seeming need for security and certitude only if one places great confidence in the One who summons.

Alternately, there are individuals who so experience life as always soothing. They may indeed be among the most fortunate of people. However, they may also be constantly seeking out buffers behind which to live. They may find life soothing because they avoid those painful experiences in which they might hear this summons to follow the Numinous One. They may be blocking themselves from being able to discover the mystery in life.

The process of expanding one's experiences to be open to mystery may challenge some to expose themselves to being stretched and pulled, to being even at times pruned. Those who allow themselves to be vulnerable to such experiences can discover that their lives unfold onto a much broader plane.

In thus encountering the mystery of suffering they can expect the manner in which they are human to expand. They will be enabled to be empathetic with a greater breadth of human feeling.

They might discover others who are so opened: those summoned in the Antarctic Circle (T.S. Eliot's reference in "What the Thunder Said"), those in the Gulf of California (John Steinbeck's reference), the playwright (Robert Bolt, who envisioned Thomas More's response to the spirit), and many individuals like ourselves (associates who have been called out by their spirit).

This range of responding individuals makes clear that in any circumstance, suffering included, individuals may be aware that they are being summoned. Individuals in any circumstance may become conscious of the interior Someone who invites them to follow into a dimension that they might not otherwise choose to go.

Because of a trust in the Someone who beckons, individuals can follow with hope, even into a forbidding experience. The Someone may dimly suggest to them that through the enigma of suffering they may advance to something better.

The critical point that must be faced by those who are aware of this summons is their choice whether to respond to the invitation or to ignore it.

ROBERT BOLT'S FAITH IN THE MYSTERY

Robert Bolt's portrayal of Thomas More manifests Bolt's desire (and perhaps his decision) to respond to the numinous invitation to turn aside—as Bolt imagined that Thomas More turned aside—from rational arguments and material satisfactions and to enter into that which cannot be empirically grasped. Bolt envisioned the summons to be able to be worthy of such trust that his Thomas More followed the summons trustingly even as it led to his murder.

If one were to seek the reason for Bolt's response, one could find Bolt's explanation of his vision. He explained in his introduction to *A Man for All Seasons* that one might find something within oneself without which life is valueless. Thus Bolt envisioned his More as choosing to respond to that "something" because he valued and trusted it more than he trusted and valued anything or anyone else. He had not, however, been able to comprehend in the summons any specific value or definite purpose other than that "something." He certainly had not followed the path into prison because it led to a perceived value or a comprehensible purpose.

Bolt expressed in the dialogue of the play the possibility that a man like his Thomas More (and apparently like himself) might respond to the interior summons out of love.

There have certainly been many individuals who have made such a response to interior invitations. Some suffering individuals have responded in their pain to a presence active within their suffering. They have responded to a presence that they could identify with no more precision than as something vaguely numinous. They had received no more than an intimation that this numinous presence bid them first to live not by the conventional values of security and certitude. Then this presence bid them to trust that there is an absolute value in responding to the interior summons.

The Continuing Enigma

The previous chapter focused upon experiencing a Numinous One who is present to the individual who suffers. That personal presence may indeed bring significant value to an individual who suffers. Nonetheless, as was evident in the raging by C.S. Lewis, even that presence does not prevent the experience of suffering from continuing to cast its shadow. Many who suffer are still devastated by the problem of evil, especially those victims who are also believers.

Thus there is more that needs to be said concerning the condition of the human person who suffers.

First of all, that person needs to acknowledge that to be human is a mystery.

That mystery can be perceived in a variety of ways. One such is available to those who respect the sacredness of the human conscience. The conscience can seek to be free from sin and to be forgiven so as to nurture one's mysterious relationship with God.

Consequently, as Karl Rahner has argued, the human person finds himself or herself to be in a relationship with an absolute mystery; therefore the human person must himself or herself be mystery. Otherwise, there would be no way that the person could be conscious of having sinned against or been forgiven by One who remains veiled in mystery.[1]

Because the human person is thus acknowledged to be mystery, any effort to reflect upon the person's relationship to suffering needs to acknowledge that mystery. If the human is mystery in some way, then all one's relationships need to be treated with the reverence that is appropriate in relating to mystery.

SUFFERING IS A UNIVERSAL EXPERIENCE

Human suffering, for example, participates in the mystery that is the human person.

Moreover, suffering can even be interpreted to belong to the very core of being human: every human being must endure suffering, sometimes acute, sometimes painful. Many suffer from bodily handicaps. Some, from injury. Some, from having too little to eat. Some, from being imprisoned either physically or psychically. Some, from various nervous or psychic illnesses.

In industrialized lands many suffer from industrial congestion or smog. In such lands some suffer from the stress of the work that is physically or psychically demanding. Others there are oppressed by their lack of contact with nature, e.g. their inability to spend time in rustic environments; others, by the demands that they organize and plan to anticipate errors, failures, catastrophes, and deficits.

Of course, the limit-event of suffering, which confronts every human being, is one's own approach to death. Even those who affirm life passionately must confront the termination of their lives.

RELIGION'S RESPONSE TO SUFFERING

A significant question that can be asked of all who thus in some manner confront suffering is whether religion functions, if not as a solution or a resolution, at least as a help in encountering suffering.

Insofar as religion is expected to make suffering disappear, to that extent Karl Marx correctly rejected religion as "the opium of the people." There have indeed been believers who assume that, if they are religiously faithful, they will avoid suffering.

However, the value of religion may be rather that it equips the believer to encounter suffering.

In the book of Job the author envisions religious faith as offering no relief from suffering; religion is not a resolution for the problem of suffering. However, the author does envision religion as providing a vision of trust.

The poet of the book of Job (hereafter, "the poet") had acknowledged that the victim of suffering eventually in some manner formulates the question "why." Those who suffer seek to understand the tragedy that, seemingly without significance, has fallen upon them. Thus Job does not complain that he has to suffer, but demands to know why suffering is his fate.

The poet uses the device of the three (and eventually four) friends to formulate the various human efforts to make up answers to the question of "why" suffering has fallen upon an individual. The poet has Job argue convincingly against all of their various formulations of the purpose of suffering.

Thus, unable to discover a human answer to the problem of his suffering, Job desires that God account for the suffering.

The God of the poem responds to Job's demand for a divine audience.

However, God does not accept Job's challenge that God must defend divine justice. On the contrary, the poet's God challenges Job to recognize the gap between Job's perspective upon the world and God's. The poet envisages God as demanding that Job acknowledge that the Lord of the universe is indeed Lord. All the events of the universe are to be left to the responsibility of God, e.g. the presence and purpose of the behemoth, the hippopotamus, the leviathan, and the crocodile.

How could Job presume that he is capable of confronting the divine wisdom?

Job bows in acceptance.

However, the poet has envisioned Job not as bowing to the superior wisdom of God—no divine wisdom has been presented. Rather, the poet's Job bows to God's goodness in choosing to permit Job to experience God. Because God is with him, he does not face the problem of suffering alone.

Yet the poet has envisioned that, although God responds to the human problem of suffering with the divine presence, God offers no answer to Job's needy question.[2]

That is a response to the problem of suffering more radical than my own. My proposal is that the problem of suffering can be addressed not by reason, not by analysis, but by an intuitive leap of the imagination.

The poet of the book of Job, however, appears to have proposed that there is no human response whatsoever to the problem of suffering. Humans must acknowledge that they remain always bounded by time and determined by history. Thus they can use neither reason, nor analysis, nor even imagination in addressing the problem. Humans can do no more than place their trust in the God who is beyond time and history. The poet appears to propose that humans can expect only this as a religious response to the problem of suffering: the response of trust.

The poet suggested that religion offers no relief for those who suffer.

SUFFERING AND THE CROSS

However, Christianity has proposed that one see in the cross of Christ (thus, that one see in the suffering of the believer) the power and the wisdom of God. Thus, the believer is to accept suffering as an opportunity to suffer with Christ. Thereby, together with Christ, the believing victim reveals God's power and wisdom.

The victim who believes in God still confronts the tension between being a victim of suffering and being a person who believes in a God who is good and powerful. This tension is at the most softened, not erased, by imagining that a Numinous One is present, or by recalling the parable that God prunes those who might bear more fruit, or imagining that the Numinous One summons the victim trustingly to enter into mystery.

THE BELIEVING VICTIM CONFRONTS A CONTRADICTION

The Lewis–Chesterton myth addresses that tension. It softens its hard lines. Formerly the angular profile of that tension blocked the light; the victim was enshrouded. The myth draws attention to a previously unnoticed curve in the profile of the problem of suffering. Because of the relationship of the Numinous One to the victim, at least one ray of light escapes to reach the victim of suffering.

Nonetheless, in spite of the softening effected by that one curve, the experience of suffering is hard and forbidding. The one who suffers can still interpret the event to be an attack by a mindless, impersonal force. Suffering lays siege with no apparent purpose. The attack appears to have value neither in itself nor in its effects. On the contrary its senseless and brutal stripping of human powers and human capacities dehumanizes the victim. In place of those lost powers and capacities it leaves only a void.

Such hard lines can, however, appear to be made more supple by the myth.

First the victim can imagine an enigmatic, numinous personal Presence who acts purposely within the occurrence of suffering.

Second, the victim can expect that, because one can imagine that there is a value in suffering, there is such a value. However, the victim is able to identify that value only as mystery.

Furthermore the forbidding profile of suffering can be softened insofar as suffering can be imagined to be a divine pruning. The victim can imagine that the divine One is nurturing the victim so that the victim may in some way become more fertile.

That is the mythic interpretation proposed by the evangelist John.

John portrayed his Jesus as proclaiming that God uses human suffering to prune the trees to increase fertility (Jn 15:1–8).

Yet the pruning, i.e. the dismembering of human capacities so as to develop a more human individual, does not appear to be a value to the victim of the pruning. The victim would prefer to remain sound as one had previously been, rather than have to suffer the pruning.

Nonetheless, there have been a number of such victims who have valued their experience of suffering. However terrible that suffering, some have come to judge it to have been their primary access to a new vision of the meaning of their lives.

These victims might wish, moreover, that they might have found a path toward such meaning that had been more of an acceleration and less of a catastrophe. They might wish that they had been able to accompany the human community in its climb, rather than to have been detoured onto a steep slide which they had to navigate alone.

Another value in suffering appears in the Lewis–Chesterton myth: the suffering individual forms many relationships.

THE INCOMPREHENSIBLE WORLD
OF ALBERT CAMUS

Albert Camus, for example, insisted that suffering be acknowledged as having a relationship to justice. He repeatedly expressed his conviction that the world, as humans know it, suffers an absence of justice and thus of meaning. Because he found the world and its occurrences to be so incomprehensible, he insisted that he could not comprehend any meaning for the word "God." In fact, he even went so far as to revolt against the presumption that humanity can presume to find any meaning within a world that is religious or rational.

Camus chose to acknowledge the incomprehensibility of the world. He thus stood on the shadow side of human life.

Within that shadowed context, he sought always to find light in the relationships formed by occurrences. When he sought for an answer to the problem of evil, he insisted upon its relationship to goodness.

Camus so situated himself that he located every meaning in a relation to persons. Thus any answer was integrated into a complex process. That process was the context for the events in the exterior world, as also the context for the events in the interior world of human consciousness.

In that relational context every secular occurrence remains contingent upon other events. Thus suffering in that integrated process could not be reduced to the consequence of human sin; that would be simply too narrow a concept. The process is much more broad. Nor could that relational context be content to reduce suffering to an appropriate stimulus for humans to grow to maturity. The event of suffering is far more complex than that.

THE MYTH'S WORLD OF HOPE

The Lewis–Chesterton myth has situated the problem of suffering in such a broader context. Moreover, it has not pretended to remove the anxieties from suffering. It has acknowledged that because suffering has the power to terrorize, many humans, like C.S. Lewis, must live within life's shadow. It has also portrayed an image of God that locates God as well on the shrouded side of life.

It acknowledges nonetheless that when humans encounter suffering, they may be summoned to hope.

Fyodor Dostoevsky has also visualized in the figure of Alyosha Karamazov the non-rational but nonetheless human value of suffering. Alyosha represents for Dostoevsky the human beauty that the people of Russia have harvested from their centuries of suffering. The Russians had been pruned into beauty. Dostoevsky projected that beauty in Alyosha's choice to be open to suffering.

Alyosha symbolizes every human's need always to allow one's self to be vulnerable to suffering.

The consequent hope is the more profound value of human suffering. There are individuals who, through their suffering, have discovered that they have been enabled to face all of life with hope.

Admittedly many of those who suffer find themselves lost in despair. They find that they need more personal presence and compassion than they had needed previously. The human community, however, may not be able to offer such presence and compassion to those who despair. Thus some of those who suffer have learned that the human community appears to be indifferent to them in their need. Yet they must never so respond with indifference.

Their choice to offer their presence and compassion to every individual is an expression of their hope.

Thus the human dispositions that some victims of suffering, like Alyosha and the Russians, had learned from their suffering have formed their attitude toward life into a hope. Those persons who so have learned from their suffering have uncovered the fertile ground from which might grow an interior serenity.

Consequently, if those individuals reflect upon their experience of suffering, they might very well perceive suffering's arcane significance. They might infer that suffering, while it may well destroy, can also nurture in persons the dispositions of desiring to be present to others, to be compassionate to others, to live always in hope, and to be interiorly serene.

That vision of the value of suffering has been shared by those who, like C.S. Lewis in *A Grief Observed*, somehow imagine that in their experience of suffering, they do not have to submit. They, like Lewis, had intuited within their pain the interior summons to demand that life be better. They had been invited to reject a life shattered by suffering and to judge that being human requires something far better. They had been challenged, thereby, to confront the mystery.

These people, in so responding, were recognizing the summons of their spirit to live not with despair, but with hope, to temper their pain with the demand that human life could be better, even if they could not see how that hope could be realized.

SUFFERING LIES BEYOND THE REACH OF REASON

My proposition, therefore, is that intractable enigmas like suffering are indeed insoluble. They are among those occurrences within the world that lie beyond the range of that which human reason can comprehend. Certainly human suffering is beyond that range; so too human love; so too the workings of the human mind; even the world of quantum physics; and certainly the divine being.

Of course, any appropriate image of God is forbidding.

One cause of such forbidding images is sin. A great many Old Testament authors assume that sin is the cause of all suffering and all evil. Some Old Testament authors also assume that God is capable of so controlling the world that God manages even the effects of sin. However, as others argue, if God is all good, then how could God have any degree of contact with sin, i.e., how could God tolerate so immediate an interrelating with sin that God manages its effects?

Still another problem with the Old Testament image of God is the manner of interpreting the suffering of God. Under the influence of Aristotle and Thomas Aquinas, Christians believe that the being of God is without any limitation. The problem then is that the unlimited being of God may leave God with no option but to suffer without any limitation.

Nevertheless, in spite of any illumination about God and sin that the imagination has so provided, in spite of any hope that might thus be fashioned for victims of pain, humans continue to suffer. Those humans continue to experience suffering as a destruction.

On the periphery of their consciousness they might catch glimpses of an attitude of hope in suffering.

Nevertheless, they endure suffering's power to disrupt their human plans and hopes, to sweep aside their concerns for their security and the security of their dependents. They are still crushed by terror when they learn that they have a fatal disease, or that their beloved ones have such a disease, or that any other tragedy is about to crush them.

As the earth upon which the victim stands is eroding underfoot, the person no longer finds a security. Then the person can no longer seriously hope. That person's goals are being shattered. That person's relationships are coming undone. That individual's self-identity is being torn apart.

Thus how else can the individual honestly judge the experience of suffering than as a destructive and evil event? The suffering individual who has heard the Lewis–Chesterton myth or who has heard in his or her own suffering the summons of the Numinous One may remain simply a victim.

The myth has not resolved the problem of evil, and has certainly not removed that problem. When suffering appears in one's life, even in the life of a person gifted with imagination, that person's life is blown apart.

THE EXPERIENCED VALUE OF SUFFERING

Still, there have been victims who have discovered some value in their suffering. Some have valued the mysterious effect that suffering has had on their lives. As a result of being swept into the mystery, they have become more present and sensitive to others. More significantly, they have become more aware of the presence of the Numinous One in every experience.

The Lewis–Chesterton myth did not intend to suggest that suffering is kind. It did not deny that suffering can indeed explode the values of victims' lives. The use of one's imagination does not remove the debris.

However, the myth did intend to suggest that the individual who suffers can find some value in that very dynamic which sweeps the victim into ruin. That dynamic appears, certainly, to be negative. It continues to appear to be negative even in the worldview of the myth. However, the myth envisions that dynamic as inverting the negative meaning, if not the negative value of suffering.

The Lewis–Chesterton myth envisions human life as of far too grand a stature to be mindlessly destroyed by suffering.

However, the myth interprets the victims' sensitivity for lost goods not as quixotic pretenses, but as interior summonses from the Numinous One to confront the mystery of suffering with hope that the Numinous One responds.

Such a vision of hope is not as impossibly distant from the victims as it might at first appear to be. Paul the apostle had found that vision to be plausible. He had urged Christians to hope that they are immersed in the Christ. In their suffering they participate in the suffering of the Crucified One, but they also participate with the Risen One in victoriously rising to new life.

Moreover, those who are able to identify with Paul's image of being immersed in the Lord can open themselves to experience both suffering and the Lord's victory over suffering.

12

The Resolution of Suffering

This study has fashioned a resolution for the problem of suffering. It began with a review of the mysterious problem that is known as evil. That mystery was articulated in the contradiction between the Judeo-Christian belief in a good, powerful God and the mindless, random destruction of human institutions and values by the power of evil.

Next the argument focused upon human suffering as the human experience in which many individuals encounter the problem of evil.

The victims of suffering must endure the consequences of evil's attack upon their persons and lives. Such consequences are multiple. Among the more evident of these are unresolved anxiety, depression or despair because of irrational enigma and isolation and alienation from the human community, then the loss of security with the subsequent loss of hope, and finally the inability to find in suffering any significant value or meaning.

At that point, the argument of this book began its positive construction. Within the context of evil and suffering, a myth was fashioned.

Myth approaches the problem of suffering from the perspective not of reason and analysis, but of imaginative intuition.

The mythical approach appears to be a more suitable approach to suffering. Every approach along the path of rational analysis has failed to resolve the timeless and seemingly atheistic problem of evil.

The myth was fashioned with the characters of C.S. Lewis, Gilbert Keith Chesterton, and Lewis' created figure, Ransom. These three were imagined to have a dialogue concerning Lewis' intentions in writing his *A Grief Observed*.

Chesterton proposed that the book's apparent expression of rage at God, e.g. Lewis had indicted God as "the cosmic sadist," was actually Lewis' response to the summons of his own spirit. The spirit had urged Lewis not to be satisfied with destruction and elimination of human life, but to expect that the conditions for life could be vastly improved.

The question that Chesterton had put before us was why Lewis had in *A Grief Observed* consciously responded to such a summons of his spirit with rage. Lewis could not have seriously concluded that anyone in the human condition could be liberated from suffering.

However, the spirit had not convinced Lewis to draw a rational conclusion by analyzing suffering. On the contrary, the spirit had summoned Lewis to approach the problem of suffering by using his imagination. Consequently, Lewis had expressed a rage that life was not as good as he imagined that it could be.

Lewis had chosen to respond to his spirit's challenge to imagine, rather than rationally to analyze the problem. If he had regarded the problem before him as a task soluble by human reason, then he might have concluded cynically that the roll of the dice had gone against him. Yet he had not so regarded the problem. He had chosen to use not his reason, but his imagination. He had heard his spirit summon him to imagine that, in some mysterious, not-yet-fashioned world, human life could be improved. Nonetheless, he could imagine the possibility of such an improvement only if he would put his trust in the Numinous One who through his spirit had summoned him.

Because Lewis had chosen so to respond to this summons of his spirit, he consequently could respond to suffering with hope.

His response had not been the despair that the casual reader of *A Grief Observed* notes. His rage at the present conditions of life was his hope that the mysterious Numinous One can and will recreate human life.

THE VALIDITY OF THE MYTH'S WORLDVIEW

That solid ground on which that myth rests is the proclamation of Jesus of Nazareth that the divine person is present in every experience.

Such a belief transforms the experience of suffering. Those

who suffer are summoned to believe that suffering is not destroying them, though such appears to be the case. Rather, they are to believe that they are being encountered by the Numinous One whom Christian faith identifies as the God of Jesus Christ.

The argument of this study paused at that point in order to defend the human value of any imaginative expression.

Humans very often experience occurrences which they cannot reduce to simple, clean categories. In order to explain such occurrences, humans have most frequently used myth. The consequence has often been that enigmatic occurrences have been represented with a degree of significance; the otherwise inexplicable had been explained by myth.

Thus there has been value in using myth to approach those enigmas which appear to be beyond human comprehension.

Extending this use of myth to the inexplicable enigma of evil, we can expect that there would be a value in using myth to approach the problem of evil as manifest in the problem of suffering.

With that defense of myth as an approach to the enigma of suffering, the implications of the Lewis–Chesterton myth were next articulated.

Those implications are principally that the experience of suffering is a mystery in which the victim encounters a Numinous One who is present in the suffering. Of course not every victim of suffering will acknowledge that he or she has encountered this Numinous One; some are so enraged at having to suffer that they close themselves off from any relationship with the possible source of suffering, i.e. from the Numinous One.

For example, in the myth C.S. Lewis had not been able to recognize his prior rage as inspired by the spirit; Chesterton had led him to do so.

As an immediate caution to its own resolution, the argument then acknowledged that the myth had not completely resolved the problem. The problem of evil, as that of suffering, remains insoluble. The occurrences of evil and suffering within human life remain mysteries. Myth is no more capable than reason and analysis to resolve mystery. However, the myth has proposed an imaginative explanation that to some extent resolves some of the human anxiety caused by suffering.

That is a review of the argument.

THE ATTITUDE OF THE VICTIM IS OF CARDINAL IMPORTANCE

However, whether or not there is value in such an argument depends upon the manner in which the victim of suffering attempts to grasp the enigma of pain. The test of the worth of the myth is whether or not it illumines experience for the victim.

The major experienced problems in acute suffering are mental and psychological. The victim fears that bearing the disease or enduring the loss has no significance to anyone. The victim is stripped of human dignity because of the isolation and alienation that must be borne in suffering.

These problems are directly confronted by the myth.

The Numinous One, dimly encountered by the victim in the experience, but envisioned in the myth, non-sensuously calls to the victim to trust the spirit as working toward a purpose. This vaguely perceived summons is a pledge that there is significance in the suffering, even if that meaning remains hidden.

However, even if there is such a significance in the suffering, it, as well as the purpose of suffering, remains hidden from the victim. Only perhaps the One veiled within the mystery grasps that which is being accomplished.

THE TRAP THAT ALWAYS LIES BEFORE HUMAN REASON

The apostle Paul had eventually approached the mystery of the suffering and death of Christ Jesus as though he were able to resolve it by using his reason. Although he had been wise enough initially to address these enigmas by way of myth, he then used his rational powers in an attempt to remove the mystery from suffering.

Thus he analyzed the rational explanation for the cause of suffering to be that sin leads to suffering. God strikes with suffering those individuals who have placed themselves in self-seeking.

He also analyzed the rational explanation for Jesus' suffering: Christ Jesus' passion and death had been part of the divine plan by which all humans receive forgiveness and thus become the adopted children of God.

Not only the apostle Paul but several others have analyzed the experience of suffering to be the consequence of sin.

The author of the second book of Samuel returns to that theme again and again. For example, he so analyzed King David's suffering at the time of the death of the child that Bathsheba had conceived. The cause of King David suffering the loss of his child was his having sinned in seducing Bathsheba. So too the author of 2 Samuel analyzed the cause of suffering during the civil war that David had to endure: David's suffering then had also been caused by David's sin in seducing Bathsheba (2 Sam 12–16).

The prophet Jeremiah analyzed the evils that were to come upon Judah as caused by Judah's many sins (Jer 8).

John Hick's *Evil and the God of Love* repeats the same theme— sin is the cause of suffering.

Conversely, the author of the book of Job argued that suffering is a mystery that cannot be analyzed.

There is no analytical cause that humans can identify as the source of suffering. No cause, not even sin, so argues the author of Job, can be identified as the explanation for suffering in the life of anyone.

Moreover, the reflective individual, especially the reflective individual who has suffered, is acutely aware that any analysis of suffering fails to remove the enigma. Even if suffering were a consequence of sin, still the experience of acute suffering remains a mystery.

THE MYTH SIDESTEPS THE RATIONAL TRAP

The Lewis–Chesterton myth has sought to avoid the trap of analyzing suffering. It acknowledges that suffering and death are mysteries and remain mysteries. The myth proposes that the victim of suffering experiences an invitation to allow one's self to enter into the unknown.

One can envision that Jesus of Nazareth, a fully human individual, responded to his torture and suffering by acknowledging them as mysteries. As a human he could have grasped no meaning in his suffering and murder other than that he was being summoned trustingly to surrender himself to the mystery.

Furthermore, the myth envisions that any victim of suffering is capable of fashioning no other adequate response to the mystery of suffering.

In spite of that, some conventionally rational victims of suffering have chosen to address suffering by rejecting as fantasy the worldview that envisions a Numinous One as summoning the victim to surrender to mystery.

Certainly the conventional, western, rational assessment of myth is that myth is superficial; the rational mind does not find myth to be an adequate basis on which to construct a response to a problem.

Alternately, a victim of suffering can choose to be imaginative, can address the mystery of suffering mythically.

In this case the victim can imagine that the self encounters the Numinous One who stands in the shadow with the victim. There in the darkness the interior spirit asks the victim to trust.

However, the most profound problem that the victim faces is the absence of hope. In some cases, this absence becomes depression; sometimes, despair.

For this, the myth offers a direct resolution.

THE MYTH REGARDS SUFFERING IMAGINATIVELY

The myth invites the victim, perhaps fleetingly and distantly, but nonetheless actually, to perceive something within the experience of suffering that bids one to look beyond the suffering. Insofar as the victim is willing to use her or his imagination and thus to be aware of that bidding, to that extent one can discover a source of hope even within the suffering.

One can imagine that the suffering will develop into something good.

However, there are less imaginative victims. There are victims who approach life only with Euclidean minds. These have chosen to rely upon the rational mind. As a result of that approach, these will find in the myth no resolution for the problems of suffering.

This mythic resolution of the problem of suffering cannot claim to be final. It has proposed that the victim trust that the divine presence accompanies the individual who suffers.

The inadequacy of this approach is most noticeable when the

myth is offered to a person like Ivan Karamazov who confronted unjustified suffering by insisting that God could not have been present there. Those like Ivan who are unable so to trust in an unsensed Presence will be compelled to deny that there is a purpose in experiences of unjustified suffering. The evil there can be too great; then such Euclidean minds will be forced to conclude either that there is no God, or to insist that, if there is a God, God is not good.

Nonetheless, the believer, like Alyosha Karamazov, imaginatively insists that God is always present and always good.

THE MYTH INVITES HOPE

Such believers have chosen to listen to the hushed bidding that they had perceived to whisper to them from within their suffering. They imagine that there is a Numinous One in their interior dynamic.

Perhaps such a conclusion had required for its foundation a prior trust that God encounters persons in every experience. We have noted earlier T.S. Eliot's "What the Thunder Said," in which he cited the Antarctic expedition that had continually, even if ambiguously, been aware of the presence of a fleeting Someone. So, too, we have noted John Steinbeck's novel in which the voyagers in the Gulf of California were conscious of a non-sensuous Presence during their passage through "bad" waters.

Many who have so encountered such a fleeting dynamic within their experiences of danger have trusted that this had been a person. Their trust may indeed have been derived from the basic Christian trust in the universal presence of God. Or that trust may have been derived from some alternate, prior commitment or value.

THE PRESENCE INVITES THE VICTIM TO TURN

In any case, the confidence in that Presence has been the crucial turning point for some individuals in their resolution of their problem of suffering. This One is imagined to use suffering as a passage into a greater vision of life and a greater hope.

For example, many people can be less than acutely sensitive to others' weaknesses. They also can tend to be less than tolerant of others' incompetencies. Moreover, they can tend to be less than generous with their time toward those who cannot legally demand their time.

Much more significantly, they can tend to expect that there is no more to be gained from experience than they could reasonably infer. Thus they may infer that human life had only that meaning and that purpose which they could confirm in sense experience.

However, if sense experience is shattered by suffering, that sensuously experienced security that held these persons in its grip is shattered. Then the victims are forced to admit that they could rely less upon their senses and their reason and their experienced security.

Nevertheless, the mythic inversion of values is not possible for the person who refuses to use one's imagination to respond to life.

Suffering has indeed forced some individuals to imagine new responses with which to live. These have been more pliable. They might have been accustomed rationally to interact with experiences. However, they were able to adjust themselves to the shattering disruptions of their life experiences. Thus, for example, some could imagine in their encounter with suffering that they had encountered dynamics other than pain and destruction. Open to imagine new responses to life, these individuals turned themselves in new directions. Some chose to pursue the new life orientations introduced by the dynamics of suffering.

For example, suffering may have introduced a change in occupation. A bread-earner, struck with a crippling disease, may be imaginative enough to become the homemaker, while his wife, the homemaker, becomes the bread-earner.

The encounter with suffering has led some so to orient themselves that they were then to find the meanings and goals of human life in entirely new dimensions of human life.

The most profound dimension that could be opened to the victim is that in the midst of the enigma of suffering, he or she could encounter the Numinous One. Some may have glimpsed a Someone who faintly beckoned to them from within their suffering. One might envision this One as inviting them to imagine a hidden purpose and significance for living that they could not rationally fashion.

However, because this Someone within those biddings remains cloaked in mystery, this purpose and this significance have to remain similarly mysterious. These may remain ever beyond the perception of these individuals. These may be known only by the Numinous One.

Nonetheless, those imaginative victims of suffering may choose to live with hope that there is a veiled purpose in suffering.

These victims can be more plastic, more flexible, less metallic, less fixed. The Numinous One urges that they flex themselves in trust. Thus they need to adjust to being thrust out of the dimension of living to which they had grown accustomed. They need to relocate themselves if they are to adjust to the events that roll over them. Those persons who are malleable enough to so respond are able to turn aside from the closed path that they had followed and to take the detour that may initially frighten them.

IMAGINING OPENS TO A NEW DIMENSION

Such a detour has led some to a worldview that has transformed the significance of life: they become persons of hope. That for which they hope may not be predictable; it may not appear to emerge from sensible data. However, the mystery of the Someone encountered within suffering invites them to hope in that Numinous One.

A second attitude that suffering can suggest to its victims is to be sensitive to any pathway that they come across as they pass through their experiences.

This might be phrased alternately. The goal of human life is to be human. Those who have chosen always to move toward that which is more human need to evaluate every event, even suffering, as a human act. They must assess any disruption or detour in the same manner that they evaluate success. Each of these can be a value.

From this perspective the meaning in all events can be fashioned no longer quantitatively, but as a result of how they have responded.

The value of this study to the current theological dialogue has now to be assessed.

This book had made a contribution both to theological method and to the theological interpretation of suffering.

There are three methodological contributions.

The first is the proposal that specific theological questions need to be addressed not only by rational analysis, but also by imagination. This is especially true for enigmatic theological questions like the problem of suffering. This study has proposed that such questions may indeed lie outside of the competence of reason and thus may be able to be addressed only by imagination.

The specific manner in which imagination was here used in responding to the problem of suffering was in fashioning a myth. The Lewis–Chesterton myth in the third chapter provides that imaginative manner of addressing the problem of suffering.

The worldview of that myth was fashioned by applying Karl Rahner's supernatural existential to the problem of suffering as envisioned by C.S. Lewis in *A Grief Observed*.

The anticipated criticism of this contribution is that I have created a vicious circle. That is, those who fashion their worldview imaginatively will be able to imagine that there is a transcendent Presence in their lives. They will be able to cite their experience of that Presence as a confirmation of the validity of the imaginative perspective of life. The criticism would be that this is a self-induced hallucination of the Presence.

A response to this anticipated criticism is first a plea to acknowledge the need for imagination in perceiving any of the more elusive dimensions of human experience. As I have argued, experience is far more complex than can be grasped by analysis or reason. Those who have a realistic hope of addressing the complex depths of experience need to rely upon their imagination as well as their powers of analysis.

Secondly, and consequentially, a "confirmation of the validity" of the imaginative perspective is not a goal. On the contrary, those who adapt themselves to an imaginative perspective need to bear in mind that their perspective remains always imaginative. It does not at some time cross over into becoming a perspective that is capable of being "confirmed." Even if it might appear to be helpful and significant, it always remains the product of the imagination. It remains in the realm of poetry, not of science. Thus its advocates need to bear in mind, especially when their imaginative perspective appears to be most illuminating, that the choice of living with such a perspective is a choice to live within a world that is insecure. Such a world cannot be rendered more firm by means of confirmation.

The second methodological contribution of this study has been its new manner of addressing Karl Rahner's vision.

Rahner himself and many of those who have written about the supernatural existential have used the refined language of philosophy. There have been many who have found that vision of the transcendent realm to be inaccessible because of the density of that language.

The Lewis–Chesterton myth presents the supernatural existential in the language of imagination. My reason for using imaginative language is that symbols appear to be more appropriate than analysis to reflect upon a vision of experience.

The apparent criticism of my study is that it has not gone beyond Rahner's interpretation of the meaning of suffering.

In the third volume of Rahner's collected writings is his principal essay on the experience of the supernatural existential. In that same volume is an essay on the meaning of suffering.

However, Rahner had not perceived the relationship between those issues. He had not proposed that the experience of suffering is also an experience of God's actively revealing the divine self. Rather, he had developed his essay on suffering by repeating the meaning of suffering that one can find in the writings of the apostle Paul. Both Paul and Rahner proposed a mystical and ascetical meaning based upon one's faith in the Crucified One.

That Pauline mysticism is principally that those who are baptized into Christ are bound to Christ as participants in his suffering. Christian victims of suffering are therefore to understand themselves as participants with Christ in the Lord's obedient self-offering to God. If one has genuinely become a branch in the vine that is Christ, then one can expect to encounter the same experiences as the vine. Their vocation is to suffer with Christ.[1]

Thus, my application of Rahner's supernatural existential to the experience of suffering is a step that Rahner himself had not taken. He apparently had not appreciated that his own assessment of God's presence within moments of experience could be so applied to human suffering.

The third methodological contribution is my suggestion that

those who hope to discover the significance of experience need to be sensitive to the hushed whispers of their own interior spirits.

These whispers may need to be brought up to a higher frequency; that is what G.K. Chesterton had done in his interpreting Lewis' profound reflections in *A Grief Observed*.

He thereby disclosed to Lewis that the meaning of the spirit's summons was the inverse of the apparent significance of Lewis' words.

Thus, as Chesterton pointed out, Lewis in his apparent rage had actually been responding to and affirming the mystery of the spirit active within suffering.

In the case of the question about suffering, the activity of the spirit had transformed the problem of suffering into an adventure. In the adventure C.S. Lewis had indeed become disoriented, even lost in focusing upon one or another distraction, not upon the bidding from his interior spirit. However, the imaginative venturer, even if disoriented, still fashioned for himself a goal.

This study's imaginative approach to suffering has radically changed the context in which to situate the problem. The context is not a situation in which there are clear categories and rigorous procedures that lead to definite goals. Rather the context is a journey on an unmapped land, i.e. a situation in which one progresses more by instinct and imaginative sensitivity to the surroundings than by reason and analysis.

In that context this study proposes that the victim of suffering can imagine within the mystery of suffering a numinous summons to endure the experience of suffering with a hope that is based only upon the summons, not upon a rational inference.

Moreover, within the mystery the victim of suffering can imagine that summons to be a call to endure the suffering with confidence. With imagination one can trust not that one can understand suffering's purpose, but that there is nonetheless purpose in suffering.

However, most significantly, the one who suffers is invited to remain confident that throughout the experience of suffering, one is not alone. Always one is attended by a Numinous Person who not only cares about the one who suffers, but is also working within the experience to fashion an imperceptible and unpredictable value.

The contribution to the content of the theology of suffering is my argument that satisfactory reflection upon the mystery of suffering is possible to the extent that one addresses the mystery with one's imagination. Mystery remains beyond the grasp of analysis.

THE REFUSAL TO APPROACH SUFFERING WITH IMAGINATION

However, mystery can be addressed by way of the human imagination. This imaginative approach to the reflection on suffering avoids the problems that had hindered the analytical approaches of monism and dualism.

Monism had appeared to deny that evil is empirically real. For example, Augustine of Hippo had taught that the world is the creation of a good God; evil is no more than a privation of good.

The problem in that is that evil can appear to be little more than the result of one's perspective; evil appears to be a mental illusion. However, the victim of suffering encounters an empirical power that disrupts and destroys human life.

The imaginative approach that I have used acknowledges that evil is empirically real. However, it insists both that evil remains a mystery and that within that mystery the imaginative victim can hear a summons.

Dualism had appeared either to reduce God's power or to deny that God is unqualifiably good. It reduces God's power in its acknowledging another equal power which is responsible for evil and which the good God cannot overcome.

In a different argument it denies that God is unqualifiably good because it assumes that, since the good God is responsible for the world, that God falters in the struggle against the evil in the world. Thus God is struggling against God's own creation. This is a logical inconsistency within God.

The imaginative approach that I have used allows God to remain good and powerful. However, the good and powerful God is present and active in the midst of suffering; from there God summons humans to enter into the mystery with hope.

Notes

To find the sources of articles whose titles appear in quotation marks within these notes, refer to the Bibliography ahead, section II: ARTICLES.

1. EVIL AS A HUMAN OCCURRENCE

1. Irenaeus, *Against Heresies*, v. vi, 1; iv, xxxix, 1,2.
2. Fyodor Dostoevsky, *The Brothers Karamazov*, p. 224.
3. Ibid., chapter 4.

2. REFLECTING UPON EVIL

1. Albert Einstein, *Relativity*, pp. 9–18, 128–137.
2. Karl Rahner, *A Rahner Reader*, cf. Index, "supernatural existential."

3. SUFFERING: A FORM OF EVIL

1. Franz Kafka, *The Trial*.
2. Elie Wiesel, *Messengers of God*, pp. 216–218.
3. Ibid., pp. 220–221.
4. Ibid., p. 222.
5. Ibid., pp. 223–229.
6. Ibid., pp. 231–232.
7. Ibid., pp. 233–234.
8. Viktor E. Frankl, *Man's Search for Meaning*, pp. 1–93.
9. Ibid., pp. 97–120.
10. Ignaz Maybaum, "Die Dritte *Churban*," in Brocke and Jochum's *Wolkensauele und Feuerschein*, pp. 9–19.
11. Elie Wiesel, *Die Nacht*.
12. John Hick, *Evil and the God of Love*, pp. 358–363.

4. THEODICIES OF SUFFERING

1. John Hick, *Evil and the God of Love*, p. 372.
2. Pierre Teilhard de Chardin, selected passages identified in the bibliography by (u).

5. A DIALOGIC INTRODUCTION TO MYTH

1. Michael Peterson, *Evil and the Christian God*, pp. 1–33.
2. Thomas Aquinas, *Summa Theologica*, pt. I, q. xlix, art. 1.
3. Ibid., pt. III, q. 1, art. 3.
4. Charles Journet, *The Meaning of Evil*, pp. 27–50, 104–115, 166, 218.
5. Martin D'Arcy, *Pain and the Providence*, pp. 7–9.
6. Pierre Teilhard de Chardin, selected passages identified in the bibliography under "Teilhard de Chardin" at (e).
7. Raymund Schwager, *Must There be Scapegoats?* pp. 1–42.
8. Hans Urs von Balthasar, *Cordule oder der Enrstfall;* Reinhold Schneider, *Winter in Wien;* Georges Bernanos, *Journal d'un Cure de Campagne.*
9. David Hume, *Dialogues Concerning Natural Religion*, parts x and xi.
10. Albert Camus, *The Rebel*, pp. 16–27, 29–35, 50–53.
11. Friedrich Schleiermacher, *The Christian Faith*, "Actual Sin," pp. 304–306.
12. Eckart Otto, "Die 'synthetische Lebensauffassung,' " pp. 371–400.
13. Griedhelm Gruenewald, "Krankheit als boeses Leiden," pp. 613–617.
14. Alvin Plantinga, *God, Freedom, and Evil*, pp. 7–24.
15. Martin D'Arcy, *Pain and the Providence*, pp. 10–30.
16. Ibid., pp. 52–53, 92–93, 101–104.
17. Ibid., pp. 125–126, 130.
18. Michael Peterson, *Evil* pp. 43–58.
19. Walter Mostert, "Gott und das Boese," *Zeitschrift fuer Theologie und Kirche*, vol. 77, 1980, pp. 453–478.
20. Rainer Albertz, "Der socialgeschichtliche Hintergrund des Hiobbuches und der 'Babylonischen Theodizie,' " *Die Botschaft und die Boten*, pp. 349–372.
21. Bernard J.F. Lonergan, *Insight*, pp. 634–696.
22. John Hick, *The Problem of Evil*, pp. 136–141.
23. Theodor Gerber, "Ein gemiedener Text," pp. 134–136.
24. Klauspeter Blaser, "Ueberalterte Fragen," pp. 136–139.
25. Arthur Rich, "Dulden des Boesen?" pp. 150–154.
26. John Hick, *Evil and the God of Love*, p. 286.
27. Elie Wiesel, *Messengers of God*, p. 211.
28. Martin D'Arcy, *Pain and the Providence*, pp. 1–31.

29. Klaus Held, "Boethius—Philosophische Existenz in Ausgang der Antike."
30. John Hick, *Evil and the God of Love*, p. 355.
31. Ernst Kutsch, *Kleine Schriften*, pp. 336–349.
32. John Hick, *Evil and the God of Love*, p. 279.
33. Kurt Marti, "Leiden, nicht Dulden," pp. 147–150.
34. Peter Steinacker, "Welterfahrung und Gottesbild bei Jakob Boehme," pp. 173–203; "Gott, der Grund und Ungrund der Welt," *NZSTR*, 1983, v. 25, pp. 95–111.
35. John Hick, *Evil and the God of Love*, pp. 292–293, 355.
36. Peter Steinacker, "Gott, der Grund und Ungrund der Welt," *NZSTR*, 1983, v. 25, pp. 95–111.
37. Kurt Rudolph, "Mythos—Mythologie—Entmythologiesierung," *Mythos und Rationalitaet*, pp. 368–381.
38. Willy Rordorf, "Sind Daemonen gut oder boese?" *Platonismus und Christentum*, pp. 239–244.
39. Anton Bodem, "Leiden Gottes," *Veritati Catholicae*, pp. 586–611.
40. Wolfhart Pannenberg, "Die Weltgrunde Funktion des Mythos und der christliche Offenbarungsglaube," *Mythos und Rationalitaet*, pp. 108–122.
41. David Tracy, *The Analogical Imagination*, pp. 429–430.
42. Hans Heinrich Schmid, "Vorwort," *Mythos und Rationalitaet*, pp. 9–12.
43. Walter Sparn, *Leiden—Erfahrung und Denken*, pp. 247–272.
44. Hans Schulze, "Reflexion ueber das Leiden," in *Der Leidende Mensch*, pp. 9–22.
45. Carl-Friedrich Geyer, "Das Theodizeeproblem heute."
46. Gerhard Oberhammer, "Mythos—woher und wozu? Zur Rationalitaet des Mythos," *Mythos und Rationalitaet*, pp. 15–26.
47. Kurt Huebner, "Der Mythos, der Logos, und die spezifisch Religiose drei Elemente des christlichen Glaubens," *Mythos und Rationalitaet*, pp. 27–41.
48. Fred Stolz, "Der mythische Umgang mit der Rationalitaet und der rationale Umgang mit dem Mythos," *Mythos und Rationalitaet*, pp. 81–106.
49. Ernst Kaesemann, *An Die Roemer*, pp. 153–154.
50. Peter Steinacker, "Das Ende der Entmythologisierung," *Alltagswelt und Ethik*, pp. 55–81.
51. Nikolaus Walter, "Geschichte und Mythos in der urchristlichen Prae-existenzchristologie," *Mythos und Rationalitaet*, pp. 224–234.
52. Peter Steinacker, "Das Ende der Entmythologisierung," *Alltagswelt und Ethik*, pp. 55–81.
53. Rudolf Bultmann, *Das Urchristentum*, pp. 9ff, 100ff, 153–156.

54. Martin Luther, *Letter to the Romans*, pp. 195–196.
55. Friedrich Mildenberger, "Das Leiden Christi und das Leiden des Christen," in *Der Leidende Mensch*, pp. 115–127.

6. MYSTERY IN MYTH

1. Mk 10:45; Lk 1:68–70; Rom 3:21–26; 1 Pet 1:18–21; there are many other possible citations.

7. THE LEWIS–CHESTERTON MYTH

1. C.S. Lewis, *A Grief Observed*, pp. 15–16, 19, 31, 33, 35, 37, 44, 46, 49.
2. G.K. Chesterton, *The Father Brown Stories*.
3. John Steinbeck, *The Log from the Sea*, pp. 300, 304.
4. Karl Rahner, "Ueber die Erfahrung der Gnade."
5. Karl Rahner, "Die Praesenz Christi im Heiligen Geist."
6. Karl Rahner, "Der Mensch als Wesen der Transzendenz."
7. Karl Rahner, "Vom Geheimnis des Lebens."
8. Karl Rahner, "Das Angebot der Selbstmitteilung als 'ueber-natuerliches Existential.' "
9. Karl Rahner, "Das Verhaeltnis des Menschen zu seinem Transcen-denten Grund: Kreatuerlichkeit," pp. 83–88.
10. Ibid.
11. Ibid.
12. C.S. Lewis, *A Grief Observed*, pp. 15–16, 19, 31, 33, 35, 44, 46, 49.

10. THE PRESENCE ENCOUNTERS THOSE WHO SUFFER

1. Robert Bolt, *A Man for All Seasons*, pp. xii–xiv, 141.
2. Ibid., pp. 81–82.

11. THE CONTINUING ENIGMA

1. Karl Rahner, "Unsicherheiten und Schwierigkeiten im heutigen Schuld-verstaendnis," in Goerres and Rahner's *Das Boese*, p. 201.

12. THE RESOLUTION OF SUFFERING

1. Karl Rahner, "Eucharistie und Leiden," pp. 191–202.

Bibliography

I. BOOKS

Aquinas, Thomas, *Summa Theologica*, trans. Fathers of the English Dominican Province. London: R & T Washbourne, Ltd., 1912.

Balthasar, Hans Urs von, *Cordula oder der Ernstfall*. Einsiedeln: Johannes Verlag, 1966.

Bausch, William J., *Storytelling, Imagination and Faith*. Mystic: Twenty-Third Publ., 1984.

Bolt, Robert, *A Man for All Seasons, A Play in Two Acts*. New York: Random House, 1962.

Brocke, Michael and Herbert Jochum, eds., *Wolkensäule und Feuerschein*. Jüdische Theologie des Holocaust übersetzt aus English: Gaetano Hassdenteufel. München: Chr. Kaiser Verlag, 1982.

Bultmann, Rudolf, *Das Urchristentum im Rahmen der Antiken Religionen*. München: Rowohlts deutsche enzyklopa, 1963.

Camus, Albert, *The Plague*, trans. Stuart Gilbert. New York: Alfred A. Knopf, 1961.

————, *The Rebel*, trans. Anthony Bower. Middlesex, England: Penguin Books, 1971.

Chesterton, G.K., *The Father Brown Stories*. London: Cassell, 1929.

D'Arcy, Martin C., *Pain and the Providence of God*. Milwaukee: The Bruce Publishing Co., 1935.

Dostoevsky, Fyodor, *The Brothers Karamazov*, trans. Constance Garnett. New York: Norton, 1976.

Einstein, Albert, *Relativity: The Special and the General Theory*, trans. Robert W. Lawson. London: Methuen & Co., 1946

Eliot, T.S., *The Complete Poems and Plays 1909–1950*. New York: Harcourt, Brace and Co., 1952.

Frankl, Viktor, *Man's Search for Meaning: An Introduction to Logotherapy*, trans. by Ilse Lasch. Boston: Beacon Press, 1962.

Görres, Albert and Karl Rahner, *Das Böse. Weg zu seiner Bewältigung in Pschotherapie und Christentum*. Freiburg im Breisgau: Verlag Herder, 1982.

Hick, John, *Evil and the God of Love*. Glasgow: Wm. Collins Sons & Co., 1968.

Homer, *Die Odyssee*, deutsch von Wolfgang Scadewaldt. Zurich: Artemis Verlag, 1966.

Hume, David, *Dialogues Concerning Natural Religion*, H.D. Aiken, editor. New York: Hafner Publishing Co., Inc., 1955.

Irenaeus, *Against Heresies*, translated in the Ante-Nicene Library, bks. iv & v.

Job, in *The Anchor Bible*, Introduction, translation, notes by Marvin H. Pope. Garden City: Doubleday & Co., 1965.

Journet, Charles, *The Meaning of Evil*, trans. Michael Barry. London: Geoffrey Chapman, 1963.

Kafka, Franz, *Der Prozess (The Trial)*. Berlin: Schocken Verlag, 1935.

Käsemann, Ernst, *An Die Römer*. Tübingen: J.C.B. Mohr, 1974.

Kitamori, Kazoh, *Theologie des Schmerzes Gottes*. Göttingen: Vandenhoech & Ruprecht, 1972.

Lavelle, Louis, *Evil and Suffering*, trans. Bernard Murchland. New York: Macmillan, 1963.

Levinas, Emmanuel, *Totalität und Unendlichkeit. Versuch über die Exteriorität*. München: Verlag Karl Alber Freiburg, 1987.

Lewis, C.S., *The Great Divorce*. New York: Macmillan, 1946.

————, *A Grief Observed*. New York: Bantam Books, 1961.

Lonergan, Bernard, *Insight: A Study of Human Understanding*. New York: Philosophical Library, 1958.

Luther, Martin, *Letter to the Romans*, vol. 3. Stuttgart: Ehrenfried Klotz Verlag, 1969.

Niebuhr, H. Richard, *The Responsible Self: An Essay in Christian Moral Philosophy*. New York: Harper & Row Publishers, 1963.

Pearson, Michael, *The Sealed Train*. London: Macmillan, 1975.

Peterson, Michael, *Evil and the Christian God*. Grand Rapids: Baker Book House, 1982.

Plantinga, Alvin, *God, Freedom and Evil*. New York: Harper Torchbooks, 1974.

Plato, *Der Staat (The Republic)*. München: Wilhelm Goldmann Verlag, 1973.

Rahner, Karl, *Grundkurs des Glaubens. Einführung in den Begriff des Christentums*. Freiburg im Breisgau: Herder Verlag, 1984.

Schmid, Hans Heinrich, ed., *Mythos und Rationalität*. Verhalshaus Gerd Mohn: Gütersloher, 1988.

Schneider, Reinhold, *Winter in Wien, Aus meiner Notizbüchern 1957/58. Gesammelte Werke*, vol. 10. Frankfurt: Insel Verlag, 1978.

Schulze, Hans, ed., *Der Leidende Mensch. Beiträge zu einem unbewältigtem Thema*. Düsseldorf: Neukirchener Verlag, 1974.

Schwager, Raymund, S.J., *Must There Be Scapegoats? Violence and Redemption in the Bible*. San Francisco: Harper & Row, 1987.

Sölle, Dorothee, *Leiden*. Stuttgart: Kreuz Verlag, 1973.

Sparn, Walter, *Leiden—Erfahrung und Denken. Materialien zum Theodizeeproblem*. München: Chr. Kaiser Verlag, 1980.

Steinbeck, John, *The Log from the Sea of Cortez*. London: Pan Books, Ltd., 1960.

Teilhard de Chardin, Pierre, *L'Activation de l'Energie*. Paris: Seuil, 1963(u).

———, *Ecrits du Temps de la Guerre (1916–1919)*. Paris: Grasset, 1965(e).

———, *Der Göttliche Bereich*. Freiburg i. Br.: Walter, 1962(u).

———, *Mensch im Kosmos*. München: Beck, 1959(u).

———, *L'Energie Humaine*. Paris: Seuil, 1962.

———, *Geheimnis und Verheissung der Erde*. Freiburg/München: Alber, 1958(e).

———, *Science et Christ*. Paris: Seuil, 1965(u).

Tracy, David, *The Analogical Imagination: Christian Theology and the Culture of Pluralism*. London: SCM Press, Ltd., 1981.

Varillon, Francois, *La Souffrance de Dieu*. LeCenturion, 1975.

Wiesel, Elie, *Messengers of God: Biblical Portraits and Legends*, translated from the French by Marion Wiesel. New York: Random House, 1976.

———, *Die Nacht*. Mohn: Gütersloher Verlagshaus, 1980.

II. ARTICLES

Albertz, Rainer, "Der socialgeschichtliche Hintergrund des Hiobbuches und der 'Babylonischen Theodizie,' " *Die Botschaft und die Boten*. Neukirchen - Vluyn: Neukirchener Verlag, 1981, pp. 349–372.

Blaser, Klauspeter, "Überalterte Fragen," *Reformatio*, evangelische Zeitschrift für Kultur und Politik. Bern: Verlag Reformatio, 1982, pp. 136–139.

Bodem, Anton, SDB, "Leiden Gottes, Erwägungen zu einem Zug im Gottesbild der gegenwärtigen Theologie," *Veritati Catholicae, Festschrift für Leo Sheffczyk*, eds. Anton Ziegenaus, Franz Courth, Phillipp Schaefer. Aschaffenburg: Pattloch Verlag, 1985, pp. 586–611.

Fuchs, Josef, "Intrinsece malum, Überlegungen zu einem unstritten Begriff," *Sittliche Normen, Zum Problem ihrer algemeinen und unwandelbarem Geltung*, ed. Walter Kerber. Duesseldorf: Patmos Verlag, 1982, pp. 74–91.

Gerber, Theodor, "Ein gemiedener Text," *Reformatio*, evangelische Zeitschrift für Kultur und Politik. Bern: Verlag Reformatio, 1982, pp. 134–136.

Geyer, Carl-Friedrich, OFM, "Das Theodizeeproblem heute," *Neue Zeitschrift für Systematische Theologie und Religionsphilosophie*. Berlin: Walter De Gruyter, 1975, vol. 17, pp. 179–194.

Gruenewald, Friedhelm, "Krankheit als böses Leiden, Seelsorge als Prozess der Befreiung," *Reformatio*, evangelische Zeitschrift für Kultur und Politik. Bern: Verlag Reformatio, 1982, pp. 613–617.

Held, Prof. Dr. Klaus, "Boethius—Philosophische Existenz in Ausgang der Antike," *Thema des Problems des Übels*. Darmstadt: Wissenschaftische Buchgeschellschaft, 1981.

Hick, John, "The Problem of Evil," *The Encyclopedia of Philosophy*, Volume 3. New York: The Macmillan Company, 1967, pp. 136–141.

Hill, John, "The Debate between McCormick and Frankena," *Irish Theological Quarterly* 49 (1982), pp. 121–133. Maynooth College: Maynooth, Co. Kildare, 1982.

Huber, Gerhard, "Die Wirtschaft zwischen Gut und Böse," *Reformatio*, evangelische Zeitschrift für Kultur und Politik. Bern: Verlag Reformatio, 1985, pp. 86–89.

Hübner, Kurt, "Der Mythos, der Logos und das spezifisch Religiöse Drei Elemente des christlichen Glaubens," in Schmid, *Mythos und Rationalität*, pp. 27–41.

Krueger, Paul, "Ein Missionsdokument aus Frühchristlicher Zeit," Deutung und Übersetzung des Sermo de memoria Petri et Pauli des Narsai, *Zeitschrift für Missionswissenschaft und Religionswissenschaft*. Muenster: Aschendorff, 1958, vol. 42, pp. 271–291.

Kutsch, Ernest, "Von Grund und Sinn des Leidens nach dem Alten Testament," *Kleine Schriften zum Alten Testament*. Berlin: Walter de Gruyter, 1986, pp. 336–347.

Mackie, J.L. "Evil and Omnipotence," *Mind*, vol. lxiv, no. 254 (1955).

Marti, Kurt, "Leiden, nicht dulden," *Reformatio*, evangelische Zeitschrift für Kultur und Politik. Bern: Verlag Reformatio, 1982, pp. 147–150.

Mildenberger, Friedrich, "Das Leiden Christi und das Leiden des Christen," *Der Leidende Mensch*, Hans Schulze, ed., pp. 115–127.

Mostert, Walter, "Gott und das Böse," *Zeitschrift für Theologie und Kirche*. Tübingen: J.C.B. Mohr, vol. 77, 1980, pp. 453–478.

Oberhammer, Gerhard, "Mythos—woher und wozu?" in Schmid, *Mythos und Rationalität*, pp. 15–26.

Otto, Eckart, "Die 'synthetische Lebensauffassung' in der frühköniglichen Novellistik Israels," *Zeitschrift für Theologie und Kirche*. Tübingen: J.C.B. Mohr (Paul Siebeck), vol. 74, no. 4, 1977, pp. 371–400.

Pannenberg, Wolfhart, "Die weltgründende Funktion des Mythos und der christliche Offenbarungsglaube," in Schmid, *Mythos und Rationalität*, pp. 108–123.

Rahner, Karl, *A Rahner Reader*, ed. Gerald McCool, "The Experience of Grace," pp. 197–198. New York: Seabury, 1975.

———, "Das Angebot der Selbstmitteilung als 'übernatürliches Existential,' " *Grundkurs des Glaubens, Einführung in den Begriff des Christentums.* Freiburg: Herder Verlag, 1976, pp. 132–139.

———, "Eucharistie und Leiden," *Schriften zur Theologie*, vol. III. Zürich: Benziger Verlag, 1957, pp. 191–202.

———, "Der Mensch als Wesen der Transzendenz," *Grundkurs des Glaubens. Einführung in den Begriff des Christentums.* Freiburg: Herder Verlag, 1976, pp. 42–46.

———, "Die Präsenz Christi im Heiligen Geist," *Grundkurs des Glaubens. Einführung in den Begriff des Christentums.* Frieburg: Herder Verlag, 1976, pp. 308–310.

———, "Über die Erfahrung der Gnade," *Schriften zur Theologie*, vol. III. Zürich: Benziger Verlag, 1957, pp. 105–109.

———, "Vom Geheimnis des Lebens," *Schriften zur Theologie*, vol. VI. Zürich: Benziger Verlag, 1965, pp. 171–184.

———, "Das Verhältnis des Menschen zu seinem Transzendenten Grund: Kreatürlichkeit," *Grundkurs des Glaubens. Einführung in den Begriff des Christentums.* Freiburg: Herder Verlag, 1976, pp. 83–88.

Rich, Arthur, "Duldung des Bösen?" *Reformatio*, evangelische Zeitschrift für Kultur und Politik. Bern: Verlag Reformatio, 1982, pp. 150–154.

Rordorf, Willy, "Sind Dämonen gut oder böse?" *Platonismus und Christentum*, eds. Horst-Dieter Blume und Griedhelm Mann. Aschendorffsche Verlag: Münster, 1983, pp. 239–244.

Rudolph, Kurt, "Mythos—Mythologie—Entmythologisierung," in Schmid, *Mythos und Rationalität*, pp. 368–381.

Ruprecht, Eberhard, "Leiden und Gerechtigkeit bei Hiob," *Zeitschrift für Theologie und Kirche.* Tübingen: J.C.B. Mohr, 1976, vol. 73, pp. 424–445.

Schmid, Hans Heinrich, "Vorwort," in *Mythos und Rationalität*, pp. 9–12.

Steinacker, Peter, "Das Ende der Entmythologisierung," *Alltagswelt und Ethik*, ed. Klaus Ebert. Peter Hammer Verlag: Wuppertal, 1988.

———, "Gott, der Grund und Ungrund der Welt," *Neue Zeitschrift für Systematische Theologie und Religionsphilosophie.* Berlin: Walter De Gruyter, 1983, vol. 25, no. 2, pp. 95–111.

———, "Welterfahrung und Gottesbild bei Jakob Böhme," *Pathos, Affekt, Gefühl*, ed. Ingrid Craemer-Ruegenberg. München: Karl Alber Verlag, pp. 173–203.

Stolz, Fritz, "Der mythische Ungang mit der Rationalität und der rationale Umgang mit dem Mythos," in Schmid, *Mythos und Rationalität*, pp. 81–106.

Teilhard de Chardin, Pierre, "Briefe au l'Abbe Gaudefroy," from Jan. 3, '24 and May 25, '24.

Walter, Nikolaus, "Geschichte und Mythos in der urchristlichen Präexistenzchristologie," in Schmid, *Mythos und Rationalität*, pp. 224–234.

Welten, Peter, "Leiden und Leidenserfahrung im Buch Jeremia," *Zeitschrift für Theologie und Kirche*. Tübingen: J.C.B. Mohr, 1977, vol. 74, pp. 123–150.

Index

CONFESSIONS

OF A CORPORATE REAL ESTATE

HIT

Killer Negotiation in Business and Life

-- Creating my Unfair Advantage

STEVE MILLER

CONFESSIONS OF A CORPORATE REAL ESTATE HITMAN
Killer Negotiating in Business and Life – Creating my Unfair Advantage
First Edition

Quantity purchases of this book are available for educational, business, or sales promotion purposes by contacting the publisher at:

Stealthy Force
A division of SiteLink International LLC
6834 S University Blvd #140
Centennial CO 80122
www.stealthyforce.com

Stealthy Force is an Imprint of SiteLink International LLC

ISBN-13: 978-1-7349444-0-2

Author:
Steve@KillerNegotiator.com

Commentary:
KillerNegotiator.com

COVER ARTWORK AND DESIGN BY NATHAN MILLER, AKA ICARUS MOTH

Author's Note and certain Disclaimers and Disclosures

This is a true story. All the events in this book and details of the transactions really happened. I am under non-disclosure and confidentiality agreements in many instances, so the identities, locations, and other specifics have been tweaked to abide by those agreements. The names have been changed to protect the innocent, as well as the guilty -- such is the nature of NDAs. The people that lived through it, though, know.

Another. References to gender are gender-specific. The guys are guys, and the girls are girls. When I refer to the entirety of a mixed-gender group, like the real estate industry or some national convention, I will use the masculine or maybe the feminine; it doesn't mean anything. The girls are as tough as the guys, and in many cases, more sinister. I'll show you my scars. Regardless, everybody is "guys" in that instance. If a person's sexual orientation, preferences, or fetishes are integral to the story, I might bring it up.

Still another. In instances where specific dollar amounts are cited, they're all in current dollars for context and consistency.

While writing this book, I was told that business books should be written for readers at an eighth-grade level, but I can't describe a four-dimensional concept to a two-dimensional brain. So, you'll exercise your genius muscle a little while reading this book. It's going to make the concepts clearer and your life better.

Technically, I'm a broker, but I'm not your broker. You reading this book does not create any sort of legal relationship between us. This *Confessions* book shares insight into what I have learned about handling people and negotiations, but is not to be considered advice, legal or otherwise, about your transactions or other dealings. I'm promoting a new way to think, not a brokerage relationship.

Finally, no humans were physically harmed or killed in the making of this book, though it might have felt like it to some. The words, "Death" and "Dying" and their synonyms and derivatives, in the context of this book, are used only as hyperbole – except when they're not.

Now, if you're ready, buckle up and enjoy the ride.

CONTENTS

1

MEA CULPA...

Prepare your mind for this impure tale. You might think it's depravity, these things that we'll learn. But it's not guilt I feel; it's satisfaction -- and pride. Welcome to adventures in the art of self-mastery.

How did I get here?

It started as a thought experiment, a way to survive a tough situation. Over time it became evident I was dealing in the realm of the unthinkable, something taboo. Experts in artificial intelligence describe "forbidden knowledge" as information that is too dangerous to disseminate because of what might happen if mishandled or fall into the hands of people with malicious intent. Some would say that's what I discovered, forbidden knowledge. I would say, "Useful as hell."

If achievement and freedom are what you're after, you're in for the fight of your life. Do you want to go up against people who know more than you do? Or do you want to stack the odds in your favor? This is not a sporting competition. You don't want a fair fight. You want an unfair advantage.

So, how deadly are you? How deadly is someone who knows how to think? I'm not talking about that brainless mush that slushes around in most people's heads. I'm talking about a stealth, strategic, thinker -- skilled at nailing his or her chosen objectives, most any objective. How powerful? Can the power of one intentioned individual with a thinking mind change the world? I changed my world, and I started with almost nothing.

I'm a deal maker, a negotiator, an entrepreneur. I built a life of independence, freedom, fun, and adventure. I did that by learning things that nobody taught, by thinking things that no one had thought. All those things and how I got here are the core of this book. It might be a little dangerous. It might change your life.

The things I know, the things I've learned, the things I've fought for, the things I have written about in this book, will put you in control of outcomes in your business, negotiations, and life. They'll make you more confident, fearless, and powerful. It's simple; you have more fun when you're free and you live life at your own direction. Deals are more fun when you know how to win.

My world has been corporate real estate and the nature and flow of people and money. It's in that context that I share with you my story. But it applies to everything. A word of warning, I don't hold back. In what I hope will be a fun read for you, there are at times dark issues and uncomfortable topics that I address because that is real life and you can't stay alive and thrive and be fully empowered by denying they exist. Just the opposite, it's those tough challenges and those painful experiences that can be the very levers we use to our advantage. We face them head-on – with a cunning smile, ample wit, and hell-bent intent. There's a lot of polite books out there; this is not one of them. You might get offended, but you're going to learn a lot.

If you're the kind of person who wants to create more success in your deals, business, and life, I wrote this book for you. If you want to be bulletproof, make more money, and have more fun, I wrote this book for you. If you want to know how to control what goes on behind closed doors making deals with the biggest players and toughest negotiators in the world, I wrote this book for you. If you're driven by pain or hunger, I wrote this book for you.

I wrote this book for the men and women who scoff at being a cog in the machine, another clone following directions. I wrote this book to show anyone with guts and brains how to step outside the norms, challenge the status quo, and experience real freedom -- a freedom that opens the doors to new potential, actual gains, and infinite possibilities. It's about being different. It's about being smart. It's about taking responsibility. It's about not being normal. It's about getting the job done your way, winning negotiations your way, and making awesome deals on your terms. It's about wielding power. It's about making your own unfair advantage and using it. Mea culpa. I wrote this book for you to unpack that raw, sovereign, power inside of you and set it loose upon the world.

With that said, I share with you my story and what I have learned. I expose things that have never been revealed. I tell you my secrets. I show you my tricks, hacks, hammers, and cheats that moved mountains for me -- as they will for you. This has been my world. These are my confessions...

2

OPENING CONFESSIONS

"Now this is the law of the jungle, as old and as true as the sky, and the wolf that shall keep it may prosper, but the wolf that shall break it must die."
-- Rudyard Kipling

I'm a corporate real estate hitman. I'm an alpha wolf in the real estate jungle. My clients engage me to do things that other brokers can't, to get things done that other brokers don't know how to do. I'm a fighter. I'm a mercenary. I get transactions done my way so my clients can win, so we both can win. With me, it's mission first. I've never done things the way they're supposed to be done. I've ignored convention, broke rules; moved ever forward guided only by my own mind, heart, principles, and passion. I've not asked permission, and I've not apologized. I am proud of who I am, that my life is what I have made it.

Killer negotiating requires having an insuperable expertise to manifest influence and change and the personal foundation to carry it out. These skills I've learned are covert, psychological, invisible, and deadly. These aren't for everybody. They're for the person who must prevail and get the job done no matter what. These are my tools, my weapons, my survival skills. These are my tricks, hacks, hammers, and cheats that I learned in my travels so I could survive and thrive and win in one of the world's toughest and most perilous jungles – deal making in commercial real estate, deal making in any jungle. In a world where few people venture beyond the safety of huddling with their familiar groups, I deliver what the adventurous free-thinker can use to make masterpieces happen.

I honestly don't know if everyone can learn to use these skills. You might have to be a little special, a breed apart, or maybe a little broken.

You see, I'm not quite normal; I'm walking wounded. I'm kind of a loner. I like it that way, mostly. I'm one of those guys who grew up in conditions where I had to be somewhat impervious to pain. I'm not afraid of risk. I seek it. I'm not afraid to act alone. I prefer it. I'm an adrenaline junky. I put it all out there on the line. What about you? Do you have the fortitude to learn this stuff and use it? Do you have the courage? Do you have the heart?

I'm writing this book for two reasons. The first is to show you the art of assuming control of every situation, every transaction, every negotiation, no matter how hard or how much the odds are stacked against you. If you're a pro already, this ability and these negotiating and survival skills will take you to a level you didn't even know existed. If you're a failure, well, that stops now.

These skills are alchemy. I've worked hard to discover and develop them, and I've used them to survive and thrive in a cutthroat world. I learned to turn shit into gold. I learned to turn bullies into putty, and you'll learn how to do it too. I will tell you things no one else is willing to say. I will teach you things no one else knows. I came from shit, and I learned how to win, no matter what the cost. I suppose I should give you some drivel now about how you should only use these skills for ethical purposes, but hey, if you've fudged on the ethics before, nothing I can say to you now is going to keep you inside the boundaries. I'm one of the good guys, though; I'm pretty sure.

These killer competencies, this mental Jiu-Jitsu, it's all legal. It's survival of the fittest, same as the athlete who's more prepared and skilled than everyone else. But these skills are not fair and not for the faint of heart. They're not meant to be. Kill or be killed. Call it what you will: manipulation, exploitation, influence, clout, juice, pull; it's the law of the jungle. It's the alpha wolf. It's the skill of a Hitman.

The second reason I'm writing this book is to tell you my story. I've carried this around with me a long time, and frankly, I'd like to get it off my chest – the start, the deals, the people, the travel, the hurts, the craziness, and the negotiations. It'll be cathartic. More importantly, though, it's how I learned to transcend the limiting constraints of the business world, prevail, and become truly independent and free. It's the exaltation of the entrepreneur in us and what one intentioned individual with an active mind can accomplish.

This is the story of my life as a hired gun for people so rich and companies so big that they don't care how things get done, only that they do get done. This is a story of triumph and victory in an industry where no one cares if you eat, live, or die. An industry where you never really know who your friends are or when an ally might put a knife in your back. This is a story about breaking things that need to be broken. This is a story about living outside the margins. This is a story of struggle. This is a story of winning.

I've represented some of the biggest organizations, corporations, and government agencies in the world -- Fortune 500 firms and conglomerates so convoluted you could spend hours with an org chart trying to figure them out. I've been just about everywhere in the U.S. and traveled around the world, from Downtown Manhattan to the Bakken oil fields of North Dakota, from the tony boutiques in Beverly Hills to the congested roundabouts of Jakarta, I've plied my trade with cunning, stealth, and skill. I've secured specialized, mission-critical sites for governments and technology consortiums. I've run transactions for portfolios with site counts that run into the thousands for ubiquitous retailers and worldwide telecommunications giants. I've negotiated headquarter facilities for military, mining, energy, industrials, law, internet, and tech.

I usually fly way below the radar, but I'm in constant contact with my clients, and I know all about my opposition. Often, it's a high-wire act because one of the reasons my clients like me fixing their problems is that they can disavow me if the need arises. There's no safety net, only my survival skills.

Many of the people I've done deals with have been smart visionaries, and I've learned from them. You'll meet them. But many, so many people I've done deals with seemed to have just crawled out of the shallow end of the gene pool. You'll meet them too. I've learned from everyone, even if only how to take them out.

By the way, if you find yourself on these pages and you don't think you were cast in a very positive light, I apologize in advance, but you no doubt deserve it. On the other hand, if you were one of those who inspired me, thank you. You get a pass, and a smile.

The high-stakes world of commercial real estate has two sides. There is the public side of smiles and cocktails, BMWs, Mercedes, and Teslas, golf games and conferences, and numbers crunching, contracts, and lawyers. But there is a soft underbelly -- greed, self-dealing, sycophants, conflicts of interest, cowardice, and incompetence. This soft underbelly is fertile ground to use to my advantage, and I do. Do you think the term "Hitman" is a little rough? Sharpen your dagger and read on. It gets up close and personal.

I love this business, at least the way I've done it. Thousands of transactions and billions of dollars, and I run solo. I've had a great time, made a lot of money, had a lot of fun, and lived an adventure. And my clients got what they wanted – as promised. The opposition has been baffled by me, bad managers have feared me, and the CEOs... they love the results. You will too.

But it wasn't always easy.

PART ONE – HITMAN 1.0
--
INFERNO

3

FROM BAD BOY TO FAILURE

IT'S A START

"If it were possible to have a life absolutely free from every feeling of sin, what a terrifying vacuum it would be."
-- Cesare Pavese

I was 26 years old, and I walked out of the conference room where I had just lost everything. My pride, my self-esteem, all my money, and my life as far as I was concerned, were gone. About two-million dollars had gone up in smoke because of my stupidity. It had actually occurred over a couple of years; the conference room meeting was just the final bullet. I felt I was right about one thing, though; I was a loser, a failure, the scum of the earth. I wanted to get drunk. How had it gone so wrong?

Perhaps I should give you some context.

My parents were crazy smart. The problem was they were also both crazy. As a young boy, my life was freakish as they both acted out with their various addictions. My father was addicted to business and power and sex and money and alcohol. He liked cars, too. His '65 GTO was my favorite. I think he wrecked it. His behavior was a long way from his Amish ancestry and Mennonite upbringing. Shunned. My mother favored alcohol and pills and washed all that down with religion. Jesus Christ. Her daddy, a protestant minister, clearly would not have approved. Both my parents functioned, in a twisted sort of way, little snippets of normalcy. They beat on each other often, sometimes brandishing weapons. I would see them fighting, wrestling over a pistol or some other firearm. Sometimes the guns would discharge; time to keep your head down. The whole thing was a fucked-up situation.

My father was a budding aerospace and computer rock star in Los Angeles in the go-go days of sending people into space with NASA and building up the awesome raw power of a new computer industry. He was a mathematician, an engineer, an entrepreneur. He helped send men to the moon and build the first supercomputers. The talk around the house, when it was civil, focused on data and algorithms, contracts and money. I made mental notes of the first two items, though I didn't understand them much at the time (that would change). I did understand that last item though, money. I had a use for that. The idea of contracts also intrigued me. I was drawn to contracts in a strange way. Maybe it was the certainty of them, the "sanctity of contract." I had no certainty in my home life; that was certain. Growing up in a family where nothing that was said could be relied on, the legally binding nature of contracts was compelling.

My family wasn't wealthy, but the money and contract talk I overheard involved capital for companies, and I knew that was the fuel that powered the world when matched with the mental spark of ideas. I loved that. Brains were everything in our house. If you were stupid, you were dead. The rules were fluid though and changed often. Good luck. If my parents were stoned, you were dead. No luck at all. I had a sibling, an older sister. She always got straight A's. Little good it did her.

I was the smart kid in the neighborhood that none of the parents liked, but most of the fun kids did. I had some strong friendships and also a small group of boys that functioned as sort of a "go-to" crew for our nefarious activities. I was pretty much the leader of that group, though there wasn't an official hierarchy. The school administrators weren't so happy with me. I was bored in school, so I just used school as a source of fun and mischief. I skipped a lot, taking friends and girlfriends with me.

I always had more money as a kid than any of my peers because I worked and earned it. I did everything I could that would make me some cash. It helped me feel in control in a world out of control. One Christmas, my father gave me a gift worth a couple hundred dollars, but I wanted to put that money into something that would generate immediate cash flow for me. I convinced him to use that money instead to buy a small tractor with blades for snow and grass. I liked nothing better than leaving the house late at night to plow snow, bundled up tight against the wind and ice. I felt whole, in flow, and in control when I was alone doing my job, just me and my machine operating as one capable unit. The heavier the storms, the better. I wrote season-long contracts with neighborhood residents – payment upon signing, thank you very much. The money I earned funded the outrageous adventures of my crew.

We would find people to buy us wine, but since that wasn't always easy, when we found someone, we would have them buy a whole case of wine and give them a bottle for their trouble. We kept the remainder of the case hidden in my closet until we needed it for the next party or gathering. We always had money and most often had booze. The spirit behind our activities was to live with excitement and push the boundaries and extremes.

The law was after us a little. They had concerns about some streetlights and some other things that had inexplicably exploded. I had to take a lie detector test with a police sergeant. The police just let the issue drop after the test; that was enlightening. I just wanted to have fun, and we had the resources to have an awful lot of fun. Girls were very welcome, and sometimes they came. I loved this part of my life. I loved the excitement. I loved the girls. I loved the action. I hated my life at home.

My life at home sucked. By this time, my dad had left, a messy divorce, and living with my mom was a never-ending horror show. Gin, vodka, and pills every day, and she was dangerous. In addition to the drugs and alcohol, there were car wrecks, violent physical attacks, weapons, breakdowns, and her endless tears and screaming. My normal was her raging red eyes while she's coming after me with a nine iron. I had to avoid her at all costs to protect myself and my sanity, sometimes sleeping in the rafters of the garage. By the time I was 13, I had learned to be self-reliant and cunning. Years later watching the Sopranos television series, I felt real empathy for Tony Soprano when his mother put out a hit on her own son. I understood his conflict. This craziness lasted until I made my escape.

My opportunity to escape presented itself when I was 15. My mother's mental faculties had contorted themselves to the point where she decided to marry a guy who was going to be a guard at the Colorado State Reformatory in Buena Vista, Colorado, and move there – a tiny, rural town -- into a single-wide trailer home -- with him and his three kids. Jesus Christ.

This guy she was to marry, Jerry, was no good. Less than a year earlier, I had escorted him out of our house at knifepoint after he showed up in the middle of the night to have sex with her a month after he'd beaten her to a pulp -- black and blue and swollen from head to toe. My mom cursed at me as I forcefully led him out the door. That was a moment of clarity for me, a turning point, the realization loyalty was lost and had likely never been there at all. She was gone. I knew if I moved to Buena Vista with them, I would either die or wind up in the reformatory myself at the small end of that idiot's gun. I wasn't going to have either of those. I called my dad and told him I would surely die if I made that move. He said he'd put me up in a tiny apartment near my high school until I was old enough for a driver's license. He even bought some liquor for the place. As crazy as this was, it probably saved my life then.

Later, I would live with him. My father wasn't much engaged with me, but this was salvation as far as I was concerned. This began the first period of my life with some semblance of sanity, way more freedom, more money, more girls, and natural consequences. The next three years with my father were probably too liberal and too promiscuous, but at least they were sane. I made money at my father's company designing simple circuit boards and building up the prototypes. The money I earned went into more parties and road trips.

I entered the workforce on my own in restaurant kitchens. Restaurants were the perfect place to work for someone with interests like mine. I liked having fun, and restaurants were a fun place to work. These were bars with good food and playful people who also liked to have fun and party. These were places with baseball cut sirloins and snifters of single malt scotch, pretty barmaids with mini-skirts, and love affairs. After hours, the real parties would begin behind locked doors with employees and our favorite special friends. Alcohol flowed regardless of age, and naked bodies hung from the rafters. For an 18-year-old with my disposition, this was ideal. The money was handy too.

That's when I bought my first property. I was on my way to college (sort of). Actually, I was 18 and wanted out of my dad's house and wanted to live with my girlfriend. I thought the idea of renting seemed like a waste. I found a vacant, run-down, 750 square foot, stick-built, old box with asbestos siding. The house had dirt for a front lawn and a broken screen door. It looked bad. There was no For Sale sign on the property, only a notice posted on the front door that read:

WARNING

THIS IS THE PROPERTY OF

THE VETERANS ADMINISTRATION

TRESPASSERS WILL BE PROSECUTED TO THE FULLEST

EXTENT OF THE LAW

For information on this property call (and a phone number)

I ripped the notice off the door and took it. I had saved several thousand dollars from the restaurant work which I used for the down payment and with a newly minted mortgage from the V.A. (I wasn't one, but the V.A. had foreclosed on the place, so they made me the loan), I moved in six weeks later and filled the house with friends and roommates. It was cash flow positive from day one.

This was a party house. It was always full of college kids, restaurant cooks, girlfriends, bartenders, cocktail waitresses, and ever-present new acquaintances. It was adjacent to the nightlife mecca of the city at the time, with bars, nightclubs, high-end strip clubs, and a myriad of eateries and trendy apartments. People were coming and going from the house at all hours of the day and night. It was a popular spot, around the clock music, drugs, conversation, debate, and everything else you might expect. I wasn't all that good at being social, but I owned the place, so I was popular too.

We were rough on that house. We'd fix motorcycles in the basement (we had to drive them up the stairs to get them out) and had a German Shepard that had the run of the neighborhood and kept the Post Office from delivering mail five doors down on either side. Years later, the Post Office became a national client of mine. I never told them this story. The neighbors hated us. The house was on Missouri Avenue, but we all affectionately called it "Misery Ave." I never fixed it up, except for some paint and carpet when I sold it. My early college stint didn't survive that house and neither did my girlfriend. But five years later, that house had more than doubled in value, an eleven-hundred percent return on my original investment, and I was hooked on real estate. It was in my DNA.

At 23, I sold that house, pocketed my profits, and I set out to make a career in commercial real estate. I interviewed at companies all over town. I quickly learned they weren't at all interested in a 23-year old kid with my rough background, untamed hair to my shoulders, no degree, and no family to speak of. One after another, they said, "No thank you, but we wish you luck." One such company that turned me away, one of the largest companies in town, I ended up running a few years later.

With my commercial real estate career plans dashed by the large firms that made up the industry's establishment, I instead started to trade properties for my own account with the money I had made on that first house. I started buying houses and then small apartment buildings. I leveraged everything to the hilt -- 95% to 105% loan to value. My going-in equity positions were razor-thin if at all. I didn't care what price I paid for the properties. I only cared if I could get them financed. I became licensed and took commissions to help with the equity. I would buy a property and move in with a mattress on the floor, just to sell it six months later for a profit. I would quickly sell the ones that would show a quick return and use the money for my expenses and hold the rest. I amassed a portfolio of houses and apartment buildings, and money was good. At the time, properties were appreciating 10, 12, 18 percent a year, so I could handle the high mortgage rates. That big appreciation covered all my mistakes, until it didn't.

I bought a large apartment property north of the downtown district on Transit Street in the path of urban renewal and redevelopment. But almost immediately, I knew I had made a terrible mistake. The city tabled the plans it had for investment in the area, and the march of redevelopment stopped dead in its tracks. Without the city's performance and without the urban renewal, the area was left to the gangs, prostitutes, drug dealers, thugs, and desperately poor single mothers and impoverished families. I would have to carry this property for many years just to break even, let alone make a profit. I had also leveraged this property to 95 percent loan-to-value, and the debt service was crushing. Time was my enemy.

I had previously moved to the 38th floor of a high-rise apartment building in the central business district to live and re-engage with the university for a work/college existence. The economics and finance courses were the only ones I found worthwhile, philosophy too, as an outlier. I could see my Transit Street apartment property from my balcony. The Transit Street property was a mere 20-minute walk from my high-rise apartment, but they were worlds apart in their reality, from comedy clubs and stylish public markets to grimy peep shows and homeless missions.

The tenants of Transit Street were the poorest of the poor. When they paid rent, they paid in cash, which was best. I had a manager on the property who would collect the rent and keep it in a locked safe. I would pick up the money twice per month and would have to go directly to the tenants to collect it myself if they hadn't paid. Frequently, I would be carrying thousands of dollars in cash in the worst part of town. Sometimes I carried a snub-nose .38 with me, a Saturday Night Special. I felt better carrying that handgun when I was there on a rough weekend night with maybe fifteen grand in my pocket and some of the tenants and their friends in the parking lots getting drunk, smoking crack, and shooting heroin. Some would offer me drugs and sex in lieu of rent. My only interest was paying my debt service.

I made attempts to improve the property and upgrade the tenants. I poured money into electrical upgrades, new finishes, new kitchens, new bathrooms, and attractive common areas, just to have them ripped out to the studs by tenants and their friends. I moved an office into the building for a daytime presence and hired nighttime patrols, but still, the midnight movers would steal the refrigerators and take a sledgehammer to the countertops and walls. The government wanted nothing to do with this property.

I personally managed the refurbishment crews and worked alongside them in the reconstructions. I once hired a gang member to act as security to keep the tenants from destroying the building. That worked well, but I lost him when he was arrested for murder (not at my building). After that, I hired a Laotian manager who did a good job of filling the apartments with Laotians and Hmong people. That worked great for a while until I learned that he was abusing the Hmong, and I fired him. Everyone moved out then, both the Laotians and the Hmong. Go figure. The building was empty, and I had to start all over again – new construction, new manager, new tenants, new problems. I could handle no new debt, and I was desperate for cash flow.

Two years I kept this going. One by one I lost all my other properties to feed this beast. Like an insatiable monster that could neither be satisfied nor killed, Transit Street devoured all my other properties, money, and assets. It also took my humanity. I didn't sleep. I didn't have friends. I was stressed to the max carrying a massive negative cash flow and debt service payments I could no longer make. I felt like shit. Two bars, a liquor store, a convenience store, and a 24-hour coffee shop were just an elevator ride from my apartment, so I didn't have to go out much. I'd sit on my balcony at night drinking bourbon and looking out over the skyline just thinking. I took it as a personal deficiency, a failure, that I had gotten into this situation and didn't see a way through it.

From my earliest memories, I'd always been able to figure a way out of bad situations; I'd done it a million times. I had thought I was young and invincible, but not this time, not this situation. It was over when there was nothing left to feed the beast, no more properties to sell, no more money in the bank, no more money to be borrowed, a giant debt I could no longer pay.

I was living in one of the tallest residential buildings in the city and having open balconies, a number of poor souls used that amenity as their last secure place before leaping off to their deaths, but that thought never entered my mind as a solution. For me, emotional pain was something I was used to; I had lived with it my entire life. It would cut deep, but only so deep and then stop. Beneath that was an odd stoic foundation, granite-like in its density and just as emotionless. I wouldn't kill myself; there's no risk in that. Risk made me feel alive.

Glimpse the Hitman

I've read that epiphanies flow from euphoria. That might be true, but that's not the only place. A combustible desperation also spawns epiphanies, and if you're dying to live, you can guess which ones have the most energy.

"Leverage" has two meanings in real estate. Financial leverage can multiply your gains because you're using other people's money. So, if you buy a million-dollar property and put 10 percent ($100,000) down as equity and finance the remaining ninety percent, if the property then increases in value 10 percent ($100,000), you've seen a 100% return on your equity. That's how I made an eleven-hundred percent return on my first property. It's a powerful tool. However, if the property decreases in value 10 percent, you've experienced a 100 percent loss because your equity is gone. Also, know that financial leverage exposes you to risk beyond your initial investment. If the property declines in value more than your investment and you're liable for the loans, you can lose two, five, ten times your initial investment and more. Financial leverage is an excellent binary tool, but only if your bet is correct. My bet was wrong on Transit Street. I was way underwater and my financial leverage exacerbated my losses. But there was a different kind of leverage that would ultimately save my ass, negotiating leverage.

Negotiating leverage is the power to increase your gains through negotiations because of a force, the lever, which unilaterally moves the negotiations in your favor. Negotiating leverage is never binary. There's no downside. Negotiating leverage prevents negotiations from moving away from you. Overt forms of negotiating leverage are obvious, such as an office leasing market that has an enormous amount of vacant space. In that instance, the office tenants have strong and overt negotiating leverage to move the negotiations in their favor because there are so many opportunities they can choose from to lease. But what if no overt leverage exists? What if you represent an office tenant in a tight office leasing market with little or no vacancy? What if you're 26-years old with a mountain of debt and no way to pay it? The only solution I saw was to create negotiating leverage where none existed. If I was successful, I would squeak through this. If not, I would be in no worse shape than if I hadn't tried, dead. I had one shot.

I was current on my payments when I entered the conference room, but that was about to end. The lenders knew some of the challenges the building presented, and I was about to tell them of my experiences over the previous two years. I sat alone at the end of a long, polished conference table. My leather satchel placed before me was my only companion. The chandeliers hanging from the tall ceiling cast a glow on the mahogany walls and made the lead crystal sparkle. The silver coffee service was brought in along with chocolate truffles and a variety of berry torts, and the double doors to the hotel conference room were closed and locked. I wondered why in the hell I had chosen this place to have this meeting.

The four men facing me were the holders of the promissory notes and their attorneys. I noticed that each of these guys wore different versions of the same tailored dark blue suit and maroon tie. I wondered to myself in amusement if they had called each other and agreed to dress alike for the meeting. I felt no pretense necessary and had worn faded blue jeans, a white shirt opened at the collar, and tennis shoes. I felt quite at home. I downed two cups of coffee and started the meeting.

If my noteholders foreclosed on the property, I would have been personally liable for a deficiency judgment, which would have been an enormous sum of money, and I was already broke. Now I was looking to be more than broke; I was going to be insolvent. My self-worth was roughly equivalent to my net worth, bankrupt. Bankrupt emotionally and financially, and the two were intertwined.

Some of the holders of the notes were the entities I had purchased the property from. The gain they had booked from the sale of the property to me was entirely tied up in my notes to them. I had a few additional construction loans as well. I'd been told one of the previous owners had exchanged sex for rent. I didn't ask for details. I did think, though, that I would wash my hands after the meeting.

I knew one of these guys knew people on the city council that had scrapped the urban development plans for the area. I asked if he thought he had any clout with the city. "No, maybe, I don't know," he said. I then told him that without a change in the city's direction, the viability of our loan was in question. I asked, "What do you think they are going to do?" "I don't know," he said again. I told him I would try to hang on until the city re-engaged its redevelopment plan, but that it would be rough going. Beyond that, I told him nothing. I let his mind run the various scenarios of what could unfold. He didn't know if I would make the next month's payment, or three months from now, or a year from now. He didn't know if I would walk from the property tomorrow or if, or when, he might have to initiate foreclosure proceedings, if ever, and what the condition of the building would be if they did take over. He didn't know if I would declare bankruptcy, then or ever, and tie the property up for ages. He didn't know. He was uncertain of everything. What he did know was things were not as he desired, and the outcome would likely not be what he had initially expected. He didn't really know anything. He was uncertain, and that uncertainty was the leverage I needed to win this negotiation.

People will do amazing things to run from uncertainty. They'll give up money, power, position, advantage, and self-esteem. To most, uncertainty means unbalanced, and impulsively they will jerk to get back their footing. Their actions are driven by impulse, emotions, and fear, not their rational mind. Their response to uncertainty is formed mainly without regard to facts. Their risk-averse nature will do what is necessary to revert to the mean of their passive harmony. If uncertainty is not dealt with using your frontal lobe, you're losing. The good news for me is that most people don't, at least not very effectively.

I was intrigued by the potential this presented, that I could influence my opponents' decision-making processes by exposing the genesis of their fear and uncertainty and guiding them out of the chaos by helping them make the decisions of my choosing. This was my first glimpse of the potential of a Hitman skill, albeit only just a glimmer. At the moment, though, I was a mess. I was broke and emotionally broken. I was a failure, and I came down on myself pretty hard.

It was a fairly short meeting. In the end, the noteholders were recommending to me that I sign the property over to them via a deed in lieu of foreclosure, and there would be no deficiency judgment. Their uncertainty led them unwittingly to take back control, and that meant taking back the property as soon as they could. This was the perfect scenario for me, as best as it could get.

Leaving the conference room meeting that day, I couldn't have predicted the lunch I would have three years later with a man who would hand me a million-dollar commission check for an office lease I negotiated in one of his office towers, not the first check he'd handed me. We ate garlic-infused herb and peppercorn encrusted rare beef tenderloin with a potent béarnaise and seared scallops. We sat in a private dining room in an old bank vault of an ornate turn-of-the-century bank building in the center of the city. He owned office towers all over the country. I told him my story of Transit Street. He told me that he had learned that you always have to make your money when you buy a property; you couldn't count solely on future market trends to make your investment right, let alone cover your mistakes. You have to negotiate terms that will generate an immediate return on your investment the moment you acquire a property and to walk away if you can't.

He confirmed what I had learned in the three years since the conference room meeting: negotiations are everything. Negotiations are at the core of what creates value. Skilled negotiations are power. The money I had lost and the time I had wasted had been my own fault and the result of my own passive ignorance. I pledged after the conference room meeting that it would never happen again, but walking out of that conference room had been a terrible low point for me. Obviously, so much needed to change. I needed to change.

Spring comes late to the high mountain country of Colorado. The mornings are cold, and the wind carries the scent of pine. The sun brings warmth to the earth.

I had spent nine days hiking alone through isolated mountain terrain. These trails were not famous. Sometimes there were no trails. I always felt most comfortable in my skin when I was in the forest, when I was out on the rocks and alone in the high country – places where the Ute had hunted more than a century before. I felt the most powerful, the most confident, the most cogent. That's why I'd gone there, as far away from civilization and people as I could. Some camps I made I stayed at several days, some just overnight, but I had been compelled to climb ever higher. The thought of the conference room meeting the week before, and everything that had led up to it, loomed in my mind.

How had I let it get so bad? What had I been thinking? Who was I? I had no answers, but I knew the fear and self-loathing weren't sustainable. So, I just hiked. I just focused on the tightness of my thighs, the placement of my feet on the rocks, and the surroundings.

On the last evening of my trek, I stopped climbing when I reached the summit of a mountain peak, 13,200 feet above sea level. I made camp there, two thousand feet above timberline. What little firewood I had with me, I had carried the last tiring stretch to the top. I'd sleep in my down bag thrown on positioned scree rock. This was not a famous mountain, either. I was truly alone, just the way I wanted to be.

In the blackness of that night, I could see the brilliance of a trillion stars and the unmistakable glistening band of this small corner of the universe, which is the Milky Way. I could feel the immensity of time and of all existence. Lying there in that surreal place and looking out into the universe, I could feel something was about to change. I fell asleep on the very tip of that peak, a dot on top of that massive rocket pointed straight to heaven.

The next morning, I opened my eyes and realized where I was. It felt like a moment out of time. I felt like I'd awakened in a new world, full of energy and possibilities open to me. My next action was typical for the trip, but it seemed more appropriate and meaningful in this new world. It seemed like a way to mark the moment. I built a fire.

That morning on top of the mountain, drinking campfire coffee and chewing the grounds that hadn't settled to the bottom of the metal cup, I could see a hundred miles in every direction. I could see the curvature of the earth. I saw the mountains and the valleys and the sky, and the tiny plants and blossoms that clung to what little soil they could find between the rocks. "Grandeur" was the word that came to me. I saw the world, the universe, and all nature as a beautiful place, and I felt gratitude for being part of it. I connected with the universe instead of cursing it. I felt respect for it. I felt its power. I learned that I loved this existence, that I loved my existence. That morning I felt a new strength and energy and eagerness to keep fighting, and I was excited to learn new things and conquer new challenges. I knew then that I wasn't a failure. That I had failed, but that it was a good thing, a very good thing. I learned that I had put my focus on the small and negative things in my life, the fear, the debt, the downside, the defeat, the sorrow, the uncertainty. I learned that what you focus on most, expands in your life. I learned I could reject the shame and let go of my shitty past and instead focus on what good I could make happen. I decided mere survival wasn't good enough; I wanted to win. I was going to take new risks, take on new challenges, and start something completely new. I was going to live autonomously and free. It was time to engage my brain and learn a new set of skills and a new philosophy to live by, learn to discover the advantages the world offered and make them my own, and then make it all happen.

4

PHILOSOPHY OF A HITMAN

PART I

UNAUTHORIZED POWER

"Once you have tasted flight, you will forever walk the earth with your eyes turned skyward, for there you have been and there you will always long to return."
-- Leonardo da Vinci

I think I knew early on my path wasn't going to be a normal one, a traditional one. I always felt a little bit like an outsider. I watched most peers go through the routines expected of them. It didn't make sense to me. It didn't resonate with me. They seemed like pieces in a board game being moved about by their families, friends, and employers; soulless almost. Brainless, though that's not fair, but certainly not autonomous, not sovereign unto themselves.

I always took a different path, sometimes smooth, often not, but it was my path to choose. I didn't want to be normal. I wanted something more.

After coming down from the mountains, I set out to build a new path for myself. This philosophy was the basis of my new start and made possible the advantages I wanted. It was the foundation for the trajectory that ultimately made me successful and the freedom, adventure, and prosperity that followed. I knew it wasn't going to be easy, but it was something I had to do.

This philosophy is the backdoor to the fundamentals of power. The kind of power that's subtle, yet devastating and unyielding if pushed against. It's not sanctioned. It's not authorized. You have to grab it yourself, without permission. You're going to learn my tricks and hacks and hammers and cheats to take the advantage and win your negotiations and more, but without learning this philosophy first, those things will just fuck you up.

This philosophy became my footing. Built over time, it has guided my thoughts and actions. It's kept me sane when the world was insane. It's pulled me out of the muck when I was stuck up to my ass. It's kept me moving forward when that seemed impossible.

I give this philosophy to you in the sequence I learned it. The sequence is important. There are four parts. Consider this first part as infrastructure, the basics to build upon, from the ground up, as I did.

I wasn't taught the values you would hope a family would teach a child: values like love, respect, responsibility, dignity, beauty, perseverance, truth, and gratitude. What I did learn growing up was how to survive. That meant cunning and the ability to withstand pain. These are useful tools, no doubt, but hardly a blueprint for life and career. My principles, my values, this philosophy, I pieced together over time without a guide to show me the way. At the time, I didn't know the concept of "first principles," but that's how my mind worked. I built this philosophy using first principles, principles that cannot be denied, raw truth without assumptions or judgment, and then I reasoned up from there.

Thinking and reasoning are the most powerful tools we can develop, yet most people deny them and abdicate their responsibility to use them. I say "abdicate" their responsibility; because, when they do, everyone suffers, especially those closest to them.

Do you want to hear the truth? Are you even able to hear the truth? Many people are afraid of the truth because they can't control it. It makes them uncomfortable, uneasy, and scared. They're like the ignorant inhabitants in Plato's story of The Cave, who, when presented with the opportunity for knowledge and the freedom to live in an unchained world under sunshine and blue skies, instead preferred to remain chained in the cave forever, watching their flickering shadows cast on the rear of the cave from the fire behind them as their total reality --because that's what they'd always known. They didn't want what was true and right. They wanted what was comfortable even though it meant hiding from the truth and giving up their freedom. They would fight, even kill, anyone who would attempt to enlighten them that their perception of reality was based on incomplete knowledge.

When confronted with an uncomfortable truth, many people will deny it, try to revise it, gloss it up, cover it over, or just ignore it in hopes that it doesn't get exposed. They'll twist themselves up like pretzels trying to avoid it, telling lies, living lies, hoping against hope that they will somehow be able to thread the needle, so the uncomfortable truths remain hidden from view. They may not even know they are doing it, content to live their lives watching their flickering shadows on the back of the cave. Are you able to hear and see the truth? It's the first damn lesson I learned.

A is A

A is A. This is a quintessential first principle.

Aristotle first described a world where things have specific characteristics, a nature inherent unto themselves which define them. This was his Law of Identity. He showed the world that logic exists, and those intrinsic characteristics in things [and people] do not change without some outside energy and influence changing them. A is A. A is not B. Someone telling you A is B does not make it so. You wishing A is B does not make it so. If A is A, yet you build your life and career pretending that A is B, you will fail. If you are an A, but you try to convince others you are a B, you are a liar. A is A. Embrace it. Live with it, even if it's hard and even if it hurts.

People are going to lie to you; they're going to tell you A is B. Accept nothing as fact until you can verify it with your own head. When they twist themselves up like pretzels trying to maintain those lies, let them. You can't fix them. It's their weakness. If you can, move on with your life without them. If you must deal with them, stay alert to their deceptions. If you are in negotiations with them, your understanding of their mangled reality will help cause their fraudulent positions to collapse in front of you. If you're the one afflicted with reality denial (e.g., lying to yourself and the world), you'd better change that ASAP, or you'll be dead. Your survival depends upon your inviolate pursuit of veracity.

Aristotle was the ultimate logic fanboy. And why not, it's pure undeniable principle; accurate reasoning determines outcomes. And we like determining outcomes. If the truth is that A is greater than B, then logic dictates that A + A will always be greater than A + B. No amount of hoping or wishing will make it otherwise. If it's a fact that the presence of A will always destroy B, then logic dictates that B will never destroy A without some additional outside force to make that occur. Logical reasoning allows you to plan for every outcome when the variables are known.

Predicting the future is not premonition. It's knowing how the natural flow of events will unfold based on the dynamics influencing them. But without understanding and accepting the truths of reality, reason and logic are impotent, and you're out of control. Knowing the truth, or not knowing or not accepting the truth, is the difference between life and death.

I know a woman; we'll call her Kristi. Kristi aspired to a life in literature, science, and academia. In that quest, she accumulated four college degrees, including two masters and a doctorate. Still, she spent most of her adult life unable to care for her own financial needs and bitter about how she perceived the world treated her. Why? Because she believed what she'd been told that those degrees assured her a job, respect, and position, and that the world would automatically provide her all those once those degrees were secured with no further effort on her part. She thought her power resided in those degrees. It didn't. The truth was those degrees guaranteed nothing except the existence of a six-figure student loan debt. Kristi had been lied to and given half-truths by the system she embraced, but she didn't acknowledge that. She wanted A to be B, but it's not, and she suffered. Kristi thought A should be B, and she spent her life trying to convince others and herself that A should be B. Kristi expended so much wasted energy only to arrive at her disappointment. What she wished for, what she thought she was entitled to, was impossible without acknowledging the truth and making the necessary changes. A is always A.

If you think I am stating the obvious, I am, but if you don't grasp the magnitude of this concept, you're missing the point. People accept as reality the crap that is shoveled to them without giving it a second or critical thought. Engage your prefrontal cortex, and cut through the clutter, cut through the emotional urgings, cut through the persuasive arguments to understand the unvarnished truth. The maelstrom is endless, so diligence is vital.

Think or Die

You can actually lose in this game of life. You can be unhappy. You can go broke. You can die. Your mind is your only real means of defense, your only real weapon, your only means of deliverance. I exalt in the potential of the thinking mind. A sharp mind is an expression of divinity. It's the prime mover.

Original thought is a rare treasure available to all but forged by just a few. The ability to think with a pronounced clarity can transcend worldly challenges and challengers and empowers you to create solutions and outcomes in extreme ways.

A dull mind is the scourge of the masses. We live in a culture where our minds are constantly bombarded with outside stimuli designed to stifle our thinking, while at the same time, arouse our emotions and pigeonhole our base instinctual urges in the direction of someone else's design. People aren't trained to think. People are trained to follow. They numb out and still feel that something important has happened. They allow the noisiest rhetoricians, be they parents, or managers, or politicians, or friends, or programmed talking heads, to imprint in their brains the tribalistic motives that direct their actions -- and not a bit of effort is required.

Fuck that. Nobody will do anything important as a numb follower. Conformity breeds mediocrity; it depends on it. It feeds on it. It's a creativity wasteland. Acquiescing and falling into conformity only serves to relieve you of the responsibility of thinking. Your mind is where your unique identity resides, where your greatness resides, but only to the magnitude of its independence, only to the magnitude of your desire and willingness to use it. Ralph Waldo Emerson said, "To be yourself in a world that is constantly trying to make you something else is the greatest accomplishment." Respect your rational thought above everything else. Critical and original thinking are the only things that will propel you forward, keep the hijackers out of your psyche, allow you to ascertain the actual truth of every situation, and create outcomes of your design.

Your critical mind powered by study is your defense. Your original thought is your creativity, your fuel, your weapon. Leave either behind, and you will lay bloodied in the field. Abdicate your responsibility to think, and you are dust in the wind, or worse, a self-described victim of circumstances. You would be a victim, alright, but the perpetrator would be you.

Nothing worthwhile is given to you; everything worthwhile is earned and taken. The mental clarity necessary to perform in a superior way requires effort and diligence. Be aware of the despoilers of clarity; the obvious ones like the depressant, ethanol (been there), and the psychotropic, THC (done that), and the more insidious ones like wallowing in the victimhood of perceived injustice or the oh-so-tempting distractions of escape – to each his own (done that too). Though you might consider each of these, the booze, the pot, the escape, as having only the magnitude of a lost hundred-dollar bill or an extra hour or two of sleep; the real difference might actually be measured in millions or billions of dollars over time because of a deal or idea missed due to a slow or dim or dull response, a plan not formulated, or something as simple as a late meeting or communication. Gold medals are won by ten-thousandths of a second. High-frequency stock trades are won by one-millionth of a second. Success in business and life is won by the sharpest edge of global and situational mental ripostes, creativity, brilliance, and action.

If victimhood is what is slowing you down, reject that toxic crap. Whatever injustice may have occurred to you, it doesn't deserve to hijack your brain now. If you allow it to keep you down from this point forward, it's a double injustice, one you can prevent from happening. Take back your power, find a workaround if necessary, and nurture your head for the sharpest of freedom and clarity.

Intellectual capability expands with deliberate and topical study and purposive use. Do you hold back placated by the cultural platitude of not overthinking a situation? Garbage. Step it up and outthink everybody. The mind doesn't work in a vacuum. It needs fuel and resources and exercise. Absorbing the world's data and ideas is akin to a baby feeding with mother's milk. Explore, study, learn, build up the synaptic transmissions and plasticity in your brain. Increase your synaptic strength. You can be smarter. Do your work and be smarter than the other guy. Outthink everybody. It's easy to do because so few do it. So many are numb followers. Instead, give yourself unfettered original thought and lead. It's your choice.

Intent to Kill

The world in which we live, all it contains, all the business and life and all other goings-on are elastic and fungible. They are the raw materials waiting for us to imprint our intentions upon it, to express our forms to it. It will bend to your plan and take on any form you provide it.

The universe has no judgment about your intention, and there is no one from whom you need to ask permission to do it. Whether you think the world is the result of some divine plan, a universe of chaotic moments and chances, or something in between, the net result is the same. The raw materials of the universe await your decisions, and once those decisions are made, and actions begin to be taken, the universe takes on the forms you intend.

Many people live their lives without clear intent, but instead are guided by fantastical questions in their heads that create fear and unease. Questions like: "What's going to happen to me? What if my boss or client becomes disappointed with me or I lose my job? What if the deal isn't signed?" Their fear becomes their reality. Their planning becomes a vehicle to avoid things, to lessen risk, to always responding and reacting to the outside world, or their perception of it, instead of making their lives into the image of their choosing. Their worried minds get knocked around every day by random events, off-hand remarks, little perceived slights, or world affairs. The energy they expend every day dealing with the seemingly infinite barrage of outside factors pushing and pulling their minds in all directions drains their creativity, happiness, income, health, and intelligence. They suffer. Their families suffer. Their companies suffer. Their clients suffer. All because of stupid fears they don't need to feel. They've given up control to their worry. They're the sad souls in Edgar Allen Poe's Imp of the Perverse as their brainless urges contort their minds to self-defeating blunder. Poe writes, "We stand upon the brink of a precipice. We peer into the abyss — we grow sick and dizzy. Our first impulse is to shrink from the danger."

Poe's description as to what happens next for these woeful mortals is no better. I paraphrase: The mind goes blank, perverse forces beyond their control flood their thinking, and they become helpless in a cloud of mush and confusion – a sorry lot.

The Edgar Allen Poe dolt falls into the abyss while trying not to. What a mess. Instead, when faced with fear and uncertainty, take back the power by thinking through to intention. Then feel the control and dominion of the circumstances and affirm: "I stand upon the brink of the precipice. My mind sharpens to a laser focus. My thinking gets clear and fast. My muscles get taut, and my power of intention takes over. Decisions are made, and I act of my own volition -- ebullient and unstoppable." Defy what's in your way. The best time to claim great things is in the face of adversity. Summon your inherent natural power and take that first step towards that greatness. The universe places no restrictions on you, only those you put on yourself.

Intention is not random. Intention is not want. Intention is not desire. Want and desire are the precursors to intention. Want and desire are the sparks; intention is the fuel needed to build the form to impress into reality. Intention is the most fundamental form of intellectual capital. It's not an accident; it's a decision. Once you decide with action, intention starts in motion the known and unknown to achieve your desired outcomes.

A timeless movie that grabs me (and worth watching) is *The Edge*, with Anthony Hopkins and Alec Baldwin. Hopkins plays a brainy billionaire obsessed with information, inquiry, and reasoning; Baldwin, a hedonistic and emotional modeling agent. This unlikely pair is lost deep in the Alaskan wilderness being pursued by a very large and angry Kodiak bear with an unquenchable thirst for human blood. As several days and sleepless nights unfold, this hapless partnership edges nearer defeat and a certain and gruesome death as their power wanes and the bear's viciousness grows.

On the last evening of their running, tired and starving, Baldwin's character is pleading with Hopkins. "What are we going to do? We're going to die." Their backs are against the wall. There is no retreat. Their ships have been burned. There is no escape. They can only give up, swiftly or slowly, or they can fight on against all odds to win. Hopkins' character thinks about the 11-year-old Maasai boys that killed lions with spears. He thinks about the young native Americans that counted coup hitting bears with sticks as a right-of-passage. He starts to develop a plan in his mind. He decides, "I'm going to kill the bear." He knows, "what one man can do another can do." He's determined. He's convinced. He's intentioned, "I'm going to kill the mother fucker." And through his intention, he's shown how to do it.

There is no defeat except the one you accept. There is no victory except the one you attempt. What bear do you have to kill? What is keeping you up at night? What's in your path and keeping you from finding your way to your own promised land? You have volition. Make a decision. Summon your innate power and start to take action. It's no more difficult than what thousands of other people have accomplished before you in one form or another. Set your intention and kill that mother fucker.

Risk, Peril, and Possibility

Growing up, I didn't get the oxytocin salve and those rewarding dopamine pops one gets from parents' hugs and kisses, so I learned to get those pops and satisfying feelings in other ways. One of the surest and most reliable methods was taking risks – risks of all kinds. Taking risks reliably produced those dazzling dopamine pops several ways. First, I would get a pop from the adrenaline rush from the risky activity itself. I loved the adrenaline. I still do. Second, I learned that almost regardless of the risk-taking activities themselves, the risks set me up for much greater achievements and rewards than were available to those that didn't take risks. With every successful risk-driven achievement came new rewards, new accolades, new profits, new perks, soaring self-esteem, the spark of freedom, and yes, another dopamine pop – an incredible score. But that's not all. I also learned I got a pop just thinking about new risks I could take and new adventures to pursue.

Even if the risk failed entirely or in part, I still reaped new knowledge, solidified self-esteem, and the dopamine pop from the effort. I was in complete control. I'm not in this life for dribs and drabs, and I get depressed when I start to feel that way. When I do, I have to shake things up and plan and embark on a new adventure.

We're taught from a young age, throughout school, and into our careers that it's okay to take "calculated risks." The problem is that everyone's own calculation of those risks are skewed safe because we're also taught to be so risk-averse. The calculations are weighted so conservatively; it's no risk at all. "Calculated Risks" have calculated out any real risk and reduced the upside. We calculate the risk to stay within our comfort zone, and you conveniently don't have to perform in any exemplary fashion. If the so-called risk lacks peril and possibility, you can be mediocre, and your outcomes will be mediocre. When you take real risks, you must perform in an exemplary way, or you might die. The onus is on you to perform. Most people can't stand that pressure, and that is why they stay in their comfort zone and accept the mundane. They quake, they fold, they fall into the abyss. You must be able to handle the incoming. I'm not suggesting you take out the calculation of risk, that would be an abdication of your thinking mind. What I am saying is that your calculations must include risk, not avoid it. They must include your willingness to exert effort and accurately assess your ability and performance. When you take risks, venture into new territory, there is a tendency to regress to old patterns and behaviors because of the fear and discomfort you experience. That's a pivotal point, move forward or fail.

Games of pure chance are games of odds, and your play is limited to your willingness to weigh and accept the odds. Games of risk include odds; but can be heavily influenced by your introduction of knowledge, skill, creativity, game theory, and logic. The degree to which you bring those things to bear determines your likelihood of success. If you aren't willing to do the work, you're rolling the dice. If you are willing to do the work, you'll win every time. At least most of the time; after all, it is risk.

When looking at a new opportunity, ask yourself: "What is the return on my money, time, and effort, and is it exciting?" Because if the return is nothing beyond mere sustenance and if the return is not exciting, why do it? The further you move away from your comfort zone, the greater your returns can be. I want to make my actions count. I want to make my life an adventure. I want to have a shitload of fun, change the world, and make a million bucks doing it. If I can't, why bother?

Fear holds most people back from taking the risks required to succeed. They fear what might happen to them if they embark on the risk. So, instead of handling that uncertainty, they opt for the certainty of what will happen if they don't take the risk – nothing. Banality awaits when fear prevails, and risk isn't exercised. Fear is common, it's built into our DNA, but it's only a tool, a guide. It's not a predictor, and more often than not, it's wrong, because it's based on ill-informed emotions. Fear is lessened with preparation, knowledge, skill, and experience. Fear becomes a fraud when you've achieved clarity of thought and confidence in your ability to ascertain the truth of a given situation and alternative logical courses of action. Fuck any insecurity and plow forward. Marcus Aurelius, the last of the Five Good Emperors of Rome, the great philosopher and student of personal ethics and logic said, "If you are distressed by anything external, the pain is not due to the thing itself but to your estimate of it, and this you have the power to revoke at any moment." If fearful, be fearless. Fear nothing; understand everything. Embrace real risk.

Gaming Nature's Meritocracy

When you dare to step out of line and to do something new and great and beyond the ordinary, you win no matter what. When you dare to start something big and worthy of profound implications, creativity is unleashed, and new options are presented to you. It unbridles your enjoyment of work and life. It shows you how to work around the obstacles. It enables you to fail, to get up, and then do it again better. There is achievement and knowledge in making the attempt. Even if you fail, your foundation is that much stronger so you can launch yet again. Your character is that much more seasoned, your confidence greater, and your likelihood to reach your goals that much more certain. Take on a challenge so great that you can feel the exhilaration of its victory or take pride and learn from its defeat.

It starts with just one tiny step.

People spend so much time and energy trying to fit in and conform. They submit to the cultural norms of the day and move through life with their uncomfortable thoughts and edges neatly tucked away, hidden from public view. To stand out is something scary to them. To go it alone is something unthinkable. They think it's better to blend in, go with the flow, respect the given authority, and be absorbed into the group. Their growth stops. Their evolution stops.

Conformity breeds mediocrity. Submission breeds stagnation and death. Your mind slows, your passion wanes, your life becomes the sludge you've accepted. For the conformists living their sheltered lives, the idea of doing something great makes them cower as did the sad souls peering into Poe's abyss. Fear of failure? Fuck it! Go fail. Go fail big. It's on the path to making your mark, improving the world, and sending your message. To become someone more, get out of the comfortable basement in your brain and start climbing stairs to the top. That's how you get to the top – you hike. If you weren't born with this imprinted in your psyche, this is a lesson you have to learn and keep learning.

Your esteem, self and otherwise, rises to the level of the challenges you put before it. Your abilities rise to the challenges you put before them. Your time on Earth is limited, what are you going to do with it? Steve Jobs had the simple clarity to say, "Everything around you that you call life was made up by people no smarter than you...and you can change it." He changed the course of the world in ways that seem commonplace now but were revolutionary and disruptive at the time. He was a giant of innovation in this and the last centuries. He took what was already known, built on it, and turned it into something new and extraordinarily beneficial.

Steve Jobs was given up for adoption, raised by adoptive parents, and he had no college degree. Jobs started Apple and developed the Macintosh computer only then to be humiliated and kicked out of his own company by the company's board of directors. He returned to Apple when it was on the brink of bankruptcy, but he was able to run it with autonomy and turned it into one of the most successful companies of all time.

Steve died when he was just 56 years old. Yet, during his relatively short life he created the personal computer industry, gave us the graphical user interface, so our screens navigate the way they do, WYSIWYG (What You See Is What You Get) computer publishing, made music instantly accessible digitally and mobile, re-created movie animation, gave us smartphones, created the tablet industry, and made the mobile computing and mobile app industries. An icon, no doubt, but Jobs was just a human being – a being who wasn't limited in his thinking. He had a thirst for learning and applying original thought to what he learned. He was always willing to work on something new and risky and better and different. Can you imagine Steve Jobs confined to a job with predetermined tasks assigned by a supervisor, or shackled in the back of The Cave? It's unfathomable because his mind, energy, and independence transcended all of that.

What do you want to do? Nature is a meritocracy. Our growth and evolution from our grand attempts, failures, and wins, afford us merit. That merit becomes our wisdom, and we score new power.

The Soul of an Entrepreneur

At the center of the heart of a Hitman is the soul of an entrepreneur with independence so fierce no other way of life is possible. For me, for a Hitman, entrepreneurship is more than a decision; it's a state of mind. Moreover, it's a state of being. Only with this sort of independence is the ability to fully act on your original thought and degree of risk possible. This independence means freedom of thought and action unimpeded by any constraints whatsoever imposed or policed by another. But at its core, independence is not the avoidance of authority; it's respecting your own judgment as the highest authority. It's respecting your own abilities to prevail without the need to plug into someone else's confidence, organization, or agenda. This is not dreaming; this is doing. This requires a level of personal responsibility and self-reliance that's not even talked about today.

Independence and freedom are predicated on self-reliance. Self-reliance is dependent on personal responsibility. Personal responsibility means taking an accurate assessment of existing truths and knowing that all appropriate courses of actions are yours to decide and implement. The obstacles before you can be destroyed, climbed, or circumvented only by your thoughts and actions, dependent on no other person or event.

Not everyone is cut out to be an entrepreneur. Not everyone is cut out to be a Hitman. The level of real risk required can feel daunting to some, and they won't go outside their comfort zone to accommodate it. Likewise, many won't muster the confidence they need to stand up and perform at a level required to succeed on their own. It's easier for some than others, no doubt, but if it's hard, so what? It's only hard for a short time. Action breeds confidence. Scars make you stronger, and the pain disappears. If confidence is the hurdle you need to clear, and you do it, your achievement is greater than everyone else's. If you cower, you fall into the abyss.

For me, entrepreneurship didn't seem like a choice; I didn't want to live any other way. When you're an entrepreneur, you're in the line of fire. The responsibility is all yours. Shit rains on you. The buck stops with you. The hungry hatchlings and chicks depend on you, but still, there is no better way of life. In my estimation, there is no higher calling for an active, thinking individual than to choose the path of self-reliance and entrepreneurship. Independence is freedom. Independence and performance is power.

Pleasure, Fun, and Gratification

I'm all about work. I'm all about hard work. I'm loyal as hell, and I work harder, dig deeper, am more passionate about my resolve and results than anyone I know. But here's what else I know, none of it makes any difference if I'm not having fun. I won't work for anyone I don't like. I refuse to work for anyone who is an asshole, is disloyal, lies too much, or is too inept for me to stand it. I have to enjoy my work. The work has to be meaningful. I have to enjoy my clients, and if I don't, I'm gone. Life is too short to give jerks a minute of my time.

Fun at work increases creativity, motivation, loyalty, and results. I'm not talking about ping pong tables and foosball, that's just distraction. The work itself has to be fun and gratifying. For that to be so, it must be inherently challenging, intellectually stimulating, adventurous, exciting, and lucrative. I tend not to work on one-off transactions, but instead build close and lasting relationships with a few clients of quality.

A loyal and intelligent relationship with the client is key. My clients have not all been entrepreneurial, given the sheer size and scope of the institutions. But my primary contacts need to have authority and a healthy degree of entrepreneurial/intrapreneurial independence. They also must be of a frame of mind that I get paid. I do a lot of free work for my best clients, stuff of my choosing, items that need to get done. But it's my choice. I don't take clients unless I think we can both make a lot of money.

The prerequisites are clear and certain. There must be good compensation, intellectual stimulation, adventure, excitement, a strong client relationship, a challenge to overcome, and fun. There must always be fun.

5

MY FIRST COMPANY

I want to live on the edge, break things, burn, live for ecstasy. I might at times be destructive, but I can build like nobody else. I'll jump off a cliff and teach myself to fly on the way down.

From my balcony on the 38th floor of my high-rise apartment downtown, I could see construction cranes high over the skyline, each one indicating another new office tower being built. I counted 28 cranes, could've been more. In the past three years or so, the office market in the central business district had nearly quadrupled in size to over thirty-five million square feet coming online. I could see welders high up on the steel frame skeletons of the towers throughout the nights with their torches sending flares like new stars cascading into the darkness. Interest rates on construction loans were already high and getting higher, so it made more sense to pay construction crews to work all night than to pay the debt service on a slower building schedule.

All this new construction coincided with a crash in oil prices. The price of oil had previously surged to over $100 per barrel but had since plummeted to just over $20 per barrel. Denver was heavy with oil companies and other energy-related firms, and the drop in oil prices decimated the demand for any office space. That, together with the Tax Reform Act, which significantly reduced or eliminated valuable real estate tax shelters, butchered the underlying value of the properties just as the new buildings were coming out of the ground. It was a perfect storm. Denver became famous for see-through office towers and giant vacancy rates. Auctions of vacant and sublease office space were broadcast media fodder around the world. Dallas and Houston were hurting too because of the oil glut, but the only office market in worse shape than Denver's was Kuala Lumpur, Malaysia. Actually, Denver and Kuala Lumpur bounced back and forth as to which city had the highest office vacancy rate in the world. All the world's office markets were suffering in differing degrees.

I sat on my balcony, looking out over the city, watching this unfold and contemplated what it meant for the future.

I realized the office building developers, investors, and lenders were going to be scrambling like crazy to cut losses as best as they could, as fast as they could. This was an extreme situation, and there were going to be extreme measures taken. This meant a huge amount of energy and money would be flowing, rushing to fill those empty office towers with tenants. Anybody proffering tenants would be substantially rewarded. The tenants willing to lease the space would likewise be rewarded. In my mind, this was a no-brainer; what is abundant becomes cheap, and what is scarce becomes valuable. Too much oil and the price of oil plummets. Too much office space and the space becomes cheap. Not enough tenants and the brokers who represent them get rich.

Supply and demand, a faultless, dynamic axiom; I decided to start a company that would represent office tenants, only office tenants, no other use, and no landlords. That company, my first real company, was one of the first pure tenant representation companies in the country, an idea that was ripe for the time. The funny thing was I knew absolutely nothing about leasing office space. It didn't matter though; I knew economics, and I knew what was about to happen. It was math (and a touch of behavioral econ). With my prefrontal cortex engaged, I decided to move forward, and set out to put together a new kind of real estate company from scratch, notwithstanding I was completely broke. I was broke, but decidedly not broken. I was hungry, driven, and determined to crawl out of the hole I'd dug for myself. I was going to take the risk, jump off the cliff, and start building my wings. I had to prove to myself my own worth. I figured success would do that.

Traditionally, commercial real estate brokerages purport to represent all sides of every transaction: buyers, sellers, tenants, and landlords – sometimes opposing sides all at the same time. Most brokers don't care about the conflicts this creates. The laws in most states at the time skewed to the benefit of sellers and landlords and screwed the buyers and tenants. The states said the property listing agreements between the brokerages and the sellers and landlords set out the totality of the agency relationships. This meant that the brokers working with the buyers and tenants were then, in fact, also agents of the sellers and landlords, subagents. The fiduciary responsibilities of all the agents flowed back up through to the sellers and landlords. None of the brokers involved in the transactions were truly representing the buyers and tenants in a fiduciary capacity. The buyers and tenants had smiling broker faces that showed them empty spaces, but nobody was legally looking out for their interests. The users were left to flap in the breeze. This was crazy. This was a ridiculous situation, a systemic absurdity, a legal catch-22 that left every buyer and tenant unrepresented by brokers in every transaction. Buyers and tenants were meat being led to the slaughter. Frankly, the injustice made me cringe. But it was the law. I thought it was nonsense. There had to be a better way. I decided I was going to circumvent the system and represent tenants, only the tenants, in a fiduciary capacity, in a market awash with new vacant office space. The established system run by the established in power was wrong. Fuck that.

I started my first company. I bought a desk and some equipment with a $750 loan from a friend of mine, and I cleared out the furniture in my living room to configure a roomy workspace. I positioned the desk so I had a constant floor to ceiling views of the growing skyline. I hot-wired cable to my apartment resulting in an endless stream of Scarface starring Al Pacino ("You fuck with me, you're fucking with the best.") while I worked on the plans for the company and set out to implement them. Ultimately, I had to turn Pacino off and turn all my attention to my new company. ("Say hello to my little friend.")

I had limited resources, actually no resources other than my brain and my time. So, I had to focus those resources on my greatest opportunity – positioning for the extreme nature of the market niche I'd chosen as my focus. In game theory vernacular, this became my dominant strategy. Focus is not just good advice when you set out to work on a project. The project itself depends on diligent focus on the principles of the project if it is to have a snowball's chance in hell to be anywhere near perfect. Without focus, entropy ensues, and destruction is imminent. The principles of my company were simple. I would represent office tenants in the central business district, and because of what I knew about the extreme market conditions and the buildings and landlords, I could negotiate for them office space that was better than they had at prices they didn't even know were possible. My data, my negotiations, their benefit. I positioned myself to where the severe market conditions became wind to my back. I represented what was scarce – the tenants.

Focus produces success because it does two important and market-shifting things. First, you become uber-smart about the data sets you focus on, which enables you to know and do things other people can't. Second, because you're so smart about those data sets and know and do things other people can't, the people and organizations that also have an interest in those same data sets are drawn to you. Your knowledge is enticing to them in almost a seductive way. When you've done your research and work and have become the expert, the specialist in your focus, you stand out in the minds of those who matter and become inextricably associated with that niche. The specialist commands all the power and attention, not the generalist. You become the obvious choice. When you're the proclaimed specialist, you're perceived as having the greatest knowledge of the data sets. When you're the demonstrated specialist, you become the leader in the niche. You had better be the best, though; because if you falter in this, your credibility will be toast.

One more thing, an over-arching axiom to know: focus without demand is dead. Only focus on what is, or soon will be, in demand in a big way. Otherwise, it's just a hobby.

Your purpose for focusing on specific data sets is to dominate the category. I had two primary data sets to concern myself with, the overabundant office space and the very scarce tenants. There was a third, too, the laws and the leases. I set out to learn everything I could, and I did. I saw the space. I knew the numbers. I researched the landlords. I grilled lawyers. I read every lease form and legal text on the subject I could get my hands on. I reached out to the tenants, local tenants at first, tenants in existing buildings, tenants in other markets. I told them what I could do for them – upgrade their space considerably, drop their rent, and have all their moving costs paid. The story was compelling -- no reason to say no. I had command of all the data sets.

The building owners did exactly as I had expected. They pulled out all the stops to lease their buildings. Lavish parties, paid trips and vacations, free BMWs, and commissions that sometimes reached as high as three and four times what you might expect were heaped upon brokers who would bring paying tenants to the buildings. Tenants didn't even have to pay anything as many of the leases I negotiated had one, two, and sometimes three years of free rent included. I had also identified fatal flaws that appeared in most commercial contracts, and I fixed those for the tenants too. I was even able to get the landlords to take over my tenants' old remaining lease payments to facilitate moves into their buildings now instead of at the end of the tenants' original lease terms. Everybody was happy. The tenants got new and better space at rents far below what they had previously been paying – and years of free rent. The landlords got new tenants in their buildings with a promise of rent to be paid in the future. And I got paid and paid well.

Clients were easy to come by because of my focus. The demand for downtown office space had been moderate, but I was making it stronger because of my activities, and of that demand, I saw my large share. The old established brokerage companies with a history of trying to be everything to everybody also said they could play in the field that I set out as my own, but I was the one known as the specialist. I was the one remembered as associated with that market. My specialty allowed me to compete aggressively against old-line firms that had been around for years and against the big nationals that wanted a piece of the pie. I was one man, but I controlled about 15 percent of the office lease-up against all the bigs. Their ability to compete in my niche was challenged because of the deep cognitive bench I developed in my focus, and my focus on real user representation and bringing down rents. You've heard the term: "tip of the spear." That's what focus does for you and your company. You pierce the noise and clutter and penetrate deep to grab their attention based on your information and knowledge. That I became known as the guy who was up against the establishment and challenging the status quo helped too.

Many of my clients were in the energy and oil and gas industries. These guys had an independent streak too. They were wildcatters, landmen, engineers; either relocating or resizing to take advantage of the rent numbers, or acquiring or expanding to take advantage of the market and do it cheaply because of the low oil and office prices. Other professional practices became interested in my office market too, lawyers, accountants, headhunters, and medical, and all for the same reasons.

I also kept my eye on tech firms because they were growing fast and because of the affinity I had with them watching and working in them growing up, particularly telecommunications firms. Communication services companies needed access to the greatest density and confluence of electrical power, fiber optic communication lines, and proximity to other communications firms. The central business district had all that in a big way.

Aggressive negotiations flowed easily because of the overt negotiating leverage I possessed. The heavy lifting was accomplished by setting up my position as the expert to take advantage of the extreme realities of the marketplace.

Because I was a small independent and I knew more about this office market niche from the tenant perspective than anyone else, I started to get offers to partner on different projects and tenants by other brokerage firms. I'm open to teams that come together organically. I want no part of the top-down formed teams, except to negotiate against.

Because of my focus, I was at the center of activity in this office lease-up rumble. Users would gravitate to me. My knowledge and positioning did all my marketing for me. I just had to perform pressing our overt advantages, and that I did. The tenants that responded to me at first were not big. I was a relative unknown, and I had no track record. What I had was a compelling story supported by great data. Those early transactions served as proof of concept, and with that, I began to secure larger, national and multi-national clients. Transaction volume increased exponentially year over year.

The first couple of years were just me and my deals. After I had traction and money was less scarce, I leased a nice suite of offices high up in one of the new towers and started bringing in more brokers and office staff to expand the company, but only people I thought were a good fit for me and my specialized firm.

Setting up my first set of offices was an exciting time for me. It was like springtime, and we were going to grow something new and great. I brought on a lot of people who were young and new to the field, but everybody was smart, and we liked figuring out the puzzles together -- make some money, and have some fun. To the staid real estate industry, we were the outsiders, the counterculture, pirates of a sort. We were all babies, but each had a strong personality and brought to the table their unique force. Some people made it, and some people didn't, but everybody recognized that they were living a free existence.

The deals kept getting more substantial, and as our name recognition grew, more companies would find us, and be referred to us, because of our unique niche and our approach to the business of representation without conflict. The laws hadn't yet changed, but we had been able to develop and implement legal workarounds so the users could get bona fide representation from brokers – mostly us.

Because of my focus and deep cognitive bench, I was put in touch with a company destined to be one of the biggest internet infrastructure and wireless carriers in the world, and destined to be the biggest office lease in the market in years. They were looking to locate a headquarters and switching facility in Denver. This company came into existence as a result of mergers and acquisitions and joint-venture partnerships that included prized rail-line properties that provided the necessary web of access to install long-haul fiber optics cables throughout the country – awesome infrastructure. I was introduced to the man that was likely going to run the place by a friend that had done some work for him. The problem was, the man I was introduced to didn't yet work for the company, and it wasn't a foregone conclusion he would. He was a candidate. Plus, they'd already been working with another broker.

The other broker, a traditional broker, hadn't shown them sites downtown yet. He didn't have my deep cognitive bench about the downtown market. He had no bench. He had directed their attention to low and mid-rise buildings in suburban areas. I knew I had better options to meet their special telco infrastructure needs. So, with the comprehensive data I had already in hand, I pulled out all the stops and put together an exhaustive analysis of the sites that were a good fit for them in the central business district and the terms I thought I could negotiate for them. I went out on a limb, and I set the mark for pricing and incentives. I told them what properties would work and how I thought negotiations would proceed. There are sometimes good reasons to be in a suburban location, but not this time. For their purposes, there was nothing comparable to a new downtown high-rise for energy, action, and awe, let alone the confluence of the ready electrical power and massive connectivity these types of firms required. I had no assurance I would be involved in any transaction they would do, but my candidate's business IQ moved higher because of the information I provided him. It was a speculative investment on my part, and I didn't ask for any guarantees. I handed my analysis to my candidate contact as he was boarding the plane to his final interview meeting.

My speculative work paid off for both my client and me. He landed the job, and I was thrust upon the real estate department at the growing company. Almost immediately, the project began to grow exponentially. The company was bringing in even bigger executive guns to run the place.

My new real estate contact at the company was smart and studious, a little geeky, and very analytical. I gave him all the information he craved and protected him from the information he didn't want. In one of the first property inspections I had put together for us early in the site selection process, we sat in a conference room prior to a tour of raw office space in one of the empty new office towers recently built. Raw office space has no walls or floor coverings or drop ceilings and often has no mechanical systems distributed. I think new raw office space in high-rise towers is beautiful, the simplicity of smooth and shiny concrete floors with maybe 18 feet clear height open to the deck above and 360-degree unobstructed views to the endless sheets of glass at all ends of the floor plate and to the openness of the world beyond. There's a bit of an echo, and if you're high enough in the tower, it's a little reminiscent of a mountain peak or standing on top of a spire. You might notice the building swaying. The unaccustomed can get vertigo.

The landlord and listing brokers at this building wanted to impress my client. The conference room in their finished leasing office was exquisitely appointed and had grand views of the entire front range of the Rocky Mountains. They positioned the leather swivel chairs so we could all face a video screen at the end of the conference table, and with fanfare and some excited self-satisfaction, the landlord and its reps premiered their new marketing video to us.

Grainy, brown images of old mining towns, old miners, and narrow-gauge railroads filled the screen, and banjo music filled the room. The voiceover detailed the hard work and hardships of the pioneering men and women who had "made this land." It had the look and feel of the Ken Burn's documentary, The Civil War, but with less carnage. The building was named after a legendary old silver miner, Horace Tabor. This video, however, reminded me of another historic Colorado mining icon, the Unsinkable Molly Brown. "Unsinkable" because Molly Brown had made it out alive in a life raft when the Titanic and most of her passengers perished and sank. The maiden voyage of this video was similarly disastrous and belonged at the bottom of the ocean too.

Shortly after the video started, my client pulled out his bag, disengaged from the surroundings, and started reviewing materials about other buildings I'd prepared for him. He didn't look at me or anyone else in the room, completely ignoring the video and everyone present. We had gone there to look at office space, not waste time viewing inane marketing videos. I told the landlord and the reps they needed to end the video, and we should instead see the space. Efficiency became the watchword for all my client relationships and activities from then on. I became the bodyguard of efficiency, efficiency in every form. Tabor didn't get the deal. It wasn't because of the video, but that didn't help.

The president of my client company came into town to tour the shortlist of properties my contact and I selected. One of the buildings we looked at was the tallest building in the city. It had big floor plates, and we all liked the building. It had an Achilles heel, though; it had double-decker elevators for some inexplicable reason. They said it was faster getting to your floor and with fewer stops, but any elementary school student with even a minor grasp of math can tell you that doesn't make any sense. If you like standing motionless in an elevator while the cab above or below you loads and unloads, this is the elevator for you. Depending upon which floor you were on in the tower, odd or even, you may or may not be able to take an elevator ride to the floor you want at the bottom, or in the tower. I would have preferred faster elevators and fewer gimmicks, but the space could have worked.

A Canadian landlord owned the building. Their local rep tried to keep me out of the pre-tour meeting for some unknown reason. Maybe it was because I had refused to be his subagent. Maybe he wanted to cuddle up with the president. Maybe he wanted to keep all the commissions for himself, or maybe he was just dizzy from having to hoof it from getting off on the wrong floor because of their elevator system. Regardless, I thought, "this is the dumbest guy on the planet." I pushed back, my contact pushed back, and the president pushed back. My client wanted me in the room; they needed me in the room. I had set the marks to achieve, and I was the only one that could achieve them. I'd already secured temporary space for my client in the building with a sublease. My data put me in the position of knowledge and control, and I ran the meeting. That building rep became a terrible brown-noser after that meeting, but he didn't make the deal either. It was the cumbersome vertical transportation, the hoops we'd have to jump through to accommodate our big parking requirement, and nobody liked the management. 56th floor? Can't get there from here. Sorry.

We looked at every building that could suitably accommodate the requirement. This was a lease every landlord wanted. Our overt leverage was enormous, but our size requirement kept growing, and with that, our overt leverage started to moderate because fewer projects could handle our bigger requirement. I kept quiet about our new size specs to keep our negotiating leverage high until we had determined our best select few properties before final negotiations. It's enticing to let everyone know your deal size is growing, but in this instance, it would hurt our negotiating leverage. I knew what each building could handle, but at this stage of the process, the landlords didn't have to know with any specificity what our plans were.

Ultimately, the client selected a four-tower multi-use project with a hotel, apartments, retail, and a health club. It was the same office project where my offices were located. I had done numerous other leases in that project and knew the ownership well. They were entrepreneurial, creative, smart, and eager to agree to super-aggressive deal terms to secure a tenant of this magnitude and lessen their vacancy risk. It helped that they had recently bought the property, also taking advantage of the record vacancies.

The final negotiations took many months, but that's common for a large deal. Not only did we need to reach agreement on rent, free rent, and tenant construction and finish items, we needed to phase in the timing of occupancy onto the various floors. We needed to handle parking for the hundreds of incoming employees, and what could become a thousand, without overburdening the existing parking garages. We needed to accommodate fiber optics access, cooling, and power for the switchgear. I'd often work past 2:00 a.m. running through the different scenarios and issues as well as track down the lawyers from both sides of the transaction on weekends to finalize verbiage details for the lease documentation. Our negotiating leverage was strong; we just had to keep our objectives clear and not waiver.

This was going to be the biggest office lease any of the landlords had seen in years. It was also going to cause a media splash that the landlord was happy about too. My power in this transaction came from the data I had put together relating to our market position and the resulting benefit from aggressively pursuing the rewards available from overwhelming market trends. It was only useful if we used it. We used it.

Even as negotiations progressed, my client company continued to be in more merger talks, and sometimes those caused additional challenges for me. At one point, there was a question as to which real estate department would survive the merger of my client company with another major telecommunications firm, one that also had their own real estate department. That was conceivably an existential threat for me, one I had little control over. If the firm I'd been dealing with lost control, I would be sidelined and have to start over regaining my footing with the company, if at all.

Another time, just when I thought we were about to finalize the transaction, the deal died altogether. One of the factions within the merged companies wanted to reopen negotiations with one of the suburban buildings that had been presented by the other broker months before. A deal is never a deal until its done. Shifting winds, black swan events, new information can all take a "sure thing" and make it a forgotten plan of the past.

Sometimes these questions lingered for months, but I survived both these existential threats. The real estate department that had engaged me proved to be the more proficient and survived the merger. The other market couldn't meet the growing size, infrastructure, and terms I had put together in the central business district, my awesome market niche and focus.

Sometimes, brokers from the big brokerage houses would try and poach my tenants, and this large telco transaction was particularly enticing for them. Maybe they felt entitled. Maybe they felt my upstart firm didn't deserve such a market-moving transaction. Maybe they felt threatened. It didn't matter what they thought; they were never successful because they didn't have the total grasp I had on this market niche. Mostly they were nothing more than just annoying. I did take more aggressive action against one broker, though, the son of the founder of one of the most well-respected regional commercial brokerages, a company I had once looked up to. Junior had never done anything of any magnitude on his own that I was aware of. I had shown a property to my telco client that had been listed by his father's company, and the son was on the listing's top-down "team." After my showing, he contacted my client directly and tried to convince them that he should be the one representing them in the market and not me; after all, he was the brokerage company's namesake, if not any of its substance.

I learned of this from my client, of course. My client didn't care what his last name was or what my last name was or how well known my company was. All my client cared about was the information and knowledge I had about the market and how well I performed for them. By this time, I had already completed several smaller transactions for their use around the city, and they had never seen rents negotiated so low. My client asked me to dispose of this guy. I called the manager of that brokerage house and shared the story with him. I told him if I was ever to show any of his company's listings again, I would first contact his company's clients and relay this story to them unless he assured me this would never happen again. He gave me that assurance. It never did happen again -- deep cognitive bench trumps empty suit. The more focused competitor wins every time.

As for my big telco client, in the end, we did a long-term lease for a mountain of class A office space with options for more. It was the biggest deal done in the city in five years. I ultimately did a half-dozen transactions downtown with this company. I was still a puppy, though. I knew I had just done a great transaction, but I also knew that I wouldn't always have such staggering market trends backing my position. I had much to learn, but I had no idea just how much I was about to learn.

My first company was a training ground for everyone, but mostly for me. It had been an enlightening journey over the last three years from my lows after the Transit Street fiasco to the media headlines proclaiming the biggest deal in years and that big commission check. That was all fun, but I was neither content nor convinced. I was flush with cash, but I was not secure. There was a lot I did right in making that deal happen and following through, but I also knew there was so much I didn't know, and my own insecurity pushed me on.

I felt good, really good, but there was something else I was looking for, some piece of information, or knowledge, or divine insight, something that would make sense of all of it for me. I hadn't found it yet. I kept looking.

The media exposure I received was fun. A big deal in a bad market when other firms were cutting back and closing, it made some news. I was in the best position I had ever been in. I had money and momentum. I wanted to grow the company more. The extreme nature of the downtown market was beginning to ebb as vacancies decreased, so I started to broaden our vision beyond the initial focus and include different types of transactions. I had loved the hard realities of the extreme market position I had taken, but circumstances were changing, and I was ready for something different. I had mastered the game downtown as an upstart, but now I wanted to compete with the bigs on their turf. I wanted to get big. The idea of going underground hadn't yet occurred to me. Still more to learn...

6

"THE MASTER" CONFLICT STRATEGY PRIMER

"Knowing these things, I can predict who will win and who will lose."
-- Sun Tzu

I was still green. I had learned to assess markets and put myself out on the front line and take business risks to exploit them. But I hadn't yet discovered and developed my tricks, hacks, hammers, and cheats to give me a radical edge and unfair advantage. That was something I wanted.

I became an insatiable student of strategy and the philosophy around war games, game theory, conflict, and negotiations. I studied the Stoics of Greece and Rome, religious leaders, business leaders, thought leaders, contemporary tacticians, trendsetters, criminal cartels, tyrants, movements, past and modern philosophers and metaphysicians, the great ancient generals and philosophers of China, and others. I learned from everyone, but of everyone, one person stood out for me as having solutions that were the most logical, enlightened, simple, and useful for achieving business and non-cooperative game dominion, Sun Tzu.

Sun Tzu was the first strategist I considered a Hitman. He messed with his opponents' minds, and he knew how nature worked, human nature and the flow of nature, and how to use those to direct outcomes. He was all about winning. Sun Tzu was a warrior general who took a small upstart nation in the southern part of China, an area considered uncivilized by the allied ruling states of the north, and he made it the dominant state of all of China after conquering and unifying all the northern states. His street cred is rightly deserved.

"Sun Tzu" wasn't his real name. That was a bit of marketing. "Tzu" means "Master" or "The Master." If Sun Tzu, himself, orchestrated that embellishment, that would give you some insight into his thinking. We would be obliged to at least consider it. Nonetheless, he was the master strategist of the time. He was alive during a very aggressive and combative time in Asia around 500 B.C., though nobody is certain of the dates. The eastern world was at war with itself, and new ideas exploring civilized life on this planet and interactions of people and societies were exploding all across Asia, India and China, and into Greece. Material resources were scarce, but exploring the mind as a powerful resource or adversary made up for that in spades.

Tzu created a treatise on his effective warfare strategies and methods that have prevailed for millenniums, The Art of War. Many of its principles and ideas enhanced my early strategic negotiating and deal-making techniques and helped refine the first requisite skills for a young deal maker and nascent hitman. I think Sun Tzu's treatise was brilliant in its way. It was a doctrine of thought and action for winning engagements that transcended establishment thinking and is still a great primer for winning conflict strategy today. These strategies should be understood and generously considered in your business dealings and negotiations, while keeping in mind it's only part of the strategy, albeit an important part.

Sun Tzu's brilliance is the way he lays out the procedural schema and mental preparedness necessary for success when approaching conflict. It provides a clear understanding of what can be achieved conceptually and shows the path to its manifestation based on his set of principles. His central premise is that you have control to be victorious by knowing the variables and knowing how to calculate strategies using them. That victory is not achieved by chance; it is achieved by a well-planned strategic course of action powered by positioning and performance. It's a matter of choice. He reasoned that if you're not well enough prepared, you don't really deserve to win. If you are well enough prepared, you will win.

New with Sun Tzu was his objective to prevail in every transaction without engaging in actual conflict or clash of ideas by setting in motion influences you control so the actual moment of victory is easy and effortless, and destruction is avoided, a natural flow of nature. In the most simplistic of terms, Sun Tzu could have said of any engagement, "You can win if you want it, and you don't have to go into battle to do it.

You can win with ease; just understand and follow these simple steps. If you don't follow these steps, however, you will likely fail."

Sun Tzu's assertion that "you can win with ease" must not be misunderstood to mean there is no effort. To the outsider, it may appear that you have won with little or no effort, but Sun Tzu's entire focus is fashioned upon the relentless pursuit of understanding the variables and complete preparedness. Sun Tzu asserts that when you've handled your intellectual groundwork competently and completely, the outcome is as known and predictable as setting a dried Autumn leaf in a pond and watching it float. No extreme force or mystery there, only beauty. The excellent fighter is not one whose victory is obvious to the crowds. The excellent fighter is the one who not only wins, but wins without fanfare and accolades because it appears to have been done so easily, so naturally. There are no cheering crowds for someone who can witness a strike of lighting and hear its thunderclap, or pick up a dried leaf in Autumn, because there are no special powers necessary or shown. The excellent fighter is one who has managed the influences ahead of time, so the victory is simply a part of the flow of nature.

Don't be lulled by Sun Tzu's simplicity and elegance. His goal is to win decisively because the alternative is annihilation or bondage. He stressed at the outset of his work the deadly seriousness in which these stratagems should be taken because of the grievous consequences that can ensue if you don't, saying it is a road to safety or ruin, a matter of life and death. At the same time, he challenges you to reconcile the fierceness with which you must act in certain circumstances with the gracious, yet unyielding, flow and cadence of the natural world surrounding all of us.

Perhaps Sun Tzu's most cultivated concept is his premise that winning does not mean destroying your opponent, but instead prevailing in such a manner that the opponent is taken intact, their resistance broken without fighting, and their provisions, assets, and people remain intact to resupply and support all. This also then presupposes a practical, productive, and disciplined ongoing relationship with the vanquished after having conquered them, but only if you choose.

Sun Tzu's process is based on the idea that all successful warfare is a result of preparation, planning, incentive, cunning, discipline, and deception. The latter of these means the leader must know how to confuse and delude the opposition while keeping his own conditions and intention concealed. Sun Tzu understood the true enemy that must be conquered is the mind of the opposing party, and that a victorious outcome is the result of our creative imagination.

Preparation and planning are of paramount importance. The current conditions of all factors dictate what the plan to victory is to entail, and it's the discovery and analysis of those conditions that you must apply the greatest focus. This includes information about yourself, your opponent, and the world as it relates to the engagement. What is the landscape, terrain, and environment in which you'll be operating, and is it suitable? What is your cause, and how aligned is the world with your cause? What are all the trend factors to be considered? How is your timing? How capable are you and your people? What training is necessary? How are they rewarded and punished? How is your opponent compensated, and what penalties do they fear? How do they hear praise? Understand the paradoxes, the motivations, debt, the physicality, outside influences, markets, laws, companies, moods, health, spirituality, training, and politics. Know it all. Sun Tzu says, "those who prevail, plan considering all these factors. Those who fail, fail to plan, or consider only a small number of these factors."

The key code to defeating your opponent resides in the character, condition, and position of the opponent itself. You must discover that code and exploit it. Your opponent will show you how to defeat it. What is your opponent's deepest desire or attachment? Therein lies its vulnerability.

Sun Tzu's overall strategy relies on achieving superior positioning relative to your opponent. You can reposition the opposition by luring with bait, seduction, and enticements, and then taking control through confusion. Their confusion is brought about by not allowing them to know the true conditions of your position, strengths, and plans. Be vague like mist in the valley. When you are successful in creating an environment of confusion and uncertainty for your opponent, they will succumb to you and present vulnerabilities you can attack when they least expect it. Sun Tzu said all warfare is based on deception. Obfuscation causes your opponent to be in a state of imbalance, and that imbalance allows you to move your opponent about at will.

Never allow the opponent to know your exact position. Appear as though you have several positions or no position at all. This causes your opponent to lose perspective and spread its defenses thin, causing it to make mistakes. This makes your opponent unable to predict or plan. Appear as though conforming, but keep your opponent off balance with subtle nuance and silence.

You dare not enter an engagement you don't intend to win, and if you don't have the proper resources available to you for the duration of your campaign, you will not prevail. Sun Tzu warns that you must adequately resource your campaign if you are to be successful. This means operating capital, people, and their conviction for the cause. The importance of this last item must not be underestimated. If the duration of your campaign is protracted, the vitality and interest and conviction of your people can wane and become dull. They can become restless and question your cause, which opens you up to vulnerability and the possibility of outside influences bringing havoc or exerting control. Sun Tzu's answer is that you should avoid prolonged sieges. Sun Tzu cautions against protracted engagements because those are toughest to resource and supply. This also applies to the need for operating capital. One concept Sun Tzu introduces to accommodate this if suitable financing is not secured beforehand is "foraging" among the enemy and allies. This calls for a series of smaller, tactical wins to provide resources you need for your campaign as well as sourcing from controlled alliances along the way. So too, with the final victory objective. Take your opponent whole and intact and absorb its organization and resources for your benefit. Compensate your people well when you win.

The need to resource the campaign also includes data and intelligence as the engagement continues. Sun Tzu put the responsibility of sourcing this needed information squarely at the feet of the leader, saying you're not fit to lead if you don't make this accommodation.

Sun Tzu said not to make plans you're incapable of completing. Incorporate your sourcing and resources into your plan. Above all, position yourself out of harm's way while the plans unfold. Positioning yourself out of harm's way allows you to move your opponent around with the promise of gain and wait for the right moment to act when your opponent is most vulnerable. You will stymie your opponent's plan of attack by keeping your own position flexible and secret. The object is to win the encounter, not engaging in the encounter itself. Being straightforward only enmeshes you in the encounter, while surprise brings victory. Do not engage when expected; engage when least expected. Allow changed circumstances to alter your plan. The skilled fighter puts himself in the position impossible to defeat while he waits for the right moment to defeat the enemy. The time and place of the battle should not be made known to the enemy, forcing it to defend numerous fronts and distributing its resources around its perimeter to meager levels.

Whoever arrives first to the field and can wait for the opponent to appear, is rested and fresh for the fight. Whoever arrives last is tired and stressed and at a supreme disadvantage.

Maintaining possession of your self-control is of critical importance because if you allow the opponent to move you about with baits and rewards, or fear or deception, you will lose your battle. Keep your emotions in check. Use your clarity, sense of destination and destiny, and your cause and motivation to keep you on your proper course. There are battles that should not be fought, roads that shouldn't be traveled, commands by the powerful that shouldn't be followed, and ideas and forces that shouldn't be contested. There is danger if you become overly reckless, cautious, angry, fastidious, or solicitous; these will bring failure down upon you. Maintain your mental and emotional equilibrium. Maintain your composure. Do not be pulled or swayed by outside forces. This is the skill of self-possession.

Sun Tzu identifies five characteristics the leader must embody to be victorious. (1) The skilled leader must know when to fight and not to fight. (2) The skilled leader must know how to handle larger and superior forces and how to handle smaller and inferior ones. (3) The skilled leader must know how to maintain vitality for the cause within himself and the ranks. (4) The skilled leader must know how to maintain self-composure and wait for the right moment to act. And (5)

The skilled leader is one with capacity, capability, and confidence to act independently of any sovereign. Hence the saying, "If you know the enemy and yourself, a hundred battles you will surely win. If you know yourself but not the enemy, for every victory won, you will lose one. If you know neither yourself nor the enemy, you will be defeated every time."

Sun Tzu repeatedly stressed the deadly seriousness that strategy is to play while conducting the affairs of the organization, including taking decisive action with autonomy and independence. Sun Tzu's king, the King of Wu, agreed and wanted Sun Tzu to demonstrate his ability to command troops using female members of his palace court before hiring him. Over 100 women were assembled for the exercise and divided into two companies, each lead by one of two of the king's most esteemed concubines. Sun Tzu explained the orders he was to give to the concubines, "face forward and face in the direction of your heart; face right, turn and face in the direction of your right hand," etc. Sun Tzu then gave the order to "face right," and the concubines only giggled. The troops did nothing. Sun Tzu then explained to the king that if orders are not clear and not thoroughly explained, then it's the commander's fault. Sun Tzu then explained the orders to the concubines again and made sure they understood. Again, he gave the order, "face right," and again, the concubines just giggled. With that, Sun Tzu turned to the king and told him that if orders are explained and understood and still not carried out, it is a crime on the part of the officers, and Sun Tzu summarily ordered the two concubines to be executed. The king was shocked. "These are my beloved concubines; spare them!"

Even so, Sun Tzu killed the two concubines and placed the next two ranking women in the vacant leadership positions. Sun Tzu again gave the orders, and this time both companies followed directions silently and without misstep. Sun Tzu then told the king his troops were now ready to do the king's bidding. Did the king wish to inspect them? The king, still in disbelief at the implacable and unyielding general, said, "no" and dismissed the exercise. Sun Tzu then said to the king, "your words are empty, and you have neither the conviction nor the spine to follow through with your intentions." From this point forward, King Wu knew Sun Tzu was a general never to be fucked with; and with that, gave him command of all the troops of his kingdom -- winning battle after battle and unifying a continent.

Sun Tzu was a paradox. He extolled grace and beauty, yet was ruthless and merciless when he felt circumstances warranted it. Regardless of his insight and brilliance in strategy, he wasn't infallible; no one is infallible. We'll later learn the extent of his shortcomings and how to move beyond his strategies and teachings to a higher level of influence. Regardless, understanding his work is important, it's solid groundwork to build on.

Sun Tzu's death is a mystery. It might have been the same year as his king's death, but some say that was just another deception because the Wu army continued to win victories for several more years. The speculation is that he had died when that ended. One thing is for certain though; it wasn't long before the influence of the Wu State began to wane, and 20 years after Sun Tzu's death, it had lost all its power and dominance and no longer reigned over China. The State of Wu had lost the competency, edge, and advantage provided by the hitman.

Pity about the concubines. Lesson learned.

7

THE BIG BROKERAGE ILLUSION

"But he isn't wearing anything at all!"
-- Hans Christian Andersen, The Emperor's New Clothes

I had built a great little company, a leading-edge boutique shop. It was small, but we were making money, and it was attractively viable. We had a good market presence, and we had market share. It was quality, and all our people were smart. I felt good about all of that. I had complete run of the show. I felt a sense of accomplishment and redemption that I had created something that good and positive after the Transit Street failure and that grim period. There are many ways to bolster confidence; succeeding at something is undoubtedly one of them.

The extreme market conditions that I had leveraged started to wane. Vacancy rates were coming down, monstrous tenant and broker incentives were less common, and the competition had nearly fully entered the market. From a quantitative decision-making perspective, the market anomaly that had been the focus of my actions was now on the backside of the bell curve, away from early adopters and beneficiaries, and sliding down the slippery slope of the fourth quintile, about to enter a world populated by laggards and normalcy, ugh. It was a full standard deviation away from anything exciting or creative. The growth and fun of the front end of the bell curve were now history. Being a statistical deviant myself, it was time to shake things up.

I had taken on the big national brokerage firms in the central business district and won, or at least won a seat on the front row of dealmakers, and my upstart firm had made a very respectable showing. Now I wanted to take on the big nationals in a bigger way. I wanted their name recognition. I wanted their size. I wanted what I thought were their numbers. I set out to build a bigger company.

I set aside the dominant strategy of pure tenant representation in the central business district, it had served its usefulness, and shifted the focus to a new strategy – getting bigger and broadening our capabilities. This became my new, albeit flawed, dominant strategy. That decision had been made by me without any scrutiny by me or anyone else. We were going to get bigger simply because that's what I wanted. Besides, isn't bigger always better? Isn't it self-evident? That is what I assumed, but I had never really thought about it, and I didn't think about it then. The only critical thinking brought to bear was how to get bigger, not whether we should. A strategy shift was in order nevertheless, and the national and international markets beckoned me, and getting bigger was my unchallenged conclusion on how to make that happen. So, I planned the expansion and set that intention in motion.

If you decide to push a boulder uphill and you're dedicated and capable, both you and the boulder will likely make it to the top of the hill, but it can be very hard work and often not much fun. It is, though, a hell of a learning experience. Sometimes the education justifies the means. It's amazing how much good work you can do when you're heading in the wrong direction.

Hiring good brokers is a challenge because there just aren't very many. Many commercial real estate brokers you meet are more like real estate valets -- five parts salesperson, two parts social gadfly, and a three-part splash of researcher, consultant, and driver. I was more interested in an immensely more energetically cerebral make-up. I wanted the smartest people, deep thinkers, creative savants, old souls, the cognitive elite, each a bit of a puzzle, all killers in their own right -- all pirates or pirates in regression. I can't stand stupid and boring people, and I don't want them around. I wanted people that would challenge the status quo and come up with new ways to look at and do things, people not afraid to challenge any system and including me. Most of my initial core group of brokers stayed on with me as I pressed the accelerator of growth. These were the best people. They were headstrong and independent. Most had moved into commercial real estate after a tamer and more mundane career in other professions. We had an architect, accountant, banker, builder, lawyer, MBA, financier, Air Force Academy alumnus, and some had prior commercial and residential real estate experience. Men, women, black, brown, gay, straight, I didn't care; I just wanted people with brains, strength, and power. I wanted people with a leaning bias for action. Some had no college degree but had a drive and eagerness to learn and succeed and mental horsepower that couldn't be dismissed. Frequently, they outperformed all the others. We'd have in-house training on the markets, lease issues, legal issues, sales contracts, math and the numbers, and basic persuasion techniques. This all can be taught; intellectual capacity cannot. IQ doesn't necessarily spell success, but it does manifest a more interesting company.

We started branching out into all different property types and geographies. We negotiated investments of all types: office, multi-family, retail, and triple net investments. We handled build-to-suits and leased everything under the sun. Office leasing was still a large component of what we did, but no longer could you call it a real focus. We had no focus other than casting a wide net for deals and trying to grow our size. Our name recognition grew, but we lost much of our counter-culture culture, and the pirate in us was tempted by the siren song of conformity – and invitations to parties. We walked, talked, schmoozed, and tailored our suits for a good corporate fit. As our hard edges softened, our profit margins narrowed.

Much of the company's early expansion was fueled organically, new people one at a time, but that was slow. So, when a friend of mine asked if I would have an interest in meeting to discuss a merger with the Chairman of a holding company that included the biggest residential brokerage company in a seven-state region, and a commercial real estate subsidiary that had name recognition but had been struggling for years, I said I would be happy to take that meeting. I thought, "this could shake things up." Besides, this was the company whose manager had turned me down for a job a few years earlier. Things certainly had changed.

The Chairman had grown his family's residential business exponentially with scores of brokerage offices throughout the region, a thousand agents, and billions in sales. His real love, I think, was commercial real estate. He had numerous partnership entities owning land and buildings, mostly big tracts of vacant land. His commercial brokerage company, however, had floundered under the management, or mismanagement, of many years of yes-men at the helm. The Chairman could have been a governor or senator; he was that well-known and popular. He had been president of the million-plus member National Association of Realtors®.

The Chairman was interested in merging with my company to bolster his own commercial brokerage with our young crew and office building prowess. I thought the prospects looked good to fix his commercial firm while satisfying my desire for a path to fast growth. I thought we could both make money. We structured a purchase for cash and stock. The negotiations moved quickly because we both had what the other person wanted, and we both wanted change. I had become bored, and this was a new challenge. Soon, we were moving people and equipment in together as partners.

I dove in to start fixing the problems of the newly combined firm and immediately bumped my head against the clash of cultures that emerged from bringing the two companies together. I hadn't anticipated that. My team of fun-loving, free-spirited smarties with a penchant for office deals, were, for the most part, happy; but the old-line brokers that were entrenched in the old firm and had been beaten down by a lousy market and dearth of deals did not want to see change. Go figure. Likewise, the legacy staff and management, except one, were equally stoic and didn't want to see change. They liked things just the way they were, "thank you very much," even if things were bad. They were starving, but their inertia had petrified their brains. They clearly weren't having any fun, and apparently, they liked it that way. They didn't want me there any more than I wanted to keep what was there. They wanted to maintain the status quo, but the status quo was not sustainable. They had been losing money for years, but they didn't care because nobody was accountable. They didn't see the truth in their situation. They wanted A to be B, but it wasn't. It never is. I was there to change things and I owned the place, at least part of it.

There was also another problem. I was used to running the show, making all the decisions, calling all the shots. But at the newly combined firm, I was number three in the hierarchy behind the Chairman and the existing President of the commercial company. Both guys were icons, legends of a sort, so I took my position in stride at first. But that I wasn't the final arbiter was something new, and eventually, unsatisfactory.

In addition to that, it became evident that 90 percent of our energies were spent on the internal goings-on and machinations in the company, not on our customers and clients and the things that generated revenue. There is a propensity in large organizations to spend an inordinate amount of time reflecting internally about the inner workings and relationships within the company – meetings about meetings, corporate naval gazing. Some of this can be useful if it's focused on process improvement and new product and profit initiatives, but mostly it's busywork, company and management narcissism, and a big waste of time. We would have a pre-meeting planning meeting to talk about an upcoming meeting. Then we'd have the meeting. Then, we'd have a post-meeting debriefing meeting to discuss what had been said in the previous meeting. Sometimes, we'd then have an executive committee meeting to talk about the previous three meetings and plan ahead for the next set of meetings. My schedule was full of meetings. Then we'd meet over a long lunch at some fashionable restaurant or private club. Managers can pretend and feel like they're working by sitting around conference and dining tables talking about weighty issues of little importance. We talked a lot, an awful lot, but I wasn't doing deals. Clients and customers weren't at the tables. I was managing meetings.

When I wasn't managing meetings, I was managing brokers. Mostly the good brokers I didn't have to manage much, they were out doing deals. The thoroughbreds, you want to cool down and check when they come back to the stables. It's the mediocre brokers you have to manage, and I had a new set of those.

Number two in line behind the Chairman, the President of the commercial company, was a very friendly, well-seasoned, traditional commercial broker, and he was a friend of the Chairman. He had done more commercial transactions throughout his life than anyone else in the company. He was a rock star in his own right. I learned from him.

The Chairman had hired him after the President had run into some hard times following financial problems resulting from ill-timed developments he'd done. Nevertheless, the Chairman thought the President's deal knowledge and sphere of influence would benefit the firm. It did, but the President had never started or run a company, and his surrendering people-pleasing personality was misaligned for the hard work and hard decisions necessary for fixing the company. There was no business or operations plan in place. Budgets weren't put together for the current year before May or June, and because the company was always running in the red, as bills needed to be paid, the capital procurement process was that the President or office manager would go to the Chairman and beg for funds to pay the bills. The company was run more like a spoiled teenager than a corporation.

On the surface, the President and I got along fine. He was supportive of my desire to up the game and restructure the company as a self-sustaining entity. But the President could never say "no" to his groupies or others, and this only served to empower their rigidity. I don't think he consciously tried to sabotage my work, but it certainly created an unnecessary headwind. Regardless, that all came to a screeching halt when the President filed for personal bankruptcy. The news cast a pall on the entire commercial company. I felt bad for him, but my new investment in this company was looking sketchy.

We loved this guy personally; he was gregarious and affable. But if the public and your clients lose confidence and trust in you or your organization, you're toast. Since the merger, we had worked hard and made some strides recasting the company in a more positive light, but his bankruptcy was newsworthy and public enough that for him to remain at the helm would have been detrimental to the firm. I told him I thought he should resign, and he didn't really have a choice. He resigned, and I became president. The personal considerations notwithstanding, this made things at the company much simpler. I could now enact all the changes needed to put the company on solid footing and back to a position of profitability. His devout group of followers in the company hated me for what had happened, but I thought that was a waste of their time and mine and not at all useful towards improving anything - just drama. I did have the Chairman's support, though, and his agreement for complete autonomy. I set out to remake the company as I imagined.

The first thing I did was cut the brokers and divisions that weren't producing. This seems an obvious step, but they were so entrenched under the old regime, it was like removing barnacles that had been attached for generations. These were people's friends that had been part of the company for years, and those that remained were angry and hated me for showing their friends the door. The brokers I let go had over the years proffered numerous plans, promises, assurances, and the best excuses for why their production was nil. Another plan or polished excuse wasn't going to make any difference. It was time for them to go. It wasn't a one-day massacre, but it didn't take long. Some people thought it was heartless, but I was running a company teetering on insolvency, not a social club. Popularity wasn't my goal. My goal was to replace them with producing brokers.

The next thing to do was to gut the expenses so the company could survive and operate within its means. This was a massacre. There was no time. I scoured the books and budgets for areas I could slash expenses. I reduced staff size and individuals' salaries (including my own), realigned responsibilities, and terminated useless tasks and processes. Reducing salaries made people angry too, but we were fighting to survive and not go out of business. Most employees stayed on, and I was able to replace those who left with better people at lesser wages. I made every line item budget cut I could. Within the year, we were operating on a break-even basis, and we could begin to grow the company fresh from a new solid footing. We set up new standards for production and boosted individual focus and goal development. I put detailed operating plans in place. I set up a new banking relationship with credit lines. I quadrupled the research and data budget. I brought in better coffee, a personal must. We ended the endless stream of meetings that didn't involve clients and customers.

I went on the hunt for the new brokers I wanted. I targeted only active brokers operating in the specialties that were relevant for the market conditions – people that were currently producing or had previously produced in a big way. I also hired a few newbies that I thought had the intelligence, desire, and drive. We reworked the brokerage compensation to incentivize top producing people and amply reward them.

I met with every top producer of every major company I could. While we were discussing if there was an actual fit, I was learning all I could from them about the operations at the companies they represented, our competitors. This wasn't the only research I did on the competition. I talked to their staff. I talked to their clients. I watched the numbers and completed transactions. I paid close attention to the market.

I started acquiring small, entrepreneurial led companies to grow our broker cadre faster. Sometimes these were single-person firms, sometimes bigger, but of those selected, the principals always possessed the self-reliance and self-determination I wanted in our staff and brokers. Entrepreneurs know they must produce to survive. They don't depend on handouts. Entrepreneurs know companies can't operate successfully as systems of redistribution where the masses depend on the few for their rationed pittance. The purchase terms were always simple cash and earn-out scenarios. Our break-even periods were usually about a year.

Some of the people I interviewed were idiosyncratic to the nth degree and didn't fit the mold of the stock image, prototypical, well-bred, in-bred, real estate agent: suited, groomed, and predictable to the nth degree. Some had previously worked at big brokerage houses. Some had been passed over by them. Some had never considered working at such a place of "plastic banality," they said.

We had doubled the size of the company when we merged, and I had since doubled it again. As the firm grew and broker talent improved, so did our financial condition. By the second year, we were propitiously profitable. By the third year, we doubled our earnings over the previous year, and we were on our way. With the new flow of operating capital, we upgraded our office facilities and equipment, administrative staff, public relations, media presence and marketing collateral, and research and data collection, all with the objective of continuing to recruit and retain strong and self-directed brokers and grow the brokerage business.

The company grew. The deal flow grew. The earnings grew. In addition to our traditional brokerage business, we started doing project work such as handling site acquisition work for the State and portfolio property dispositions for the Feds, auctions too. We also did some M&A work, such as a roll-up of emergency medical service (EMS) companies to be taken public. We were firing on all cylinders, and I thought it was time to take our program on the road to handle national and international transactions. I thought that was the future of the company and something that piqued my interest personally.

My existing oil and gas and communication and telco services clients supported my interest to solidify our global reach quickly because those companies had a growing need for representation in markets across the U.S. and internationally. Initially, to satisfy those needs, I set up a network of brokerages to support us in that business expansion. I also researched companies to partner or merge with that had purported global reach as well as the networks of independent operators. I crashed some of their global conventions so I could get an unencumbered look at how they operated. I was not always welcome, but I always learned a lot. The network I ultimately selected, though already large, was going through its own growth spurt at the time and eager to have a company of our size as part of their network. They were already tied up on an exclusive basis with a smaller brokerage company in my region, so I bought that company too. With the global network in place, I set out to grow the global business. We now had access and could launch from offices in over 300 different markets around the world.

My desire to manage projects and transaction business worldwide with the network I'd just acquired was somewhat dashed when I started including the network in my book of business. As it turned out, within the network there were many who felt proprietary about some of the multi-nationals with which I had good relationships. My communications with these clients chafed my new network partners. Prior to my arrival, a group of prominent players in the network had been assembled to make presentations to these same companies and solicit business, and since I wasn't part of the original group, they were finding it a bit cumbersome to make room for me, let alone see me spearhead the relationships. That was frustrating. I had brought the new network on board to use it, not have it restrict my activities. Additionally, notwithstanding the network's lofty promotional talk about taking care of the needs of their clients and customers, it was apparent their priorities, in reality, were not aligned with what was best for the client companies. I moved forward on my own, nonetheless. I did agree to carve out a portion of my early telco business and stand down from that, allowing the network group to pursue it. I did this for the sake of keeping the new relationship with the network on a positive tone. It was a gift. They eventually lost that business and my heart. I would have to pick up the pieces of that business later.

As the presence and prominence of my company grew locally and nationally, so did my own. I was on the Advisory Board of the new global network comprised of the 30 or so of the biggest and most active member companies around the world. I was president of the regional Commercial Association of Realtors®. I traveled around the country with the National Association of Realtors® training brokers and rolling out new technology and legislative initiatives at their events. I sat on economic development councils and charity boards. I had media visibility. I MC'd civic events, did speaking and university engagements, and promoted new airports to a global audience. Life was good, mostly, but my dissatisfaction grew.

The top performers, alpha performers, about 16 percent of the overall group on the bell curve, always outperformed their average peer by factors of 5x to 10x. On the other side of the curve, those performing within one standard deviation of the mean, I considered still deserving of their positions if there was realistic evidence they were potential high-performers, and their production was consistent over the periods. I always looked to replace and upgrade the bottom 16 percent unless there was a compelling reason otherwise. I never understood why more of this bottom group didn't exit themselves.

The pace of recruiting new brokers never subsided. Finding the right fit was a challenge and slow. I wasn't alone in this. All the big brokerages experienced this as they climb over one another trying to recruit the others' good performers. The joke is on everyone, though, because there aren't very many good performers and if brokers for hire are good at anything, its image and self-puffery. If they were on "teams," which was generally the case, they would often claim the entire production of the team as their own. Their real productive value was some small fraction of that number, and during interviews with me, there was no shortage of baby chicks with their mouths wide open waiting for some new momma bird to disgorge her lunch into their trembling beaks. I think some of these people still had their umbilical cords attached, and they were wandering around trying to find a place to plug it in. Not everyone was like that; I always looked for those with the spark of self-reliance.

Regardless as to the quality of talent recruited and retained, as companies grow large, the Law of Large Numbers starts to exert is numbifying influence and discounts the benefits of outstanding outliers to the marginal mean of the mediocre middle. The beauty of the elite group of alpha achievers you assembled gets diluted, marginalized by the middle mass. If the organization gets big enough, it's all middle, ballast that keeps the high fliers from reaching their full, unencumbered potential.

In big brokerage companies, this becomes the perfect manifestation of the Pareto Principle -- the 80/20 rule, the common manifestation that the most vital 20 percent of causal factors produce 80 percent of the results. This holds true in an infinite number and types of systems, including in my own experience. Anecdotally, 20 percent of my actions produce 80 percent of my results. In big brokerage houses, 20 percent of the agents produce 80 percent of the revenue. This means, of course, that 80 percent of the agents produce only 20 percent of the revenue. The bulk of the business is handled by a small, vital, percentage of the workforce, one in five, at best.

Today's model in the large commercial brokerage houses is for management to bundle the most vital brokers with the less vital brokers, along with the non-vital brokers, and call them "teams." This works well for everyone except the two most vital entities in the transaction: the vital broker and the client. The vital broker loses because he or she is saddled with the human ballast on his or her team that eats an unearned share of the fees that the vital broker must disgorge. The vital broker also has the added management responsibility and time drain required to keep the non-vital people productive in some way. The client loses because she's saddled with the human ballast that's been off-loaded to her by the vital broker trying to justify the added expense of carrying the less capable brokers on the team and keeping them loaded with tasks. Studies have shown this causes something called "social loafing" on the part of the vital broker wherein he or she instinctively withholds their competency because they deem the system unfair to themselves. The client thinks she's hiring a top professional, what she's getting is an eager neophyte at best, a seasoned lackey often. What do you think is really going to happen with your business after six well-groomed people walk into your office to make a presentation, but only one seems to have a deep cognitive bench about anything besides sports?

I was experiencing first-hand how the Law of Large Numbers and the Pareto Principle were bringing down the effectiveness of our top producers. I first addressed this by bringing in a professional sales manager to work with all the brokers, but particularly the bottom 80 percent. This helped at first because of the added attention (a phenomenon found in most tests), but it waned. More importantly, though, the truth I discovered was my interest in supporting the bottom 80 percent of brokers was nil. Right or wrong, and I'll probably be trashed by every HR and management consultant out there, but my interest, we'll say 80 percent of my interest, was focused exclusively on the top 20 percent of performers. That was the world I chose to live in. Those were the people with energy and ideas. The bottom 80 percent of the workers need to be managed, but not by me. Someone else needs to do it. I choose to focus on the top 20 percent and learn and support what makes them special.

I came to realize that big isn't better. More capable is better, and that is more difficult to achieve the bigger an organization becomes. I realized I needed to make a drastic change, and that change would be to leave the big company I helped create and start a new one, a smaller one, one where the alpha outliers didn't have their special powers and skills diluted.

Coincidental with that thought, a large multi-national firm was rolling across the continent "rolling up" real estate companies into a global behemoth and initiated conversations with us to acquire the residential and commercial companies. As I thought my correct path was to get smaller to be able to focus solely on alpha performance, the prospect loomed that I was about to become part of this global behemoth. There were arguments to be made to stay with the behemoth. It's easy to make the argument that big is better even when it's not. It's easy to make the argument to be cushioned and protected by a big company even as your own authority and autonomy are diminished. Staying with the behemoth, my career path would be set, seemingly with almost no risk. An easy "yes" for most, perhaps. I would have to make the decision soon because the growing conflict in my mind was wearing on me and my performance.

Our network was having a global convention at the Fontainebleau Hotel in Miami Beach. The Fontainebleau is nice, but it's not chic like The Breakers in Palm Beach, and it doesn't have the crazy iron outside of valet parking you'll find at The Breakers. They're both old, but it's definitely more Sinatra and less Vanderbilt, and probably better suited for my purpose at that time. I decided I would expand my trip so I could drive down to Key West for a couple of days of scuba diving and relaxation and weigh my options between staying at the company, riding the wave the merger would bring, or leave and start my own company again. I would make the final decision on the trip.

I felt like I was on autopilot at the convention, doing everything I needed to do and everything expected of me. My people were in Miami, too, making the rounds and contacts they were supposed to make.

On the last evening of the convention, after all the events and post events and last calls, little crowds of well-dressed people still huddled in small groups scattered around the lobby. There were periodic loud laughs. Mostly they were telling each other stories of the best of the best or the worst of the worst, all magically turned into a joke because, in the end, it didn't really matter in any important way anyway. More laughs. The people are happy, for the most part, a little loose, but the scent of perfume in the room that had pleased me earlier in the evening now seemed stale, and I'm feeling antsy. I'm bored. I need something different.

The crowd is a little drunk. I'm not. I'm stone-cold sober. I'm in decision mode. My original plan was to drive to Key West in the morning, but that wasn't going to happen. I was going tonight. I went back to my room, took off my suit, packed my bag, got in the rental car and headed south. It was about one o'clock in the morning.

The road is dark most of the way to Key West in the middle of the night, only two lanes and not much on-coming traffic. It took about four hours, time I had in the car just to think, also relishing in the thought that I had the next two days alone to just relax, reflect, ponder without interruption, and do a little diving. (I passed through Key Largo and gave a nod to Bogie and Bacall.) I disconnected from the world and that stale business scene in the Fontainebleau lobby I had left behind. The ocean air was bracing. I felt free and excited.

I got to Key West just as the sky was turning dark orange, pink, and gray. I checked into my motel room, just a cinder block box really, but it was on the water. That was all I wanted or needed. That, and a place to charge my laptop. I walked out onto the wooden boardwalk at the pier, sat down, and watched the sun come up.

Five hours later and after a little sleep, I'm back at the same table, coffee in hand, watching the seagulls and the activity on the boardwalk. I had come to Key West to make the decision as to whether I should stay at the company or start a new one. That question was moot now. That decision had been made the night before in the hotel lobby when any desire to sleep had vanished and replaced with the desire for new adventure – and the need to leave that place and drive all night on a two-lane road across open water, my face and chest pounded with warm, salty air. I was here to plan my new venture. I was energized, my neurotransmitters firing decisively on the fuel of adrenaline, my vision sharp, my thinking clear, I'm excited and ready to be challenged. I have a new venture. I have a new risk. A natural hit of dopamine is icing on the cake.

I had wanted my company to get big because that was the paradigm I had bought into for success. But that was based on the myth and devoid of any satisfactory definition of success. I'd seen the big companies up close. I'd run them from the C-suite. I'd partnered with them around the globe. I'd researched them, competed against them, and poached their brokers. I'd been one.

There are three basic business models of global real estate companies with purported reach: corporately owned offices, franchises of independently-owned offices, and independently-owned offices partnered with others as part of a network. Most are a mixed smash-up of all three. Offices of all three types share branding, logos, media, and marketing collateral for show. Management is disparate across offices and markets. The strength of each company is no greater than the weakest link of the broker on the street who was handed the clients' business -- the proverbial handoff. In this day and age, the big brokerage company is an anachronism.

Big brokerages are often riddled with conflicts of interest, large and small. The states have largely legislated away any illegality or dereliction in those conflicts or requirement for the broker to perform as a true fiduciary with duties requiring the highest standard of care and loyalty. The truth is that clients are getting less representation now than ever, and they're handed a stack of disclaimers to sign for the privilege. Now the laws state the brokers can just represent themselves and only owe their customers and clients what amounts to the lowest standard of legally fair business dealings. That's a very low bar, indeed. They could stumble out of a bar and satisfy that requirement, or just as easily ignore it with the unconscious slip at the mouth. Real advocacy has been conveniently stripped away. The laws give brokers safe harbor in most dealings. It would be speculation to say that a huge political action committee infrastructure has an impact. Nonetheless, the clients are left to flap in the breeze, again -- still.

Sometimes, big companies compete directly with their clients without their clients' knowledge. Some companies have investment funds to buy the best properties, in competition with their clients, and then turn around and lease those same properties, again in direct competition with their clients. If you're a tenant and you've picked a big brokerage to "represent" you, there's a chance they have an ownership interest in the buildings you see. It's maybe a different entity, but the conflicts exist nevertheless. Big brokerages are comfortable with the deal churn used as fuel to keep the engine of self-dealing running and a way to feed their less competent brokers. Does that sound harsh? In my opinion, there's only a whiff of loyalty to the client and little respect. They attempt to control transaction business of the buyers and tenants while working their best to be in the good graces of the sellers and landlords so they can gather more listings. Some good people work for those companies, but the system they work under is misaligned and misguided. Façade is what is provided to clients. I think they should want to deserve more.

The Hans Christian Andersen's fairy tale, The Emperor's New Clothes, tells of an emperor who hires two tailors that told him they would weave for him the finest new clothes, clothes so special that they would be invisible to anyone incompetent or stupid. The tailors were smooth talkers out to make an easy buck, and their client, the emperor, was gullible. He was taken in by the swindlers' trap.

The tailors set up their looms and pretended to go to work, looking very busy. When checking on the progress of the clothes (that didn't exist), the emperor and all his friends exclaimed how beautiful the emperor's new clothes were because they all feared they would be labeled too stupid or incompetent to see the clothes. While the charade continued, the tailors asked for more money and resources for their work, but really just to line their own pockets. No one wanted to deny them because no one wanted to say there were no clothes because of their fears of what others would say. The tailors praised the emperor for his brilliance. The emperor awarded the pretenders medals and the title of Lord because they told him he was special, so special.

On the day of the big reveal, a procession took place with the emperor showing off his new clothes. When the emperor made his appearance, everyone in the crowd exclaimed how beautiful the emperor's new clothes were, except one, an innocent child who trusted his own mind and wasn't afraid of what others thought. He shouted out, "But he isn't wearing anything at all!" The crowd was stunned. The boy had said what everyone knew but had been afraid to say. The emperor had no clothes. He was bare-ass naked, not a garment in sight.

The conclusion of this tale is what I find most remarkable, because, you see, the emperor then continues and pretends as though nothing was exposed. The bare-assed naked fool wants A to be B. The bare-assed naked fool wants to suspend his judgment, wants the crowd to suspend their judgment, swallow what they've been told, and move in lockstep just as they had been manipulated to do by the pretenders.

The child looks on in attentive amusement.

Scuba diving wasn't so great. Hurricanes had kicked up the sand, and visibility was only about five feet. My "dive buddy" assigned on the dive boat disappeared the minute he hit the murky water and never returned. Since I was a kid, I've always assumed I was on my own. "Goodbye," I thought, another top-down team drowned despite good intentions.

I said goodbye, too, to the real estate establishment that I had become a part. It wasn't good enough for my clients or me. It wasn't principled. Leaving the established way of doing business wasn't going to be hard. This was going to be easy because it was natural and right, bright, not toxic, brilliant, not sludge. I had wanted to grow my company and get big. I had wanted to take on the big nationals on their own turf, and I had become a big national in the process. I'd gotten what I had intended. But it wasn't what I had thought, and there was no satisfaction or passion in me. It all felt like swimming in the murky middle. These were people that wanted to convince others that A is B and that original thought is unnecessary, to give up any thoughts of independence and accept the mundane. I wanted out of that muck.

A psychotherapist once wrote a book that claimed the majority of men suffer from subtle and covert depression because of cultural claims placed upon them and then blamed for that very behavior. They attempt to cover up that depression with things like acquiring power, sex, success, prestige, and big companies too. I can't say definitively if he's right. It kind of fits together, though. It might explain some things and why some men do what they do. So, what's the argument for getting big? If there is no tangible benefit resulting in profit and joy and benefits to clients, then the idea is flawed. I was at the top of the hill, the boulder I had pushed at my side -- time to go.

In the establishment, the 80 percent wash away the full alpha potential of the top 20 percent, and alpha outliers are all but invisible. I had wanted to get big, but not at that cost. The clients weren't better represented. I knew I could supplant the global network and exceed the total production of the entire company with just me and a small, intelligent, support group. By leveraging skills, technology, and unidirectional partnerships, without the cost, management, conflicts, and human ballast of a big company, I could give the clients the representation they deserved, anywhere, when others pretended.

My desire to get big had been vanity. It had been a big brain fart, and it stank. I hadn't used my frontal lobe to decide to get big. I wanted to grow for growth's sake and have the world see what I built. My self-image had become a reflection of what others saw. It built up my external reflection at the expense of my core. That sucked. Fuck that -- time to go.

It's funny how much good work you can do when you're headed in the wrong direction. It's incredible how much you can learn and grow when you're headed in the wrong direction. It was all perfect at the time, I suppose. I had helped a lot of people make a lot of money. Nevertheless, it was time for me to go. I knew what the new venture would look like. I knew it would be everything the big nationals weren't. I knew I could do what the big nationals couldn't. It was time for the clients to win. It was time for me to be free.

It was time for me to take what I had learned and go underground, to go stealth. I was a free agent with a radical new way to win. It was time to take on the big nationals, not on their turf, but my own. I wanted to be autonomous, anonymous. I wanted to be in flow.

It was time to go.

PART TWO – HITMAN 2.0

--

OFF THE CHAIN

8

PHILOSOPHY OF A HITMAN

PART II

STEALTHY FORCE

"You are the sky. Everything else is just the weather."
-- Pema Chödrön

Now we get to play with more lethal tools. The world is laid open for us, and we start to design the future and make it happen. It's the basis for the rise in income, control, and nearly effortless defense. Production jumps 10x. Your enjoyment jumps 10x. Now we start to use our innate power against the imposters. You can guess how that turns out.

I know that I am fortunate in that I have always been at ease with taking on risk. It's natural for me. I'm drawn to it. It's not just the thrill that pulls me; it's that creating new things drives my interest, and that's what keeps me engaged. I get bored easily. Taking on risk, I get to play with new ways to use what I've learned. All of it, the good and the sad, and apply all of it to a new project. It's like old coals with fresh kindling, and what starts to flame is something new and unique and accompanied by a new passion.

I don't know if there is a single moment one becomes a Hitman, maybe it's a decision or a plan, but this is about the time in the story it happened for me. I knew it happened when I realized I had control of the important outcomes because I only needed to concern myself with the strategies and tools I could fashion with truth and logic, and I could leave image and the pursuit of the counterfeit to others. How they handled their fear and insecurities would merely be fodder for my success. It's substance over image.

Now we start to design the course ahead with new tools of expansive creativity and original thought, free from any boundaries anyone has tried to impose on us, including ourselves. Now is the time to start something new.

Start with Zero

Start with zero. That should be easy.

Start with zero. Your expectation for what you need to start should be no greater than that.

Start with zero. Everything you have learned in your life up to this moment is merely a backdrop, a benchmark you may compare to or not, an education that may be useful or not. What was good yesterday may not be relevant today. What didn't exist yesterday may wreak havoc today, or tomorrow. Change is alive and constant. Let that wash over you as you know the one thing that doesn't change, zero. Start with zero.

Zero is nothing, but it's enough. It's half the binary code and that's something, and the other half is irrevocably dependent upon it which makes zero everything. It's the placeholder for the Big Bang. It's the one thing the Big Bang didn't create. Start with zero. Start fresh.

A glass needs to be empty in order to be filled.

The Hitman questions everything. Start there.

Knowing the truth in every situation means scrutinizing the things you haven't questioned before: teachings, messages, concepts, and ideas you've accepted as truth throughout your life without any scrutiny. The paradigms perpetuated by groupthink, societal think, the society of which you are apart, your culture, your tribe, your company, your club, and your own habitual thoughts, those are what you must question. Start with zero and examine the beliefs you choose to accept as truth and fact. Ferret out all your misconceptions. Release all your preconceptions. One of the most important things you can learn from this book is that zero is your best friend.

Start with zero. Go to zero. Meditate. Pray. Unleash endorphins with exercise. How ever you choose to do it. Go to zero. Empty your mind. Release your thoughts. Release your feelings. Release your self-image. Release yourself. For a moment, let it all go.

Release the negative catalysts, the emotions and drivers you've been carrying around and using as ineffective defenses and excuses: fear, insecurity, uncertainty, confusion, indecision, anger, envy, resentment, revenge, rage. Release it all; go to zero. Use the opportunity to release all your other shit too: your diseases, your addictions, your shame, your sorrow, the rest of your excuses. Release it all.

What do you find at zero? Certainty, clarity, optimism, confidence, an awareness of self, a bit of indifference, infinite possibilities, the wisdom of maturity, the playfulness of a child, the guidance of the universe, harmony with the Tao, and the hand of God; that's a handful, but it's easy and transcendently powerful. At zero, you can begin to design a new creative path and build its foundation on solid truths determined by you. There's an eagerness for purpose.

When you do this, you might decide to change your path and direction, a little, or a lot. Either of those is a new track. You create that new track unencumbered by the ballast you carried before.

You feel exhilaration from starting something new. The new track and planned trajectory will be perfect for its time, and you will recognize that anything is possible, that you direct what's probable. Create a new business and a new way of life of your design based on your desires and aspirations.

Before the Big Bang, zero was less than nothing, yet it was infinite potential, and all there was, a singularity of infinite density and nothing at the same time. Zero launched the Big Bang; it's a good place to start your new plan, new track, and new trajectory. It's the only pure place to go to start.

Start with zero. It's the beginning of everything. It's all you need.

The Fraud of Power and Position

Hierarchies are everywhere. When you open your eyes to them, you see they're more prevalent than you ever considered. Every corner of your life and business has a hierarchy of authority, power, and position layered upon it. Most everybody accepts those without scrutiny. They plan their days around them.

Hierarchies are supposed to provide some organization to the systems to which they're attached. The organizational structure can be helpful, such as setting out a legal or cultural track to cite the function of responsibility, scope, and procedures for the (hopefully) smooth flow of operations. There is, however, an insidious downside inherent in hierarchies, a rigorously imposed and blindly accepted caste system associated with each. These meted out castes invoke an authority and power of position that impose a relative ranking, a pecking order, on those subject to it – and people subject themselves to it, to them, without thought or scrutiny. Sometimes subtle, sometimes not, this silent caste system of relative ranking and pecking order should be ignored and shirked by you because it's a fraud.

The good the hierarchies are supposed to provide are communication and lines of service, but the caste systems attached are a throwback to a tribal existence that only serves to limit challengers. Ignore it. Position is merely province and not a natural, overarching, actual authority. Actual authority, natural power, is not bestowed by position and does not require the reflection of others. Actual authority and power are a result of a rational mind applying logic and original thought to a situation. It doesn't require subjects or subordinates, or their willing or unwilling sanction. True authority and power are not dependent upon subjects or subordinates, only reflected authority is, reflected power is. How many people do you know in positions of power without enough intellect, principles, or values to oversee that which they are responsible for? Yet, those around them carry on as though the power and authority are real, sanctioning the fraud, and thereby making their own fears real and subjecting their lives to it.

Even those that claim empowerment by "speaking truth to power" are taken in by the fraud because the concept "speak truth to power" presupposes there is inherent relative power in the entity to whom they are speaking. The term "speak truth to power" conjures the mental images of the meek standing up to the mighty, the lamb risking life before the lion, the flag-waving protestor to the oppressive government, the peon to the pontiff, the victim to the perp. But in each of these scenarios, the meek, the lamb, the protester, the peon, and the victim, all acknowledge the relative power given to the entity to whom they speak. Fuck that.

Power exists. Power is real. Real power is that which is only joined with nature and only to the extent nature intended and for no other purpose. It flows according to the laws of existence. Anything else is a fraud. Don't willingly or unwittingly choose to subjugate yourself to it. Real power, nature's power, resides in you. It's innate. The only question is whether you choose to recognize that and allow yourself to express it.

You are not subject to any relative ranking, caste system, or pecking order. You get to pick who's pecking and in what order.

There are some good people in positions of power, and if you want to extend a respectful deference for a person in position, do it, but only if you choose knowingly. You can be polite to the others or not; at least know the difference. When dealing with different cultures, it's valuable to understand their imposed caste systems, and to what extent you choose to abide by them.

Some decisions are the responsibility of those with position in a hierarchy, but that is not real power, not real authority. It is merely province. When dealing with hierarchies, understand them, understand the province and responsibilities of the positions within them, but ignore any imposed caste system or ranking because that's only a fraud to stifle conflicting ideas and keep those with position and province unchallenged.

Go challenge them.

Martial Arts of the Mind

Jiu-Jitsu is the martial art developed to defeat a larger opponent. You do this by taking the fight up close, by "going to the ground." You cause pain and disable your opponent by applying leverage and chokes. If you master this, it can save your life.

Decisions about the world are made by people with position. Most of those people make those decisions in inefficient ways. Their decision-making process is broken. Their programming is buggy. It's transparent when you learn to see it.

Their decision-making process is compromised because they automatically perform predictable behaviors and have predictable knee-jerk reactions to outside stimuli. These stimuli can be either associated or disassociated from the decision at hand; it makes no difference. They are compromised by their internal responses to their fears and uncertainties – also predictable, also often disassociated from the decision at hand. Predictable behaviors, knee-jerk reactions, fears, and uncertainties, these are like giving you the passcodes to access their decision-making programming. It's so remarkable because people don't even know they're exposed this way, and almost everybody is. This applies to individuals as well as to decision-making groups such as boards of directors and committees. Regardless of what other leverage you may have for a given situation, you also have massive leverage once you know what causes their fears and uncertainties and what triggers their programmed behaviors. This is the most effective leverage available. This is a realm not impacted by the size or heft of your opponent. Using these is "going to the ground."

Sun Tzu touched on these vulnerabilities of the opponent, but he didn't follow through and stopped short before he understood what he had. I glimpsed the benefit of exploiting these vulnerabilities while negotiating the deed in lieu of foreclosure for the Transit property. That just scratched the service of how powerful this knowledge could be, but it whetted my appetite for what more I could learn, and I set out to find out. I researched and developed new techniques of influence and subjugation by taking advantage of those vulnerabilities displayed by the opponents by understanding what triggered their programmed behaviors. I found what worked best and kept improving upon them with training and practice and trial and error. This was the beginning of an applied influence methodology to control negotiations that would later and include my Tricks, Hacks, Hammers, and Cheats. With this, the exposed become outgunned. You can prevail in virtually any encounter, avoid and survive the most brutal blows, and direct outcomes to your design.

You'll keep your opponents off-balance, off-center, uncertain, and confused. They'll follow the plan you laid out for them. Never lie, but never be specific. Learn and practice the martial arts of the mind to subjugate even the most powerful. Train your mind and body to understand and use it. I gave this the highest priority and has become the basis for my consistent negotiating success.

Living [and Surviving] with No Controls

When you live and operate with no controls and complete independence, there needs to be a fitness and cohesion of principles guiding your actions and maintaining your personal integrity and congruity if you're to survive and excel. You need self-governance since you are governed by no one else. There's no cheat for this. You need to perform at a higher level than your peers and opponents, and that requires congruity and integrity in action and thought that operates in agreement with nature and is devoid of discord or distraction. Without that integrity, that congruity, you'll falter. On the edge of the abyss, you'll hesitate. You'll start to wish that A could be B. Your core will fragment.

Does the idea of a code of honor for the life of a Hitman sound strange? Your life and sanity depend on a level of precise support provided by such a code.

The idea of a code may seem to you like an anachronism, perhaps, but it's the glue that holds everything together. It's the glue that holds you together and nurtures your success. It keeps you righteous, bulletproof, and supplied and aligned with nature.

I didn't invent the idea of a personal code. Many groups of successful individuals with a warrior prowess, a cleric's calm, and a track record of accomplishment and extreme performance have done so supported by a code: elite operatives like the Greek Spartans and the Roman Soldiers and their Stoic ethical doctrines, the SEAL Ethos, the Shaolin Monks' and Chinese Martial Arts' teachings of Wu De exploring the morality of deed and mind, the Samurai virtues of Bushido, the Knights' Code of Chivalry, and the Rangers' Creed. For my purposes, and theirs, the code is not a set of limitations, but a foundation and design for clarity and empowerment. It fosters distinction, grace, and excellence in outcomes. None of the codes are group-centric; they are all keyed to individual behavior. They all support the singular agent, the free-spirit. Make your code an intelligent model for honor. It not only gives you an edge of incalculable value, but it also gives you the internal congruity and alignment that strengthens character and creative and original thought. It gives you an advantage.

I'm far from perfect. I fall short, make mistakes, and fail to live up to my own ideals, but I know what my ideals are, and I'm closer to living them and more successful because I've defined them. They're important to me. I know what perfection looks like. I know my true north. It is:

Unleash tenacity, perseverance, and endurance in your chosen endeavors. Own and take responsibility for your self-governance, self-respect, self-trust, and self-confidence. Make decisions with wisdom and your prefrontal cortex, not your emotions or your reptilian brain. Award absolute loyalty to deserving clients, family, and friends. Act with a sense of justice; return good for good and justice for bad. Understand honor and merit and temper your own with humility. Perfect your skills without ostentation or show. Make use of your skills and power only for the fulfillment of your mission and only for good, only to the extent required, and never upon innocents. Take action in the face of fear. Have deliberate patience securing your outcomes. Embrace your mission and purpose without reservation. Speak seldom, but only the truth. Comport yourself in the design of your ideal. For all your troubles, blame only yourself.

Loyalty and Advocacy Proviso

Loyalty is an agreement and expression of values that resonate among two parties based on underlying principles understood by them. Growing up in an insecure environment where there is no loyalty, you become hyper-attentive, super-diligent, and critical. If you aren't raised in an environment of loyalty, it's something you have to learn. If you grow up in an environment without loyalty, you also have to learn to be loyal to yourself. I didn't learn about loyalty growing up, maybe that's why I think it's so important. Maybe that's why my idea of justice for broken loyalty is so harsh.

All people crave loyalty because they seldom get it, and they get shot at from all sides. They need to know that they have someone they can depend on. They need to know they have you to depend on. It's probably not a coincidence that with my desire to give ardent and steadfast advocacy and loyalty, I've chosen an industry where there is so little; that now I travel in circles where there is so little loyalty, so little advocacy, so little truth.

The concepts of honor and loyalty are on the wane in our culture and all but forgotten. They've become something transient. They're not taught. They're not even understood. The expediency of the moment is what reigns supreme; but the cost of that, though initially hidden from view and out of sight and mind, is very high, and very expensive (and not just financially). To paraphrase C.S. Lewis, "They laugh at honor and then are shocked to find traitors in their midst."

Loyalty is about ethics; it's about integrity. Loyalty makes you powerful, but it's a two-edged sword.

For all my lofty talk, here's the rub. Loyalty is conditional. If your loyalty is given in a situation and then broken in return, then fuck it and fuck them. That material consideration means you have no further obligation to provide your loyalty, legal considerations notwithstanding. When engaged, loyalty is absolute; there are no gradations. If gradations in loyalty are present, it's a virus, and no good can come of it. If your loyalty is required because of a legal responsibility and you receive no loyalty in return, then you need to end the relationship.

Loyalty is absolute when you choose to grant it. Loyalty in gradations is merely a game, a game you must play to win; otherwise, you lose. Gradations have a way of sliding ...into the abyss. The expediency of the moment will prevail if the underlying principles of loyalty aren't absolute.

Loyalty requires a measure of resonance of principles between the parties. This doesn't have to be absolute, but they cannot be in discord. Giving your absolute loyalty to a person, client, or cause requires that there is an alignment of values and principles. Without that alignment and resonance, keep your powder dry. Give your loyalty as the highest honor only to those who deserve it.

Goofproof Goal Controllers

If you're going to get good at handling a weapon, you've got to be able to hit what you're shooting at. This, of course, presupposes you know what you're shooting at, knowing what your targets are in advance.

I had goals as a kid. Not lifetime goals mind you, thinking about a lifetime was way too fuzzy for me at the time, but short-term targets that focused on my immediate priorities like sanity, survival, and fun. I spent most of my time in pursuit of those goals, and mostly I achieved them, or at least made advances towards them. I achieved the moments I was looking for back then -- sanity, survival, fun, and a little natural dopamine.

Goals worked for me, so I kept using them as I got older. After the Transit Street fiasco, I realized I had to be much more precise and discerning about what my targets should be, and I started using goals in my planning with greater diligence as I started my first company. I learned more about what types of goals worked and what didn't and how best to use them in my business, and then later in my life. Having targets increased my performance dramatically. They're super effective and cost nothing, so it's stupid if you don't use them. The opportunity costs are infinitely high if you fail to use them. Goals are the simplest and surest thing you can do to get what you want. Conversely, of course, you can just numb out instead and achieve nothing.

There's plenty of data that shows how to make goals that work to boost incremental performance improvement, and more importantly, make major gap up advances. Self-management and self-determination are needed skills if you're truly independent, and goals are an integral part of your self-governance.

Here's why identifying specific targets make you more successful and happy (assuming that's what you want):

You have powerful little subroutine programs called cognitive motivators embedded in your head. They sit idle until they're confronted with an incongruity that has enough strength to disrupt your life, causing a gap between your present state and your desired state, your ideal state. If the gap is unsatisfactory, unacceptable, existential, a threat to your life or happiness, and you care about those things, then those little cognitive motivators switch on. When they switch on, they initiate the release of the resources necessary to close the gap and move you closer to your desired state. If there's no goal, there's no gap. If there's no gap, your little cognitive motivators stay idle, and so do you.

That's why specificity is important. If the target is fuzzy, you don't know what you're shooting at, the gap is ill-defined, and nothing gets triggered. If the target is fuzzy and the gap is not well defined, there's nothing for you to care about, so nothing is triggered. When you've defined your goals with specificity, then you know what it means to hit them, what it means not to hit them; and this creates expectancy, an expectation of outcomes, and a well-defined gap. A well-defined gap that is meaningful to you is the incongruity needed to trigger the cognitive motivators. When the cognitive motivators are triggered, energy, creativity, and perseverance are all set loose to close the gap. Perseverance perseveres when happiness is attained in pursuit of your goals, not just in their achievement.

Your perceived value of the target will also help define the gap. The higher your perceived value, the greater the gap, and that sends a strong signal to your cognitive motivators. Goals of little value to you will put you to sleep. Goals that are valuable to you help create a state of expectancy and are the catalyst for action and persistence.

The data shows that a higher level of difficulty of goals results in higher levels of performance. If you want real achievement, pick goals that are challenging, difficult, audacious, and potent, goals that make you stretch to reach them. The thing that sets the most successful companies apart from their less successful peers is that the more successful companies have audacious and awe-inspiring long-term goals, at least one. Use your imagination and have fun, but avoid pure fantasy, because you must believe the achievement of the goals is possible for them to work. Have confidence in your outcomes. Expectancy drives their manifestation. Believe in your own efficacy, and don't short-change yourself. Go to zero and let the deepest and calmest part of you guide you. The guy that built the biggest hedge fund in the world meditates every day. He bought his first stock for $300 and now runs funds worth $160 billion. That puts the Om in OMG. The more capable people believe themselves to be, the greater the expectancy and the higher the goals they set for themselves. The higher the goals they set, the more capable they become. The higher the goals they set, and the more capable they become, the greater the performance. Believing yourself to be capable doesn't mean you're not afraid sometimes that you might fail. It just means you use that fear as motivation. It helps define the gap.

That same data shows that written goals with the most detail and specificity produce the best results. Articulate each target with enough detail to stimulate a vivid mental image of its realization and have it quantifiable and measurable so you can assess your on-going progress. Detailing who, what, where, when, why, and how is a good place to start. Ambiguous and vague goals fade and are forgotten. The more specific and explicit the goal, the more dramatic the performance improvement. Having a system in place to regularly assess your on-going progress so you can make needed course corrections, helps assure your targets will be reached, but that's secondary to just doing a good job defining them in the first place.

The level of detail and specificity of my goals increases when I write them down, and that causes those little cognitive motivator subroutines in my head to take off and go to work on the problems and challenges presented without conscious effort on my part. My mind works the subroutines in the background 24/7 while I carry on with my other work and life. When it's time for a decision, the work and answers have largely been completed, ready for my conscious intervention and implementation.

I started carrying a shortlist of goals in my wallet after the Transit mess. I know that sounds simplistic and pedestrian, but it worked. It made the recovery from my Transit fiasco happen. It made my first company happen. It made each subsequent company happen.

A Chinese proverb says the best time to have planted a tree was twenty years ago, but the second-best time is now. The time is now to set your targets. Write down the top 20 or 30 things you want or want to achieve in your life and career, your aspirations and ambitions. Don't be shy. Have fun with this. Let it all out. Be audacious.

After you have your big list, then pick six of the most meaningful items on the list that resonate with you and that you can to put your mind, spirit, and effort behind accomplishing. Pick only six. Let all the others go.   This is about building focus for your most important priorities and setting boundaries so you don't get distracted.   You're choosing your highest-priority targets, the most important things that matter.   Time or energy spent on any of the leftovers on the list steals from your highest-priority targets, regardless of their merit. Affirm and say "yes" to the six you picked as your highest-priority targets and release all the others.   It means you will have to say "no" to most everything and most everybody; otherwise, you're pulled in umpteen different directions and further away from your real goals. They won't help you get to where you want to go. Clarity as to which projects you're willing to work on and which projects you're not is important. People pleasers will have a hard time with this, but you have to make that choice. Do you want to be a people pleaser and not reach your goals, or do you want to hit your highest-priority targets? Being successful is as much about what you choose not to do as it is about the things you choose to do.

After having chosen my six highest-priority targets, then daily, I'll pick six things to do that day that get me closer to one or more of my targets -- including one that supports body and mind so I can be sharpest in the hunt.   If you do this, your accomplishments each day will snowball. I get a little dopamine pop each time I check off a completed item. You can roll over or re-evaluate items that are not yet completed. This is core to amping performance immediately. Pick your enduring six high priority targets and pick six daily tasks. Write them down and start making things happen. There is magic in writing down six things to do today that will move you closer to your goals and doing them.

Some things will kill even the best goals, things that fuck your brain like addictions, bad relationships, and conflicting goals. The best goals in the world become impotent if they are in conflict with your behavior or with one another.

Also, be aware that the performance boosts you get from your individual, self-relevant goals apply only to individuals, not assembled groups.   It's the social loafing problem I mentioned before.   Some psychologists call it the Sucker Effect. But no matter what you call it, top performers are less effective working in assigned groups than they are working alone. Their loss of motivation is caused by the perceived injustice that they're contributing more to the group than the others resulting in unfair distributions of gain and credit. The unfortunate solution is for them to contribute less; the winner then being whoever can work the least. The "suckers" in these studies are the higher performing team members contributing more than the others for an unfairly small share. The real "suckers" are the clients that unknowingly hires one of these groups.

To improve a group's performance, the goals must be group-centric, not individual-centric. The individuals, including top performers, must subordinate their goals to those of the group. That is why groups convened organically are more likely to thrive, because the goals and values of the group and the individuals are aligned. Top down, management-formed groups flounder because of the misalignment of the goals and values of the group and the individuals.

Why do people not set targets? Perhaps because they don't know they work. Perhaps because they're afraid to commit to something they don't know they can reach and are afraid of failure, or they are afraid to commit to something they may learn they don't want later. Perhaps because they're schmucks and they want to talk and fantasize about being successful, but they don't really want to put forth the effort. Goals do work. There's no improvement without risk, and you can always change your goals later if you want. If you're a schmuck, you might consider changing that. If you're not willing to do the work to develop the details of your targets, ask yourself if you are really willing to do what is required to reach them.

My original family's expectations for me were pretty low. Nobody inquired as to my aspirations for life or career. Nobody inquired or made recommendations for education or purpose. None of them ever acknowledged an achievement of mine, small or large, or said they were proud of me, at least not until I had my first million-dollar year. I thought that was pretty shallow of them. It didn't matter though; the time had long since passed that I cared what they thought. Set high expectations for yourself; that's what matters. Underachiever, overachiever, it's all bullshit, all transitory. Those labeled as underachievers sometimes make great success of their lives. Those labeled as overachievers sometimes stumble and fail or burn out early. The past is not prologue. Set your goals high and know you can achieve them with effort because you can. And then go do it.

Some people are embarrassed or even ashamed of their ambition and aspirations because society wants you to stay small, stay humble, and not stand out. They might even label your desires a moral failing unless they approve. Fuck that. Be proud of your ambition and aspirations and goals. Don't hide them. Embrace your aspirations and dreams. Respect your ambition. Take aim on your targets; you can hit them. Pick six. Hit six.

Heat

If you're going to call something hot, you need to feel some heat. Thermodynamics describes the darkest voids of space where temperatures approach absolute zero, entropy approaches its maximum constant, and virtually all motion and activity has stopped -- literally cold and dead in its tracks. These are places of no movement, no heat, no hope. There might be the tiniest hint of thermal energy locked up in the matter present, but it will likely never see its potential realized because there is no catalyst to release it. These places aren't necessarily light years away in deep space; they might be right here at home, in your office, or in your head -- no heat, no movement, nothing new, flat-line entropy.

If you're going to make something new happen, you're going to have to bring a catalyst. You're going to need to bring radical stimulus. You're going to need to bring the heat. In the absolute sense, heat is the flow of energy from the sources of the greatest movement and action to the destinations deprived of it. It's a law of nature.

The greatest sources of motion and action are in your aspirations, ambition, purpose, and passion. These are the fuel and the spark, and there's no limit.

Intensity, fervor, spirit, and drive, these are the things that breed momentum and success. These are the things actualized by purpose, passion, aspirations, and ambition. Passion is a result of the confluence and resonance of your purpose, values, principles, goals, interests, and enjoyment. Passion creates motivation. Passion creates flow.

Your purpose is a destination, a reason, a cause, a guide. Your purpose is the "Why?" the "What's the use?" the "Why am I doing this?" It's the rationale and motivation to keep things rolling, to keep on going, even when things are rolling against you. Purpose is the intersection of your values and your goals. It's the segue from your values to your goals. It's the compass to know if your mission is still on track even if your goals temporarily fail and your results suck. It's the map; it's the mode, it's the lab churning out your ideas, it's the blockchain that holds and carries your disparate ideas to a unified end. If you can't name your purpose, you're floundering. You don't "find" your purpose, and it doesn't "find" you. You determine your purpose and why. It's a decision you make. Name it.

Reach beyond your comfort zone and choose a purpose that inspires you and is meaningful. Embrace extremes. Embrace risk. Make the decision with your frontal lobe, without boundaries and without fear. Shrinking from this and clutching for the ground for security for fear of falling into the abyss is anathema in my mind. Even a fall into the abyss would provide some definition to life (its end). Determine your purpose, a good one, a challenging one. Name it and articulate why it's it.

Determine your purpose as though you have no limits because none of the limits you may perceive you have are absolute. There are always workarounds, adaptions, adjustments, cheats. Make your ideas challenging, disruptive, market-changing, world-changing, and important. You don't need to limit yourself to a single purpose. No reason. Have multiple purposes. Have purposes that you engage and then later dismiss if you wish. It's your decision. You don't need to ask permission of anyone. You don't need to care if anyone casts judgment on you. It doesn't matter. Only your values and your decisions matter. Decide on your purpose and then make it better later. It's simply an investment in yourself. Name it. Say why, and own it.

Passion is a river that runs deep, far, and fast. Unlike anything else, its power shapes your world, always moving, always changing. Nothing seems to stop it. Nothing seems to slow it. Everything that ventures near it becomes part of its strength. Passion unleashes energy as nothing else can.

Passion is the most powerful motivator. It's more powerful than fear.

Passion is the incentive that keeps you driving forward. Passion brings excitement and makes self-confidence a moot topic. It transcends any of that. Passion finds ways to overcome any objection. Passion gives you a pipeline of dopamine and keeps you resolute to press on.

Passion requires you to feel. You can't numb out and be passionate about anything. You have to be fully engaged. If you don't have passion for how you live, the work you do, or how you do it, pack it up and change it up; it's not worth it. Your time on this Earth is limited; spend it engaged and enjoying the objects of your passion.

What are you in love with? Choose it and use it. Let it out. Consciously let it out; let it run. Express it. That's real power.

I have a passion for learning new things, a passion for understanding everything, and a passion for creating great outcomes. Do you think perfection is the enemy of good? It's not. Good is a good first inning. A passion for perfection is the end game.

Be careful, though, because passion can be a wild stallion, and you can get bucked or trampled. If you become a slave to your passion, you are out of control and no good will likely come of it. If you find you have a passion for something or someone that will hurt you, you need to pull out. The power of misguided passion has the potential to destroy you. You need to put a stop on it. Select instead, your passion that has a richness and potency for life.

Enjoy your existence.

I like to cook. I like to cook things I like to eat. And what I like to eat explodes with flavor and texture, things I've discovered in my travels around the world that have an uncommon robustness of taste and substance and bring their own unique ambiance without the need for anything else. One such dish is a rich, red, spicy, and peppery, stew-like ambrosia called Pozole Rojo. It's hot. The Aztec descendants of Mexico perfected it. You can change it depending upon your mood. The basics are posole (hominy), seasoned pork and/or chicken braised and cooked low and slow, so the collagen has broken down and transformed the meat to the point that it is so tender it falls apart and off the bone, ample onions and garlic, some roasted green chilis, enough chipotle for a little smoke, enough powdered red chilis to start making it thick, aromatic herbs like oregano and cilantro, and enough salted meat stock to make a stew. Add fresh black pepper. Cook it all night. Here's the point you need to grasp: you handpick the best ingredients for your outcome in mind and put them all into the pot with intelligence, intention, and love. Let it simmer, walk away and forget about it. It's perfect when it's ready. It's ready when it's perfect. Life's the same way.

Set in motion the things that will change your life, your goals and subroutines that go to work for you 24/7/365. Your power of intention creates the business and life you want without all the shit. Pema Chödrön was partially right; you are the sky. But you're not separate from the weather. You make the weather. Life is good.

Enjoy your pozole.

9

SHIT CANCELED

NEW FREEDOM WRIT LARGE

"Everyone who has ever built anywhere a new heaven first found the power thereto in his own hell."
-- Friedrich Nietzsche

After I told the Chairman I was leaving the company to start a new firm, the behemoth started looking for my replacement and wanted me to sign a non-compete agreement. I refused, of course; I had every intention of competing. The sale proceeded as planned. Some people thought I was nuts for leaving the protective cocoon of the large company and venturing into the jungle alone, but I didn't care. I couldn't wait to get started on my new venture.

I was acquainted with the man who took over my position at the company after the sale; though, admittedly, I was ambivalent to that info. It occurs to me now that I never heard again from that man and haven't heard of him since. I guess he was consumed by the behemoth. Sometime later, that company would be purchased by a friend and partner of mine and folded into his operation.

The Chairman understood my reasons for leaving that company. He was gracious, but many of the people that worked for me at the old firm didn't understand so well. Some were resentful I was leaving. Some apologized for being difficult -- all silly drama as far as I was concerned. Don't get me wrong. There were a lot of good people at that company, and some were my friends. But I was happy to move on and not have to worry about the laggards and their ballast, or spinning messages so a contrived image was convincing to the public. Shit canceled. I didn't ask anyone from the old company to join me, not even the top performers. I started fresh from zero -- unencumbered. There were several that went on to start their own companies after I'd left. Kudos to them.

The sale closed with the behemoth. I got my check for my share and was free. I relished in my freedom and put my mind to my new task, building another new company from scratch.

Off the Chain

I leased a small office high in a tower with floor to ceiling glass that looked down on the building that housed my old company. It was a great feeling. The old company occupied two floors of the building I had just left. I had one small office now and was much happier.

Starting my new firm unleashed a new flow of energy in me. I could bring all my new knowledge to bear and plan out my new company and build it just the way I wanted. I knew all about my competition. I knew all about the markets and what was driving them. I knew the economics. I knew my strengths and weaknesses. I knew the resources I had at my disposal. I took all that and designed the plans for the surest path to fun and success. I felt like a kid that had just discovered Aladdin's lamp, and I was about to decide which wishes were to be granted to me. Starting something new from zero heaps on you the raw, infinite, potential the new venture opens and merges the infinite possibilities of the universe with the creative energy of your mind. It can be a rush.

I had learned first-hand at my first company the benefits of exploiting markets that had extreme supply and demand dynamics, those markets that are fueled by unrelenting trends and high-velocity capital. I had learned at my second company that there is no reason to compromise your focus, unless you're choosing instead to fall into the generalists' trap and degrade your superior strategic differentiators to the marginal mean of mediocrity, to depend on the fraud of image over substance, presentation over performance. That would be stupid, but people do it all the time.

I had learned at both companies that the most important decisions you make at the outset of any new plan are those concerned with what the focus is to be, what the dominant strategy is to be. Where will the focused strategy lead? Is it the right decision for the circumstances? Is it the right decision for the time? Does it resonate with you and will the world embrace it or reject it? Prefrontal cortex engaged, I critiqued my own decision-making processes and then picked my focus; one that would stoke my passion, one that I would be resolute about in its undertaking, one that was interesting and adventurous, and one where I could do a lot of good and make a lot of money.

Months before, I had given a speech at an economic forum to a group of assembled commercial real estate people about how the ubiquitous nature of information technology and the cloud were changing the industry. The reception I received from the group was polite, but indifferent. They knew this trend was changing their world, but they didn't seem to care much. They were curious about the latest app, but that was about it. What I chose not to share with them during my talk was something that I'd had my eye on for a while, the growing demand for a new generation of internet infrastructure. This was about to surge because of exploding demand for bandwidth capacity and a newly de-regulated telecom and internet environment. The floodgates had been opened. Smart money, and a lot of it, was flowing into new companies to build out this new mission-critical infrastructure – the backbone of a massive global internet upgrade with significant increases in speed, capacity, and efficacy. It was a million times faster, a million times bigger, a million times better, a factor of 10^6x. This was an exploding trend, and I wanted to be part of it.

The companies playing in this new arena were entrepreneurial. These were startups, well-funded, massive, startups, with an insatiable appetite for the right kind of buildings in the right locations in the right markets. Each of these buildings required massive and redundant electrical power and fiber optic internet connectivity. This was a land grab. This was "Go Time" for these companies, and these companies were the fastest of the fast. "Build infrastructure and market share now at any cost," was their mantra. NFL cities were what they wanted first for their nerve centers. That didn't seem very scientific to me, but hey, there's a lot of NFL cities and that was just the start.

The buildings they needed would be used for central office switch facilities, colocation and cloud infrastructure centers, data centers, network operation centers (NOCs), telecom hotels, and hubs and point of presence (POP) sites. The companies needed these to connect their broadband products to their customers and all the other internet service providers (ISPs) in the world.

These were monster bunker-type buildings able to withstand anything nature or invading armies could throw at them. Each one of these buildings required the power to run a small city, enough cooling to quell hell's fury, floor loading capability to support the gravity of a black hole the backup battery stacks would require, and a clean fire suppression system that would stop a fire instantly and save the equipment from the havoc and destruction that traditional water fire suppression systems would wreak. (The favorite systems absorbed the heat to a temperature below the fire ignition point and displaced the oxygen so nothing could burn – no muss, no fuss, no water.) The mission-critical nature of these sites required backup and redundant systems so the networks, essentially, would never go down. "Nine nines" they call it, 99.9999999 percent probability the network would never go down. If a system has only 90 percent reliability (.9), one nine, it might go down 2.4 hours in a 24-hour period, obviously unsatisfactory. Nine nines allow for only 0.8764 milliseconds of downtime in a 24-hour period. Nine nines reliability is what these companies wanted for their network infrastructure.

Thousands of these specialized buildings were going to be built, acquired, and retrofitted over the next couple of years. Very few people knew what was required, how to find them, how to secure them, and how to get it all done fast – the convergence of telecom engineering, construction, and the disparate real estate markets and owners across the nation and around the world. That knowledge was scarce, and there were billions of dollars funding the hunt. I had found another extreme market anomaly to exploit.

It was easy for me to develop passion for this focus because I had a passion for the technology and the expansive geographical aspect of it. I embraced the importance of the mission-critical infrastructure for the global internet, and I loved the challenge of the hunt. As before, I had to build a new cognitive bench from scratch. If you're not learning something new in your work, you're sliding backward, and the world will pass you by. I set out to learn everything I could about the industry, its requirements, and the environment in which I would be operating, a new knowledge set that translated into intellectual capital, an investment in the future, and my critical deep cognitive bench.

The companies mounting this massive demand were run by entrepreneurs with swashbuckling swagger who sometimes made up the rules as they went along. One of these guys was a lanky Texan who gravitated to the rarified air of the New York and Washington D.C. haut monde and dated a New York City publishing and fashion icon of worldwide fame to the chagrin of many, particularly her husband. One was a Colorado oilman and railroad tycoon, solidly placed in the Forbes 400. Another had his start operating a construction company in Omaha, still another was a Silicon Valley engineer who traveled around the country piloting his own plane with a suitcase full of cash so he could make fast deals to set up his POP sites nationwide to build out his market share fast and first. (I had to clean up those deals several years later.)

Others flew less straight and found themselves facing legal turbulence; like the guy who transformed himself from a milkman and motel chain operator in small-town Mississippi to acquiring over 60 independent phone companies and climbing his way on to the Forbes 400 list, only to perpetuate one of the biggest corporate frauds of all time, according to the FBI and the federal courts. Still another, the son of a longshoreman, spent time in prison for insider trading. Another was sent away for racketeering. And yet another for tax evasion. Even Enron had more than its toe in the pond. It was the wild west, still yet untamed, and they wanted to get theirs while the getting was good. I wasn't at all involved in any of the antics that got these guys into trouble. My involvement focused solely on securing the awesome rare sites suitable to bulk up the internet infrastructure capacity and grow these startups into solid companies for their customers and investors -- the things these guys should have been doing instead of letting their hubris cloud their thinking. A Two Million Dollar roman orgy toga party on Sardinia partially funded by Tyco, a major fiber optic cable manufacturer, exemplified how out of control this had become.

Many of these companies seemed to burn through CEOs faster than the light pulses moving through their fiber optic strands. It wasn't uncommon for me to be the only one standing after the change of regime and the requisite movement of the department heads, personnel, responsibilities and other game board pieces after the new guy took control. I was the only one left standing because I was then the only one that knew all about their properties. One company changed CEOs four times and department heads three times in one year. When the new department head showed up for their first day on the job and asked, "How do we handle all the leases for the switched sites portfolio?"; the answer was simply, "call Steve Miller." But I get ahead of myself.

Taking Aim

When you start to lay your plans for your new venture, starting from zero is the best place to start, the most creative place to start, the most fun place to start. All that potential that is opened up to you as you start your journey is just waiting for you to claim it and deploy it with direction. Keep in mind Sun Tzu's guidance about knowing the landscape, terrain, and environment of your new venture because it significantly impacts the level and ease of success of your project -- one of the most critical and basic concepts he taught us. The beauty of creating a new venture from scratch is that you get to choose the environment and design the backdrops for your activities, ones that will be supportive to you, tailwinds for you and your negotiations. You get to pick your battles and their locations, the locations within the supply and demand push-pull continuum, the situations where scarcity puts the wind at your back and makes your offerings more valuable.

Your positioning relative to market dynamics is highly predictive of your outcomes. I had already pushed a boulder to the top of the hill once, no reason to do that again. If you come online with a project model that looks like a thousand others, nobody is going to care. Like my friends in West Texas say, "That dog don't hunt." Know the truth about your market dynamics and position yourself to take advantage of the ones that will set you apart. This is the purpose of planning and focus. The generalist is always nursing a sick dog. Select a dominant strategy that takes advantage of nature, markets, and overarching trends, and your focus will be supported and rewarded. All other dogs get left in the pen.

My first company had been an answer to an overabundant supply of office space and a heavily financed demand for new tenants. Killer. Supply and demand, that unyielding axiom, had been the foundation of my success then. Times change, catalysts change, but the axiom doesn't change. Only the variables in the equation change. My early success had been driven by understanding the dynamics of the relationship of what was abundant, office space, and what was scarce, the tenants to lease it, and the level of demand and price elasticity to acquire what was scarce – the willingness for landlords to pay greatly for tenants in terms of fees and incentives and slash rents to pennies on the dollar. I mined the scarce tenants, delivered value to them as promised, and was paid handsomely by the hungry landlords to relieve their pain.

But now, something new was happening that was creating an even greater market shift, a global market shift, a radical sea change. My new company was going to answer the demand for a new mission-critical infrastructure to connect the world. Again, supply and demand, that beautiful, faultless, dynamic axiom. Connecting the world, a macro-trend that was changing every persons' life. The right space was rare and so were the skills needed to find it, secure it, and configure it. Killer.

I immersed myself in learning about this focus and developing my deep cognitive bench. I organized meetings with telecom engineers and lawyers and interviewed them. I read the books and white papers I could find on the subject. I interviewed construction companies specializing in the niche and studied Construction Documents (CDs) of the specialized spaces. I attended every conference on the subject. I developed a database with the "lit" buildings in the United States that had fiber optic cable supplied to them. I learned how to determine the location of the fiber optic cables in all the municipalities. I acquired access to ownership info for every building in the nation. I had the data. I had the knowledge. I became a guru, and I was willing to travel. The result was I became one of the most knowledgeable brokers about the communication services industry, the internet, switching facilities, data centers, pop sites, hub sites, long haul capability, and what's called the "last mile" into the buildings and to my clients' customers.

The deals started small, just like at my first company; a hub site in San Diego, a POP site in Walnut Creek, a hub site in Chicago, a POP site in Monterey, a switch in Denver, one in Fort Collins, another in Wilkes Barre, and others. But even though they were modest in size, I would travel to each location and inspect and document all buildings and spaces and markets. I knew more about the physicality of the sites than either my clients or the landlords. I treated each transaction as mission-critical, because it was for me, and it was for my clients. My methodology was proof of concept, and the concept worked.

The big national brokerages again made attempts at working in my niche, often with poor results. One client asked me to locate a switch and data center site in Washington, D.C., after they had floundered with one of the big nationals. Those brokers had uncovered only one site in all of D.C., one of the densest internet infrastructure areas in the country, and it was ridiculously expensive. After I did my own research and site visits, it was obvious that the best sites for the requirement were going to be in the Sterling/Herndon/Reston area, so I configured a shortlist for my client to visit. I arranged for a town car and catered lunch to tour the sites. We secured a better site at a quarter of the price.

Having established the proof of concept, the projects and remuneration got bigger. The clients liked the quality of the work; no one could reproduce it. I took on a portfolio of about 300 sites a client had acquired through a merger with another ISP. This portfolio represented about 10 percent of the public switched telecom network internet traffic in the country at the time.

When the sites had first been assembled (by the guy with the airplane and suitcase full of cash), no thought had been given to when the leases expired, and they were all now expiring at about the same time. Virtually none of the leases had renewal options. About 80 percent of the sites in the portfolio expired within a six-month window. This meant my client was at risk of losing the critical infrastructure they had just acquired and that so much internet traffic was dependent upon. These were mission-critical. My client was dependent upon my success for the continued existence of its network. It was an existential threat to them. I loved the challenge. I loved the adventure. The money was good too.

There was a huge amount of work to be completed in a short period of time. I needed to bring on additional staff and assistants to help with this project and the others that I knew would follow. I've had a lot of different assistants over the years, some more effective than others.

Man-Eaters

"In Sicily, women are more dangerous than shotguns." This was said by Calo in the Godfather. Calo was a young and respectful shepherd from the old country, a deeply loyal mafia bodyguard. He was a simple man, but he knew there were forces of nature for which there was little defense.

Before anyone can dip their electronic devices into the endless stream of pulsating data to do something insanely productive, or more likely, satisfy their immediate gratification, there is the functioning internet infrastructure that nobody notices, and everybody takes for granted. There are the hard realities of hard people dealing with hard circumstances who re-shape the world according to their plan so that it is a more useable, productive, and livable place. The kind of place the privileged complainers complain about because they don't know what it took to build it or what it takes to maintain it. Engineers, heavy construction, power installations, and people with their own money on the line – a lot of money. These are not people that sit in cubes all day. These are men who wear boots, real jeans, and don't give a shit what you think. They get out of their trucks and walk through the dirt to see if their orders are being followed and their money is being spent well. This is a male population with a capital "T," except for the lawyers. This is testosterone territory, tough guys who are used to getting their way because they usually do. And just so you know, testosterone and brains are not inversely correlated. Brains and testosterone, when found together, are a potent mix. These are wealthy men. This isn't merely weapons-grade machismo; this is world-domination machismo.

The best assistants, for my purposes, do great research. They have a sixth sense for finding the back story for people, situations, and property and bring that story to life so I can know what I'm dealing with, and they've begun to handle the details even before I've told them what I want. We were about to do a huge volume of work with coarse properties and callous people, so any new assistant had to support our ability to reach and maintain the alpha performance I was looking for. They had to be a massive net positive. They had to enjoy the work and be able to handle these men with ease.

My assistants have almost always been women. Sometimes they've been true personal assistants, administering the details of my life and business. Sometimes they've been junior dealmakers, either in the back office or on the front lines of transactions with me. I always expect them to think for themselves.

They've all been smart, all who lasted have been brilliant, and they must have a personal power and presence that more than hints at their depth, strength, and survival skills. They have to be able to travel with me with ease, and I have to be comfortable spending a lot of time with them. I don't mind so much if they don't take orders well; I might prefer it. I don't want anyone who'll just roll over, and I find the banter stimulating. Besides, I might gain a new insight or perspective. They do have to get the job done, though, regardless, and I must be able to trust them implicitly.

Interviews with assistant candidates have been the oddest things, like speed dating for a job. I'll have sixty or more respondents requesting an interview from one posting, 95 percent are women. I just hope to be able to whittle that down to a handful to see.

Some women have been sexually aggressive during the interviews, from not-so-subtle innuendo to blatant offers for sex, and one once pulled up her olive-green sweater to show me her boobs. She was a free-spirited, bohemian blonde, and she just set hers out on the conference table for me to see. I still remember the sweater. I found it more amusing than titillating, though. I didn't invite it, or them; they were just presented to me. An accomplished temptress, no doubt, but I knew this wasn't who I was looking for to help me further my business. I did appreciate, though, that she wanted to be a pirate. It would've been fun to help her. She probably got a job somewhere, but that was not the type of person I was looking for. I was looking for someone more exceptional, more reserved. The woman I hired first for this project said that if I hired her, she would be my "day wife." Was that the reason I hired her? No. There were many.

My assistants deal with my clients, contractors, brokers, and others that come into my world. They must be able to handle themselves in conversations and situations where they may find themselves in over their heads. They have to be quick on their feet and be able to deliver an even quicker riposte. They must possess a quiet sophistication and reserve, yet be easily approachable, maybe because of, or sometimes in spite of, their colorful past. Almost all have had pasts that accentuated their subtle worldliness and depth, though they never talked about it much. They're never a cog; it's not in their DNA. They're determined to be their own force of nature. They were pirates themselves before we met; I just helped them value that side of themselves more. They've survived their own trials, which helped develop their own, budding, hitman tendencies. They easily and naturally connect with and influence other women, but even more easily and naturally move men. They would never use the term "manipulate"; because that's not friendly, and if there is a common thread among them all, it's that they're friendly and professional when they want to be. They are equally adept at asking hard-hitting questions walking through a job site in boots and a hard hat, or keeping people engaged in conversations in a cocktail dress at a party or reception. They've all possessed social skills I don't have. If heads turn, all the better. And as reliable as the chorus of birdsong in the early dawn, the men on the opposing sides, those hard men shaping the world, just want to attend to them.

Women have certain powers and skills that men just don't have, couldn't have, not in their nature. Sun Tzu taught us to understand the nature and landscape settings of our engagements. The nature and landscape we were dealing with in this internet infrastructure rollout were that men were running the show everywhere. Men ran the companies that were rolling across the country and around the world laying their pipes to connect the world, and men ran the companies that controlled the land and buildings where the pipes would have to penetrate to leave their information load. Men controlled the money, and men controlled the plans. That wasn't by design; it naturally evolved that way, an extension and manifestation of our hunter/gatherer prehistory DNA. We did learn later as a species that an agrarian society was more stable and efficient, but some guys never forgot that the fun was in the hunt. Those that could never forget, strode out every morning and took the risk to push out the boundaries of civilization ever farther, conquer ever bigger challenges and discover new ventures, adventures, knowledge, beauty, and open new worlds. For them, this became their passion, their honor, and the source of their self-esteem. It became their definition of themselves, and they longed to be recognized for it – at a core personal level.

That's just part of the story, though. The other part is the undeniable fact that part of their longing is that these men find women desirable. If you think I shouldn't say that, take it up with your biologist or your theologian; it's true. Sexual desire, like hunger, is a part of every man's physiology; it's in their DNA. It's hormonal. But its more than just biological, there is also a psychological component that drives motivation, affection, and action. Men admire and desire women they find attractive. Men want to take care of women that are nice to them and are engaging, and the men want to help them. They want that connection. That's just the way they're built, the men. That's just the way it is. That's every man with few exceptions. Nice girls, pretty girls, smart girls, engaging women move men; sometimes in ways they don't want to be moved. The men know it. The women know it. You can try and deny it, bury it, reject it, hashtag it, call it names, but it's nature, and it won't be denied. I'm not talking about the men who behave badly. I'm talking about the men who behave well. I'm talking about the men who behave normally. I'm talking about the modern-day hunters and adventurers.

Men looking upon women as objects of their sexual desire is not misogyny, chauvinism, or sexism; it's nature. It's the connection they're after. The motivation of these men to protect and care for the women they desire is also part of their nature. Chivalry is an outgrowth of their longing and a sign of respect and admiration. It's a manifestation of their longing for connection and recognition.

The men we were dealing with in our internet infrastructure rollout were the present-day versions of those men who walked out of the prehistory camps, risking it all in search of adventure. And like the first versions, they too carried the desire for recognition and connection. Buried deep perhaps, but it was there nonetheless. These were hardened men, those present-day hunters and adventurers, and as nature would have it, they became more agreeable in the hands of my assistants. This is so powerful and true, just writing the previous sentence will cause some men to want to meet my assistants knowing full well their own decision-making capability may be compromised, but they will want to come nevertheless. Hormones are powerful drugs. That penchant among men to consider women in a sexual way, without understanding why, is a ripe vulnerability indeed.

No touching.

The fuse was burning hot to get the 300 site portfolio lease re-negotiations done so our client's new network wouldn't collapse. We laid out the plan to get them done on time, and fix the terms so the future lease expirations would be staggered over time so our client would never again be faced with all the expiration dates on top of one another. We also added renewal options and termination rights to increase flexibility for our client. Protracted negotiations were not an option because of the short fuse on all the current lease expirations. My assistant handled the administration, communications, and relationships with the landlords and their brokers, keeping them happy and accommodating. I traveled, handled the markets and sites, negotiation strategies, the final contracts, and communications with my clients and their attorneys. In addition to the 300-site portfolio, we also handled the new switch and data center requirements as they came in. It was an effective streaming operation.

The cash flow was good. Hundreds of payments flowed in for the hub and pop site transaction, and more substantial amounts for the bigger switch sites and data centers also arrived. Life was good. We were building something important, impressive, and improving the world at the same time. In the C-suites of my clients, the positive energy was palpable, and all the employees throughout the organizations felt they were doing something important and fun – building a massive new communications and internet backbone, the likes of which no one had ever seen.

Carpe Tempore

Time is money, and how well you leverage your time with high-impact moments determines how much money and good you make for you and your clients. The SVP in charge of all the real estate at my most active client company was a process and procedures guy. His resume and street cred were impressive. He had helped build out the worldwide real estate infrastructure of one of the biggest overnight delivery companies in the world. He'd also built the headquarters campus for one of the biggest enterprise software solutions companies on the planet. Smart guy. He rode the tidal wave, we both road the tidal wave, at this company as it changed CEOs at each new gust of wind. He laid out the process for an even bigger national expansion, which included mergers with other companies and opening new markets fast by retrofitting existing structures and building new ones from the ground up.

He used three firms to handle all the real estate work: my firm, one out of L.A., and a third out of Houston. None of us had an exclusive relationship with him. This was smart because he could select which firm from his preferred list he wanted for each project, and each of us was incentivized to bring our best performance forward because of the on-going competition. Competition doesn't bother me at all; I thrive on it. I'm eager to compete. I think companies that limit their willingness to compete to the initial presentations (image over substance) and demand exclusive tie-ups with clients, lack energy and initiative. They're chickenshits. I think they're lazy. They may win the assignment, and they'll revel in their victory, but they don't bring their best game forward then, and the clients that agree to this are naïve. This SVP was smart, and the three of us competed on actual metrics, not on what we promised we could do, but what we actually did do locating, negotiating, and securing those rare sites. The Houston firm, the biggest company, was dropped from the list in fairly-short order.

As the new market rollout intensified, my client decided to divide the transaction work by facility type between my company and L.A. I would get the majority of sites, the hub and pop sites, because we were already performing on the 300 site ISP portfolio they had acquired. L.A. would do the new switches and data centers. He explained his plan and the details to us in a meeting in his office with the members of his real estate team present and then adjourned the meeting.

I wasn't happy with this new plan. The portfolio I was responsible for was a good project, but my upside was capped, and if the company released the funds to go get the bigger sites in a big way, I wouldn't benefit. Not only that, the switches and data center transactions were worth ten times the value of the smaller sites from an income perspective.

As the meeting adjourned, I accompanied my client to his office and asked him if he had a problem with my work. "No," he said, "I'm happy with your work. Why?"

We talked for a couple of minutes about the workload required for each of the different types of sites and the difference in potential revenue associated with each. We recounted the successes we had had with the number of switch and data center sites we had already put on the scoreboard for his company around the country, including build-to-suits, and the money we had saved them. We had a good relationship, and he acknowledged my concerns and my good work. After asking if I had the capacity to take on additional switches and data centers as well as the hub sites, he told me that I would be included in on the larger rollout along with L.A. if it happened.

The company did subsequently release the funds for the bigger rollout. I ended up doing half or more of the new switch and data center sites across the country over the next 18 months, generating savings to my client over Ten Million Dollars and an additional Million-and-a-Half Dollars for my firm and me. If I had kept quiet and been happy with what I had initially been told, that wouldn't have happened. You have to advocate for yourself and your client because no one else will if you don't. I stepped up and asked for what I wanted and what I thought was right. That ten minutes and a half-gram of initiative was worth Ten Million Bucks to my client and a Million-and-a-Half-bucks to my company and me. If he had turned me down, I would have lost only ten minutes. Get out of your chair and go ask for what you want.

There are a couple of takeaways worth learning from this event. The conversation I had with my client took place at a time when change had been initiated by authority, in this case, my client. Things were in flux. When things are changing, that's the time to change things. If I had waited days, weeks, or months, to bring it up, the first change would have become the accepted norm and a new change less welcome in favor of legacy and lethargy.

Also, that conversation took place in person, face to face, stomach to stomach. The outcome might have been different if it happened on the phone or other messaging. There is a human connection that is present when two people are face to face, and unless any rapport is damaged, people are more accommodating to others in their physical presence. It's harder to say, "no." They're more likely to say "yes."

Lastly, my work performance had shown the advocacy I exerted for my client. Though that doesn't guaranty a place at the next event, smart clients, the ones you want to keep, acknowledge what you've earned.

Seize the moment. That ten minutes at my client's office door was high-impact time. Identify those moments, and don't waste them.

Wired

Well-planned and well-funded rollouts can be some of the most fun and lucrative projects to work on.

I combed the country looking for the right properties. With few exceptions, local brokers weren't much help because they didn't know the importance or details of what those special buildings possessed. The owners found themselves alone without a way to connect with the new internet players in the market. I was the connection.

In the early days of this rollout, most sellers and landlords didn't even know they had properties that could be converted and made suitable for this type of requirement. Some of the best buildings were products of the old savings and loan meltdown the Feds had disposed of by the Resolution Trust Corporation through auction. Like the old 1930's concrete buildings that housed "C" quality tenants paying low single-digit rents with fifty percent vacancies; but had the extreme floor loading capacity, clear height, and access to redundant fiber lines and proximity to big electrical power. These buildings were often scattered along the fringes of downtowns across the country, but some were located right in the densest part of the cities. Many investors accidentally found themselves having won a lottery without even knowing the infrastructure potential. One building I dealt with, the ownership had paid only $22.00 per square foot for the building at auction, but after a several Hundred-Thousand Dollar electrical upgrade, internet network tenants lined up willing to pay $38.00 per square foot per year for the space. A seven-month payback and pants-wetting future returns.

These buildings were diamonds in the rough, and I scoured almost every inch of installed fiber in the biggest markets in the U.S. to find them. I hit all the major markets in 32 different states during this time.

Often the governing municipalities didn't even know how to deal with the new use requirements. As part of our redundant systems requirements for reliability, our clients always needed large backup diesel generators, fuel tanks, and battery stacks to maintain redundant sources of power. But in Lower Manhattan, there's no open land to place them. They would have to go on the roofs or elevated floors of the buildings. But the city disallowed large fuel storage tanks in elevated locations, allowing only for piping to transport the fuel from the tanks to the backup generators. One block from Wall Street and Broad, the solution was to keep the fuel tanks small, but install fuel pipes that were 36" in diameter eleven floors up, giving us plenty of fuel volume stored in the "pipes" to run the generators.

I saw hundreds, maybe thousands, of buildings that had the potential for our use. Some were the hardest of fortifications like the former Federal Reserve vault that extended seven floors underground with walls of reinforced concrete 36" thick in Minneapolis. Some were historical linchpins like the old art deco monster in Manhattan, AT&T Long Lines Building, that had once carried all of the overseas communications during World War II over the vast web of copper wire still hanging from the ceiling in its underground tombs. Others presented special challenges like the abandoned high-cubed warehouse in Jacksonville, FL, that had been taken over by bats that had deposited nearly a foot of guano on the floor and walls. Some buildings presented unique dangers. I remember looking at an ancient industrial power panel in the moist basement level of an old 30's era mid-rise concrete building on the edge of downtown Philadelphia with a group of about six men. We stood in a row about three feet in front of the 12-foot electrical panel made up of giant copper plates and a dozen or more massive circuit breakers, all old copper throw switches about a foot long, all exposed. Nothing was enclosed; everything was exposed. The buzzing of the transformers was almost deafening, and the 13,000 volts so near and exposed made the hair on your body stand up. I thought it was exhilarating, but the water dripping down the walls kept my attention. I decided to step out of the puddle that had formed at our feet.

Three years into my new company with only a researcher and an assistant, we were doing a bigger volume of work than my former company with 35 brokers. We did it with almost no marketing. I turned new business away. We were operating in stealth mode. We didn't advertise our capabilities, and we didn't advertise our clients. While other brokerages would gather for their annual galas, patting each other on the back and handing out plaques to put on their walls showing how much money they made (even the low producers got plaques), we threw the invitations in the trash, stayed stealth and focused on the mission. We had almost no competition. Those who needed us found us. Our performance spoke volumes. We didn't need accolades, nor did we need manufactured image or spin. We had a rare skill. The people in those ballrooms weren't celebrating their clients; they were celebrating the income they had extracted from them. Their clients weren't in the room, except to the extent they were being served up as the main course on the buffet table. The brokerage community partied as co-conspirators. I celebrated with my clients and our work together.

Don't get me wrong. I like money, and we were making a lot of it. Our production would certainly have been applauded at those parties. It just all seemed like nonsense to me, and misaligned.

Making a lot of money can go to your head. You can start to think you really are smart enough that you don't make mistakes. Hubris sets in, and you bask in the warmth of your own dopamine and oxytocin cocktail as you share your brand of genius with the world. New entrepreneurial ideas flourished in my head, and old competitors came calling offering signing bonuses and glory. I remember one recruiting call I took in my AMG coupe as I accelerated passed 100 mph leaving the Santa Fe city limits on my way to my next data center deal. "What could I do to entice you to come on board?" the caller asked. "A million bucks maybe," I said. The truth was, I wouldn't go back to the bigs, ever. I figured I couldn't be stopped. It wasn't all open road ahead, however. Mercedes had put a 155-mph governor on that little street machine to keep people like me in check. Damn.

Over 100 million miles of fiber optic cable was installed during that period, but at its most oversupplied point, only five percent of it was being used. More than 100 telecommunications companies went bankrupt in spite of nearly a Trillion Dollars a year invested in new fiber installations and capital and operating leases. It was like the railroad companies that opened up the wild west, most failed. Industries flourish then fail; some flourish again. Companies flourish then fail; some flourish again. Everything cycles. Everything changes. Everything reverts to the mean, eventually.

10

HUBRIS

"Life would be tragic if it weren't funny."
-- Stephen Hawking

The ancient Greeks were deeply attuned to human behavior. It was a central theme in their philosophy, teachings, and pastimes. They well defined the characteristics, causes, and unpleasant outcomes of hubris. Though mostly in a thespian portrayal, their observations of this malady were dead on nevertheless.

In simplest of terms, the Greeks defined hubris as extreme arrogance that challenged the gods, which in turn brought about the downfall of the perpetrator. In real terms, hubris is an estimation that one's competence and skills defy the laws of nature. The consequences are easy to predict. The lack of humility is a tell. Being equal to the gods is one thing, thinking you're better than the gods is ignorance. After all, one should always remember that Hippocrates, the creator of the Hippocratic Oath, and who cured so many people of discomfort and disease, eventually fell sick and died.

I had overcome so much, I thought. I'd made my point. Focusing solely on a dominant strategy determined by market scarcity to drive alpha performance had worked. There was no ballast or shit to deal with; less was more. Clients sought me out. People I didn't know came to me asking advice about real estate and technology, some offering co-ventures, some peddling startup ideas. Money flowed in, lots of it. New horizons beckoned. The constant dopamine feed masked any insecurities I felt. Lots of people wanted to be my partner. Lots of people wanted to be my friend. Oxytocin kind of blurred the lines between right and wrong, between rational thought and emotional urgings. I was feeling good.

My playing field had become the world, and I was feeling free and fueled with resources as I'd never experienced before. I made angel investments in new startup ventures: an internet recruiting company, a venture fund of venture funds startup, and an emerging market commodities exchange. I pursued other projects as well around my knowledge of real estate and technology, like a discounted pure-play buyer rep residential brokerage and an array of micro data centers in the smartest small towns in America.

The Houston company that had been dropped from the telco rollout had developed a database to track properties and leases for clients. It was clunky and cumbersome. One of my communication services clients had hired another small company out of Chicago with a similar product to handle the administration of the docs and money for their portfolio. There were several companies backed by venture capital bringing their lease administration applications to the marketplace. Other small companies were coming out with their own products, too.

My work with property portfolios had been extensive and lucrative. I thought adding portfolio administration would be a complement to my existing business, but I wanted some control as to the functionality of the program. I reached out to a number of these software firms to see if we could structure some type of partnership where I could brand their application and customize it for my own portfolio work. To my surprise, they were reluctant. They didn't want to give up that much control, and I think they were a little embarrassed about what their programs could actually do. When I explained my needs and plans to them, mostly they demurred.

I decided to build my own simple lease administration application. I started designing the logic, algorithms, and interface. I liked the work. Days turned into nights, turned into days again. I was in flow. I used as many off-the-shelf tools I could find, and in about two weeks, I had a working desktop beta version.

It was a sleek little stand-alone program that housed the critical dates, compliance issues, lease abstracts, rent payments, and keyword searches of the documents in digital storage. It was clean and useful. I hadn't intended to market this version as a product, but soon I had several clients on board, including one of the growing online travel companies.

About that time, I was introduced to the group handling the portfolio of one of the biggest retailers in Indonesia. They flew me to Jakarta to demonstrate my software to their real estate and IT people, and their senior staff. Most liked the program, but the IT people were underwhelmed with the off-the-shelf platforms I had used. They wanted something more robust and scalable. I said I would have it rebuilt. Doing that, we could also add new functionality that wasn't included in the original program and put it on the web. The remainder of my week in Southeast Asia became a giant brainstorming session and torrential download of everything they could want an application to do. I met with dozens of people within the firm discussing all sorts of new functionality and potential. It would be a massive expansion of its capabilities. I was confident I could build the logic and algorithms, but I would have to bring on strong programming talent to handle the code. I built a new stand-alone-prototype which demonstrated much of the new functionality, and some clients started to use that as I worked on putting the new web app together.

I entered into contracts with programmers. First, one U.S. company, then another, but neither company could figure out how to adequately program my algorithms or how to build suitable workarounds of their own. I'd given both my functioning stand-alone prototype, but months and money burned, and progress was almost non-existent. I had nothing that was useful. The work was second-rate, and I decided nothing was salvageable. Into the trash it went, as I worked to figure out what my next steps would be. I thought about offshoring the programming work to places like India or Vietnam, but I didn't have any contacts there and wasn't excited about signing on with yet another third-party contracting company even though they had purported ties there. Then providence struck.

I walked into a Starbucks for a caffeine fix, a double doppio with cream. There was a man at a table near me engrossed in a computer science book. I leaned in and asked if he was a SQL programmer. He said, "not really," but said he had a friend who was. These two guys became a central part of my project. They were both from India, super smart, and soon I felt confident that with their help, I could build the web-based lease administration program I was wanting.

One of the things that impressed me about these two was how they approached the work. The first thing they did was take my expanded prototype of the software and what documentation I had and started breaking it down to its most basic parts. Then rebuild it using my algorithms and new algorithms they created after learning the program. Not only were they able to program my algos, but they improved on them and had new ideas on how to make the program better. They did months of work on spec without asking for compensation.

After I did hire them to do all the programming, I asked why they did so much work up-front without compensation, considering I had previously burned through two U.S. companies. One of these guys told me his Hindu grandmother taught him as a child that if you mistreat people in this life, you'll come back as a rat in the next. I believe him. I know a lot of rats.

Over more than a year, we worked on fully developing the app and expanded its capabilities beyond what we discussed in Jakarta. They used programming talent in the U.S. and India. I love the logic of how expansive databases work and the creativity developing the algorithms to take all the stored information and combine it, parse it, compare it, gauge it, display it, move it, report it, and stow it. You build an inner world of your design, and it does your bidding.

I would spend hours in my office late at night reviewing the programming, algos, and interfaces wanting to make it work just right. I spent nearly a hundred percent of my attention and effort trying to make this thing work the best it could. My consulting and transaction work began to dry up because I was concentrating on this project. My brain was focused on the tiny details that had staggering implications throughout the app. It was compelling, and I tuned out all other info and life, including my angel investments.

"Get all the information you want in 18 seconds or less" was our aim and tagline, and we succeeded.

The technology notwithstanding, lease administration was a labor-intensive business. All the commercial leases had to be abstracted and manually entered into the program. You couldn't count on the quality of the old abstracts provided by our clients. Over ten percent of the critical dates they provided were wrong. Commercial leases are 40 to 140 pages long, and you need a real estate or legal background to comprehend them properly. To correctly abstract a lease can take three or four hours with a skilled lawyer or paralegal doing the work. Add another hour and a half for adequate audit procedures. There were many thousands of leases to abstract. No AI was available, and offshoring that work was sporadic at best. Files provided by clients were often missing pages, missing data, out of order, and often a mess.

One of the largest private security companies in the world hired us to manage their portfolio. They were a prison operator and immigration enforcement company, and we had to convert all their hardcopy lease files to digital form and enter the data. Their hardcopy files were a mess. We had to reconstruct most of their records to even start. I wondered if they knew who or where their prisoners were if their record-keeping was so bad for their facilities. This group was a major government contractor, and their records were a disaster.

The web-based program we rolled out was extraordinary. It efficiently and elegantly tracked all critical areas of portfolio administration and produced cogent and timely alerts and action items. Included was detailed information on the physical sites, lease abstracts, subleases, ownership rights, obligations, critical dates, budgeting and accounting, contact information, digital document management, special projects management, facilities maintenance, key performance indicators (KPIs), and on and on. It did everything. The software was first-rate and enterprise-grade, utilizing triple tier architecture – a user interface layer, business logic layer, and data access layer. It was fully scalable. State of the art, it was a work of art.

The world had changed. The markets had changed.

The competition in the lease administration space had become outrageous. In addition to the existing companies offering similar products, more and more new companies were coming online, each with their own product model and some with massive funding. I had financial partners, but we weren't prepared or willing to match the many millions being spent to service the burn rate of the venture-backed operations. There was also a shift towards full enterprise software. Massive programming was required to stay in that race, and the lease administration function was becoming commoditized.

We had created a beautiful program, but we didn't have a true strategic differentiator that set it apart from all the other lease administration apps that were available. As beautiful and elegant as our program was, without a strategic differentiator that put it into a class by itself, it was in the same class with everyone else, and this class was over-crowded. That dog don't hunt.

We had built an application to help companies scale their businesses and bring economies of scale to the administration of their property portfolios, but there were no economies of scale in my company. The bigger we got, the more money we lost; but in order to compete, we had to get bigger, and bigger meant more capital burn. I was pushing a boulder uphill, but the top of the hill kept getting farther away, like a Hitchcock nightmare.

I had ventured into the world of programming as an adjunct to my core competency of site selection and negotiations, thinking the lease administration would be a strategic differentiator. It wasn't. It wasn't my primary purpose, but it had become all-consuming, and my real estate business languished as a result. The burn rate was stupefying, and there didn't seem to be a way to close that gap. All my competition was 100% focused on their software as their sole product, and they were burning money to grow, but nobody was making any money. NOBODY WAS MAKING ANY MONEY! Transit Street loomed in my mind. Lease administration had become ubiquitous. It was like we were all digging our own graves, and some had really big shovels. It was going to turn into a mass grave. I looked around and thought maybe we should stop digging. It was time to refocus on where strategic differentiation and true alpha performance could be achieved.

When You have to Launch a Comeback

If you've ever found yourself in circumstances that you need to speak in terms of a comeback, then you know that it sucks.

Shit happens. Markets change. Black swan events occur.

Sometimes things don't go according to plan. Sometimes forces beyond your control move against you. Sometimes you burn out. Sometimes you're the victim of friendly fire or a self-inflicted wound. Sometimes hubris interferes. Sometimes you might fail. There is only one bit of insight you need to understand before you can make your comeback. It's always your fault. If you failed, it's your fault.

You don't want to hear that, do you? It might even piss you off. You might like having excuses. Excuses let you off the hook. They let you be a victim. As a victim, you can shirk responsibility and lay the blame at someone else's feet. Let me make it abundantly clear. If you failed, it's your fault. It's not that your mom or dad wasn't there to rescue you or even love you for that matter. It wasn't because you didn't go to the right school or because of the pigment of your skin or how many X chromosomes you have. You failed to find the way around the obstacles that were in your way. If you failed, it's not because you've been oppressed or denied or criticized or mocked. It's not because your lover left you or because you don't feel you have had the chances that other people had. You failed because you failed and it's your fault. You failed to objectively understand the landscape and act on it. You failed to do your research and your homework so you were more prepared than the other guy. You failed to take responsibility to find the workarounds to beat the obstacles. You failed to properly game out the various scenarios, find the right dominant strategy, and follow it. You failed to get the job done. No use whining about how life is unfair. Take note: Life is unfair, and nobody is going to make it fair for you. So fucking what? To paraphrase Ted Turner, stop complaining about the wind and adjust your sails!

So, you've failed. So what? You're lying in a bloodied heap on the ground, a failure, what do you do? You're standing on the precipice of Edgar Allen Poe's Abyss, what are you going to do? Are you going to shrink and fall in the hole, or are you going to get big and own the facts and get ready to fight on? There are people that have had it way worse than you that have done extraordinary things. Were you dealt a worse hand than Steven Hawking? The facts are simple. Life is unfair, and nobody is going to make it fair for you. You failed to understand the landscape and see the failure coming. You failed to work around the obstacles.

Jack Ma, the founder of Alibaba, said, "Never give up. Today is hard, tomorrow will be worse, but the day after tomorrow will be sunshine." Never give up. You can fight your way back. Make a plan; it's the launching pad for your next success. Your plan helps you articulate your intention. Failure isn't the opposite of success; it's part of its foundation.

Take an accounting of your current situation. Know your landscape. Take an accounting of your current resources. Take an honest accounting of your knowledge and training, your strengths and your weaknesses, but never short-change yourself. You can do more than you know. With the right dominant strategy, you can do just about anything except go against nature. Build your goals and make some audacious. Where do you want to go? What will muster your passion? Reach beyond what's known and create something new.

Peak Abyss

If you've never failed, you're special – probably lying. If you're like me, you've been bloodied more than a couple of times.

Failing at something important can cause an oscillating response of disappointment you feel over and over again, and sometimes interspersed with resurgent grief from prior setbacks. This only serves to reinforce and bring into focus weighty feelings of fear, shame, and self-doubt – all gravity. That all sucks. If you can shirk that crap, do it. If it's your nature to be hyper-critical of yourself, or if you just plain like feeling bad and you can't quit that, you'll need to engage a different course of action for your successful comeback or turnaround. Learning from defeat is too obvious to mention, but your head and heart must be in the right place to leverage those learnings into your next new thing.

Failure is an excellent catalyst to help define the gap for your goofproof goals, but the associated weighty feelings are counterproductive. Instead of reliving the disappointments of your setbacks, go back to all your prior disappointments and defeats and focus on your subsequent recuperation, rejuvenation, regeneration, and reconstruction that took place. Most failures don't last, but your regeneration does. And if the impact of the failure does last, your regeneration is the strength that moves you beyond it and live free in spite of it. Explore those moments of recuperation, rejuvenation, regeneration, and reconstruction. Go to zero and re-experience them. Create them new again. I often think of my solo trek into the mountains after the Transit mess, and that night spent on top of the peak and the subsequent morning there. I'm always moved. I'm always lifted up. I've created other moments like that too.

I remember when I was building my first company and money was tight and I didn't always know we'd survive. During the toughest times, I was looking down the barrel of another failure. I'd think and plan what I wanted the company to be and what I wanted my life to be, but I felt I was missing something, like the last crucial piece of a Chinese puzzle, a Kongming Lock, that makes it solid and whole. I worked hard trying to find the answer, sometimes putting myself on a 100-hour per week work schedule to shore up against failure and not miss anything. I didn't want to take the time to sleep. I'd work into the night, sometimes all night. But sometimes the work didn't come, and it was just a sleepless night.

It was winter, and on some of those sleepless nights when it would start to snow, and it looked like it would be a heavy storm, I would take my 4-wheel-drive, leave my house in town, and venture alone into the mountains. I liked the pristine environment late at night with the new blanket of snow and no tracks except the wild animals that had roamed through. I would drive old railroad grades, abandoned mining trails, high-mountain off-road passes, places I had no business being that late at night or with a heavy winter storm upon me. I liked the challenge. I liked the solitude. I liked the feeling of the slow surf across mounds of white and the deathly quiet as the snow absorbed all the sound except the grinding of the engine. I marveled at the extreme beauty, power, and energy of the natural world in those extreme circumstances. I liked having the skill to be able to navigate it, survive it, and master it. I never really thought about the risk, only what needed to be done at every moment so I could keep moving forward and not get stuck or slip off into a ravine or off a cliff. I enjoyed the confidence I had in myself and the machine I was driving, and the knowledge of the capabilities and fitness of each.

When I would reach the top, and there was always a top, I'd stop and get out and just feel the immensity of the moment and the place – to feel the cold wind and ice against my face, alone on top of a mountain in a winter storm, surrounded by the stillness and blackness of the night except for the endless snowflakes bearing down on me like a friendly vertigo. I felt alive and free. It was often two or three o'clock in the morning. I'd then head home, sometimes forward and the hundred miles or more the big loop might bring, or back down the lonely tracks I'd made on the way up, not always to be seen under the piles of more new snow.

I would get to my house and crawl into bed just as the sun was coming up, refreshed and confident. I'd sleep well.

Those late-night winter drives in the high country might not have been the smartest things I could have done, but I'm glad I did them. They helped shape my life. I remember every one of those late-night trips. Those drives were moments carved out of time that gave me peace, joy, and serenity. I didn't know it at the time, but it was a reset to zero for me, and I would start the next day rejuvenated and confident and ready to build new.

The work I did in Indonesia was right after 9/11. I stayed at the Intercontinental Hotel south of Jakarta. The soldiers guarding the driveway entrance to the hotel were equipped with automatic weapons and bomb-sniffing dogs. They would check all the passengers and look under the vehicles for explosives before they would let us pass into the serpentine maze they had created with concrete barriers leading to the hotel.

The company I was doing work for insisted that I be accompanied by an escort or driver whenever I was in public, in route to their offices, or returned to the hotel at night. Since I stood nearly a foot taller than most of the population, my client discouraged me from being out alone during that tense time, particularly at night. Volatile elections were approaching too, and police riot gear lined the streets in anticipation of impending anarchy. Nevertheless, after I was safely deposited at the hotel after the workday, I would venture out into the city on my own to see what there was to see, leaving the hotel grounds by walking out the serpentine maze and passed the armed guards.

I tell this story because it was during those evenings wandering the crowded streets as the cars inched their way through throngs of street vendors and skinny cattle between the lanes, that I discovered something beautiful. It was a version of Tom Yam Soup unlike any other I had ever tasted. It wasn't the Thai version made with crushed chilis and sour paste you find in most restaurants in the U.S. This was a deep fish, lime, ginger, and cilantro broth; steaming, spicy with tiny Thai peppers and scallions. Coconut milk is added for body and to round out the edges. The soup is white and green, smooth and hot, accompanied by some of the biggest prawns I'd ever seen. I kept coming back for more.

The disparate ingredients coming together in unison is what intrigued me initially. It wasn't just the soup, but the culture and tension and squalor and aspirations that this soup emerged from, that it could be prepared among all that and served in a porcelain bowl on a white tablecloth. The taste is why I keep making it. Life is hard sometimes, but there is always beauty somewhere. If you're missing it, go find it.

11

STREET SKILLS

"Look well into thyself; there is a source of strength which will always spring up if thou wilt always look."
-- Marcus Aurelius

When I was first growing my businesses, I tried to distance myself and escape from that part of my life where, as a young boy, I had the role of a street urchin and lout; maybe not a true street urchin, maybe not a true lout, but enough of a delinquent where the street became part of my DNA. All authority was to be suspect, and I made things happen for myself by my own force of will and mental acuity. As an adult, I tried to put that period down, keep it hidden, pretend it had not happened. I didn't respect it and assumed others didn't either. Business was my new business and the street was not to be a part of that, or so I thought. The truth is, though, no matter how far removed from the street you become, no matter how much money you make, no matter how educated, powerful, respected and accepted you become, the street is always a part of you. It's part of your core. The street makes you resourceful like nothing else can.

The street teaches you things that nothing else does, skills to keep you alive and moving forward with no support other than your own mind and intention. When my young life was falling apart, I thrived on the street. My family said I was shit, but on the street, I ruled the day. The skills I developed there were sharp and effective. Because of the dangers on the street and at home, I learned to develop a cutting intellect that ignores distractions and focuses on the situation and objectives at hand. Anything less leaves you open and vulnerable, and that's not acceptable. Risk is a way of life; you learn to accept it. In fact, you learn to accept risk at levels few are willing to embrace, but that's only possible with a robust and focused intellect. Because of this, I learned to respect my brain. That was the first glimpse I had of real self-respect and self-esteem and probably the only reason I was able to get out of that early shit-hole life.

I started out as a scared little kid, but I learned to overcome fear. The threats and risks were ever-present back then, and I was afraid much of the time. But that's not sustainable. You either succumb to it, or you overcome it. For me, fear became almost meaningless. A will to take advantage and live in a supreme way is what replaced it.

I became resilient to pain and uncertainty. I felt those to the core, but my capacity to withstand those pressures became nearly boundless. I plowed through pain and defeat, sometimes denying them, sometimes overcoming them, but always learning from them and moving forward. I climbed back up every time smarter and stronger. Uncertainty was just the constant backdrop to be gamed out for patterns and likely outcomes.

I learned to be self-reliant because I didn't think I could depend on anyone.

I learned to persevere – never stopping, never giving up, never succumbing; because to give up meant to die. It meant my life force, the thing that keeps me independent and whole, would be extinguished.

I was angry, angry at everything and everybody, including myself. But I learned to use that anger and channel it outward and for productive ends. Anger became a source of positive energy to plow through any interference.

I learned to use creativity to overcome obstacles, and there were so many obstacles.

I learned how to fight – my own demons and anybody else that stood in my way or needed to be taken down in my estimation.

I learned to protect myself at any cost. Foes needed to be rendered inert. In an odd paradox, however, that left only me remaining as my own greatest challenger.

I learned to embrace education and expand my knowledge always. I became an insatiable learner and voraciously consumed data and information, yet at the same time, I became critical of all information. I learned to accept nothing as fact except what I could independently verify.

I learned to be loyal because it seemed to me that was the most important thing in this world.

I developed a hunger, a hunger to build a great life, a life better than the one I'd been dealt.

Finally, I learned to appreciate and have gratitude for the few blessings that would come my way or that I would bring my way. And through it all, I learned to laugh regardless of the shitstorm. The tragedies and triumphs, the trivial and the consequential, each just another color in the collage of my life. Though, all to be taken seriously, I learned that seriousness needn't interfere with my joy and fun because life is fleeting and what purpose could there possibly be other than to enjoy it and have gratitude for the privilege of the moment.

I have lived my life knowing I've had these skills, but thought they were in spite of that scared little kid and how he lashed out. The truth of the matter is, I have these skills, and they are honed as well as they are because of that scared little kid attempting to break out and live. My fierce independence and sovereignty, and willingness to accept nothing less, are part of the result. Some of the best of me, maybe most of the best of me, are the skills and philosophies that street kid made for himself to survive. Those too, are what would take me to the next level. Whether making a comeback, or gapping up to a higher plane, I've been training for both my entire life. The insight of Marcus Aurelius is clear, "The impediment to action advances action. What stands in the way becomes the way."

PART THREE – HITMAN 3.0

--

BRAINS AND INFLUENCE

12

THE REAL VALUE ALGO

AND

WEAPONIZABLE MONEY BLUNDERS

"Those skilled in mathematical analysis know that its object is not simply to calculate numbers, but that it is also employed to find the relations between magnitudes which cannot be expressed in numbers and between functions whose law is not capable of algebraic expression."

-- Antoine Augustine Cournot, as translated by Nathaniel T. Bacon

The goal of every negotiation is your opponents' compliance with your objectives. The level of their compliance is a logarithmic response to how closely aligned their objectives are with yours, and the effectiveness of your applied influence on the former – your level of effectiveness moving your opponents' objectives to be more in alignment with your own. These changes occur in their brains, so we'll start there. You can't use outdated tools and worn-out tactics; they're useless. You're going to need new precision tools and the skills to go with them, like the precision of a new gamma knife to operate on their brains. That is what I'm going to give you.

Before you can get good at strategizing your negotiations, you need to know what most people get wrong in their decision making, particularly their economic decision making. When you know what they do wrong, you can avoid it yourself. When you know what they do wrong, you can weaponize it.

Too many times, I've been brought into situations where my clients have been saddled with the results of bad decisions by their people or advisors, and they ended up paying twice what they should. Too many times, I've been brought into situations where my clients have been saddled with subpar locations but were paying premium prices for the privilege. The objective of any negotiation is the optimal fusion of price and terms, and so-called professionals miss their chance to connect all the time. Mostly those failures go unnoticed and stay hidden from view. Nobody knows because nobody shines a light on it. They want A to be B, but you and I know it never is.

How could such feeble attempts and poor decisions have been made, and how do you fix them? The answer to both questions is the same. Understand the mistakes everyone makes in their economic decisions and learn to use the nature behind those negative influencers to make them work for you, and those you choose to represent. But before we can go there, we need a quick and cogent understanding of the unvarnished economics behind value and price.

Valutility

(I made up the name, and I expect a Nobel for the concept.)

Price discovery is determining your side's proper price for an asset, product, or skill, irrespective of market drivel or your opponents' desires. There are other definitions in financial academia, but you can ignore all those. All the material considerations in your negotiations are derivatives of your proper price discovery. The first and most important concept to understand is that price does not equal value. Value is intrinsic. Price is transactional, and it's a muddled mess; perfect for you to manipulate, if you don't get manipulated first.

Price discovery in a world swimming in market inefficiencies and confounded by meaningless data, misinformation, misdirection, and mistakes, is a skill few possess. Approach any decision about pricing and value of any asset, product, or skill with the same skepticism and scrutiny as that you apply to any hierarchical authority or position. Don't accept any of it that is shoveled to you -- none of it – ever.

A course study in microeconomics will teach you that the price of a thing is a function of the drive to equilibrium of supply and demand; the optimal price being the point where the number and demand of capable buyers is equal to the immediate supply and costs of the sellers. It is a simple binary principle that allows the market to accommodate adjustments of both demand and supply as the point of equilibrium is naturally, constantly, and automatically sought by market forces. This principle underscores most of the foundation of economic theory. It's a nice idea, simple, cute, and the principle works. But it's only partially true, and if you've ever had a conversation with a fellow traveler on an airplane ride comparing the cost of plane tickets, you'll know many other unseen variables impact pricing beyond simple supply and demand. Intended and unintended influences exist in the pricing of every asset, product, and skill, and make for inherent inefficiencies of every marketplace. More importantly, though, it's the inefficiencies in the brains of the market participants, the distractions, distortions, and cognitive biases of the participants, that have the most profound impact. That's where your biggest opportunities are. That's what you can leverage to create your biggest advantages. But you need the foundation of your proper price discovery first.

Value is not price, and likewise, vice versa. When the two are the same, there's parity, which rarely occurs. They're usually not even in the same ballpark. When they're divergent, which is most of the time, there's opportunity. There's always opportunity to negotiate better terms.

Value is inherent, innate, like one of Aristotle's essential characteristics. Price is driven by a messy mix of market supply and demand, intended and unintended influences brought on by the dynamics of human emotions and biases, and ultimately negotiations. The inefficiencies of all those are multitudinous. Value exists for the user, because of the user, and varies by user. Value is a function of the needs and desires of the user, and the utility provided by the asset, product, or skill, through its operational functionality or profitability as an investment vehicle. It's the qualitative and quantitative aspects of the utility that determine value, and therein lies the importance of valutility.

Valutility is the level of force inherent in the utility that satisfies the specific needs and desires of the user. Think of it as the thrust. Valutility takes into account all positive causal factors such as consistency, efficacy, and efficiency (including time) of the utility to be derived. These are the things that provide the thrust to make your company or investment fly. Valutility also takes into account the negative causal factors that produce drag. The probability of outcomes and level of risk or risk premium are also factored in. Valutility is the excess thrust, the amount of thrust which exceeds the drag, adjusted for the level of risk and probability. Value = Valutility (thrust) x Utility. The complete mathematical expression is posted on the web.

In this model, value is the benefit overtly driven to the user by valutility. The price will be a derivative of that. Without the value certainty derived from this model, the transactional characteristic of price will continue to drive market volatility and keep all the less-informed humans up at night.

Everything cycles. Everything always cycles, and the so-called market price of any asset, product, or skill at any point in time is either trending up or trending down on what is best described as a bubble/crash continuum, it's just a matter of degrees. Usually, the cycles are moderate, like the gentle waves of a rolling surf. Sometimes the earthquake of extreme volatility will hit and cause the rare, destructive, tsunami, but not until after a fantasy ride through paradise. Always know your own determination of value, and always keep an eye on the horizon.

The Lemmings' Ride
Bubbles First, ask Questions Later
Fear and Greed and Fantasy Thinking

Lemmings are adorable little creatures, but I don't take financial advice from them. They kill the executive functions of their little prefrontal cortices and instead look to their peers for instructions on how to interact with markets and commerce, ignoring the fact their peers have also shut down their executive brain functions and are blindly following the group. No matter though, they're in the group, part of the herd, and they feel comfortable being part of the herd and can joyfully, blissfully, with brains fully disengaged, excitedly squeak in unison: "Whoo Hoo! Here we go. Where we going? We don't know. Okay! Let's go!!!" Secretly though, each little lemming worries, "I hope this is the right thing to do," but they don't really want to find out because they're moving with the crowd, and their little brains are comfortably disengaged. They wouldn't know what to do differently anyway. They're infected by a form of groupthink that overrides rational thinking. Useful, critical questions aren't part of the plan. The only "plan" is to do what others are doing, and they feel safe because others are doing it. When challenged to justify and rationalize their non-decision decisions, they point to the "momentum" of the herd and the price action that's occurred. They don't acknowledge that the momentum is just the manifestation of the herd behavior, the very behavior they need to be questioning. In essence, their proof that what's happening is appropriate relative to the risk relies solely on the fact that it is happening; provided, of course, the momentum is running in their favor.

Without the benefit of the executive functions of their prefrontal cortices, the lemmings let their greed, desire to belong, and their fear of missing out (FOMO) run the show. They're left to the whims and hormones of their limbic systems as their most basic emotional urgings make their decisions. Fear, greed, pain, and pleasure, the most basic and primitive of all human emotions, are driving the bus, and not one rational thought gets through. Every lemming accepts the range of prices shoveled to them and are ecstatic if they've "saved" a couple of "discount" points from that.

This is the experience in an ascending bubble cycle. It's not investment, its speculation, sometimes just gambling. It's relying on the hope there is at least one more person more foolish than they who will pay more for the overpriced asset they just bought. No asset class is immune. In some instances, there is no valuable asset, just a belief, an appealing pile of shit. Bubbles are fairly easy to spot. What you don't know is how long they will last.

Following a basic S-Curve (think of it as the left half of a bell curve), early investments are made in an asset prompted by an appealing business case (or fraudulent business case). Then, because of increasing positive sentiment, it attracts more investment and speculation. After more speculation, there is greater media and social attention on the asset and its attractive price appreciation, which then fuels more enthusiasm and even more speculation. This manifests an exponential rise in the rate of pricing increases as the wave of lemmings step in fueled by their fear of missing out and the talk of a new pricing paradigm. Prices rise 10x, 100x, maybe more, and some people get rich, but then it peaks and starts down the slippery slope to reality.

The descent that follows, and the resulting inverted S-Curve, is a compressed version of the rise because the descents are usually much faster than the ascents. The mass of people that fueled the dramatic rise in prices then see a rapid decline in pricing, which can be devastating, maybe 99 or 100 percent or more if the adventure was funded with borrowed money. A lot of dumb and smart people alike have been caught up in this scenario and have been ruined.

Price does not mean value. Price does not mean utility. You can't fool nature by speculation. Nature, on the other hand, allows anyone to fool themselves long enough for the lesson to be learned over and over again.

It's after the bubble, after the crash, after total capitulation, that the scattered remains of disillusioned investors dot the landscape, and smart money then comes in with a vulture's eye to feed on the now underpriced assets (if there ever was any intrinsic value in them in the first place) to build new solid platforms that create profits and wealth and accelerate those along the new ascending S-Curve into the future, until it too, plateaus.

In varying scale and intensity, bubbles are always occurring, and the subsequent crashes likewise are always forming. Current market pricing is just a result of present expectations of future events. In rising markets, the bias is for continued rising prices. In declining markets, the bias is towards continued declining prices. These biases create the propensity for fundamentally overpriced assets in rising markets and underpriced assets in declining markets. Markets always tend to overshoot.

Everything cycles, through recurring cycles and supercycles, but everything eventually reverts to the mean. Benjamin Graham, Warren Buffett's teacher and mentor, said that in the short-term markets behave like voting machines, what's popular and what's not; but in the long run, markets are weighing machines, assessing the real substance and value of the asset.

Faulty pricing and people's willingness, sometimes eagerness, to succumb to it, is caused by their misguided mental machinations. You don't want to get caught in these traps. But you do want to know how to take advantage of them, so it's important to know what they are. Besides, it's a fun romp through these mortals' brains. Let's have a look.

Homo Economicus – Pure, Proud, and Extinct

In the early days of promise of free markets in the U.S., the prevalent economic thought assumed that commerce and markets were driven by thoughtful actors, making decisions in a rational and fair way, with relatively complete information, so to capitalize on, and capture, maximum utility and value of an asset, product, or skill. Sounds good, the smart human hominid, Homo Economicus, they were called, a pure and innocent creature. H. Economicus had the starring role in the Rational Choice Theory of economics.

It turned out, though, H. Economicus was a myth. The creatures who now stumble out onto the streets of L.A. or Beijing, with various payment methods at the ready, are more complicated mortals who have to deal with increasingly complex markets. They are driven not only by utility, but also by a need for self-identity, which they try to cobble together by their consumption, consumerism, and facade. They want to make decisions quickly, without complete information, in order to satisfy not only the actual needs of utility, but also behavioral and psychological needs of the self. But they are afflicted with a variety of internal and external biases. Their transaction decisions are used to try to fill the inescapable holes in their souls. Enter Motus Humanae, the emotional (economic) human. These are the teen girls from Pasadena, the hedge-fund managers from Greenwich, the tech entrepreneurs from Shenzhen, and basically everyone. These gamers and players and participants of modern-day markets are not rational beings, far from it, they are *rationalizing* beings. They invent the rationale necessary to support the "rightness" of their emotion-driven economic decisions.

Motus Humanae
"Manipulate me, please! Because it just feels right."

Notwithstanding the raw power of intellect, humans are subject to a nasty set of reason-depleting disorders that wreak havoc on any rational decision making. They're like some bug in a Stephen King-esque novel that bites people on the ass and then takes over their brains – and everyone gets infected. These humans are going to trip up, make mistakes, and make bad decisions for stupid reasons they're not even aware of.

Your understanding of these reason-depleting disorders and their role in distorting economic decision-making needs to encompass two perspectives: first, knowing of their existence so you can avoid having them impact your own decision-making processes, and second, knowing how to exploit them for your own benefit and that of your clients. These distortions pervert and corrupt any rational approach to optimal solutions, and they infect parties on both sides of any negotiation. These pesky human proclivities and the resulting deformity to optimal pricing and sentiment are so common that humans are predictably irrational in their economic behavior and decision making.

These reason-depleting disorders, these mental money blunders, are the fuel that makes my Tricks, Hacks, Hammers, and Cheats work. I've divided these disorders into four basic categories: Social Suckers, Lazy Brain Defects, Fear Fallacies, and Cognitive Coding Errors. Enjoy, and learn.

Social Suckers

Social Suckers deprive the mind of the critical thinking necessary for optimal decision making by suppressing the prefrontal cortex executive functions and replacing rational thought with the unconscious and powerful primitive desire to fit in and belong to the prevailing tribal caste by any means possible. It's an outdated survival instinct, but Social Suckers are what makes lemmings, lemmings.

Here are the worst offenders:

Social Contagion and Convergence. Social Contagion and Convergence is a phenomenon whereby sentiment and behaviors are adopted and shared among people through a process more like that of an infectious disease than reasoned choice. It's like a mind virus. It's clustering of similar human behavior in the absence of any coercion or rationale. This manifests as dumb, predictable, consumer behavior, the extremes of which can turn into buying frenzies fueled by easy money (bankers and politicians get infected too) and then selling panics.

This outbreak of human behavior spread by social means (and memes) doesn't even need to have a perceived benefit to the participants for the behavior to take hold. A wave of suicides occurred in Europe in the 19th century by people who had all just previously come in contact with Goethe's tragic tale, "The Sorrows of Young Werther," in which the hero, Werther, takes his own life.

Other examples of the contagion phenomenon include worthless initial crypto-coin offerings, worthless dot-com stocks, leveraged speculative housing with variable-rate mortgages, drug use, and teens eating laundry detergent pods. Don't let fiction or dumb shits influence your behavior.

Imitation Ethos. Humans are most comfortable being part of a group, almost any group. They'll willingly outsource their thinking and decision making to their group even as one lone critical thought would make them understand the fallacy of that non-decision decision. They want to belong to something; they want to be included. The fear of missing out, the fear of being ostracized, the fear of standing alone with nothing but their own mind and decisions, makes them shut down their brains and go with the crowd. This is how bubbles are formed and why they crash.

The colloquialism "drinking the Kool-Aid" refers to this non-thinking, group-joining, brainwashing phenomenon. It's instructive to know where this phrase came from. Jim Jones, a religious psychopath, convinced over 900 people that, in protest against legal action facing some of the leaders, it would be a good idea for everyone to kill themselves and each other, an act of "revolutionary suicide," by drinking cyanide-laced grape-flavored drink (it wasn't really Kool-Aid). It became known as the Peoples' Temple Jonestown Massacre. It was the ethos of the group that drove them to it. They'd previously voted as a group that suicide was a viable solution. They practiced the act ahead of time. You have to believe that of those 900, there must have been some people that thought maybe this wasn't such a good idea, but hey, everybody's doing it, so off they went and offed themselves (and their kids).

The next time you want to buy that over-priced asset in hopes of finding nirvana, or easy money, and think it's probably okay because everybody is doing it, think of Jim Jones.

Social "Proof." A derivative of Imitation Ethos, Social Proof allows humans to numb out, subordinate their thinking, and feel confident in their bad decisions and behaviors because other humans of the same social group, or friends, or people they respect or want to be like or otherwise follow in some way, are doing the same thing and that's "proof" it's a good idea. It's like an opioid that masks the hard realities of having to think. Social Proof doesn't have to be real to be effective, just believable. So-called "influencers" and spokespeople thrive on it. Companies use it to trigger your "aspirational" purchases. Salespeople tag you with it and try to sell you all kinds of shit because "people that think just like you" have bought it before.

Confirmation Bias, and its corollary, Denial of Unfavorable Evidence. Humans crave information that confirms previously held beliefs, information that confirms the rightness of previous actions and decisions, even if its isolated and even if it's been contradicted by valid information to the contrary. They're drawn to it. They lean into it. Humans crave an echo chamber, an endless feedback loop of information they can interpret as validating their understanding of the world above all else, not the integrity or veracity of that information, and not new information that may shape their understanding. They don't want their understanding shaped; they want it endorsed. Have a chuckle and help them endorse it. It'll clear your path and cost you nothing. I don't feel compelled to share my principles if my opponents are going to cherry-pick and manipulate evidence.

Inequity Aversion. As selfish and greedy as many humans are, they still have some inherent semblance of fair play at work and will, perhaps unwittingly, try to fix the inequities presented. Appeals to fair play on a personal level work because it's part of their DNA. It works even better if the entire process is on public display wherein the respondent may be subject to criticism.

Reciprocal Altruism. A derivative of Inequity Aversion, Reciprocal Altruism refers to a built-in mechanism that naturally tries to fill the perceived vacuum created by being the recipient of an altruistic act. This natural inclination is not satisfied by paying it forward, but by paying it back... to the person that first proffered it. Give your subject counterpart some act of generosity; you will create a vacuum that your subject will be driven to fill by making a gesture of giving in return.

Lazy Brain Defects

Lazy Brain Defects prevent people from understanding the details of the decisions facing them and push them to make decisions with incomplete or inaccurate information. The following are the most prevalent culprits:

Propensity for Simple Solutions. Many humans have simple minds, and they don't want to exercise them much. They find complex solutions tiring, and they don't want to take the time and energy to figure them out to see which is the best; it's just too hard. Humans like to keep it simple. If a satisfactory solution presents itself that's simple, well, you can forget the complex one no matter how good it is. Present your complex solutions to your counterparts along with one simple one, the one that leads to the outcome you desire. That's the one they'll likely select in order to avoid the effort involved analyzing the others.

Propensity for Minimally Satisfactory Solutions. Humans are lazy creatures. They will accept the first acceptable set of circumstances that come their way instead of waiting, persevering, and exerting the effort necessary to achieve better, more optimal results. Most humans likely will not even know what their optimal result might look like. It's important for you to know yours; it might very well be an acceptable one for your counterpart. If not, resist and make your counterpart work and work and work some more to get theirs. They'll eventually tire and succumb to your way of thinking.

Reliance on Heuristics. Virtually every decision made by humans relies solely on mental shortcuts, not facts; estimates, not calculations.

Heuristics is an approach to decision making that relies on what's easy to discern, not what's complete or accurate. The purely rational is set aside for the sake of ease and simplicity, just enough to suffice. It is important for you to know the math and details, but your counterpart will not want to bother. So, help yourself by helping your counterparts save themselves from the anguish of having to understand the data by presenting them a clear and easy path to the outcomes that satisfy their most basic estimates of their needs.

Typecasting and Stereotyping. This is heuristics at their worst. Typecasting and stereotyping is the mental misfiring that mislabels other humans, groups, or companies of a certain type, or that have common characteristics; by assuming they all have the same characteristics, needs, requirements, problems, or other attributes without actual knowledge or supporting information that such assumptions are true. They assume that a corollary of one characteristic with another will always be true within the group, when, in fact, it is not.

Whenever I enter a new transaction, the people involved usually expect me to act like every other broker they've ever met with the same triggers for fear and incentives. That suits me fine. I use it to my advantage, as you'll see in the next chapter.

External Reference Dependency. People often have some benchmark or outside reference point with which to base decisions as the sole metric in their decision process. For instance, a landlord might think any rent that covers his mortgage nut is "good enough." Or any rent that is higher than what his neighbor got for his space a year ago is "good enough." Learn what your opponents' outside reference points are because they can be mitigated, substituted, disproved, and ridiculed. If an external reference point suits your purpose, use it.

Price Equals Value Fallacy. Humans almost always equate price with value. Humans assume the $1,500/hr lawyer is more effective than the $150/hr lawyer. Humans assume the diamonds in the $10,000 pair of earrings are of a higher quality than the $6,500 pair. The reverse holds true as well. People will assume the lesser-priced item is of poorer quality than the more expensive one. That is why discounting is often not an effective strategy and can be self-defeating.

Limited Attention Capacity. People have limited bandwidth, and if faced with too many options, they will overload and short circuit. When you see the smoke coming out of their ears, you'll know their decision-making is regressing and falling back on emotion-driven biases such as typecasting, stereotyping, and heuristics so to bypass the brain and avoid any actual thinking and the resulting feared meltdown. You can use this to your advantage, of course. The integrity of the decision-making process of the afflicted is severely compromised and open to your manipulation.

Fear Fallacies

Fear Fallacies can be the most powerful blocks to the decision-making process, creating a false, but urgent need for humans to move their avoidance strategies into high gear. Their dominant strategy can be summed up in one word: Run!! If they're running from situations because of unfounded fears, that limits possible positive outcomes and prevents the most optimal solutions from being achieved. These blocks block critical and creative thinking.

Loss Aversion. Studies have shown that humans will fight more than twice as hard to keep from suffering a loss than they will to gain an equivalent amount. The fear humans feel at the prospect of suffering a loss, significantly outweighs the drive they feel to gain an equal amount. Unless there's a passion at play, the greatest motivation for action is to prevent loss, not secure gain. Structure your games accordingly.

Stress Response to Market Volatility. Volatility in the marketplace is felt in the nervous system of the players. Fear and greed take over, and a flood of hormones disable their prefrontal cortex executive functions. The act of critical thinking is replaced with reptilian compulsion. Greed is a powerful motivator, but remember that fear of loss is the greater catalyst. When volatility is high, stress is high, and humans will be less rational and act with hyper-diligence to defend against their feared loss or to satisfy their fear of missing out.

Perceptions of Scarcity. Humans want what they can't have. Their fear of missing out is heightened when perceived supplies of an asset, product, or skill are low. It's merely the perception of scarcity that drives their FOMO, not necessarily the facts. Given a fixed demand for something, as the object becomes scarcer, the price goes up. If the supply of an object is fixed and demand goes up, the price goes up. There are also structural causes for scarcity, such as lack of funding capacity or availability or logistics problems. Regardless, all these real forms of scarcity, merely perceived scarcity triggers an emotional response which heightens drive and demand at a visceral level. Their fear of missing out on something scarce will move them to action to fill that vacuum and reduce their resistance to price, create greater pricing elasticity – prices go up.

Fear of Criticism. Most every human you deal with will be a cog in the hierarchical machinery in some way, whether it's at work or family, lender, or other social or business systems. They will readily choose to go down paths of least resistance, meaning least criticism, in order to avoid that conflict. They don't want any criticism. They don't want to be ostracized. They don't want to be cast out. In the tribal past, that would have meant death. Today, it's merely social insecurity. Nevertheless, asking your subject counterpart to undertake actions that would bring on scrutiny is pointless. Your desired course of action must be one your subject thinks will be free of criticism.

Fear of Shame. Fear of Shame is the real reason Fear of Failure is a thing. Fear of Failure can stop the smartest humans in their tracks. It's the most shameful of all the reason-depleting disorders because what's really holding the people back is not the failure so much as fearing the associated shame they'll feel for being exposed as a loser for their failure. It's all over-amplified in their heads, of course, but no matter, it's done its damage. It's not a surprise, though; it's one of the byproducts of living a life of image over substance. They'd lessen both fears if they didn't rely on reflected esteem so much, but instead did the research and actual calculations and trusted in their own judgment and worth.

Cognitive Coding Errors

These gems are the product of faulty internal programing that can have the victims believing that down is up and day is night, and yes, A is B. They become blind to the reality of a situation until it hits them squarely in the face, and sometimes not even then.

Relative Advantage Sham. This is probably my favorite of human mental foibles. It completely disengages rationality and supplants it with fake rationality. Here's how it works: Let's say you need to determine drive times from a distribution facility to several different locations in and around Los Angeles at different times of the day and night. You find an online database that can provide the information you want, and it has three pricing options. "Basic" gives you one day access for $100. "Pro" gives you seven-day access for $200. And "SuperPro Special" gives you one-year access for $250. If you know you will only need the information one time, you will probably choose the Basic $100 scheme. If you think you might use the service more than once, you might very well buy the SuperPro Special for $250 because, for only $50 extra, you get the entire year, quite a bargain if a single day costs $100. But here's the rub, the marginal cost to the vendor is nearly $0. The data cost the vendor almost nothing. Their only costs are for marketing and programming their web user interface. If you found the right database yourself, you could have had all the data for nothing. The three-price strategy takes your mind off what the real price of the data is. Instead, you're focused on the relative "value" of each scheme, when in fact, all three were losers.

The relative Advantage Sham can also be perpetrated with only two options presented. A friend of mine recently asked me about a retail space where the landlord was asking $25 per square foot. The space had less visibility because it was located in the back of the center. The landlord told my friend the sites with greater visibility were more than $30, which made the space in the rear look like a good value. The problem was the average price in the market (the price the lemmings paid) was only $26 per square foot. $25 in the rear was no bargain.

Humans gain satisfaction not just from the utility of the object, but from the perceived quality of the deal. This is faulty. What really counts is not a relative advantage, but an absolute advantage.

The Decoy Deception. Similar to the Fallacy of Relative Advantage, the Decoy Deception comes into play when a pricing strategy is deployed to guide the buyer to a specific option using a decoy that creates a perceived dominating relative advantage. When there are only two options to choose from, humans will rely, to some extent, on their perceived relative utility of each to make their decision as to which has the better value. But when a third decoy option is added, it will significantly skew the humans' perception of value because of the false relative advantage introduced. For example, consider a user looking at office suites, and they're presented with these alternatives: 1) $20 per square foot for a nice suite, or 2) $25 per square for a nicer suite. Given these two options, they'll probably choose the one that best suits them. Now, what if the landlord instead presented three options? Option 3, the decoy, is a suite comparable to Option 2, but it's priced at $32 per square foot. The tenant will likely get caught in the trap of relative advantage because of the decoy and their perceived value of Option 2 will rise. Option 2 gets leased. The decoy never does; it wasn't intended to.

Who buys a medium popcorn at the movie theater? Nobody. It's not intended to be bought. It's only there as a decoy to support the pricing strategy of the large size.

Anchor Influence and Hypnosis. The dependency humans have on perceptions of relative value gives rise to the importance of the starting point or perceived initial value that is used as the reference point. This first reference point is an anchor that significantly influences decision-making. The asking price of the first property a client looks at, or the closing price of the last property a seller disposed of, will serve as anchors to each party in turn. But other unrelated numbers can also have a priming effect, such as directing your subjects' attention to their birthdays or phone numbers or anything. This is what make anchors so dangerous, and so useful to you. It doesn't matter where the number comes from. Lower anchor numbers yield lower result numbers. Higher anchor numbers yield higher result numbers. Both results are biased towards the initial reference point anchors.

In typical negotiations, a declared market price or asking price of an asset is an anchor. Presenting the numbers of a recent sale or lease of a building is an anchor. A Price/Earnings or Price/Sales ratio of a company can be anchors when comparing stock prices of two similar companies. The amazing thing is presenting numbers of dissimilar assets or even something totally out of context, such as calendar dates or random numbers, create a cognitive bias in the decision-making process towards those numbers. It's like a magnet, and humans don't even know they're being influenced.

Well-designed and deployed anchors have a myriad of uses, from helping influence the price paid for something to how many items are purchased and when.

Operant Conditioning and Reflex Responses. Pavlov had his dogs, and Skinner had his rats. I won't say whether these test subjects are suitable proxies for those you'll find on the other side of your negotiating table, but your counterparts' responses to known stimulus (which sometimes you proffer) and their subsequent association with reward or punishment (which you may also proffer) hold true to shape their behavior no matter what their whiskers look like. Make sure though that you're the psych-scientist and not the lab rat.

Sunk Cost Shackling. Everyone knows throwing good money after bad is a bad idea, but humans do it all the time. The reason they do it is because they have a bias to assume the rightness of their previous decisions, even after new evidence to the contrary may show otherwise. It's like sticking with a bad spouse. Humans will go to great lengths to support, protect, and affirm projects where they previously expended capital and effort. The greater the capital and effort, the greater the depths they're willing to go to save it and not walk away; notwithstanding, walking away might be the optimal choice.

Probability Problems. Humans over-assume the likelihood of small probability occurrences and under-assume the likelihood of large probability occurrences, thereby inappropriately exaggerating the probabilities of any possible outcome and exposing vulnerabilities you can exploit.

Over Reaction Infractions. Humans tend to overreact to either good news or bad news resulting in actions and over adjustments that aren't called for. The fight or flight stress response manifests itself in ways that often-times aren't helpful. In the context of market movements and catalysts, humans have a tendency to react to new, seemingly binary information with extremes of magnitude out of proportion to the news itself and its possible ramifications. Its either full-on throttle or standing on the brakes. Once it occurs, there is always a predictable bounce back the other direction to correct the over-reaction. Keep that in mind. Everything always reverts to the mean.

Nudge Budge and Default. Humans are easily influenced and manipulated into specific behaviors by gentle and innocuous nudges that alter the environment or circumstances in a way that triggers an easy, thoughtless, automatic response from the victim. The most basic example of this is an image of a black housefly etched into the bottom of a urinal of an airport men's room to help keep the place clean. Another example would be a list of options, one of which is a default option, that requires the subject to take overt action to opt-out of the default option. The default option will most often be selected (by default) as no energy, effort, or decision is required of the human.

Don't be lulled by the seemingly innocent implications of these examples. There are teams of behavioral psychologists working on contextual designs so you will make decisions in "predictable and preferable" ways for all kinds of public and private, profit and political, policy-making ends. I should emphasize that the "preferable" part of that equation is from the perspective of the designer of the environment, not you, the decision-maker.

Adversary Source Aversion. Most people are programmed to recoil from solutions provided by an adversary, the more contentious the relationship with the adversary, the greater the aversion. This is irrespective of the quality of the recommended solution. They merely succumb to the mistrust and fear triggered in them by the adversary. This creates a mental block that limits the number of viable options the humans would otherwise consider. If you're considered an adversary, knowing your opponent will likely recoil from a solution you proffer is quite useful. Creating a path to your desired solution that they discover on their own as their idea is the best solution.

Intended Misdirection

The first four types of reason-depleting disorders may occur naturally, or they may be created by either party to take advantage of the other, but using little or no coercion. These next intended misdirection techniques are more overt and malicious:

Dishonesty. If making rational decisions wasn't hard enough because of the onslaught of mind-twisting dynamics and manipulations, we also face the dishonest acts of the "honest" people. I've uncovered landlords charging my clients twice for property taxes, math that doesn't add up, fake comparables, forgotten "promises," fraud, deceit, graft, and a copious quantity of other criminality.

Price and Product Comparison Obfuscation. When price and product comparison research is difficult, prices go up. When complexity in price or product information increases or is difficult to find or analyze, the cost of research goes up, and prices go up. Consumers that understand deliberate product complexity and pricing and detail obfuscation as a pricing strategy, pay less.

A.I. Purchases made solely interacting with machines subject humans to unseen price manipulation (think airplane tickets). Algorithms are built to extract as much money from humans as possible, and the more information the programs have about the prospective purchaser, the more money they can extract. Hold all information close. Release nothing that isn't necessary. Don't be lulled into simplicity, e.g., shorter lists, more specific options, they each are accompanied by a tick up in pricing. Keep all your information secret unless absolutely necessary.

<u>Bonus Bias!</u>
<u>The Dunning-Krueger Effect</u>

You must make yourself aware of this exciting cognitive bias so you can add it to your arsenal. Plus, it can be an endless source of laughs (or tears) for you, while you're at it.

The Dunning-Kruger Effect is a psychological phenomenon wherein humans with low skill levels and ability incorrectly assess themselves as high performers, and humans with high levels of skill and competence tend to underrate their own performance. The low-ability humans make an internal error about themselves; they lack the self-awareness and knowledge to accurately determine their level of competence. The high-ability humans make an external error about others, assuming that others have a high level of skill that approximates their own.

You can assess yourself to determine where you fit into this little continuum. Try to be objective.

These reason-depleting disorders cause the volatility and mispricing of assets, products, and skills. They ravage the uninformed, but create opportunity for those in the know. I'll show you how I weaponize these in the following four chapters, but remember, what matters most is your determination of value. What is the acceptable pricing scheme for the thing under consideration, the price and premium you're willing to pay to acquire it, or the compensation and discount you're willing to accept to release it?

Any identification of value other than your own is just noise. It's unreal. It's just a distraction. It's alien for your purposes. It's a "Lemming Value" because it's a value identified solely based on what the vast number of lemmings are saying or willing to pay for the privilege of closing their minds and jumping off a cliff en-masse. Lemming Value gets presented to you in the form of list price, ask price, market price, competitors' pricing, proposed price, and a myriad of other ways. It's a copy-cat value useless for your purposes and to be ignored.

Primate brains evolved with a predictive capability principally to find food, shelter, and sex – not necessarily in that order. It's capacity to attempt pricing in a free market scenario stems from its ability to determine patterns presented historically. It's a backward-looking calculator. Your calculator should be, must be, re-calibrated to be forward looking. The past is just that, past, and has little if any bearing on the future.

You can't be a lemming and beat the herd. You can't do what everyone else does and achieve alpha performance. You need to do the research to determine your own values and know the reasons the pricing is where it is. You need to do the intel on the humans on the other side of the transaction and their story, desires, capabilities, and weaknesses. You need to know the markets you're playing in, and how and why they move if you're going to manipulate them. You need to build your deep cognitive bench. Determine the valutility.

What are your counterparts research costs, costs to develop prospects and customers, what are their transaction costs? Construction costs, delivery costs, legacy costs, what's the cost to them for not doing your deal? These are all opportunity costs and can easily be credited to your side of the ledger.

You needn't be too concerned about the wild price fluctuations of volatility, though price fluctuations and high volatility drive lemmings crazy. They head straight for the cliffs. When you know the intrinsic value of the asset, and you know what is currently driving the pricing pressures, you are able to relax and just watch the show. Timing is sometimes difficult to predict with precision, so be careful not to put yourself in a box by tying up all your capital in a volatile market. You can get pinched. It can suck if you find yourself in a predicament that you need liquidity to handle extraneous capital requirements, take advantage of underpriced assets, meet a margin call, or just survive, but your money is tied up in a market that's moving away from you because your timing is off. Give yourself room, both in timing and liquidity. It's best to keep some powder dry.

13

TRICKS

POSITIONING THE OPPOSITION

"The human brain is an incredible pattern-matching machine."
-- Jeff Bezos

"I like nonsense; it wakes up the brain cells."
-- Dr. Seuss

The two statements above, when taken together, beg the question: If nonsense wakes up the brain cells as Dr. Seuss suggested, are they asleep when the "incredible" pattern-matching is going on? I think it's likely, and why Jeff's so rich.

For all the seriousness and drama and pain and joy, life is a game. It's full of mystery, hints, clues, and house rules. Your experiences program your thoughts and move you in predictable patterns of feelings and behaviors. The house always wins, unless you are willing to step out of line and change how the rules are applied.

As we venture into these covert strategies, I should warn you of a vulnerability that may beset you when you learn to use these skills and internalize them. You might start to get overconfident in this. You might start to think that everyone will do your bidding by merely thinking that they should. You might start to think that you can make people think what you want them to think merely because you want them to think that way. This is understandable because as you start to use these skills, it will appear to you that they do. Make a note of the following: You can't. Your diligent effort applying these skills and developing a sharp insight into the status of your deals and your counterparts' mental and emotional states, as well as an accurate gaming of your next steps, are required to succeed. Managing your own behavior is key. In the end, what we're talking about, what this entire book is about, is managing your own behavior and mental and emotional states so you prevail. Sometimes your only friend is your frontal lobe. If you have one, pay attention to it.

Applied Influence

I first realized that it might be possible to develop a method for winning any negotiation when I rejected the bloated brokerage company model and started to think about how to build a more artful and adroit method of negotiating than the tactical crap we've seen a thousand times before. I realized that the right approach for winning any negotiation would be one that naturally changed the mental and emotional states of my opposition. I wanted to achieve super-high levels of performance and way more consistent outcomes, so I set out to build it.

The winner of any negotiation is the one with the best algorithms, the one that has the clearest signal inputs and knowledge, and the willingness to convert those into actions that maximize their outcomes. The losers are the ones making suboptimal decisions based on less good algorithms and accepting lesser outcomes, blind to their own deficiencies, biases, and wrong or null actions. The same can be said of life. The advantage goes to those who consciously decide which role they will play. It's an unfair advantage. But hey, life's not fair.

Early in my career, I had learned first-hand that I could easily win by capitalizing on active trends that were themselves supported by massive resources resulting in predictable economic consequences. I realized the key to developing a method for winning any negotiation was to exploit the most obstinate and unyielding trend there is, the inevitable flow of nature and human behavior -- natural law. Natural law, by its very nature, is supported by the most powerful resource and force in the universe, itself. Ignore natural law, and you lose. Learn to use it as your vehicle for changing the mental and emotional states of your opposition, and you win. It's unavoidable.

The skills and strategies I developed leverage natural law, and in particular, human nature and human behavior. They became these Tricks, Hacks, Hammers, and Cheats, and the guts of what I call Applied

Influence. I designed it to flow with the cadence of the propensities and principles that govern everything. It's minimalistic and simple, but nearly impossible to counter. It would be, well, unnatural. Natural law becomes the wind at your back in all your negotiations and endeavors. I soon discovered that I didn't need to limit myself to just winning negotiations. I could use Applied Influence to win just about anything if I was willing to put forth the effort.

My clients hire me to fix their problems. I do. Clients are sometimes slow admitting to problems, at least the ones they helped create. It's hard to admit to your shortcomings or mistakes, I guess. They're always happy when the problems get fixed, though, and Applied Influence does that. It's like having a suite of influence devices programmed to alter the code behind your oppositions' decision making.

This is a martial art of the mind and emotion where your primary objective is to maintain your balance and control while disturbing the balance and control of your counterparts. It's a nuanced and strategic form of negotiating that leverages the inefficiencies of your counterparts' cognitive functions, emotions, decision-making processes, and the inefficiencies of the marketplace, to compel your counterparts to help you achieve your objectives. These skills and strategies are covert, stealth operations that won't be recognized. It's like pulling sticks and rocks out of an earthen dam so the water flows your way. It's a beautiful example of less is more, but it's so powerful and so much more. You'll learn how to set up, position, and guide the negotiations and your counterparts so that the natural outcome of the negotiation is your targeted outcome. Some of this might seem counter-intuitive, but it works.

This is not "Win/Win" negotiating, per se. In my opinion, Win/Win negotiating is only perpetuated by the lazy ones who don't want to have to think very much and can instead coddle everyone in the negotiations in hopes of avoiding conflict. Win/Win negotiating is the fast track to the mediocre. I'm happy when everybody wins, but we need to keep our priorities straight, particularly if you're a hired gun. Applied Influence is "You Win" negotiating. If you intend to separate yourself from the masses, you need to have a higher level of performance to win for you and your clients. The problem with Win/Win negotiations is that you have to accept the premise of your oppositions' expectations of a win entering the negotiations. I say you may want to change what your counterparts perceive as a win. They'll be happy at the end of the negotiations, but happiness is relative. You might have to disappoint them first.

If a new counterpart approaches you promising a Win/Win negotiation, assume it's a lie, or just unzip your pants now and bend over. Proposed Win/Wins are never intended to be fair; they're intended for you to lose. Win/Win is easy because you do lose. You and your clients should expect more than so-called Win/Win. You Win negotiating takes skill.

Applied Influence is an aggressive method of negotiating, but your behavior is not. The amazing thing about this methodology is how simple it is to execute once you realize the flow of nature does most of the work. There's no lying. There's no dishonesty. There's no discord with your values. You subtly change the world with your informed and intelligent actions in accord with natural law and its flow. You bring your own style, your authentic self, and stone mountains will crumble at your feet. Your negotiations are not only more effective, but they're also easier.

For the most part, all your interactions will be non-confrontational. Though sometimes, confrontations are warranted. But you'll know when to use them and what the outcomes will be ahead of time.

Maybe you've approached new negotiations wanting to be liked, trusted, and respected by your counterparts, but that's just a way of compensating for your own insecurities. If you're approaching new engagements with that as your objective, it's a disaster in the making. The fact is, in the beginning, your counterparts probably won't like you, trust you, or respect you. They expect you're trying to negotiate better terms than they want to give you, which you should be. Get over it. They also expect you to enter the engagement trying to manipulate them in having them like you, trust you, and respect you because that's how they've been approached a thousand times before you showed up. They habitually assume you're not sincere. Don't go there. Having them like you, trust you, and respect you is NOT your objective. Your objective is to negotiate the best terms for you and your client. As the deal unfolds and you've got what you wanted, that's when they'll like you, trust you, and respect you. That all is a by-product of these strategies, not the objective. You'll see how that all comes together as the process unfolds.

There will be ideas and strategies presented in this chapter and throughout my entire Applied Influence confession that may momentarily confound your thinking and appear paradoxical. Paradoxes exist in life. Embrace them; you will use them to your advantage.

Finally, there will be instances, though rare, when the human you're dealing with will want to give you what you want at the beginning of the negotiation. If after you've looked at all the evidence you decide that they're for real and are sincere, accept it as the gift it is.

Presynaptic Positioning

Before you begin any negotiation and engage your counterparts, their future response to your actions is pure potentiality. They may have a predetermined propensity to go positive or negative based on their previously established patterns of thought because of the neural pathways in their brains set up in similar previous encounters. The more often that type of interaction has taken place and the pattern of thought reinforced, the stronger that neural pathway becomes. If this happens often enough, that pattern of thinking and feeling becomes habitual. Once those patterns are in place, they run pretty much consistently until the pattern is interrupted. This is the environment we find ourselves facing when entering a new negotiation. Your counterparts have predetermined ways of thinking, and you often approach them in a way they fully expect, again, reinforcing their thinking and their established patterns. Worse yet, you may be operating within your own habitual neural pattern, and it may be so commonplace that it triggers the established pattern in your counterpart, entangling the two of you in a predetermined dance of automatons destined for mediocre outcomes. Fuck that.

Until the initial interaction, it's pure potential and subject to your creation. If you're as prepared as you should be entering the engagement, as the Sun Tzu lessons taught us to be, you'll have a sense of the likely propensity for patterned responses from your counterparts. If their likely patterned responses are not constructive for your objective, take the counterparts out of their patterned behaviors and reset them to zero so you can proceed unencumbered by your counterparts' old trodden pathways, their worn-out predetermined patterned plans for you. This is simpler than it sounds because becoming part of the flow of nature is the easiest thing there is. What is difficult is you breaking out of your own neural programming you've been following like a robot day in and day out.

One of the most important things you learn when running white-water rapids high in the Colorado mountains is what to do when you get knocked out of your boat so that you don't die. In Class 4 or 5 rapids, you're in the water before you know what happened. You have just the next second or two to save yourself. If you fight, grab, or resist, you're dead. Your head will smash against the sharp edge of a wet boulder, or you'll get pinned down beneath the water in a churning hydraulic and drown. They'll find your body a mile or two down river some following August when the water levels have receded. The answer to a continued happy life is simple and applies not just to the white water and rocks, but to everything in your life. When you're out of the boat and you hit the water, you have just one second to turn on your back, point your feet down river, sit up best you can so you can see where you're going, and enjoy the ride. Use your hands to protect yourself from the visible hazards. The natural flow of the water through the rocks will support you through the journey until the river has calmed. Your butt might take a beating, but it's worth it, you lived. Let nature work for you; to resist it is futile.

The overarching concept for Applied Influence is understanding the natural flow of nature, truth, and consequences, so you can use them to achieve your aim. Most everyone you encounter is fighting the current, trying to impose their will on the river. The "trick" here is not to try and beat the river, that's the loser's path to discredit and death. The trick here is that you become part of the flow of the river.

Resetting your new counterparts to zero so you can proceed unencumbered by their previously established neural pathways is achieved by simple and natural changes in how you engage your counterparts initially and throughout the negotiations, ways they have never encountered before. Set aside any cookie-cutter negotiation strategies and processes you've learned before. They won't serve you well because your counterparts have been faced with these strategies and processes a million times before and will trigger the previously programmed responses from your counterparts that will throw you both into that dance of automatons destined for hell. You need to change it up. Take them out of the game they're used to. That's not just changing the approach and the script so you can slip back into your regular patterns later, it's changing how your counterparts view the engagements and their emotional and mental responses to it. You need to position yourself, your counterparts, and the game at hand such that your counterparts' natural response will be, "I've never encountered this before. I'm curious about this. How do I deal with this?" You're going to help them figure that out.

One example that comes to mind of resetting my opponent to zero was a 300,000 square foot mixed-use building near Beverly Hills. My client had asked me if I could reduce their occupancy costs in about a half-dozen properties they leased and occupied; this was one.

I always have a complete photographic record of properties I work on as well as other properties in the markets that are comparable or have some other use for my project. These aren't images for marketing purposes; it's the nitty-gritty for later reference. These are pics of the mundane. They're like crime scene photos. For this Beverly Hills property, I put together a small collection of the pictures to send to the landlord along with my introductory email. They were pictures of side doors and back doors, dumpsters and parking entrances, pictures of the lobbies with poor lighting, and photos of the exterior with trash and homeless people. It had been a cloudy day, so everything was a little grey. Some of the shots were a bit out of focus. These were not glamour shots. They would never appear on any piece of collateral material the landlord would produce, and they wouldn't want them circulated on social media either. They were more like what the building would look like if it had a hangover after a rough night of afterparties in the Hollywood Hills.

In my email to the landlord, I made no comment or judgment about the pictures, other than to say they were attached, and that I had pictures of many buildings in the area.

The response I got was swift. He immediately sent me all his professionally prepared glamour shots of the property as well as his glossy marketing materials, and he asked what other buildings I looked at. I had taken him out the familiar control of his habitual patterned response, and he found himself in the position of trying to play catch up and regain some control in a situation he knew nothing about.

Playing Their Prefrontal Cortex
for Maximum Receptivity

The frontal lobe, including the prefrontal cortex, integrates the brain functions of judgment, problem-solving, planning, anticipation, organization, abstract reasoning, insight, attention, expression, and self-awareness of limitations and ability. These executive-level thinking skills that everyone takes for granted are highly susceptible to disruption when you withhold the data flow and information that your counterparts are expecting. Being starved of the data and information they expect will cause them some uncertainty and confusion, and denies them the hit of dopamine they're expecting from feeling in control of a familiar situation. When information and dopamine deficiencies occur, information that is provided to them later is a welcome relief and accepted with less scrutiny.

I purposefully create uncertainty and doubt in the minds of my counterparts through opaqueness, ambiguity, aloofness, and paradox – keeping them enough off balance so I can focus them in the direction I choose. I'm usually friendly and usually keep things friendly. Uncertainty, though, is a ripe asset; and the paradoxes, ambiguity, aloofness, and general opaqueness I present to my counterparts create plenty of it. The certainty I do present to my counterparts is limited to the principles and causes behind my mission. My preferred outcomes are never revealed, at least not yet. The uncertainty I foster in my counterparts' minds is a result of their inability to ascertain how they fit into my equation or what my equation even is. At this stage, and throughout the negotiations, I never reveal my side's desired outcomes, metrics, details of procedures, alternatives, or the competition. I only allow them to know that those all exist, but never forthrightly. I merely allow them to surmise. I create a guessing game for my counterparts and never confirm anything. Their hunger for certainty, confidence, and the status quo builds.

This reminds me, I never responded to the Beverly Hills landlord asking what buildings I'd looked at. I just let him wonder. I took my time before I engaged with him again at all.

Lighting Up Their Limbic System
to Support Your Objectives

The Limbic System is a collection of brain functions that govern emotion and motivation. It sets the course for future behaviors that are in accord with your counterpart's values, principles, and beliefs. You can help initiate desired behaviors in your subject counterpart by setting out a narrative framework of your purpose in such a manner that it aligns with your counterpart's values, principles, and beliefs -- plug and play.

At the start of your engagement, its outcome is pure potential. You know you have a job to do and what that job is. Your counterpart is, meanwhile, going on with his or her life and has their own expectation of the near term. It likely doesn't include you. If at the outset of your interaction, you explain your presence and purpose in a way that doesn't resonate with your counterpart, you will find yourself positioned on the outside without an easy path in. By explaining your presence and purpose in the negotiation in terms of core values and guiding principles your counterpart can agree with and embrace, a small but critical affinity is formed that allows further access to your counterpart and their receptivity.

Be clear in stating the fundamental axioms behind your mission. But be equally clear that the possible outcomes may include outcomes that don't include that counterpart, that you are open to a myriad of possibilities that may be suitable. You don't want them to think they're a target, that you're taking aim at them. You don't want to provide them any certainty, good or bad.

I've been involved with thousands of commercial lease renegotiations. Renegotiating existing contracts can be challenging because the tenant is already occupying the property; relocation costs are generally substantial, and often the go-forward terms are already set out in the original lease. The landlords have no interest in changing terms, particularly if they consider our new terms to be detrimental to their bottom line. This is an area where few brokers are willing to tread.

Consider the following two statements:

"We'd like to extend the lease ten years, but we want to renegotiate the terms of the option, reduce the rent, and also ask that you fund a million-dollar tenant finish package for our renovations."

Or:

"My client asked me to review this market and make recommendations on how best to move forward after the lease expires, given the changing circumstances. This is an important decision for us, so we want to make sure we have all the information we should have in order to make the best decision."

Both statements accurately reflect why you're there negotiating. But with the first statement, you show your hand without getting anything in return. It pigeon-holes you into a path of limited outcomes and even less leverage, immediately setting up disagreement and defenses with the landlord. Your counterpart's response to the first statement will likely be something to the effect of, "I doubt that."

Conversely, the second statement makes clear the principles behind the purpose of your presence, but also elicits from your counterpart an obvious agreement as to those principles and their validity. His response to the second statement will probably be something like, "Obviously, that makes sense, as you should. I wonder what happens next." People tend to side with people that think like them. People are more trusting and willing to bend for and engage with others that believe what they believe.

State your purpose in terms of principles, values, and fundamental axioms, not outcomes. At the outset, your counterparts won't agree with your desired outcomes, so don't tell them. They can and will agree with your principles and values if you state them correctly. Desired outcomes should always be kept private between you and your client throughout the entire negotiation. Every time a desired outcome becomes known to a counterpart, the price of that outcome goes up, and you lose leverage and negotiating position. Stating your purpose as a principled mission your counterpart can agree with increases your esteem in their eyes, elicits agreement, yet maintains uncertainty of outcomes in their mind. Maintain that uncertainty until the point in the process when it's advantageous to release it, which is pretty much never.

Set the tone of the process moving forward. Tell your counterpart that you need to do your homework and research. Tell them you expect to be talking with lots of people to get the information. Tell them you don't know how much time it's going to take but that you're going to take your time and get all the facts you need. Tell them you're going to be fair but that you need to understand the economic circumstances.

Injecting Oxytocin for a Killer Bond

Everybody feels a little abused. Everybody feels like they don't quite get the recognition they deserve.

When entering a new negotiation, you need to have a good understanding of who you're dealing with, their successes and failures, as well as the benefits and liabilities of the objects of the negotiation. Observe people objectively and without emotion.

Amateur (soon to be dead) negotiators are always focusing on their counterparts' weak spots, some kind of opening, something they can leverage to cause harm, all the while missing and ignoring their counterparts' strengths. It's those strengths that can kill you. Find them. Find them and praise them. Search your counterparts for their virtues and acknowledge them. Find what there is to respect in your counterpart; you'll learn more, connect more, and be better prepared. State your honest recognition of their qualities, and their strengths will become their weakness.

There's also a tendency to focus on the negatives of the thing being negotiated, go right for the jugular, and avoid pointing out the positives or breeze through them quickly. It doesn't work. You're convincing your counterpart of nothing when you do that. You're only making your counterpart more entrenched, defensive and resistant. Plus, you would be doing precisely what he or she expects you to do, reinforcing their habitual negative behavioral responses.

Stating the obvious benefits of the object costs you nothing and elicits further agreement from your counterpart in the negotiation. They'll appreciate your honesty and your esteem in their eyes will rise as they see you understand the qualities of the object of the negotiation, something that's important to them. If you feel this moves you further from your goals, worry not; it doesn't. It's changing the mental state of your counterpart to move away from their habituated neural pathway behaviors and will allow you later to guide them into the direction of your chosen outcomes.

Understand the situation, condition, and footing of your counterpart and learn to genuinely empathize with their state of being, not to further it necessarily, but for your own knowledge and the recognition provided to your counterpart. Empathy allows you access to their emotions and thought processes and can help you anticipate their thoughts, feelings, and moves. The connection will help lower their defenses. Praise your counterparts' previous decisions as being correct at the time they made them. Find the qualities of your counterpart that you can respect and articulate them from an objective point of view. You might have to hunt, but you can discover the things perhaps others don't know or understand. Don't embellish or make it up, and don't move into sycophant mode. That's a disaster, and then you might as well shoot yourself. You can't stand alone if you're kissing butt. But acknowledging the worth of the individual on the other side of the table is important for your own knowledge and will help guide you moving forward. Just as important, though, it releases an oxytocin salve in your counterpart that creates a bond with you that functions as a bridge to your desired outcomes.

Your counterpart's treatment of you or your deal at any one moment is not necessarily related to you personally or the deal, but instead some other emotional baggage or indigestion they're feeling at the time. Things are not always as they seem. Appearances can be misleading. Acknowledging the positives of the object of the negotiation and your counterpart improves your knowledge and understanding of the conditions at hand, the landscape, your position, and it costs you nothing. It will open new neural pathways in your counterpart more aligned with your desires. Everyone is susceptible to the moods and emotions of those around them. They'll know that comfortable, warm glow and stress relief they feel from the oxytocin release came from you; they just won't know what it is. They'll fear you less, be less anxious, trust you more, and feel way more generous thanks to the oxytocin – and it's all subconscious. The oxytocin bond you create will allow them to bend for you. The name is bond, oxytocin bond.

Diffusing Their Defenses

Because of the type of work I do, sometimes a new counterpart might be a little worried and defensive, a little on edge, at the beginning of our interaction. The oxytocin bond will certainly help turn down the heat on that. Sharing a weakness of mine helps deepen that link as well as serve to lower their expectations of me and lower their defenses.

I've witnessed with amusement, the bizarre process of two opposing sides initiating communication and early positioning with the stiff presentation of the plastic façade of their choosing in hopes of impressing the other side with the benefits of the proposition or successes and skills and kills they'd like the other side to know about. Chests puff out, plumage shakes, and each engages in a prancing dance in hopes their social media persona is somehow personified, their collateral materials or branding made real. Everybody is operating at 50,000 feet with little oxygen, and no real connection is possible. It takes a long time for this nonsense to dissipate. I don't have that much time or patience.

You can bring everyone down to earth, not by showing off the notches on your belt or the scars on your hands, but by showing some of your weakness. Let them win the puffy chest, paroxysmal plumage, and the prancy-dance contest; that's not your objective. Show some weakness, some vulnerabilities, your imperfections. You'll appear more human and accessible, which in turn will set your counterpart more at ease and less defensive. They'll let their guard down, lessen their security, remove some armor, and be more open. Let them think they're winning the plumage game; it doesn't matter at this point. It serves you.

My work takes me to many different markets with lots of different types of real estate. Upon meeting a new counterpart, one simple statement I often make to show weakness and lessen their tension and defensiveness is: "I've been asked to work on this market; but frankly, I'm still learning about it, and I have to rely upon what other people tell me and what I've been able to uncover on my own."

Regardless of the deep bench I've already created for the project, the statement is basically true for its purpose, and what usually follows is a download from my counterpart on what he wants me to think about the market as he shows off his knowledge. Sometimes I learn something new about the market. I always learn something about how he thinks. Since I've already done my research, I usually know which of what he is telling me is truthful and what is not, and that helps me understand more his own vulnerabilities.

This, together with the oxytocin salve you apply, lets him feel safe and freer to open up to you. You no longer appear to be a threat. He feels more in control, and at this stage of the game, that's a good thing. His lowered expectations of you allow you greater access. I stay low key. I want to be underestimated. I'd rather they didn't see me coming. Use moderation, of course. Don't wallow in your debility and decrepitude. A little self-deprecation goes a long way.

There's a successful (and sinewy) Chinese entrepreneur who also conducts personal physical defense classes for executives, so they can learn to survive an unexpected street attack. His process is simple. Even for the well-trained fighter, responding in a fashion that announces your skill level, such as raising to a defensive posture or a fighting stance, will only serve to alert your attacker and give him time to think and act, likely to your detriment. The sinewy entrepreneur teaches how to strike a devastating blow to your attacker from a cowering position, when you look most vulnerable and defenseless, without announcement, readiness, or thought – only the lethal blow as your response when your attacker has lowered his expectations of you.

Triggering Synaptic Sympathy

Successful human interaction is lubed with communal behavior. Communal behavior flows most easily among people with common interests, beliefs, and characteristics – people who think and act alike, people part of the same community, a shared social group. Activities, language, religion, politics, charity, parenting, and lifestyle, are obvious outward examples that foster communal behavior. The similarity of thought is what creates community, an alignment of neural pathways pertaining to at least one subject. People are most at ease dealing with other people in the same community, and their focus is more on their own reputation within the community than economic gain. Conversely, people often are less comfortable dealing with people not in their community of thought even if there is no impending threat by the other. Simply being an "other" can put you at odds. You can be perceived as a threat, even if there is none. And if there is a possibility of a real threat, such as reduced money, you're challenged indeed. The analytics show that people that share a common community are more likely to offer "fair" transaction terms than not. It's up to you to help your counterpart understand the common community to which you two belong and what is "fair" in your circumstance.

"Let's take a ride." My little AMG was a convenient object to build some community around. At the time, it was the fastest car on the road from a standing start. Fast cars, at least for most men, strike interest and bring pleasure. If you hadn't driven this car, you hadn't experienced the explosive, rifle shot acceleration, the g-forces that pinned you to the back of your seat. For the uninitiated, the driver might have a little fear the car would get away from him; it was so fast. I'd let people drive it, at least the ones I thought wouldn't let the car get away from them. Those that drove it were hooked. Community doesn't have to be deep, just aligned.

I was asked by a client to step into a negotiation for a monster distribution facility near Phoenix. The lease was about to expire, and my client had previously sent one of their in-house real estate people there to negotiate terms with the landlord. When the real estate person demanded that the rent be reduced, the landlord threw them out of his office. That's when my client asked me to step in and help.

From the dossier I put together on the landlord, I learned he liked amateur club car racing with his Porsche. When I met him in person, I initiated a conversation and explained why the Mercedes AMG was preferable to his lowly Porsche. He immediately became fully engaged and proceeded to educate me on the subject. We debated the merits of Porsche versus AMG for some time, and soon his early dissatisfaction with my client's behavior vanished. We were then able to start a new relationship and begin a new negotiation with a least one grounded community bond.

Notice your counterparts' habitual mannerisms, gestures, mood, tonality, patterns of speech, and the words they use and learn. That will give you clues to the communities they have an affinity with and where there might be some natural congruency. Your counterparts are more likely to bend for someone like them.

Bezos was right. The human brain is a pattern-matching machine, and we can use that to guide our opponents in the direction we choose. Dr. Seuss was even more insightful, though, because nonsense, like chaos, opens the brain to be more receptive and it clamors for the patterns we then provide it.

To close out the discussions on the Beverly Hills and Phoenix deals I've mentioned, after my initial positioning of the landlords, creating a little community with each, and using the strategies in the following chapters, I reduced my client's occupancy costs by 35% in Beverly Hills and more than 42% in Phoenix. Positioning your opponents so they move away from their habitual patterned responses is critical to opening the doors that allow them to be more aligned with your thinking. The smallest nudges, the innocuous tweaks, the calculated causal factors you apply, are all that's necessary to change the course of negotiations or your life.

In the positioning stage of any engagement, you never talk about outcomes. You only talk in terms of process and principles. This requires patience, sometimes massive patience. You only talk about outcomes when you start talking about the structure of a deal, never beforehand.

Now it's time for your counterparts to start thinking your way.

14

HACKS

TRIGGERING YOUR OPPOSITIONS' AUTOMATIC BEHAVIOR RESPONSES

Go exploring and make discoveries. Define your targets and choose your actions. Exploit when you're ready to cash in. This is the journey that determines your character, freedom, and dominant strategy.

———

These hacks breach the firewall of your oppositions' brains, gain access undetected, browse their mental schematic, and reconfigure as necessary. It's not a complete system reboot, but enough of a cleanup to get your job done. Admittedly, you're not really an authorized user, so go softly.

Starved of the information and data your counterparts expected, they will be anxious to have this new and unfamiliar uneasiness go away so they can get their footing again and get back to the familiar circumstances they're used to. They'll be eager to get that stream of info they're now craving, so they can again feel in control (and maybe get that dopamine buzz they're missing). In this emotional state, they don't much critique the data coming in; they're just happy it's coming in. You can take pleasure knowing that you're going to help them, just not the way they expect. They'll be excited, though, and they'll want to help you help them get what they need, a flow of information to fill the void.

My Tricks opened your counterparts' minds to become more receptive to your way of thinking by helping them step off their trodden pathways of thought and onto new and more creative adventures aligned with you. Our counterparts naturally help configure the new story you two create together. They become co-architects because of your novel insight. Through your applied influence, you compel them too move forward with you and establish new thoughts, feelings, perceptions, and behaviors more aligned with your objectives.

Every negotiation is a relationship. The nature of that relationship impacts the outcomes. It's a human connection, but it's riddled with tests and rewards and challenges and scrutiny that must be navigated and directed. It's a game, like it or not. You can play it on a beginner's level, but it's much more rewarding if you play it as an expert.

Mind Mining and Mapping

Get people talking, and they'll tell you their secrets. Elicitation is the art of getting your subject humans to talk so you can download their information, ideas, concepts, plans, fears, feelings, and anything useful and instructive. Ask questions, ask lots of questions. Answer questions with questions. Question their answers. Question their questions. Acknowledge, then question their concerns. Above all else, listen to the answers and question what you've heard. Ask questions three, four, and five times. Ask the same question three, four, and five different ways. The data dump is useful in determining and strategizing your vectors implementing Applied Influence.

You don't want to come off as though you're interrogating your subject and running a criminal investigation. You don't want to appear strategic. You want to get them talking and keep talking. Use the points they make to bring up other lines of questioning. Use the words and mannerisms they use to prompt communal behavior to help foster a greater flow of information.

Of all the research you can do on your human subjects, the empirical data you get right from the source is the best. Keep them talking. The more they talk, the more they reveal, and the more you learn that can help your cause. If you're talking, you're not learning. Nurture the flow of information from your counterpart that reveals for you the correct courses of action.

This cannot be hit and run. Be easy to talk with, not harsh. Acknowledge their answers and build rapport around the give and take. You want to develop a relationship that has substance. What you learn helps create that substance. Be open and frank, upfront and honest. Remember, though, your job is not to share information but to mine it. Ask questions. Elicit answers. Make no presentations.

Executing the Uncertainty Loop Advantage

Hold all your information close to your chest. Nobody needs to be apprised of any of it: its scope, its content, its source, none of it. Everyone is on a need to know basis only, and it's your need, not theirs.

Don't divulge any information until it suits your purpose. You do, though, want to maintain the relationship throughout the negotiation to keep the conversation flowing and your subjects talking. I would never advocate that you feed them misinformation, that's not principled and opens you up to damage later. What you need to practice is the art of obfuscation. I can be generous with an inquisitive human, but the information I choose to provide them is ambiguous, precisely imprecise, and a little confusing. It's like feeding your subjects carob instead of chocolate. They want to like it and try and make it fit with their chocolate desire, but it doesn't quite satisfy the same way. When the time comes, you can always use beneficial information in trade for something you want. Don't succumb to those impulses to share information because it would be appreciated by another or make you feel good. All information is valuable and to be treated strategically.

Maintaining a cloaked presence also prevents your counterparts from planning either their defensive or offensive moves. Providing vague and ambiguous information makes your counterparts' discernment and comprehension of the situation difficult at best. They can't strategize, game out, or exploit. Your use of unexpected and inconclusive descriptors increases your subject's uncertainty and confusion, and that opens a path for you. When humans are immersed in uncertainty and confusion, they crave a simple solution to follow, the simplest way out of the uncertainty. That, you will provide... later.

Priming Your Oppositions' Generosity Cache

Push and pull and yin and yang, humans need recognition, but the minute they get it, they have an impulse to give it back. Nature abhors a vacuum. When a human receives a gift or a compliment, whoosh, there's a new vacuum the recipient feels bound to fill. Your generosity leads to a drive for reciprocal action on the part of the receiver. *"Thank you for admiring my nose; you have quite a beautiful schnoz yourself!"* The human mind is pre-wired to correct an imbalance that confronts it. Gifts received by humans trigger an immediate drive within the subject to provide reciprocity – to make things even.

Give your human subject something tangible, a bit of privileged information given on the sly, the granting of an ask, a personal desire of theirs, something that is unexpected and personalized -- the more personal, the better. The value of the offering is of little consequence. But if it's something that makes the recipient feel as though they've received an undeserved reward, they'll feel more indebted. Make it something that is useful and makes the subject feel good. The automatic response from your subject will be to give you something in return. They can't help it. Their desire to provide reciprocal generosity will continue unabated until satisfied, and you can show them how to quench that desire.

Reconfiguring the Oppositions' Win Criteria

In any negotiation, your counterparts' perception is their reality. When your subject human is happy and content, they are confident in their plans, confident in their thinking, and less open to your direction. But when your counterpart is uncertain, unhappy, confused, or discontent, then their own plans are subject to suspicion in their own mind, they're not confident, and are open to change.

The adage, "good things come to those who wait," is incorrect. It should read, "good things come to those who are disappointed first." That's because "good things" are relative and a matter of perspective. We can recalibrate what the opposition deems a win by introducing disappointment into their equation. By re-shaping their landscape away from the familiar, they become open to our way of thinking because it settles their problems and uncertainty. You must disappoint them first so that you can relieve their pain later. A shift in your counterpart's perspective is achieved. This technique is subtle but powerful.

Happiness is relative to expectations. Disappoint them first. Promise dates, then delay. Promise information, then delay. Promise decisions, then delay. Allude to agreements, then delay. Make conditional agreements, then; well, you get the idea. Your counterpart will think through all the scenarios of your misses, each one making him less comfortable and off-balance. They won't know what's going on. Be subtle and friendly and a little apologetic. Rest assured, you'll fix their pain shortly, just after you redefine the scale your counterpart uses to measure their wins.

Your goal in every negotiation is to shift your counterparts' perception in such a way that they feel your terms are simple and viable solutions to their problems and insecurities. Disappoint them first.

Remotely Accessing your Counterparts' Cognitive Dissonance Filters

Each human has a set of beliefs, core values, and a perception of their own self, their self-image. They will strive to have their self-image remain consistent over time and will take such action as necessary to defend it. Self-image, or self-schema, is how humans define themselves. If they are acting in accord with their belief systems, core values, and their self-perception, everything is fine. If they are acting in a way that is discordant with their self-image, all is not fine, and they will make the changes necessary to remove the cognitive dissonance. It's like a set of guardrails that keep behavior and decisions inside the boundaries that will maintain the self-schema. It functions as a set of "if-then" parameters that dictate the next steps: If positive for self-image, continue; if not, abort.

Frame your process and objectives so they align with your subject's perception of themselves and their beliefs. You're not trying to change them. You're taking them as they are and building a pathway for them to your objectives guided by their own character and principles. Ascertain your counterpart's self-image and aspirational self-schema and get them to confirm those concepts of themselves. Helping them to make "I am" statements will reinforce their sense of self, and they will act in accord with those associated principles and self-image. What self-image do they need validated?

Being in a state of cognitive dissonance causes discomfort because of the innate drive to maintain internal consistency. Presenting your subject with choices that confirm their self-image and help maintain internal consistency are easy choices for your subject to make. Ignore this issue altogether, and you will find yourself butting up against a wall you didn't even know existed. Get agreement on who they are, their core values, and build your negotiations around those. Have them affirm their set of values and behaviors, and they will be compelled to conform to you by default.

I was disposing of prime re-development acreage on a busy interstate (180,000 cars) in a major office market. It was a beautiful property, but there were some hazmat issues associated with the site. It was contaminated. The universe of potential buyers was limited because of the necessary remediation issues, but we had priced the dirt to accommodate that cleanup.

I received an offer from a developer with environmental remediation experience. He knew he was a unique buyer, and his offer came in about ten percent under my asking price, saying his price was justified because of the scarcity of qualified buyers. I didn't respond to his offer and waited for him to start calling me to ask what was going on. I told him I wasn't going to respond to his offer because it was too low, but I kept the discussion fluid, encouraging him to talk about his experience and ability to capture value on properties with similar contamination issues. After a couple of weeks, I sent him a counterproposal at a price that was about six percent over my original asking price (almost 18 percent more than his offer). I pointed out that this was the highest quality property he had ever had the opportunity to use his unique skills on -- and right on the interstate for all to see. He accepted my counteroffer.

Using Request Rationale – Because it Works

Try this. Walk up to someone standing in the TSA line at the airport and ask to step ahead of them in line. They're likely to point and say, "The end of the line is over there."

Now walk up to someone and ask to step ahead of them in line, saying, "I'm late for my flight." Their response would most likely be, "Sure." The rationale you provided has considerable merit. No problem. But now, walk up to someone and ask to step ahead of them in line and say, "Because I have to get to my gate." Again, the answer probably will be, "Sure." But why? Everybody standing in the TSA line has to get to their gate. Or try saying, "It's been a crazy day." Again, no problem. Or maybe, "My dog ate my homework." They're still letting you in line even though your rationale has no merit. Why?

When faced with a request, the human brain confronts the [daunting] challenge of weighing the merits for granting or denying the request. "Why should I grant?" and "Why should I deny?" Both are open-ended questions, and the myriad of answers to each question must then be weighed against each other to determine the calculated net answer, yes or no. But humans are lazy and often will deny a request simply for the reason of not having to go through the effort of weighing the merits. The human brain knows the default "no" is disingenuous, but it's simple and usually ends the task. Simplicity accomplished. However, when you make a request accompanied by rationale for granting that request, your human subject can choose to simply grant your request because the rationale has already been provided. Otherwise, they'll have to go through the mental exercise of weighing the rationale you provided against the counter-arguments they will have to develop themselves. You've changed the landscape by providing an effective nudge to your subject human. The simple default answer has been shifted to a "yes" irrespective of the quality or merit of the rationale. The human brain is lazy. The default answer, "yes," wins the day. The request will most likely be granted, obviously scaled by importance.

If you have good rationale, use it. It helps assure your success. For instance, "We would like to secure all the parking in the rear of the project because we need a place to park our service trucks."

If you don't have good rationale, find something. Have fun with it. "Can I get you the contracts on Monday? It's the day after the weekend."

By the way, if the TSA traveler rebuffs you when you say, "My dog ate my homework," follow up with the "It's been a crazy day" rationale. They'll let you in line for sure.

So, link prescribed rationale when making all your requests -- because it works.

Triggering your Counterparts' People Pleasing Programming

This is simple to do, but you might have to get on an airplane. (At least you'll get to your gate on time, right?) Meet with your counterparts in person, if possible. It's much more difficult for them to reject you if you are in their physical presence. Most people have automatic people-pleasing programming, which turns on when the two of you are together, unless something is broken in them or in the relationship. The people-pleasing mechanism is so strong, it might even turn on if the rapport is challenged.

There is a story of a Japanese public official responsible for a massive transportation infrastructure project in Tokyo. After having completed the project, he was asked how he had navigated the stoic bureaucracy that threatened to stop him at every turn. His explanation was simple. He credited his success winning over the entrenched bureaucrats to "Over two-thousand cups of tea." Do the calculus; it might be worth your while to get on that plane.

Performing Pre-Negotiation Negotiations

These are covert one-sided negotiations you control. Seasoned business people don't want to negotiate against themselves; they want the back and forth of a sequential series of give and take. No problem, when you execute with Pre-Negotiation Negotiations, your opponents won't even know they're doing it.

You know by now that pushing or telling your counterparts to do anything is counterproductive. It just leads to more resistance. Remember Newton's third law of motion: for every action, there is an equal and opposite reaction. Productive play occurs when you ask leading questions of your counterparts that pull them in the direction of the important issue items you want to resolve early. The decisions they make are based on conclusions they arrived at themselves. You simply need to show them the path.

For instance, "I was wondering what your thoughts were on how to address the need to upgrade the HVAC control units." You've created a vacuum with that question your counterpart is compelled to answer. If they don't think the control units need upgrading, they'll tell you, and you'll know that will have to be addressed in a proposal or trading of concessions later. But if your counterpart agrees the units need upgrading, they might very well say that they will handle that task because they want to keep you moving forward to make an offer. A win for you out of context, and it costs you nothing. You can sweep up all the little shit before you start the offer phase of the negotiations. But be careful that you're not the one who gets pulled into negotiating issues one at a time, at any time. It's almost never a good idea.

These pre-negotiation negotiations can also be used to get early agreements on items you expect will be contested or debated during the offer phase. The human mind has a bias to defend and support previous decisions and will do so by continuing to make decisions that are aligned on the same vector. So, ask your counterpart for the smallest increment of that thing, something easy to grant. Once granted, they'll have a propensity to expand on it. For instance, if your objective is to secure four, five-year renewal options, initiate your discussions in the pre-negotiation negotiations with the concept of an option, not how many. Once they've made the decision to support an option, they'll likely then agree to sequential options.

Ordering up Oxytocin Compelled Conclusions

As you approach the offer and proposal phase of the negotiations when actual numbers and terms are presented, rejected, tabled, modified, traded, and finally accepted, praise your counterparts' previous decision making. Tell your counterparts their earlier decisions were correct at the time and correct given the information they had. Tell them they'll make the right decision this time too. You'll release a load of oxytocin in your counterpart. Studies have shown the presence of oxytocin increases generosity on the part of the subjects when compared with placebos. When you present your offer, state your message using the same beliefs, values, and principles as what you've ascertained helped deliver your counterpart to their earlier decisions. They'll subconsciously thank you for it by being more accommodating in their responses.

The Mind-Altering First Offer
with Autosuggestion Triggers

We make money, and we make money for our clients, because markets aren't efficient and decision making is not efficient. We take advantage of those inefficiencies. By executing the Mind-Altering First Offer (MAFO), we trigger our oppositions' autosuggestion responses that change their behaviors and advances our desired objectives. This is a quintessential Applied Influence move.

RFPs suck. The first formal volley in negotiations in most organizations is the request for proposal (RFP). RFPs are basically a list of requirements and requests, then finished off with the mind-numbing, open-ended question, "How much is this going to cost for what we want?" Big and small organizations alike use RFPs because they don't know the market as they could, and they assume they can learn what they need to know by "going to school" on the respondents. They don't have to think very much or do any real research. It's like composing a Dear Santa letter. They mistakenly believe that the respondents will feel the pressure of competition and respond with their best deal terms. Wrong, wrong, and wrong; companies using RFPs are flushing billions of dollars down the toilet in lost negotiating delta.

RFPs are a flawed version of the classic game theory standard, the competitive ultimatum game. In the competitive ultimatum game, multiple offerors responding to an RFP submit offers to one offeree. Then the offeree accepts the offer they deem most to their liking. But in the real world, the results are corrupted because the drafter of the RFP, the offeree, can accept more than one of the offers. Even if the RFP states the offeree will accept no more than one proposal, everyone knows that the offeree can and will, perhaps sequentially, if necessary, so the offerors don't offer their best terms because they know they'll eventually be asked to improve upon what they proposed.

The information received in response to RFPs is mostly worthy of the trash. It's rehashed marketing materials, and the pricing isn't competitive in any meaningful way. Offerors don't give their best pricing unless they think they're going to get the deal, and nobody reaches that threshold responding to an RFP. If they do believe they're going to get the deal in response to an RFP, it won't be because of their pricing, so they won't give their best pricing. The only results organizations achieve by collating responses to an RFP is to reaffirm what the opposition already wants you to think is a market price -- the anchor they happily set for you. The process reaffirms that anchor, and the drafter of the RFP is in a worse position than before. Nothing gained, leverage lost.

List price, ask price, market price, it's all shit. It's not value. It's the Lemming Price. It's not real, and it's not your price. It's your counterparts' anchors that are mindlessly accepted in hopes of then being able to negotiate some morsel of a discount away from it as if it's chiseled in stone. Their anchors loom over the negotiations for the duration of the talks. The lemmings ask for "some scraps, please." If you enter any negotiation and you consider any price given to you ahead of time as any sort of benchmark, you've screwed yourself and you've screwed your client. Disregard and discard all of that and start over with the Mind-Altering First Offer.

The Mind-Altering First Offer resets the anchors, so your counterparts are negotiating away from your anchored numbers instead of you negotiating away from theirs. This is not just offering a lower or lowball price; that's not a sufficient strategy and may work against you. If they consider your first offer to be ridiculous, you'll lose credibility. Their defenses will go up. Instead, disengage their anchors, the "list price," "asking price," and "market price," and replace them with your anchors. The MAFO sets new anchors, yours, and they're chiseled in stone. Throw away any thoughts of using an RFP. Let the RFP RIP.

Resetting the anchors is accomplished by initiating thoughts and actions that trigger new autosuggestion responses in the mind of your counterparts and unseats their prior beliefs about the pricing of their product.

Before you can change their anchors and their perception of value and pricing, you first need to establish, from your price discovery, the real value to you of the product/asset under consideration from data you determine pertinent and weighted accordingly. Your value of the thing under consideration is your price target.

In any transaction, there is a range of possible pricing. The top end of the range is the most you're willing to pay, and the bottom of the range is the least your counterpart is willing to accept. This is the range of acceptance. The bottom price, the least amount your counterpart is willing to accept, may have some hard constraints influencing it such as fixed costs, debt service, or loan conditions, and you'll need to ascertain best you can what those are. Achieving a number lower than the bottom price of the range is possible, but would probably involve workout scenarios with the lenders or others.

Consider the negotiations as a tenant for a well-located, big-box retail site in a major city. The local brokerage community will eagerly tell you what they consider "market" for the space, which is likely the price the dumbest tenant in town is willing to pay for it and is probably near the landlord's asking price. These "market" prices are all skewed high because brokers generate most of their income representing landlords, and the skewed higher rents turn into a self-fulfilling prophecy. The tenants get screwed. Skewed rents equal screwed tenants.

The MAFO unlocks the previously untapped lower end of the pricing range – achieving the lowest rent numbers the landlords could possibly accept.

Pricing ignorance is a tremendous source of market power over tenants by landlords and brokers. Pricing ignorance is an enormous source of market power over the uninitiated in any transaction type by those that control the flow of data. As market obliqueness and market research costs rise, competitive equilibrium devolves into one with monopolistic or oligopolistic characteristics. Spare no effort in your proper price discovery to break the hold that ignorance supports. Use your price target to benchmark success for your negotiations and not your counterparts' anchors.

Your price target is not an anchor. You don't reveal it outside of your circle of confidants, but it's going to be your likely outcome as a result of this process. You set new, strategic anchors to trigger your counterpart's autosuggestion responses, so to arrive at your price.

With the Mind-Altering First Offer, you set three or more new anchors by saturating the contextual settings of your opponent's mind with new information. The first anchor is the Deep Anchor. This is a number significantly below your target price and well below the bottom of the pricing range. This number can be an anomaly, or a first quintile number based on your research and market pricing scatter chart. It doesn't matter where this number comes from, but it helps if it's related to the market you're dealing with. You don't propose this number in your offer. Using the Deep Anchor number as an offer price might only result in offending your counterpart and further entrench their position and bolster their rationale for their pricing. It might also be perceived as a nonsense bid, harming your credibility. Instead, project the Deep Anchor number so it is heard in a non-threatening fashion.

"I was surprised to find in my research offering rents in the $5.00 range. None of those have risen to the level we think is a fit yet, but we think we have a pretty good understanding of the market now and look forward to your favorable response to our offer." A statement such as this doesn't scare them, it doesn't offend, they don't become entrenched, but the jury heard it. That's all that's necessary. They start to think in terms of moving away from your low Deep Anchor number. There is also a pinch of uncertainty for the landlord in that statement, and they wonder what happens next. Present several Deep Anchors if you choose.

The next step in the saturation process is setting the next two or three anchor numbers by proposing two or more scenarios for pricing in your offer, any of which would be suitable for you and your client. I like to present a multiple-choice offer with two or three answers to choose from. The multiple scenarios I structure will yield a constant net present value (NPV), but the structures and incentives vary. For instance, one offer scenario may be a clean, simple, flat rent for the term. The second scenario may be at a higher face rate but also include some free rent and a landlord funded tenant finish allowance. A third offer might start at a substantially lower rate with periodic increases arriving at a higher face rate at the end of the term. The NPVs of each rent stream are the same, so all else being equal, we like each of the three offer scenarios equally as much. I might choose to incorporate into the pricing schemes a Relative Advantage or Decoy operant. The landlord's process of analyzing and comparing each scenario against the others further saturates their subconscious with your numbers and solidifies each scenario presented as a new anchor.

Also, structure your MAFO to prepare for trading and concessions later in the negotiations. Front-load your offer with soft issue asks that you can use as trade-away concessions. These predetermined concessions include items that would be nice for you to get, but that you're willing to walk away from so you can trade them for your most important items and targets. If little or no trading occurs later, then you can chalk up those asks as additional perks in your win. Put those into the offer up front because you can't add them later. Protect your important issue items by trading away from your predetermined concessions list.

Set a hard date for their response, but assume that fifty percent of the time they'll miss it. Don't let that concern you. It's their feeble attempt at fighting against you.

The U.S. Postal Service asked me to check out a regional distribution facility they had in the Blue Ridge Mountains. The lease was scheduled to expire, and they had an option to renew it, but it was expensive. I reviewed all the details, and it was obvious the Postal Service was paying too much for the site, so I went to work.

I did all the in-market research I usually do and put together a dossier on the landlord. I thought the tenant was paying twice what they should. The landlord was a trust set up by the developer, and they had a local lawyer playing defense when I came on the scene. The lawyer's boring old strategy was to not talk with the tenant or me and try to force the Postal Service to exercise the option (it always is). I structured a Mind-Altering First Offer that contained two scenarios: a five-year term and a ten-year term, both netting the same net present value rental rate and both acceptable to my client because both scenarios cut the rent roughly in half. One of the deep anchors I used was zero rent, pointing out there were several high-profile bankruptcies plaguing the market, including a regional grocery chain that had been the center and foundational part of the community for decades. Though the chain had just declared bankruptcy and no decision had yet been made as to whether or not that particular store would close for good, that was just the uncertainty I needed. The landlord feared if we vacated their large site, it might be vacant for years. Still, the lawyer was reluctant to respond to my proposal. I figured he just couldn't bring himself to the realization that he'd have to recommend to his client to take a fifty percent haircut. What lawyer would?

So, I got on an airplane to Atlanta, enjoyed the drive through the beautiful Blue Ridge Mountains, and walked into that lawyer's office unannounced and politely asked to see him. The receptionist scurries off to tell him of my presence and then comes back saying, "He's very busy; it's going to be awhile." "How long?" I asked. "Could be hours," she said. I said, "Okay, I'll wait." She was obviously stunned. I sat down on the couch in the reception area, pulled out my laptop and other materials, took over the little coffee table setting their mags on the floor, and started doing my work. I was set up for the afternoon. I can work anywhere, you know.

After maybe ten minutes, the receptionist disappeared again. She reappears in short order and says, "he'll see you now," and she shows me into a stuffy, musty, dark, dank conference room that made me think of a 1970's man cave. I don't remember if there were any dart boards or framed mirrors with beer company logos painted on the glass, but there might as well have been. I sank about eight inches into the cracked black leather chair as I sat down. A few faceted brass buttons were missing from the upholstery. I told him I was surprised I hadn't received a response from him yet and asked if he had one? He mumbled something but had no real response. I reiterated that I was 18 months into a staunch cost reduction initiative for the Postal Service and that I'd seen many sites closed and merged and relocated and that I was in town to take another look around. I thanked him for his time and left.

It was just a coincidence that I was standing in the parking lot of the grocery that had just filed for bankruptcy when the Trustee called me 15 minutes later. She wanted to talk with me personally, and soon we came to terms on a new ten-year term. The cost savings to my client was over 50 percent off their option price. I had more than cut their rent in half.

If you question the efficacy of the power of spontaneous autosuggestion, do this exercise with a group of your friends or business associates. It's enlightening.

Give everyone a piece of white paper with two perpendicular lines drawn sectioning the paper into four quadrants. Mark each quadrant with a number, beginning with the number 1 in the upper left quadrant and then clockwise with 2, 3, and 4. Give each player a pendulum made of a washer tied at the end of a piece of thread about 12 or 14 inches long. Tell each player to hold the pendulum over the center of the page for the entire exercise. That's the only instruction you'll give them. Then begin to speak in a calm voice, "one, two, three, four; one, two, three, four; one, two, three, four"; and so on. This is not instruction; you'll just be talking aloud to the room. Your players' minds can't ignore it, though, and soon you'll see the pendulums in the room begin to swing clockwise, following the path of the numbers 1, 2, 3, and 4. You'll also hear some chuckles of disbelief and "whoa." Fun, but then change your message, "one, three; one, three; one, three"; and so on. You'll see the pendulums change and start to swing diagonally across the page tracking the numbers 1 then 3 then back to 1 then 3 again. Then change your message a third time, "four, three, two, one; four, three, two, one; and so on. The pendulums will start to swing counterclockwise. At this point, everyone in the room will be amazed at what just happened. If you now told them to pick up the piece of paper and eat it, half the people will laugh, but the other half will look around the room looking for support as to why they shouldn't.

This is not just a parlor game; it shows the power you have to influence and actuate desired behavior in your subjects that is driven by their subconscious. It's a fun example of Applied Influence.

15

HAMMERS

PRESSURE, TENSION, AND DENIAL OF SERVICE

"Cry 'Havoc!' and let slip the dogs of war."
-- Shakespeare, Mark Antony in Julius Caesar

In *The Dark Knight*, Batman's butler and alter-alter ego, Alfred (Michael Caine), bemoans, "Some men aren't looking for anything logical. They can't be bought, bullied, reasoned or negotiated with. Some men just want to watch the world burn." The statement is insightful but incomplete for our purposes. Being perceived as such a person is an extremely consequential negotiating strategy, but you have to be able to take the heat. I have a high threshold for pain. I'm nearly impervious to it. Though I don't necessarily want the world to burn, I don't mind watching while the world does burn, and those around me scramble to find ways to get me what I want so the world doesn't burn down around them. This is dangerous ground.

When your counterpart is moving in the direction of your desired outcomes and all you need to do is navigate your ride down the river and close the deal, enjoy it. Conversely, if your counterpart has instead gone a little insane, had a giant brain fart, or let some innate incompetence take over and run things off course, you'll want to give them an extra push so they will become more aligned with your thinking. These Hammers will help.

If you think I've been too nice up to this point, you'll enjoy this chapter. This is when you get to go hard.

The Four Horsemen of the Apocalypse

You've got to give it to the Four Horsemen and the doom, dread, dire, and gloom they rode in on. They got their point across. Those killers are a perfectly reasonable hyperbolic analogy for the shit I'm prepared to rain down on my opposition when the circumstances warrant it.

The first of these restless stallions brings conquest, and my unwavering determination and willingness to bring about the results I intend and to bear my full acceptance of risk to do so. The second horse, war, unleashes disruption of the status quo, convention, complacency, certainty, satisfaction, and smugness. The third horse wreaks famine, causing discomfort and pain by upending supply chains, funding sources, allies, and employees. And fourth, the pale horse, the last and most feared, portends death as I strategically and deliberately dismantle anything unacceptable.

What follows are some of my tools I set lose on my opponents to haunt their sorry asses and fill their nightmares with the doubt and fear they deserve if they become unreasonable beyond my patience.

Flame the Cockroaches

If I'm not getting satisfaction in my negotiations because of my opponents' inaction, ignorance, incompetence, intransigence, ill-will, or lack of communication for any reason; I'll flame the cockroaches by lighting up their chain of command, supply chain, food chain, external source of esteem, and social order. I'll be persistent. You needn't follow the hierarchy you've been dealt. Ignore it and start talking to their boss and their boss's boss and everybody that has an inkling of authority, their higher-ups, customers, clients, or other third parties. Expand out to include their friends, their cliques, their tribes, their industry. They can all get included. Take it to the press, big or small. Everybody has hierarchical higher-ups they answer to whether it's their bosses, boards of directors, partners, shareholders, lenders, spouses, families, the community, governmental entities, or their social circles. You don't need to abide by the hierarchical norms, but your counterparts will always be under the collective hierarchical thumbs. I'll take their unacceptable behavior and its negative stain and throw it on everyone associated with them. I'll put it on display for every entity in the hierarchy and won't be shy about it.

Incompetence, inaction, ignorance, intransigence, and ill-will flourish best in the dark, in a vacuum. The cockroaches scurry along, thinking they're protected by the 200 million years of evolution that made them so gross, and the moist, dark crevices they hide in. But they're not safe. Flame them and expose them to the authorities that oversee them; the people they report to; the people they polish their image for; the people they lie to in order to get support, a leg up, their paycheck or next measly meal, or whatever their little cockroach brains might want. Spread the word, turn on the lights, and watch the cockroaches run. Light them up, and don't be shy. Expose them and the situation to the light of day. Spread the word like an insecticide cloud. Be harsh or be gentle; it's your call depending upon the circumstances. You neutralize their fake intimidation and other nonsense those entitled little shits depend on for control and turn it on its head. The change you want happens almost immediately.

I was negotiating a new lease renewal term with a landlord in a Southern California coastal town for a huge health club facility. My client was paying way too much for the market, so I was looking to reduce their costs drastically. The landlord knew he'd been getting a windfall and wasn't happy with my presence in the deal. He made every attempt to avoid me. He wouldn't return my phone calls or emails. Even a personal trip to his office proved unproductive -- not there and no return call.

My research dossier on the landlord showed a community bank in the area held his mortgage for the property. I walked into that bank, found the landlord's personal banker, and explained that I was considering signing a new long-term lease at the property the bank held as collateral, but had been unable to do so because the landlord was MIA. That was gentle, but that was all that was needed. Humans don't like you talking to their authority, their hierarchical higher-ups, especially their lenders. The landlord called me within two days. We worked out terms, saving my client over 20 percent in occupancy costs.

Lenders are particularly useful for cockroach-flaming purposes. In another instance, I had signed a new lease for a big home improvement retailer in an affluent suburb south of Chicago. But after the deal was signed, the space built, and the retailer occupied the property, the landlord wasn't paying my company the agreed-upon fee. Then the landlord and his staff started avoiding me. Cockroaches. I pulled the mortgage note, deed of trust, and the associated assignment-of-rents to the lender and studied them. These documents had provisions that required the landlord to professionally manage the property, including paying the bills, and do nothing that might create any encumbrance on the rent stream or title to the property. Close enough for me. I called the mortgage company, pointed out the provision to them, and the current default. I had my check within the week.

Stalking Horse Assault

A stalking horse is an alternative course of action perceived by your opposition as being particularly viable for you. Perception is a funny thing. The validity of one's perception, your oppositions' perception, for instance, is of no consequence. The only thing that matters is the intensity of it, not whether it's valid. Perceptions are most intense when conjured up in the fearful minds of those doing the perceiving. If you say it, it's suspect. If they think it, it's true.

There are three types of stalking horses I find useful. (1) True alternative solutions: These I nurture parallel with any on-going negotiation as a backstop if I need to kill my primary target. (2) Attractive alternative solutions: These may or may not be true alternative solutions but are attractive as stalking horse picks because their pricing, value, or utility is particularly impressive and useful for comparison purposes. And (3) the virtual stalking horse options, and my favorites: These exist only in the mind of your counterpart's imagination which you happily foster and allow to grow. This third type is particularly devastating because it's impossible to defend against.

They're all nearly impossible to defend against because you never disclose the details of any of your stalking horses. You don't even tell your counterparts overtly that you have any, but you allow them to come to understand through your words and actions that they exist, maybe many of them. You're never specific about your stalking horses because if your counterparts know what they are, they can always find ways to poke holes in them. Without specifics, they just worry about them and imagine the worst-case scenarios. Conversely, if your counterparts keep yammering on about the market and comps or alternatives that support their positions, invite them to send over the information. If they don't send the info, they are either lying or ill-informed and have now lost credibility. If they do send you the info, you can poke holes in them, rendering their arguments moot. Nothing exists that you can't poke holes in, only what isn't revealed.

Subtlety and nuance are important. If you brag about your stalking horse picks and don't reveal the information, you lose credibility. If you reveal the details, they're rendered less useful. It's when your counterparts are guided and allowed to conjure up the details themselves, that the pressure builds, doubt and uncertainty increases, and the stalking horses manifest the most benefit for you.

Executive Action
(Threats are for Stupid People)

On-going negotiations are best kept in a fluid state. When one side or the other becomes overtly entrenched or vested in a position, forward energy in a transaction can slow down or even stop, making a successful outcome more difficult. You can make matters worse by making threats. The absolute worst is an unenforceable threat. If you make an overt threat against your opponent, you will see them respond with energy of equal magnitude and force. Their response will be of disdain, defense, closed-mindedness, and entrenchment. You will have achieved nothing. You will have forced your opponent to reaffirm their prior positions, rightly or wrongly, to the detriment of you, your client, and the transaction. Always keep the transaction in a fluid state.

If you proffer an unenforceable threat, you have only set yourself up to be discredited and ridiculed. If your counterpart calls your hand and you're unable to perform, you're toast. With your integrity and credibility in shambles, your ability to negotiate further in any meaningful way is mostly gone. Never threaten.

When I first started handling the U.S. Postal Service occupancy cost reduction negotiations, I was partnered with one of the big national brokerages. As that work got underway, I started organizing the network to handle the business and internal and external communications, processes and procedures, and scheduling meetings in the eight different field service offices (FSOs) the Postal Service staffed around the country to manage their 25,000 locations. Alan, the liaison with the big national I was partnered with, immediately got started ordering 250 Kleenex box covers shaped like little mailman delivery trucks for some silly purpose. I can't tell you why he did it. He couldn't even give them to Postal employees because of rules against accepting gifts. This may have been the apex of Alan's contribution to the project.

As I started doing Postal Service deals across the country and meeting with more FSOs, it became apparent that the big national's local people weren't up to the task. So, I started using my own network. The Postal Service was pleased with this new arrangement, but Alan, with his tiny Kleenex box covers shaped like mail delivery trucks stacked high on his desk, was not at all pleased. He called me on the phone enraged and said if I didn't stop doing the transactions with my own network and if I didn't stop meeting with the Postal Service without him, "There would be consequences!" This conversation took place about 30 minutes before I was to meet with the decision-makers in the Southeast FSO, the biggest region in the system at the time. The only consequence that came out of Alan's threat was that he froze himself and his company out of any of the transactions I did with the Postal Service moving forward. I went to that meeting with the Southeast Field Service Office that morning alone and secured 50 new assignments, hundreds then followed.

Never threaten; your outcomes are never as you anticipate. Do you want to threaten you'll walk from the deal? Don't; instead, just walk from the deal. Your outcomes will be resolutely more productive. Do you want to threaten you'll call a supervisor? Don't; instead, call the supervisor and call that supervisor's supervisor. You get the outcome you're looking for instead of looking like a shmuck. The weakest forms of power are coercion, threat, position, and force. Vacuous aggression is suicide.

I was in the process of selling an office tower in the central business district. It was a quality building with strong tenants, mostly military and government. There was a lot of interest in the property. The first credible group to come forward was a public pension fund. Discussions about the price and leases and maintenance were going well, and they wanted to set up a meeting with their board of directors and me, which we did. After I gave the board the basic information about the building, the conversation turned to the structure of the deal and pricing. Several of the board members immediately pounced. They launched into telling me our asking price was too high and asking how much would I be willing to reduce it. Usually, I represent commercial buyers and investors in these types of transactions, so I was a little amused by the amateurish approach they were using. Plus, I think the whole "pounce" thing had been planned. I had no interest in playing along. I told them we knew what we wanted for the property. If they didn't want to pay our price, we would sell it to someone else. I knew that would be true. Many of the board members became offended that I wouldn't negotiate with them. Some even complained to my client directly that I had been so rude to come out and tell them, "take it or leave it." I knew what we could achieve in the market, and I didn't want to mess around with half-baked negotiators. They did buy the building at my price. It was "take it or leave it," but we had the guns to back it up. They're lucky I didn't raise the price.

There may be times when it does come down to an ultimatum, but then it must be purely objective, and you can't be vested in one direction or another. If you are, you haven't handled the transaction with the skill required. Never attempt to use more power than is necessary to influence your desired outcome. Less is always more. Veiled threats are equally amateurish. The only threat your counterparts should be feeling are those they conjure themselves.

Hellfire Haboobs

At any stage of a negotiation, or renegotiation, your opposition may start to act as though you're operating within a closed system, that your options are limited, that your only or best option is them. When this happens, they'll become much less accommodating than they ought to be. There's a fix for that.

There are giant storm fronts in certain parts of the world that cause walls of dust and debris 5,000 feet high and 50 miles long that bear down on every town and farm and animal and human in its path. You can see it coming ahead of time, but not with enough time to do much of anything about it. In the Middle East, they're called "Haboobs," but they occur in many arid parts of the world. Texas and Arizona have them. Also called "Black Blizzards, they were a central feature of the Dust Bowl of Oklahoma and throughout the Great Plains that wiped out millions of farmers during the Great Depression. Those were an unintended consequence of bad U.S. government policy that incentivized farmers to use ag practices that didn't protect the topsoil. But that's another story. The point I'm getting to is that I can create information storms that can obliterate everything anybody understands as normal in the negotiation and gum up the machinery just like those Hellfire Haboobs.

My haboob hammers inundate the market with eager alternatives for my requirements, making my opponent an insignificant part of the equation, and they know it. I do this by opening up my requirement parameters, making them known ubiquitously in the marketplace, and soliciting engagement from all the players regardless of their perceived fit ahead of time. I get the word out to all participants and influencers in the market, making my presence and requirements known. You create chatter. You become news. There's a rumble. If there's a viral component, all the better. The buzz that's created starts to build pressure on your counterparts as they wonder what is going on without them. You're everywhere, talking to everyone. You'll drive your counterparts crazy, and their uneasiness will grow.

I will fly into a city and set meetings with everyone except my subject just to create unbalance and uncertainty in my counterparts. Robert Ringer, in his book, *Winning Through Intimidation*, postulated that the further one travels, the greater the esteem is bestowed unto them at their destination. The "expert from afar" he called it. I have found that to be true in my own travels, and it also applies by extension to the implied importance of the trip. Your counterparts assume that if you're flying into the city and not meeting with them, there must be something else of importance going on. There usually is; I make it so. But the hammer of uncertainty and concern comes down on your subject nonetheless, as planned.

The Postal Service had a big distribution facility outside of Houston that was coming off a lease they needed to renew. Negotiating USPS sites can be a challenge because it pretty much takes an act of congress to close or move one of these things, so the landlords think they have the Postal Service over a barrel and can dictate terms. The Postal Service was looking down the barrel of a big rent increase, so they brought me in to fix it. As an aside, this was one of the assignments I secured after the vacuous threat from Alan with his little mail-truck Kleenex box covers.

This landlord was no dummy. He was a grand poohbah in the CCIM organization. CCIMs are educated, though I'm the only one I know that ever aced their bedrock Financial Analysis test with a perfect score. At first, I couldn't even get him to return my calls. He figured he didn't need to.

I found that this guy owned big tracts of vacant land, and he also carried a significant debt load. I also learned that he had liquidated some of his holdings. I assumed he had done that because the debt service was becoming a problem. I didn't know the exact extent of his financial condition, but I knew enough to know that he was counting on the Postal Service deal. It looked to me that he had a fuse burning.

I flew to Houston to do my research. I walked into his office without telling him I was coming and introduced myself. These surprise visits can put the opponents back on their heels a bit. It puts them a little off-balance, particularly if they've been trying to avoid you. They're not prepared and a little out of control. They might become a little anxious. Some get intimidated. You get a more honest view of their humanness. You get a more real interaction.

I started asking him about his land. He became very uncomfortable with this discussion. He didn't want to talk about that topic, so he started talking about the Postal Service to deflect the conversation. I told him I was in town to look for sites, and then I left. I loosened the parameters of my requirement for a replacement site, and blasted that information throughout the market, making it known ubiquitously. I made three more trips to Houston, making him aware each time I was there, but never meeting with him, or even attempting to. I just let him sit and stew and wonder.

On my last trip, I sent him a message that I was coming and that it would probably be my last trip there; that I didn't think I would need to come back. He was eager to meet. In short order, we came to an agreement that dropped the rent to the U.S. Postal Service better than 16%, even lower than our target price.

This landlord thought he had us over a barrel, but he didn't. His insecurities got in his way, and I made it our advantage. I didn't chase him, push him, or plead with him; that all would have been useless. I did just the opposite. He wanted to avoid me, and in answer, I avoided him and made my presence known ubiquitously in the marketplace. I was patient and aloof. A pair of balls beats any hand in Poker.

I worked on hundreds of transactions for the U.S. Postal Service, saving them millions. I stopped working on Postal Service deals when they signed a no-bid contract with a national brokerage whose chairman was married to a U.S. Senator. That didn't work out so well for the Postal Service or the taxpayers. The Postal Service budget exploded, and the taxpayers got stuck with the bill, but that's another story. It's insane the Postal Service loses so much money. I could put them on a profitable footing in a year.

Smack, Thrash, Pummel, and Bash

Herb Simon was a Nobel Laureate, and prolific economist, computer scientist, and sociologist. His work encompassed extensive study in the cognitive processes of decision making. This was instrumental in the foundational work and algorithms behind artificial intelligence. He coined the term "Satisfice" as a means to express people's propensity to accept the first set of tolerable terms because of their desire for expediency rather than work harder to achieve a more optimal solution. The name "Satisfice" is a conjunction of the words "Satisfy" and "Suffice."

Humans are lazy; they want it easy. You could also say that humans are practical; they don't want to waste energy if they can get their basic needs met easily. They'll take a satisfactory solution to a problem before they put forth the effort to pursue a more optimal one. It's the principle of good enough, happy enough. If the decision-maker is strained, they'll clamor for the first satisfactory solution; everything else be damned.

The skill required to impose this on your opponent requires diligence, patience, and resilience. If your optimal outcome is not the same as your counterpart's, and it rarely is, position yourself between your counterpart and their optimal outcome, increasing their strain and the energy and effort required to achieve that solution. This will trigger their cognitive expediency response and a willingness to accept a lesser outcome.

Strain signals a threat in humans. Large threat or small, they'll immediately start to seek relief. The decision of expediency is an easy one for humans to make provided a level of sufficiency is achieved – the minimal needs of your counterpart.

If you're getting a negative response to your asks, don't give up. Never give up. The first "no" your opponent gives you may be habitual. The second one, reflexive. The third "no" requires more effort, and your counterpart will need to start to build a supporting argument because they're starting to feel the strain. The fourth time you make your ask, your subject may become flummoxed. This is new territory for them as the strain increases. Five, six, and seven is territory under your control. The most productive thing you hear might be the fourth or fifth or later "no" because the next response you hear may very well be "yes" because they can't hold up under the strain any longer. Persevere. When you've been turned down, don't recoil or retreat; reload.

Never concede; instead, delay and trade. You have your predetermined concessions list. Use it to protect your required and most essential outcomes by trading from your concessions list.

Killer Crib Notes:

Keep your negative emotions in check. Stay calm, cool, composed, and in possession of yourself. Fear nothing.

Never use more power than necessary for the influence you need.

Do elicit fear only if you provide your opponents with a clear means to avoid the negative outcome. Otherwise, they will "block out" or "numb out" to the danger.

Focus on your opponents' loss aversion. Leverage the people's fear to losing something they already have. It's more potent than the drive to move forward to something they want.

Remember, don't make demands and don't be absolute.

In direct negotiations, don't offend, insult, criticize, or belittle. I'm referring to the asset, product, or skill, under consideration, as well as your counterpart or his ability or processes. Your objective is to win the negotiation, not who can be the biggest asshole. Being an asshole just puts obstacles in your way.

That said, there is a place for anger in competition and negotiations. There are some productive outcomes that can come from it, but it's got to be kept in check and directed. Anger is an approach emotion because it causes you to be proactive, to move toward the subject and attack it. It fires you up to take action and make change. It enhances your persistence. That's why coaches trash-talk opposing teams. Careful, though, because it can harm the relationship. And though it can fill you up emotionally, it can drain you emotionally as well. It must be measured and well-articulated. Get mad right before the fight. Assess your audience and gauge the reception. Focus on the objectives. Believe it will work. Focus on what is not fair. Use blame as fuel. Ruminate on it; it will empower your attack. Just don't become enmeshed with it and know how and when to let it go. If it becomes chronic, you're the one who gets ill.

Studies show that our expectations influence our outcomes. Our expectations make us take actions that create results that are in line with our expectations. If we think our anger will help us win a negotiation, we're more likely to do so. It's a self-fulfilling prophecy. Nonetheless, if your anger causes you to lose self-possession, steer clear.

None of this is going to work for you if you're not prepared. Bluster, arrogance, and blatancy is just bullshit, and nobody cares. It's counterproductive. You'll just look foolish. Real success is based on your knowledge of the cognitive and emotional catalysts the markets ride on. You might be able to slough off once or twice or even get a string of wins with a scripted spiel, glad-hand sweet talk, outright fraud, or offensive threats, but you'll never reach consistent alpha performance if you don't do the real work to build your deep cognitive bench about your chosen focus and the players you encounter there.

Existing market conditions will be strong tailwinds or strong headwinds depending upon your positioning. If market trends are against you, ask yourself why you're there in the first place. If you don't have a compelling answer, leave. Find the markets that can support you. If that's not an option, you can still win negotiations, but you had better know this stuff, and sometimes you're going to pay a premium, pay a price, and it might be out of your hide.

If you can, find those markets where you can take a position that invites your success instead of fight against you. If straight math is on your side, use it. Pile on the logic and reason. If not, bring on the creativity. Logic can show you the path from A to B, but imagination can take you throughout the universe. When you have the facts, pound the facts. When you have the trends, pound the trends. When you have neither, compel your creativity and consciously finesse the constraints surrounding you – or crush them. You choose.

16

CHEATS

SIMPLE STEPS TO OPPOSITION ACQUIESCENCE

"Intellectuals solve problems; geniuses prevent them."
-- Albert Einstein

"It doesn't seem that there is any life left in this deal. Is this deal dead?"

This is one of my favorite questions. It reveals nothing of your position other than a simple request for objective information, and it conveys a sense of your ambivalence and aloofness as to whether the deal gets done or not. Your counterparts are programmed to habitually answer "no" to questions they're faced with during negotiations, and they might be a little surprised in themselves as the word is coming out of their mouths that they've just confirmed they're moving forward with the deal. It's fun to watch them backpedal then, but it doesn't do them any good.

You've revealed nothing, they've revealed everything. If they answered "yes" to the question, then you have some objective information you should have known before. It's time to deal with it.

Your job is to keep your counterparts a little off-center, a little off-balance. Your counterparts' comfort is not your objective. If you're new at this, you might feel that tug as your own insecurity seeks more communal belonging. But don't be distracted. Keep your eyes on your targets. Be attentive, but aloof, professional, but vague. You've brought your counterparts into your sphere, and you might want to treat them as guests. They are in a way, I guess, but remember they are the opposition and your job is to win the negotiations. You don't suppress your needs in favor of theirs. You don't limit the satisfaction of your needs to the level of satisfaction of theirs.

It's also important that you don't fall for the lie of relativism wherein victory is declared if the loss you suffer is less than that suffered by your opponent. A win must be determined in absolute terms for your purposes, irrespective of its relativism to your counterparts' results. If your counterparts win, great. It's not your objective, but it's not your objective that they suffer either. Your objective is achieving your optimal results in absolute terms for you and your clients, not in relation to anybody else.

Romantic Entropy

There is nothing like the charge you get when romance is in flow. Dopamine and oxytocin are set loose in your body and build feelings of power, invincibility, satisfaction, and fun. Throw in a taboo or two, and it's turbo time – speed-obsessed, tunnel vision, endorphin empowered. Just the two of you against the world. But what if it starts to crack, or a third party enters the picture? Emotions can go into overdrive.

The Boy/Girl phenomenon is fairly predictable and extends to areas outside of gender, love, and sex. Its dynamic is found in almost any human interaction.

Business deals track like interpersonal relationships. Two entities entering negotiations for a possible deal can be a lot like the Boy/Girl phenomenon. Boy meets girl; girl meets girl, whatever. They come together. They talk and get to know one another. They play, but stay non-committal and keep dating other people. Then one side perks up and takes the casual acquaintance to another level, offering a level of commitment, making a proposal to formalize and bring greater definition to the relationship in some form or fashion. Both entities are on their best behavior. Groomed, polite, endearing, and making promises they mostly believe. Romance blossoms while the union is considered, and if one side plays hard to get, it just intensifies the lobbying effort. Eventually, if value is given for value, the deal may get done, and the committed relationship is consummated. Good intentions abound, and then for some relationships, entropy has a starting point.

Both parties settle into their comfortable positions, bliss turns into happiness and contentment. But then something odd happens. One party starts to feel entitled, owed something more than their original value for value transaction, feeling more deserving than their mate. Their earlier romance with the powered tunnel vision to make the other one happy turns into a narcissistic exercise of "you owe me more." This often happens in on-going business relationships, and I have found it is often the state of affairs in commercial lease renewal negotiations. Who is usually the self-proclaimed entitled one who thinks they deserve more? The landlord.

I've been brought in hundreds, if not thousands, of times to represent the newly beholden party in such a transaction, the tenant. The landlords had slipped into the role of the domineering boyfriend, girlfriend, or spouse with a casual willingness to under-appreciate, if not abuse, their partner and demand more favorable terms in their relationship. The solution is easy. Rekindle the romance. Bring back the feelings they had when they first got together. This is accomplished by pulling back, backing away, making steps towards greener pastures. Let the self-entitled party feel a bit of separation. Let them see you out with your new friends having fun. Let them wonder what the future holds. Let the longing build. Let some jealousy fester. People will work more than twice as hard to keep from losing something they already have than to replace it. Have fun with the actions you take so the newly self-entitled party gets a better appreciation of value for the other, and the quality of relationship they had. Boy meets girl, again.

How Big is your BANANA?

If you've studied negotiations at all, you're familiar with the acronym BATNA, the Best Alternative To a Negotiated Agreement. I think the term was first coined by William Ury and Roger Fisher of the Harvard Program on Negotiation and made popular in the book, *Getting to YES*. It was described as an alternative to your least acceptable deal terms and what to do next if your deal fails. The problem is that markets aren't static, and it's unlikely you'll have a backup solution of any merit in your back pocket unless you've been working on it all along.

That said, you need to have a sense of what your oppositions' BATNAs are so you know their opportunity costs for losing you – what it's going to cost them not to do a deal with you. Time on the market, commissions, legal fees, new TIs, whatever, but again, know none of it is static.

My program, the better program, is to **Be Always Negotiating Another New Agreement**, your BANANA, parallel with your target negotiations, and the bigger, the better. Better yet, have a bunch of BANANAs. You should always be looking for better leverage and valutility.

You can let your opponent know that you have a BANANA or more, but not what they are.

Having quality BANANAs lessens your risk and instills greater confidence and solidifies your negotiations. Run two or more negotiations parallel for the same requirement so you can move seamlessly between them as necessary. With no BANANAs in place, failure to achieve your primary objective can be devastating. That danger can impact the level of risk you're willing to accept to achieve your objectives.

BANANAs can, of course, be stalking horses, but as with stalking horses, the details are always to be kept confidential. Your counterparts' knowledge as to the existence of your Stalking Horses can be helpful to you, but any specificity as to details or identities of either group must remain confidential. Revealing your BANANAs, stalking horses, or any alternatives can cause you to lose leverage and mystery. BANANAs are for your protection, in case you need to stick it to your counterpart.

Killer Compound Strategy

In the Hacks chapter, I introduced two effective influence techniques: autosuggestion and cognitive dissonance filters. As you move towards consummating your transaction, you will find these two techniques particularly useful when combined. It creates one killer compound strategy and takes things to the next level.

In the first discussion of cognitive dissonance filters, you leveraged your counterparts' self-image to influence their actions. But you don't need to limit yourself to the self-schema your counterparts present to you. Using waking suggestion and autosuggestion, you can imprint in your counterparts, consciously and subconsciously, self-identity elements that aren't currently being brought forward by them. These might be existing components that you want to expand and emphasize, or they can be new identity factors altogether. As you do this, the cognitive dissonance guardrails form naturally, and your counterparts led in the direction of your choosing.

New and emphasized identity elements are impressed on your counterparts' self-schema by verbalizing a positive rational linkage of the elements you choose to decisions your counterparts have made in the past, and can make in the future. Because your statement shows support for their previous decisions, the linked rationale will be accepted without scrutiny and become part of their identity schema. Following on our earlier cognitive dissonance example: "The buildings you've developed after your remediation efforts have put you in the top tier of office developers in the region." Or, "I think it was smart how you took control of the situation to get a better product by choosing to do a built-to-suit instead of buying an existing building." Or, "You were one of the first to get in on that investment. The early adopters reaped the rewards. Nice job." Or, "The people you hire seem to be cutting edge, super creative, out of the mainstream. That sets your product apart from the competition as an early adopter."

Link the rationale you want to emphasize that suits your purpose with the decisions they made in the past. They'll naturally embrace the identity component you affirmatively link with their prior decisions, and their future decisions will likewise be influenced by them.

Deal Suicide Help Line

Managing your counterparts' esteem needs is particularly important at the end-stage of the negotiations. Your opponents are going to give up a lot in your negotiations, so you have to help give them the rationale, the excuse, to allow them to justify arriving at your target objectives. If there is not a path for your counterparts to complete the transactions and maintain some self-respect, honor, and respect from their constituents and hierarchical overseers, the deals will be harder to close.

The terms will be less favorable for you, if the deals happen at all. If you leave your counterparts with no means to save face, they might fight to the death, which will likely be the fate of your deals. If you feel you need to destroy your opponents when the stakes are not life and death, then your priorities are wrong and misguided, and you are harming your positions in this and future negotiations (with anyone). There are few instances when total destruction is appropriate. If your actions are driven by the emotions of revenge, hate, your narcissism or self-aggrandizement, and not actual freedom or life, then your thinking and behavior need modifying.

It's in your best interest to help your counterparts protect their dignity and manage their own esteem needs. You make better deals. It makes for an easier path to your optimal outcomes. Keep in mind, too; this might not be the only transaction you'll be doing with these parties.

Using Neural Integration
to Remove Opponents' Reluctance

The amygdalae (plural for amygdala, there's two) are a part of the limbic system and the source of feelings of fear and anxiety caused by threatening events and things and out of your human subjects' control. This pair will likely light up in your subjects' heads as a result of your skilled negotiations, Mind-Altering First Offers, and the unfamiliar territory your counterparts now find themselves in. This new stress can cause the neural pathways in your subjects' heads to shut down and trigger defensive behaviors like freezing, aggression, and active avoidance. Expect it, you're uncovering new ground, but none of this helps achieve your objectives. Deal neglect is often the result of conflict between the parties. You need to help your subjects re-open the communication pathways by applying a form of cognitive behavior modification. This will calm the stress and allow their acceptance of the new norm you've imposed, enabling your subjects to move forward. Neural integration occurs when your subjects express their negative thoughts and emotions and have them heard and acknowledged so as not to be confined and fester. "I understand you feeling this way." Your affirmative empathetic statements presuppose and further the inevitability of the situations you've created. It's the nudge, the default option.

You need to elicit a complete response as possible, particularly their emotional reaction. It's the fear and concern that must be acknowledged before any substantive headway can be made on deal points in contention. Empathize with the feelings of your subjects and name for them the emotions they are feeling. This process helps neutralize and diffuse the power of the emotions and negative feelings.

Naming those emotions and expressing empathy brings certainty to them through reassurance. Permit them to say, "No." You don't want them to feel trapped. If they feel trapped, the outcome will not be in your favor. They must feel they still have sovereignty over their decision making. It's okay if they feel angry, it just shows that you are negotiating in the right territory. Having them express their negative feelings, and having those acknowledged by you, diffuse their power and causes the neural integration necessary for them to move forward unencumbered by their initial emotional response.

Preventing Deal Remorse

It's common once an agreement is reached that your counterpart might begin to feel some remorse about that agreement, a distressing emotion that arises from worry that their actions caused them to accept a deal that was not as good as it could have been. They might feel that they left money on the table, or they didn't get the terms or deference they now feel they deserve. They might begin to think that they wish they hadn't made the deal in the first place or that they should have fought harder for some of their issues. This is natural, but it can be problematic if contracts haven't been signed or contingencies fully met.

If you accept the final terms of a negotiation with smiles and celebration, you're inviting your counterpart to question the rightness of the final resolution and come back later to try and claw back some benefit or kill the deal altogether. It's not an intellectual response on the part of the remorseful, it's an emotional one and not at all rational. It needs to be prevented from happening to protect your position and the deal.

People want what they can't have. A little scarcity goes a long way. As you approach the final stages of your negotiation, pull back a little. Don't be too eager to cross the finish line. Slow the process down. Allow your opponents to feel what it would be like not to have the deal go through as planned.

Never accept final terms with a smile. Only accept final terms begrudgingly. Make your counterpart fight for that last inch. Let your counterpart feel the effort and sweat of the brow. Make reaching the agreement be an achievement for them. They will feel better about the deal themselves and will be less likely to revisit the terms later.

One method you can use is to go after a new deal point, or revisit an old one, just as all terms are about to be finalized. This might seem counter-intuitive, but it works. If your counterpart begins to think they are giving up too much in the deal, that's the time to ask for more. "Jacob, I know we've just about covered all the points, and I really appreciate your effort in this, but I'm afraid that issue about timing might gum things up. Is there any way you can change your mind on that?" It doesn't matter if he changes his mind or not. If he does, you get a perk. If he doesn't, he gets the last win in the negotiation, and the deal can close now. Use finesse, though. You don't want to appear greedy. It's like meds: the right dose can help you; the overdose will kill you.

Why Your Counterparts Will Help You Win

Humans seek to finalize a transaction when it accomplishes the following:

It settles their uncertainty to the extent it applies to the immediate or near future.

It handles the most immediate utility requirement, regardless if that is rooted in rationale or not. Most humans operate with a present bias preference, meaning they will choose a marginal solution today over a more optimal solution tomorrow.

You're part of the same communal group, and they want to belong.

It results in some relative gain, regardless of how small it is. This is not absolute gain mind you; it's relative gain, some improvement in immediate circumstances. Out of the frying pan and into the fire might be considered an improvement.

The action appears safe from unintended loss, ridicule, or expulsion from their chosen community.

To secure a "gain" relative to the low expectations you've anchored.

To "satisfice."

To feel safe and accepted.

17

PHILOSOPHY OF A HITMAN

PART III

THE CREATIVE POWER PREROGATIVE
(FIRST PRINCIPLES OF CAUSALITY -- METAPHYSICS)

"Float like a butterfly, sting like a bee. The hands can't hit what the eyes can't see."
-- Muhammad Ali

"They can conquer who believe they can."
-- Virgil

This is not magic, but sometimes it's going to feel like it. It's not religion, though some religions have touched on it, then mostly missed its foundation. It's not a cult; you don't follow anything or anybody. You create everything yourself using principles few people know, but you can learn. With these, you can change the future and the effects of the past. You can change your world. You can fashion your fate when you're good at it. It's best to start with zero.

Math is beautiful, as to its certainty. Science is beautiful, as to its certainty and wonder. Metaphysics is beautiful, as to its certainty, wonder, simplicity, and what it can unleash.

Metaphysics is the exploration and practice behind the causality of everything. It examines the genesis of action, being, and movement of all things (physical, mental, conceptual, and behavioral) and how it all changes and evolves. It holds the key to creating, influencing, manipulating, and transforming everything. It controls the programming, the algorithms, of how everything works and why. It provides you root access to invent and create your outcomes. It's like jailbreaking your life.

So, what do you want?

Let's again go back to the Big Bang, that point of singularity when all that ever existed and all that was about to exist was without size or mass, beyond definition, nothing; yet, unequivocally everything, where zero was infinite. It wasn't merely the explosion of matter that became the material stuff of the universe; it was much more than that. It was the source of all possibilities and potential, time and concepts, emotions and logic, conflict and accord, beauty and ugliness, good and evil. More precisely, it wasn't the source of all those things; it was all those things. All those things being just one thing at the beginning. You were there, albeit in quite a different form, but you were there nonetheless.

All that was to flow and expand from that moment of release and expansion was, and is to this day, inexplicably and forever related. Joined together by that invisible field of creative energy that caused, then emanated from, that one minuscule, infinite, singular point. All things impacted by all other things. All things connected, including you. An incomprehensible web unfolding and expanding, increasingly exponentially complex, each point linked to every other point by the same energy that created the singularity in the first place and then released the flow. This is your energy.

Einstein knew this, of course, but his attempts at quantifying this in his theories of relativity included only a few variables: space, time, energy, and mass. Stephen Hawking then added a few variables of his own while attempting to reconcile quantum theory with general relativity, trying to reconcile the properties of the infinitesimally small with the vastness of the infinite. Hawking's variables were the presence of matter and anti-matter, temperature, information, and entropy. Those last two items are particularly interesting for our use, but there are an infinite number of variables all impacting and relative to one another in this thing we call the universe and the experience of our lives.

Quantum field theory shows us there is ever-present energy that permeates everything, exists everywhere, always: zero-point energy. There are no vacuums. There are no voids. Pardon the double negative, but nothing doesn't exist because zero-point energy is always there.

Zero is boundless, infinite, vital. Zero-point energy exists irrespective of any dimension, including time, and changes by mere observation. It is the field of all possibilities, pure energy of origin in stasis until engaged, and a part of you.

The takeaway is that everything impacts everything else, bound together by the same energy, each a part of the singularity. No firewalls exist, no silos, no vacuums, no real separation. Everything is subject to influence, your applied influence at will.

Deterministic Chaos aka The Butterfly Effect

Our lives are part of a net of intertwined, deterministic, dynamic systems where the present impacts the future, and the smallest causal factors of seemingly insignificant importance will cause dramatic changes in major outcomes because of a series of interconnected actions and events building upon one another over time and space. The Butterfly Effect, a term first coined as a result of computer modeling of weather patterns which showed that something as insignificant as the movement of a butterfly's wing in Brazil introduced enough change in the atmosphere that subsequent effects compounded over time so that a tornado formed in Texas. That minute change in the initial condition, impossible to track in the physical world with conventional means, yet infinitely powerful in its potential to change anything. Given the smallest of causal events, the movement of the butterfly wing, and the outcome, the tornado in Texas; you can assert that the flap of the wing is not insignificant at all, but of the greatest importance because without the flap of that wing, that tornado would not have occurred.

The flap of the wing in Brazil was a random event, but you can introduce those small causal factors yourself as specific catalysts, thoughtfully, strategically, targeted, and with the intention for a specific effect. You build momentum. You start a chain reaction. You change outcomes. You influence the impact of the past. You create new. The smallest of causal events you create can upend the status quo and change the future. To others, it may initially appear as chaos, but it's not out of control. It's a clockwork universe; events unfold as a result of your influence.

So, what do you want?

Deity Level 10 – You Win!

Wow, so in the game of life, you've reached Deity Level 10! Congrats! You've totally arrived! Well, actually, there was no real accomplishment on your part that got you here, other than the fact that you were born and lived long enough to become sentient. The only thing that comes with this state of being is responsibility, and there's no cheating that, though people try all the time. They fail. The fact is, you're responsible because you're creating your reality all the time, whether you want to or not. You'd better own it.

This macrocosm we live in is made of existing, unyielding, and unending processes churning out the reality we create. This constant creation goes forward continuously. These creation processes carry on irrespective of the participants' knowledge, or sanction, or agreement. These processes relentlessly advance, creating, shaping, and reshaping the reality of our world, whether we like it or not. We influence it, whether we want to or not -- manifesting the forms, patterns, and outcomes we impress upon them by our thoughts, words, and actions.

You're always influencing, shaping, and guiding existence. So, do it purposefully, cognitively, consciously impress your intentions upon it. When you do this purposefully, it's fun. But if you don't, you subject yourself to the ebb and flow of the unintended consequences your random impressions create because of your lack of conscious direction.

So, what do you want?

We're confronted with infinite possibilities. Consider the number of thoughts you have in a day and consider that each thought has influence and meaning. Consider the number of atoms that burst forth as endorphins on-demand as you hear the sudden screech of tires or a lover catches your eye. Consider a field of wheat and within each stalk, each seed, the ability to create a trillion more fields. You have the same ability to create an infinite number of ideas, companies, products, and concepts, but even more potent because they can be fueled and directed by your conscious thought. Consider the number of all possible events and conditions in your life and the abundance the universe offers. It's full of adventure and an endless supply of good for you and everyone that chooses to accept it. Your options are without limits, except for the limits and boundaries you place on yourself.

The only question is, are you creating outcomes you intend because of your affirmative, cogent, clear, thoughts and actions, or are the results formed from a muddy mashup of numbed-out misdirection and confusion? Your call. You're always creating. You're always shaping energy. There's no "off" switch.

The only constant is creative energy and its infinite potential. There are no "things" per se, only the continual and ever-changing expressions of form. This provides for an infinite number of things in an infinite period of time and with no limiting rules whatsoever. Zero is the beginning of everything, infinite potential, the field of all possibilities. Just as water seeks its own level, and air rushes in to fill a vacuum, and plastic surrenders to the form of a mold; so too does creative energy follow these same principles and reaches its own level, fills any vacuum present, and neatly fits to any form presented through conscious and unconscious thoughts. There are no limitations. There are no constraints. There is no cap on the number of things, just as there is no cap on the number of thoughts and ideas. This is because thoughts are things, and thoughts create things. It is not a zero-sum game. The supplies are as limitless as your creative thought and energy are limitless.

To consider your life experience to be lacking in anything is to deny its true nature. This is not a universe of lack, but one of growth, change, and expansion. What you need is provided to you, though it may not be what you expect. When you think you need money, you may first be provided with a new incentive or a new skill. When you think you need control, you may first be provided with a new way of looking at things. When you think you need power, you may first be provided with humility. When you think you need love, you may first be taught how to love, or learn to love yourself. The need is provided for if you call for it, articulate it, and collect it. Learn to look for the good in all things and marvel at the help that is provided to you every step of the way.

We live in an infinite field of potential and possibilities. While anything is possible to you, what is probable is what you hold in your mind as the truth. This abundance is subject to your direction. If you select lack, distress, and poor performance as objects of your thoughts and accept that as your reality, then that will be your experience. If instead you select flow, prosperity, abundance, happiness, and freedom as your reality and act on those vectors, then these will just as effectively be created. All possibilities exist; select the outcomes you wish to bring forward. Creative energy is always at work manifesting new forms. If you think you can, or you think you can't, that's what you get. If you need to change your thinking, change it.

Choice, Catalyst, Cause

So, what do you want?

This is not an idle question, not a rhetorical question, and is not to be taken lightly. The question and your answers are central to your success. Answer the question with the weight and importance you deserve.

Conscious choice is the tool provided to you that enables you to be, or have, anything you can conceive and believe. Choice is the catalyst and cause of your reality. It's axiomatic, fundamental. Choice is the catalyst and cause.

You have free will and the ability to make your own original choices. Choice unlocks all potential and directs your creative energy to manifest the outcomes you choose. Turning your choice over to external influences negates your power and destroys your ability to reach your goals. You'll be unhappy. To tap into potential and realize your desired events and outcomes, consciously make choices as though they dramatically alter your life experience, because they do.

So, what do you want?

Are you afraid of what you want? Do you feel guilty or a little ashamed about what you want? Do you think you don't deserve it or that you shouldn't want it so much? Fuck that. If you have ambition, scream it to the world. If you have desires, let them be known. Tell somebody. Tell everybody. Ignore your detractors no matter who they are. Build a mastermind.

Decision is an outgrowth of discernment. Discernment is possible only with intelligence. Intelligence is meant to flow and enables you to create your future by creating the present at will. The power of choice transcends all boundaries you are accustomed to: time, the concept of past and future, emotional and psychological tendencies, and all others. Your choice is the first step in the manifestation process. Without it, the directed creation process cannot begin. Without a conscious choice, the manifestation process is left to flounder. It's then guided by your unconscious tendencies, fears, and habitual thoughts. Choices are being made by you constantly, consciously, and unconsciously. As conscious choices prevail, you are the director of your life experiences. As unconscious choices prevail, you are subject to the unbridled thoughts of your subconscious mind. Those too, you can change.

Choice and creation are synonymous when your choices are well defined, specific, and believed as possible by you. A force of will is not necessary. Have confidence in your knowledge that your outcomes are being determined by your choices and unity with creative energy. Have confidence in the outcomes.

The key to manifesting your desired outcomes is to understand that the answers to your questions are embedded in the questions themselves. The solutions present themselves as a result of asking the questions. If you want to succeed in any endeavor, ask the right questions, ask a lot of pointed questions. We each draw from our lives what we put into them and what we put into them comes from the answers to our challenging questions. The tougher the questions, the more creative the answers, and the more creative the answers, the more likely real change will occur. That's where thought becomes creation.

If you've tried for something before and come up short, then the image you have in your mind of the events to unfold is not always constructive. Though educational, you might still follow that same path time and again hoping for a different result but getting the same result. New questions need to be asked so new answers can be revealed to cause new creative thought. What you manifest is limited only by the audaciousness of the questions you ask. Even if you doubt you have the ability, or doubt your willingness to follow through, you can still prevail in the end and win the successes you want. Those doubts of ability and follow-through are overcome by moving forward regardless. The little successes you start to see will breed more success.

What You Focus on Most

Let me be concise. What you focus on most expands in your life. Focus on what you want to grow in your life. The focus of your stream of conscious and unconscious thoughts is what determines your reality. What you think about most, programs how you act, how you use creative energy, the forms you imprint on that energy, and what you create as a result. This works continuously with your agreement or without it. You might agree with it intellectually and still let your mind wander and fashion a life of worry, fear, poverty, and desperation if you fail to consciously compose your outcomes. Context is important.

If you're thinking about money, is it its lack or its abundance you're thinking about? That's what you'll get. If its love you're thinking about, is it its lack or its abundance you're thinking about? That's what you'll get. If its freedom you're thinking about, is it its lack or abundance you're thinking about; because that's what you'll get.

It's easy to know what you don't want, and often it's those thoughts that are prevalent in your mind. That's what expands in your life. You don't want loss, fear, lack, addictions, or worry, but focusing your attention on those will cause them to grow and expand.

Maintain diligence to release negative thoughts and instead focus on the healthful, helpful, nurturing, and prosperous thoughts and have those expand and manifest. They will manifest for you if you focus on those and actively pursue them. If this comes naturally for you, be thankful. If not, affirm the outcomes you desire and then let your creative energy do its work. Impose your intention upon the universe. This is not the random flap of a butterfly's wing. This is choosing the constructive tornado you desire.

Your Creation Algorithm Architecture

Each of us carries a potent seed of incalculable potential and possibility, the beginning point and source of all new things. Do we nurture it and allow it to grow into its potential and sprout subsequent generations to be realized; or do we stifle it, starve it, abuse it, and let it die? I don't think it can die, but it can certainly lay dormant forever.

How you treat it initially is how you were treated early on. How you treat it now is up to you.

You define the fulfillment of your potential. What is the achievement bound up in your core you want to release? Is it prosperity, athleticism, notoriety, new discoveries, benevolent works? Why not all of it? Your being is made of the stuff of that first singularity, all its potential, all its energy, ready to explode with performance when you bring the catalyst and release it. There are no limits; it's your own big bang.

Are you awed by the infinitely expansive nature of the beginning point and source of all new things within you? Just like the grain of wheat that can spawn a trillion wheat fields and each grain within each stalk in each of those fields the ability to give rise to a trillion more, your seed too can spawn a trillion new universes.

You are the source of that potential. Your expression of that potential achieves the realization of it. The trickle, flow, or flood is released by the magnitude of your expression, by the detail of its form. Let it loose. Hide your expression, and the potential stays confined. Express yourself fully, consciously, and your full potential is released upon the world. When you're expressing yourself fully, you're in flow. And when you're in flow, all is right.

So, why haven't you expressed yourself fully up to now? What has held you back, kept you quiet, dampened your outreach? Was it fear? Was it apathy? Was it a feeling? Were you told your work wasn't good enough? Were you told your worth wasn't worthwhile? Was it worth it, staying down? Fuck all of that. Take it back. Take it all back. Show the world in a big way how perfectly imperfect you are and manifest your greatest desires.

Your creation algorithm architecture is a simple systems design that shows how your defined wants and desires trigger the processes for their eventual satisfaction. This is a great tool in the Hitman's arsenal to bring about positive change in your life and negotiations. Your programming is already encoded (it's part of nature), you just need to understand the info and format you need to provide it to make the whole thing work. Don't forget you've reached Deity Level 10, Hotshot, so this should be easy for you. You already have your augmented reality apparatus in your head, so it's time to augment some reality literally. Just a couple of quick checklist items as we get started:

1. You know that your ever-present creative energy is continuously, relentlessly, evolving, and changing your world. Check!

2. You know that you are an expression of that energy and that you influence its direction and what it manifests, always. Check!

3. You know the smallest conscious changes you make today cause ripples in creative energy and reality, and those will make profound changes as the creation process compounds and unfolds over time. Check!

Okay, ready?

Like any good design, such as in architecture or software, industrial or product design, or your negotiations and life, enduring success creating your outcomes stem from the degree to which they follow the principle of "form follows function." Forms that manifest in the real world satisfy the functional demands first presented. A beautiful example of this is a soaring eagle sweeping in flight. Solutions are presented as functions are defined. Objectives are met as details are pressed.

Take the targets and goals you've chosen and imagine the details and emotions working the solutions and having achieved them. Create and own the conceptualization, feelings, surroundings, and imagery of the activities achieving and having achieved those outcomes. It's stepping into an augmented reality scene you create of how you intend to have your reality augmented. Assert and affirm this experience as you intend it to unfold and your role in it. Dwell on the details and accept that this is part of you and the legitimate flow of nature. Go to zero and accept that the world you choose with your creative thought and energy is unfolding. If doubts surface, understand those are just natural insecurities, and you can let them fade. You're creating something new now, and that's all that matters. Make your activities moving forward appropriate for this new world you're creating.

Have fun with this process. Be playful with it. Include your emotions and intellect and creativity and expand on it. You get better at it the more you use it. If you haven't done it before, it might seem awkward at first. No matter, keep playing with it and have fun. You'll get good at it, and you'll get good at engaging your creative thought and impressing your desires, functions, and forms into reality. This isn't wishing. You're programing yourself and building new neural pathways, engaging your creative energy, influencing nature, and driving new creations. See yourself at your best.

Few athletes today get to elite status without practicing some form of conceptualization, affirmation, and visualization like I've described. The most successful also use it to expand their endorsements, brands, and public presence. It works for anything.

Billie Jean King, Michael Jordon, Tiger Woods, Lindsey Vonn, Mikaela Shiffrin, and the sports psychologists with the U.S. Olympic team all acknowledge the key role visualization and affirmation have in making them successful in their skills and business.

"I am the greatest," yelled Muhammad Ali. "I am the greatest!!" Muhammad Ali powerfully affirmed again and again and again. He wasn't quiet about it. He shouted it to the world in interviews, in the ring, in speeches, and in his writings. At 21 years old, he said he would beat the then heavyweight champion of the world in eight rounds. He beat him in six. Ali's opponent, the then champion, gave up; he'd gotten the message about Ali ahead of time. Ali was the greatest. Ali affirmed this message relentlessly, and he changed the course of his life. "I am the greatest!" Ali told us time and again.

We learned something more private from Ali before he died. He told us a secret. He confessed, "I said that ['I'm the greatest!'] even before I knew I was." Obviously, Ali and the world got the message, and it stuck. He only ever lost one title fight in his entire career.

The world evolves, after Ali came Floyd Mayweather, Jr., who tagged himself "TBE," -- "The Best Ever." He told the world he was the best ever, and he worked harder than anybody else. Floyd finished his career undefeated.

These guys internalized their message. Their entire focus was on improving their craft and winning. It was more than just belief. It was creating certainty. When you say, "I can" achieve these goals, you make progress because you affirm your ability and efficacy. When you say, "I will" achieve those goals, you make progress because you set in motion the intention. The most progress is made, though, when you say, "I am" achieving those goals because then their manifestation is unfolding. Whether you think you can, or you think you can't, you're right. When Ali said: "Float like a butterfly, sting like a bee. The hands can't hit what the eyes can't see." He set in motion an unknowable number of butterfly wings and expectations that helped support and create his reality in and out of the ring.

I remember years ago when I was breaking down the greasy commercial kitchens after a long and busy night preparing meals for the restaurants' clientele, I would think about the companies I wanted to create and the office where I'd do it and its detail. I would visualize being on the upper floors of a high-rise building with sheets of glass and views of other office towers and the mountains. I could see my big workspace with computer screens and contracts piled high and depositing big fees. That imagery in my head and what I felt seeing myself sitting there was a representation of the companies I would create. It happened. Later I visualized my travels to far-flung locations working on challenging transactions for multinational companies. I could see myself on airplanes, working out plans and strategies as a representation of that lifestyle and global reach. It happened. Still later, I saw myself developing the key to unlocking negotiations in a way that had never been done before with clients reaching out for my help. It happened. And then, more recently, I visualized myself working entirely on my schedule in settings that I love. I've written a lot of this book in my cabin high in the Rocky Mountains and late-night sitting in a gazebo on my property at home looking out at an expanse of fields and trees and pasture. That's where I am now.

Visualization works, I could cite hundreds of examples, from companies built (I've built three) to deals consummated, brilliant people hired, vacations, love, and my own salvation. See and feel the outcomes you seek and create a vivid image of them. Ponder that image, enjoy it, play with it. Feel it and let it be a part of you. Augment your reality. This is the process of creation.

Visualize first, then plan. Form follows function. It's a self-fulfilling prophecy.

Alpha Prime Ethos

Since your own conscious and unconscious thoughts are what shape your life experiences and create your existence, you might as well choose to provide for yourself only the best of all things. Why wouldn't you unless you thought you didn't deserve it? And if that's what you're feeling, fuck that, go do something nice for yourself right now and enjoy it, then read on.

Living an Alpha Prime Ethos is living the principle of best first, and that means that you bring into your life the very best, first, and always. You deserve that. After all, you were part of the origin of the universe. It's part of your nature. Focus and put your thoughts on quality, perfection, abundance, gratitude, and appreciation, and that is what will manifest for you. Choose to be best in class or in a class all your own. If you accept a lesser standard on any level, you downgrade yourself, and this will cause your brain to operate at a lower level, bringing you lower level achievements, goods, relationships, and enlightenment – maybe no enlightenment. When you open yourself up to the finest of all things, reality answers with the finest of all things. Compromise for nothing. You deserve the best. Acknowledging this truth helps tear down your self-imposed barriers so more good things will exhibit in your life. Do you want to live up to that low opinion of yourself, or something higher?

Do you ever tell yourself that you are not worthy or deserving? Is that what you've been told or believe? Challenge it. Never tell yourself that the success you desire is for other people or not deserved by anyone. Never tell yourself that you are worth less than your peers or your clients or your competition. The truth is that you are an original expression of perfection and part of nature's creative energy. A thing cannot be withheld from itself, and your success cannot be withheld from you. A is A. Never accept a feeling or image of lack. Challenge it. Never accept anything less than what is rightfully yours. The fruits of creative energy are yours for the taking. If you ask for less, you get less, and this tends to repeat itself. If you ask for the best, take the best, you get the best, and this also tends to repeat itself. What you focus on most expands in your life. Tell yourself that you are the best, that you expect the best, and that you get the best. Tell your clients that you are the best, that you expect the best, that you get the best, and that they get the best. Tell your family that you are the best, that you expect the best, that you get the best, and that they get the best. A is A.

Perfectly Imperfect

There is good in everything. No matter how bleak or awful, sad, desperate, or evil a situation or something may seem, the good is present. Everything is perfect. There is good in all things.

Back at the singularity, when there was only one thing, all of nature condensed into a singular, infinite point, and there was nothing else that existed to which it could be compared, could it be possible it was anything other than perfection? It could not. You were part of that. From perfection, flows perfection. You are at once a conduit of perfection and perfection itself. There is good in everything, even when you don't see it and can't even comprehend it. It is there, and in time, the good will present itself. Sometimes you must look for it. When it's obvious, it's fun. When it's not, it may be even more important and impactful. The good may present itself immediately, or it may only be revealed after time, but it is always there. It might be a new lesson learned, a new path required, a newborn concept, a truth understood and acted upon, ballast to be jettisoned, an enemy revealed. It might be a struggle you experience to show you're alive.

There is good in all things. Everything is perfect because the universe is perfect. If there was even one imperfection anywhere, then the universe would be imperfect. Compared to what? It's impossible. A is A. All is perfect. When I learned to accept the truth of this concept, my life and business moved to a more solid footing because it showed that every circumstance was foundational for new improvement, gains, and joy.

Sometimes life is hard. Sometimes deals are hard. Sometimes you screw up.

From grief, we learn gratitude. From sadness, we learn solace. From shame, we learn the meaning and importance of dignity.

In the uninformed, the reptilian brain will say, "This hurts, so it's not perfect. I feel bad, so this is not good. I'm scared, so I want to panic." The enlightened will say, "There is good in all things. Everything is perfect. If this hurts, what am I missing? Where is the good? I know it is here. I will find it."

Practicing this, the hurt and fear of even the worst situations get diffused, and you're far better equipped to move forward. Some people like feeling bad, though. They get something out of it. It might be because feeling bad is most familiar to them. If that's you, you might want to change that. Make feeling good the most familiar thing to you. You deserve that. What you focus on most expands in your life, no matter what it is.

Allow yourself to feel gratitude for what you have, what you've created, and what you are creating now. All that is a gift from the universe, and you are the universe. It's a gift you give yourself.

The Theory of Everything

Applied Influence works because it sets in motion everything necessary for the creation of the outcomes you intend. The Tricks, Hacks, Hammers, and Cheats open the minds of those around you to see and feel the benefit of your way of thinking so they will act towards its achievement. The metaphysical principles in the Creative Power Prerogative open your mind to the richness of creative energy you can harness to achieve your aims. Taken together, it's a unified method for creating anything. It's the Theory of Everything.

PART FOUR – HITMAN 4.0
--
THE FIXER

18

SUN TZU'S MISTAKE

"If you would be a real seeker after truth, it is necessary that at least once in your life you doubt, as far as possible, all things.

-- René Descartes

I need to close the loop regarding Sun Tzu. Sun Tzu's teachings were integral to my early development as a negotiation strategist, but someone smart once said, "You can't use an old map to explore a new world." My experience, work, and study have taken me passed Sun Tzu to a new world of strategy and influence. Creating Applied Influence and the Theory of Everything, I discovered new concepts and strategies beyond his realm that would prove to be life-changing, things that would bring my effectiveness to new heights.

Sun Tzu had clarity in his vision and thought which guided his principles and actions, and served him well. His guidance would sometimes move his actions to extremes, but he was resolute and unapologetic. His work is solid as a foundation, but it doesn't come close to being an all-in unified theory of negotiating strategy. It's too elementary, too two dimensional. Taken as a whole, his principles and strategies are incomplete and leave open vulnerabilities that are dangerous to you and miss opportunities for you to disarm your opponents by more efficient means.

Sun Tzu was brilliant, but he wasn't infallible. Nobody's infallible.

These are the initial fixes, corrections, and enhancements I applied to his strategies in my own work.

Game Theory

Sun Tzu's approach to conflict was from a purely two-dimensional perspective. Army against army. Force against force. Win and Lose.

Our conflicts tend not to be that simple, often with three or more vested parties involved in an encounter, each with different priorities and self-interests. Our games are not binary. Our conflicts take on the characteristic of being three dimensional or multi-dimensional. It's enticing to boil each encounter or pending conflict down to just two players, it fits easily into a narrative and doesn't take very much brainpower, but that is usually not the true condition – and we need to accommodate for the true condition. Conflicts will have at least two principals, but there will often be a number of characters on either side that have a vested interest in the outcomes and influence decisions. In my transactions, in addition to the principals, I'll have other players such as lenders, creditors, investors, lawyers, agents, powers of attorney, government agencies, brokers, COOs, CFOs, and other third parties that all have a vested interest in how the conflict plays out. Each is a potential and likely force of influence.

Game theory analysis is the tool for determining the most beneficial course of action in conflicts, transactions, and other games that have two or more players, and The Art of War was devoid of any game theory thinking. Hugely beneficial in a two-dimensional game, game theory is critically important as the complexity of the games and the number of players increase. John Nash won a Nobel Prize in Economics for his insight into non-cooperative games. Nash Equilibria is a combination of strategies that incentivize each player in a game to support your move because any other direction will be detrimental to them, or perceived as such.

You can determine your optimal dominant strategy to impose by knowing the self-interest priorities of each interdependent player in the game, and considering each of their possible moves and resulting consequences. You influence the outcome of the game by changing the other players' perception of their upside and downside to the various possible decisions they can make. It helps if you have a mind that runs fast all the time to visualize how each move by you and each player impacts the decisions and subsequent moves of all the other players, and you. Game out in advance how each move influences all the other players' moves and the outcomes that result. The proper algorithms to achieve the objectives you're after will present themselves. Game theory analysis is a game-changer.

Game theory is logic applied to foresee your opponents' actions. The goal is to achieve your outcomes in a non-cooperative game where your opponent is trying to achieve their outcomes at the cost of yours. It's a valuable skill to be able to correctly interpret the information you have and reveal only selective information to your opponent.

In commercial real estate and many, maybe most, other industries, negotiations often don't take place in a vacuum, and there may be a prior and subsequent relationship with your opponent. Any negotiation should include a suitable mix of cooperation as well as self-centered competition for long-term benefits for you and your clients. Some cooperation can help foster creativity of solutions in an impasse.

The Benefit of Conflict

Much of Sun Tzu's teachings center around achieving victory while avoiding conflict, winning without struggle, defeating an opponent without bloodshed, using influence to change the opponents' behavior as the primary weapon. I agree, but we must recognize that today engagements come at you swiftly and often without warning and that the influence used to change the opponents' behavior must include all of nature's resources, and conflict is a prominent change agent in nature.

Conflict is a cornerstone of how our universe evolves. Conflict forces improvement and kills dead-end experiments. Conflict exalts in the essence of real power, while anything less gets ferreted out. Conflict challenges theories, motivations, and results, and the ultimate victor is so only as a result of merit. Armed conflict is not so good, but mental and emotional conflict can be perfect for you and one of the best catalysts for change in negotiations and behaviors there is.

Conflict creates pressures that can be exerted when time is of the essence, or when managing the setting or terrain is not practical. There is a correct way to impose conflict, but before you do, you must know the outcome.

Humans hate conflict. Most everyone will go out of their way to avoid conflict. People will sacrifice their values, integrity, honesty, and principles to avoid conflict. Those simple sapiens, they'll sacrifice the truth. They'll sacrifice money. They'll sacrifice themselves to avoid conflict. Their conflict aversion is a handy tool we can use to get our way. The perceived damage of impending conflict is useful to extract benefits for your side.

Conflict is dangerous and can be damaging, but you can prepare and manage the conditions such that your opponents view the potential damage inflicted by the conflict to be more detrimental to them than to you. That is the catalyst you want.

Your opponents will pay for risk avoidance, conflict avoidance, making the moment conflict is averted a great opportunity for you to benefit. Create scenarios where the very action that averts the conflicts benefit you. Game that out ahead of time. Your opponents have conflict aversion already programmed into their DNA; everybody does. Instead of you averting the conflict ahead of time, thereby relieving the pressure on your opponents, embrace the conflict. Increase the pressure and threat on your opponents, so they feel the experience and worry of the damage and resulting loss from the conflict. Pressure builds as the moment of conflict approaches, and the likelihood of damage or loss looms. These should not be overly overt threats or attacks. Those can be counterproductive. Think of it as manufacturing diamonds through the application of extreme heat and pressure on a basic carbon source. Only it's you bringing the heat and pressure. Your opponents are the carbon source, and they will gladly tell you when the diamond is ready. In the most simplistic of terms, people can't stand the pressure. Make sure they feel the pressure and be ready to collect your prize when they're ready for relief.

A client with a portfolio of hundreds of big format stores called and told me that he had lost a lease for a big box retail space in a wealthy New Jersey suburb and was being forced to close down operations and vacate. Repeated attempts to contact the owner had produced no communication and my client was becoming frantic. My client wanted me to step in and fix the situation so this one store wouldn't have to close.

This shopping center, and about a dozen others like it in New Jersey, New York, and Pennsylvania, had been built by a self-made man who had since passed and willed his fortune and real estate to his son, Levi.

Levi didn't care much for real estate, preferring to party with skinny models in skimpy dresses and paying to play with a large group of hangers-on in Ibiza and Manhattan. Ibiza Boy's social media posts were full of images of night clubs, neon lights, rented Humvee limos, and videos of pretty people moving in synchrony and shouting over the electronic music, "Thank you, Levi." Presumably, because he was paying for everything. He also anointed himself the "new arbiter of culture and art." Maybe he was referring to the "Thank you, Levi" t-shirts prominently displayed in his posts.

His father's company was being held together by the COO, who was a good soldier who soldiered on, and the head bookkeeper, a woman who should have retired a while ago, but stayed on to try and protect the legacy of the father. But regardless of their stoic attempts at keeping the company intact and profitable, Ibiza Boy was the final "arbiter" of the real estate decisions, too, as he continued to ignore the business and burn money.

At first, I didn't get a response from anyone, either. So, I walked into their office. The COO and head bookkeeper were initially defensive and said they wouldn't be able to talk about a new lease because Levi wanted to redevelop the shopping center. I started showing them the titillating imagery I had of Ibiza Boy and his friends. I asked why the banks holding the mortgage and assignment of rents would be willing to watch the rent stream go to zero or add funding for new development if they knew how their money was being spent.

The COO and head bookkeeper started to open up to me about their frustration and concern for the company. They said their hands were tied, and they only talked with Ibiza Boy, I mean Levi, only once a week.

I stayed in close contact with the COO and head bookkeeper over the next couple of weeks. I forwarded to them whatever new info I found on Ibiza Boy, such as the new companies he was forming to promote musical artists and fashion models and the great parties he was throwing for them – all with no revenues, of course. The pressure started to build, and they started pressuring Levi, fearful of what the banks might do if they knew.

I eventually got the new lease I was looking for and a deal on the rent too. My client is still there to this day. Can't say the same for Ibiza Boy. As I was writing this book, I checked in to see how Levi and the company were doing. Ibiza Boy didn't make it. I never did find a cause of death, but I can guess. He threw a hell of a party, and it made a useful example story for my book. Thank you, Levi.

Altered States

Sun Tzu's most famous quote is: "All war is based on deception." Yet, he avoids the greatest deceptions of all, those that require the boldest mastery and skill, and that reap the most rewards – those which change your opponents' states of mind and cause them to feel the fear of uncertainty and defeat.

In the Art of War, Sun Tzu says, "when able, appear unable" and "when contented, appear disadvantaged." In these and all his examples of deception, he presupposes that your ability is greater than that of your opponents and that your deception should be to appear less able, thereby luring your opponents through the expectation of gain and feigned disorganization, and then attacking with strength – essentially, set the trap and strike swiftly. In these, Sun Tzu is entirely dependent upon a superior strength and position to win, the position achieved through his dance of deception, though he is silent as to where the strength is derived. He goes on to say, "when the enemy is stronger, or its position is superior, evade it." This is flawed, incomplete, and sometimes not possible.

Appearing less able may be a good strategy in situations where your army strength is greater than your opponents, but the rewards and victories he deems unachievable because of lack of strength or position can indeed be won when you are skilled at changing your state of mind and those of your opponents, to wit: When unable, appear able. When disadvantaged, appear contented. When the enemy's position is stronger, engage it. Sun Tzu articulates, "the key to defeating your opponent resides in the opponent itself," that it is a condition or result of a condition inherent in the opponent. But he then doesn't exploit those vulnerabilities if they are not manifest by lack of size, strength, or tactical condition or position. I do. You can. You do not need a superior force to prevail. You don't need a superior position. What you need is the ability to change your opponents' perception of your plans and position, not with any certainty mind you, with uncertainty. Those vulnerabilities can take on many forms and may be completely unrelated to the transaction at hand, but exploiting those vulnerabilities can cause unease and uncertainty in the opponent. That is the leverage needed and can be the key to winning the transaction.

Humans judge their ability relative to their perceptions of the circumstances surrounding them and their perceptions of their opponents' abilities in the situation. What they believe to be real manifests itself and becomes self-fulfilling. What they think is their relative position becomes their relative position. Shifting the perception of your ability to be greater than previously perceived, causes your actual relative ability to be greater -- reality changes. Your opponents think they are less able to handle or control the situation, and therefore they are. Their state changes, and they become less capable. Your state changes, and you become more capable.

Intangible Timeline

Albert Einstein said, "The only reason for time is so that everything doesn't happen at once." I say, since time exits and everything gets spread out, make it work for you. It worked against Sun Tzu.

Sun Tzu cautioned against a prolonged campaign or siege for several reasons. A prolonged campaign is difficult to supply and re-supply. There is a greater likelihood the vitality and commitment to the cause within your ranks will diminish. Also, his position favoring a swift encounter was easily received as preferable by his audience from a pure "get-your-head-around-it" perspective. It's easy to digest. It sounds good. But there are times you want a prolonged siege. There are times when you are ideally prepared for such an undertaking, and the factor of timing you control can be the death-knell for your opponent.

As part of your practice to keep your position and conditions unknowable to your opponent, this should include the critical dates associated with your plan and encounter. Your opponent must not know your timeline. If your timeline becomes known because of circumstances such as a prior contract, lease, or other published requirements, you then also need to encourage it to be known that those dates are not the drivers of your decision making and of little consequence. So too, it is your responsibility to stay out of harm's way while you wait for the right time to act when your opponent is most vulnerable and least expects an engagement. You accomplish all this by advancing your campaign start date many seasons before anyone would expect you to. Depending upon the conflict or transaction at hand, this could be many months or several years. Be alert to the needs to keep your stakeholders' interest high for the cause and not be diminished.

When you are subject to known critical dates and those dates are within the typical time cycle of the type of transaction you're working, you are disadvantaged at the outset, and all tactics and strategies will have the pall of the looming critical dates over them. Take that off the table by initiating your campaign well in advance of the typical transaction cycle. Be first to arrive rested and ready to fight. Be unknown by your opponent as to your timeline and critical dates. Be out of harm's way by having time on your side and working your BANANAs. Your opponents' vigor and resolve diminish with time, and their unease and uncertainty increase. Your opponent becomes unsure by your actions, or what comes next, and moves to settle the uncertainty. When you control the timeline, you control the outcome.

The Lone Wolf

Sun Tzu's biggest mistake was failing to recognize that one lone individual could bring down a nation. He did use secret agents, double agents, and spies to gather intelligence, but not to conduct decisive action to bring the opponent to its knees. Sun Tzu was myopic. He depended entirely upon a large, superior, well-positioned force to vanquish an opponent, oblivious to the deadly surgical strike that could be unleashed by one lone figure. It's kind of a mystery. Sun Tzu's strategies primarily focused on manipulating the mental processes of his opponents, yet in the end, he relied entirely on the raw power of his force to prevail.

The lone wolf has many advantages over a large force when engaging an opponent. A lone wolf is more nimble, quicker making decisions and changing directions and plans, more focused on the objective without the need to manage subordinates and their welfare, and subject only to his or her own ability without the liability of the weakest link of an organization which could slow down the operation or bring it down altogether. The lone wolf can be stealth, quiet, and invisible if necessary. The lone wolf can be non-obtrusive and move and change without notice or alarm, or be like fire engulfing all in its path. The lone wolf needs little in the way of supplies and capital, just enough to stay alive, nothing like the needs of a large organization.

That's just the beginning, though. I used the imagery of the lone wolf because I expect the readers easily understand it. However, there is an even more cunning and more dangerous solitary hunter and skill set we will soon learn: that of the puma.

19

FRIENDLY FIRE

"Master, what is it that I hear? Who are those people so defeated by their pain?
And he said to me: This miserable way is taken by the forgotten souls of those who lived their lives without disgrace and without praise. They now commingle with the coward angels, the company of those who were never rebels nor faithful to their god, but instead just stood aside. The heavens, so not to have their own beauty disgraced, have cast them out; Hell will not receive them either – for even the wicked cannot glory in them."
-- Dante Alighieri, Inferno

"You know what? Fuck you! How about that?"
-- Scarface

My sentiments exactly.

There's nothing friendly about friendly fire. There's nothing friendly about being shot at by someone who's supposed to be on your side, being shot by someone on the team you've saved over and over again. Accidents occur, but in this context, it is almost never an accident. It's fratricide, the killing of a brother or sister for some mal-intended narcissistic end. This is a hostile act, one worthy of repercussions and consequences. It's an act of cowardice perpetrated by the most loathsome of creatures, devoid of principles and loyalty, a spineless weakling, a vacuous soul not worthy of the air that you and I breathe. You can take revenge, or expel them from your life, or play with them as a cat plays with a mouse before leaving it to die. It matters not. Their lives have little value you need be concerned about. My empathy for these slimy creatures ends at the muzzle end of the gun they're pointing at me. Fortunately for us, we can usually spot these traitors ahead of time, usually by the piss running down their legs. Fear is what compels them; they don't handle it well.

These perpetrators suffer from serious character flaws. Sometimes just one; but often an entire buffet of defects like narcissism, megalomania, grandiosity, corruption, dishonesty, sadism, lethargy, victimhood, passive aggression, the knowledge they haven't learned to overcome their poor work ethic and don't care, and full-throttled stupidity which then culminates into a banquet of anxiety, fear, and resentment of you because you do take care of business. You do get the job done. Take an assessment of everyone you work with, and don't be fooled by the level of their expressed admiration; it might just be part of their deception. Know what lurks behind the smile. Judge them by their actions in the toughest of circumstances.

Sometimes friendly fire injuries are caused by the incompetence of an incompetent manager, you just become collateral damage, a waste. You might find that these people can be rehabilitated and trained to follow a more productive path, one that is more supportive of your objectives and their company, unless they're a lost cause.

There's also a darker, more pathological, more dangerous kind of perpetrator. This is the guy that shoots you because he can, and he feels pleasure from doing it. He's the guy who doesn't want to work very hard, and he doesn't care if he wastes his company's money or your time. He just wants to roll over on everything because it's simple. He's not held accountable. He thinks he runs a fiefdom that exists solely to give him title, identity, position, and a small stable of brown-nosing sycophants he can slap around once in a while. He doesn't want to create. He wants to destroy, but he keeps his numbers just above the threshold that would cause a review of his actions by his superiors.

The Spineless

When you're an alpha-performer, too often you'll find those who will become threatened by you because of your performance or simply your presence. They won't be pleased with the benefits you bestow to the company or see ways they might be able to up their own game and contribute more. All they see is that you outshine them, and in that light, they appear dull. Fear rises-up within them because they know that by comparison, they look like yesterday's lunch. By contrast, you've exposed their laziness, ineptitude, and bad results. Their twisted calculus of self-preservation will make them willing to resort to any means necessary to take you down a notch, or two, or try and take you out all-together.

It's absurd that when you're successful in your negotiations or any endeavor for any organization, some managers and staff will hate you for it. The confident ones will appreciate your work, but the bad managers and staff will fear you and resent you because you make them look, lazy, ignorant, and far less capable. They look that way because they are. They'll do whatever they can do to derail you, defame you, discredit you, block your success and income, and will trot out any method they can dream of to control you. Their priority is to have you fired, broke, and bloodied, so they can feel better about themselves, all while you're trying to help their company. If you tell them to stop, they'll deny it's happening.

I was contracted to run valuations for a global wireless carrier so their inhouse real estate people would know what their properties were worth as they negotiated lease renewals. At first, everyone was happy with the program, and rents were coming down. Managers were happy because they were hitting their numbers. But as the program proceeded, the real estate people started to argue about some of my valuations in Puerto Rico and then in Columbus, Ohio, saying they were too low, and they wanted me to go back and find evidence to support higher numbers. I offered to show them how to negotiate the lower rents. But they didn't want lower rents; they just didn't want to work that hard. The managers called me and asked if I could lighten up some because their real estate people were grumbling. I thought that was insane. Eventually, they bought me out of my contract so they could hide the fact they were failing in their negotiations and paying higher rents than the markets warranted.

The Big Swinging Dick
and other Threatening Genitalia

The title of this subsection is a bit misleading because most of the dicks that come out swinging aren't all that big. What is protruding notably from these offenders is their insecurity. When their position, esteem, or decisions are challenged, their impulse is to drop their pants and start marking their territory with piss flying everywhere. Their only source of power is reflective, their perception of how they're being viewed and treated by others. Since their view of themselves is sketchy at best and needs constant support, their perceptions are usually skewed to worse by their paranoia and anxiety.

When they're triggered, and the zipper comes down, they try to regain the power and prestige they think they have lost. This is difficult for them since it was fake to begin with. It's all emotional. They do this by exerting what feeble little powers they do have control over. They try to lessen your power by putting you down, withholding information, making stupid demands, and otherwise throwing grenades in the works and gumming up processes. They'll try to subvert you in any way they can, even if it harms their own company. It's not about the company; it's about them, and everything else be damned. They're frustrated human beings, and they figure shooting you will somehow fix that. It never does. These are the guys that wanted to leave the camp and journey out on to new adventures, but they didn't because they were too afraid. So, they try to lessen you somehow because they think if they can make you crawl back to camp, then they will have won, and their power restored.

There is no deal or client worth that nonsense. There are too many good clients and new adventures for you to embark on. You can face the BSD head-on, but be careful not to get wet. He may back down after being confronted, but that usually only lasts for a little while. Then his insecurity takes over again. Take none of it to heart. It's not about you. I might just prefer to stay out of harm's way, not engage, and let the harm the offender is perpetuating on his company start to unfold. Let nature do its work.

The Wounded Animal

Animals were put on this world to breed. They like breeding. They're driven to it, sometimes uncontrollably. Left unchecked, all that breeding would engulf the world in animals because of the exponential power of the process. The irrevocable math would have swallowed the world in offspring. Nature, however, saw fit to put in place checks so this wouldn't happen; most notably, dying. Dying, however, came with its own brand of unpleasantness, not the least of which was being killed and consumed by other species -- bummer for the eaten.

This gruesome scenario made an impact on the survivors. Animals that became wounded had a heightened fear that they too might be eaten. In a frantic attempt to avoid this outcome, their brains would flood with hormones, and they would lash out at anything and anyone that came near. It was a biologically adaptive response – fight or flight. It was a crazy survival instinct that manifested a crazed wild beast in the field, and it worked, at least for the short term, but works less well in the corporate world. Unfortunately, the flood of hormones that flood the brains of wounded animals followed the humans into the present-day workplace. In the corporate world, the wounds they experience aren't of the flesh, but instead of the mind and emotion. But they are wounded nonetheless, and they too become crazy.

Wounded, trapped, and cornered animals are the most dangerous. Those extreme stressors create desperation and flood of hormones in the afflicted that cause them to lash out with a fierceness unbridled by any rational thought. Their fear and anxiety create their extreme reactions. Regardless if you are friend or foe, if you're in close proximity to them, you're likely to get attacked. It doesn't matter if the wounded is a mule-deer, rabbit, COO, or a Director of Real Estate; when the stress comes, they're hit with a nitrous boost of unmanaged adrenaline, and they want to hurt you.

We're all just animals. We like to think we've evolved to a higher level of self-awareness, but in a pinch, most people revert to those reptilian impulses that have controlled their actions since the dawn of time, the modern-day version of curling up into a ball to make yourself small, snarl and show your teeth, and snap at whoever gets too close. For those in the real estate departments and C-suites of corporations, it's bad numbers, missed metrics, companies teetering on the brink of bankruptcy, new supervisors with a penchant for maltreatment of their subordinates, family problems, health problems, addiction problems, or a whole host of other personal issues that can cause that person for whom you've saved millions of dollars and had a great relationship with for years, to turn on you in an instant and go for your jugular before you know what's happened. You'd like to think these supposedly sane people are whole enough to handle the stressors and they wouldn't make such a stark, irrational, behavioral shift, but you'd be wrong.

Their fear and anxiety and the combination of the steady stream of adrenaline and cortisol turn their brains to mush. They make decisions to hurt and maim, instead of fixing the problems, building up the company, and making a profit. Any relationship capital you've built up along the way is tossed aside by the wounded animal as he flails trying to understand his situation, fearing he'll fall into the abyss or be eaten. Their misguided efforts at self-preservation make all matters worse, not better, and are amplified by the level and significance of their personality deficiencies and disorders.

Merely being aware of this concept is no protection for you. I've been slashed and bitten by friendlies more than enough times to know this is true. True protection comes from assessing the stress responses of the people you're working with by seeing how they've handled smaller stresses in their business and life in the past and how they react to little challenges to their thinking and decisions. How do they treat subordinates? How many disgusted or discarded spouses have littered their home life? Do their kids speak to them? How tender is their ego? How false is their pride? Have they overcome challenges in their lives, or is their propensity to create challenges, then blame others and run away? Know who could break easily and find others in the organization you consider more stable that you can depend on when the shit hits the fan, the steadfast ones, the ones who are unflappable. Your other protection is to not take any of the attacks personally. Know it's their disorder causing the malfeasance, not you. In extreme situations, you may have to extricate yourself from the situation altogether or put the wounded animal out of its misery.

The Corrupt

I'd been doing transactions for a global retailer for several years. I probably worked on a hundred or more transactions of different kinds: distribution facilities, big-box retail, and high-end showrooms, all over the place. They were putting together a new concept store they wanted to roll out across the country and asked me to research big-box retail locations in an affluent coastal town. I already knew the market well because I'd done several similar projects there. I put together a list of suitable sites for their requirement. They narrowed the prospective sites to a shortlist of preferred locations, and we began negotiations on those. As that progressed, they started to identify sites on the list that I would not be responsible for, and likewise, not compensated for.

One of the company's executives (someone I had never dealt with in my years handling transactions for the firm) said he had previously entered into an exclusive representation agreement with another brokerage company. This was news to me. That other brokerage company had been started by a nationally recognized star athlete, and their grand opening had been presided over by the mayor of the city with much fanfare. Everybody loved this celebrity, and the story told by the exec to everyone in my client company was that he'd hired this star ballplayer as his broker.

I'll step aside in some situations if there is a good reason, but this situation didn't make sense to me because the other brokerage company had no experience in this kind of work that I could find. My interest was piqued when one of the landlords called me and asked who this other group was that had just contacted them. She sent me copies of the emails she had received from the other company's rep. The rep told her I wasn't to be involved any longer in the deal and that his company would be handling the transaction. The rep's surname was the same as the exec's. This smelled like bad fish, so I decided to do some research.

The first thing I did was a deep dive into the exec, the same kind of research I do building a dossier on an opponent of an important negotiation. I learned his father had made a small fortune with an office products company, and the exec and his brother were never wanting for money. They both had a string of various companies they had started and ended with limited success. The exec had done a stint at one of the big national brokerages as a typical glad-handing broker – super friendly on the outside, but always looking out for his own interest. I also learned the brother had a son, the exec's nephew, the same guy whose name was in the email that told the landlord not to deal with me. The nephew was a pup; to this point, it looked to me his real estate career hadn't yet expanded beyond showing small residential condos. I'm sure he's a nice guy, blah, blah, blah.

What I learned about the principals of the other brokerage company was more interesting, though. The star ballplayer had provided funds to start the company. But there were two other founders that had previously been found to be part of a ring that perpetrated a mortgage fraud scheme that stole millions of dollars from thousands of victims. The state Department of Justice and other agencies had raided their offices with over 60 agents. "What the hell," I thought. At this point, I didn't want to step aside. This exec wanted to sideline me and use the company run by these goons, so his young pup nephew broker that knew nothing could collect a six-figure commission. I couldn't help but wonder if a kickback was also part of the plan.

I exposed this guy's conflicts and the situation to my client company together with the documentation I had. I thought the exec should be tarred and feathered and run out of the company. What happened was less dramatic. He was indeed removed from any responsibility as to the markets I'd been working on, and I was re-instated to handle the sites there. Ultimately, in short order, he was gone from the company too. I never did ascertain if the ballplayer knew about the fraud ring or not.

The Coward

One of my biggest disappointments of human character occurred at an ICSC convention in Las Vegas. The guy in charge of managing all the real estate of a company with hundreds of big-box health operations explained to me that his boss had just told him that he wanted me to handle all the lease renewals and renegotiations in their portfolio because of the performance I'd shown on about a dozen recent transactions for them. I'd saved them almost 30% off their previous rents on all the deals. Nobody in their company had ever approached savings like that. Usually, there hadn't been any savings. The guy was of a different mind, though. He feared for his job since his boss wanted to turn all those transactions over to me.

It was a stupid fear. He wouldn't have lost his job. Instead, he would have been able to bask in the glow of my great results. Nevertheless, his plan was to not turn over all the transactions and instead to discredit and sideline me. But I had the support of his boss, so he slow-walked and sulked. He wasn't stupid, but he was like one of those lightbulbs that flicker on and off. You don't know if the bulb is going bad, the bulb is not screwed in all the way, or there's a screw loose in the lamp. Either way, it's a dim bulb and doesn't work the way it's supposed to -- and it's annoying. Up to this point, Dim Bulb's lease renewal process had been asking the landlords for a reduction in rent, and when the landlords said "no," Dim Bulb could report back to his boss that it couldn't be done.

We both worked on the leases, but the decision as to who handled which lease fell under his purview. Increasingly, the properties Dim Bulb selected for me were the toughest of the bunch. They were locations where we were least likely to have the cooperation of the landlord and most likely to be stonewalled on any attempt to renegotiate, let alone get free or reduced rents, or tenant finish allowances. These were the situations where there was no obvious leverage for us and the least likely that I would get paid.

Funny thing, though, I kept hitting my numbers. My Applied Influence methodology was working great. Another dozen sites and I was still generating savings of 30 percent off the occupancy costs for my client.

I don't mind doing other people's toughest jobs. I might even consider that to be a core competency. But I would prefer if the client was honest in that selection and not use it as a means to subvert me. Regardless, my performance didn't suffer, and every lease I renegotiated for this client showed a sizable reduction in occupancy costs -- every one. The boss continued to sing my praises, but Dim Bulb got increasingly frustrated and hostile. He doubled down trying to take me down.

It was about this time that Dim Bulb asked me to write an instruction and procedures manual on how I conducted the negotiations. I didn't mind really. I found it amusing. I knew he wouldn't do what I would outline. You can lead a horse to water, but you can't make him think. I did figure he'd put his name on it, though.

To my detriment, the boss left the company for greener pastures, and Dim Bulb was left to his own devices. He didn't want to get rid of me entirely; my data was too good, my performance too outstanding. But he hated me doing deals the performance of which could be, when compared to his own, superior. Meanwhile, the company started to splinter as executives left for different positions. It was eventually sold to a new group of investors. That didn't stop Dim Bulb from trying to subvert me, though. It got worse.

In one instance, after I had negotiated a new lease term for a site in Denver at terms far superior to the renewal option they had; with amendment prepared, negotiated, and waiting for signatures, they inextricably exercised their original option thereby wiping out the million-dollar savings I had arranged for them and any hopes I would get paid after a year's worth of work. It was the most bone-headed move I had ever seen.

The landlord and I were both shocked. The landlord was delighted. I was in disbelief. When I got Dim Bulb on the phone, I was laughing at how incredulously stupid this was. "Stop laughing," he said. He got increasingly mad and frantic, "Stop laughing!" he shouted! How could I not laugh at such buffoonery?

The landlord, to whom I must credit with integrity and character, agreed to stand by the earlier agreed-upon terms and set the option exercise aside. The amendment got signed, I got paid, and my client, in spite of their ineptitude, reaped the rewards of my negotiations, the million dollars saved in reduced occupancy costs. Later, Dim Bulb accused me of strong-arming the landlord to get this deal done. I hadn't, but I thought it was such an odd accusation. What if I had strong-armed the opposing side and prevailed? So what? I thought Dim Bulb was losing his grip on reality. Whose side was he on?

About that same time, I had renegotiated another lease for this client with a New York landlord, again with substantial rent savings. After several months of negotiating the verbiage of the document itself, during the final legal review, my client's in-house counsel at the last minute removed my representation reference and fee from the final set of documents. They told me it was another internal communication error. They apologized and it got fixed, but it was inexcusable, nevertheless. The wheels were coming off the bus. The bus was about to go off the cliff. I was looking for the exit.

The last straw for me was a renegotiation of another site in Denver. This lease had an option the client could exercise at fair market value. The landlord had a bogus "appraisal" he had bought and paid for from one of the nation's biggest brokerages. It purported the value of the property to be twice what I thought it was worth. It was a stupid document that pulled comparable properties from as far away as sixty miles in its feeble attempt to support its claim. Convenient for the landlord and the brokerage, it might have been just one of a number of properties to be included in a blanket mortgage brokered by... you guessed it, the big national brokerage that wrote the appraisal.

During negotiations, I had ignored the bogus appraisal and absurd rents the landlord was demanding. My offers amounted to about half of what he wanted. The guidance I was receiving from the tenant was that they would be willing to vacate the building if we weren't able to reduce the occupancy costs and juice the site's profit margin substantially. This was perfect overt leverage for hammering our position home, particularly if the landlord wanted to re-capitalize some of its debt.

I had met the landlords in their L.A. offices. They were incensed that we would have the gall to pursue lower rents, let alone half of what they were asking. I listened to their whining and even acknowledged their hurt feelings (boo hoo), but this conflict, this disparity, wasn't going to go away until they accepted our terms or something similar. It would have happened. The landlord would never be able to lease or sell their building for anything near what they were demanding. We held the power in our hands. That's when Dim Bulb folded.

He called me and said he now needed the space and asked me to stand down because he was going to go to the landlord with "hat in hand," no more negotiations, total capitulation, and totally out of the blue. That's when I fired him. The last I heard of him, he and his family were living out of a guest house of one of the company's landlords -- rent-free. There was no way this guy wasn't conflicted. How could he negotiate optimal rents for his company when he's personally receiving these types of material perks from their landlords? I think it's unacceptable.

Ass-Kissers, Boot-Lickers, and those that Love 'em and Need 'em

We'll finish this section with a special category devoted to the brown-nosers and the assholes that excitedly receive them. Picture that docking exercise. It's driven by the need for them both to cover up their core insecurities. The sycophantic brown-nosers jettison their own integrity because they have such a low opinion of themselves; they think this is the only way to get into the game. The assholes take them in so eagerly because the gooey adulation heaped upon them by the sycophants is the opioid they need to mask their low self-esteem by giving them a fraudulent patina of self-worth. They don't care it's fraudulent; it makes them feel good. It's a sickening dance. As for the terms of the deals these two might put together, they don't care at all about the terms of the deals. They're a narcissistic, parasitic mess. It's all about them and the holes in their souls. If you find yourself anywhere near these bloodsuckers, you're bound to get splattered. Terminate them.

Unfortunately, friendly fire is a reality you're going to run into if your performance is better than others. Expect it. Plan for it. It's an unnecessary obstacle, but hey, life's not fair, and nobody is going to make it fair for you. Watch your back.

20

PHILOSOPHY OF A HITMAN

PART IV

BEYOND CHAOS, BEYOND POWER

To learn how to think and to learn how to play is to learn how to live and create.

"If things seem under control, you just aren't going fast enough."
-- Mario Andretti

Real mountain biking is a raucous symphony of muscle-blowing, cardiac-crunching, oxygen-starving, endurance-climbing, limit testing effort and intention; interspersed with moments of calm and jaw-dropping beauty and awe; then culminating in maximum, high-intensity crazy. It's another amalgam of man and machine pushing the boundaries and challenges of nature all for the adrenaline rush and fun -- provided you and the bike stay together. You're never really in control, but you're not out of control. You let go of your addiction to what you imagine is control in order to win your optimal velocity.

The descents, and regardless of any lofty talk about aerobic exercise or appreciation of the alpine wilderness, all true, but the descents are why you do it. Down narrow, steep, dirt, single track at speeds faster than safe, taking advantage of every rocky ledge to leave the earth and fly a little, keeping your center of gravity low and leaning in deep to dig into the turns, hoping, counting on the knobby tires holding the arc, then unweighting, as if on skis, to move the bike to the other side and lean in on the reciprocal switchbacks and more sliding rocks, slipping tires, and dust. Then out over the flat rock and off into space until once again, your tires hit the sandy earth of the hardpack trail. Flying low past the trees and boulders, pulling the bike up into your loins to jump over the rocks and holes you can't avoid. Faster and faster you go, and you just glory in the moment...and hang on. You've got to keep your eyes on the trail if you're going to survive -- and the horizon.

Not being in control is not the same thing as being out of control. Not being out of control is not the same as being in control. Between those four points is flow. It's like the whitewater ride out of the boat. Too much dependence on control, and you die. Understand, embrace, and work with nature, and you win.

Nature, by its very nature, by definition, is omnipotent. It's not arbitrary. It's not capricious. It's the harshest meritocracy around, and you're its agent. Not only its agent, but its handler. And not just its handler, but its beneficiary -- an expression of its omnipotent power. You have access to all possibilities. Legacy systems, hierarchies, cultural biases, and dull minds be damned. The matrix for the developing future is you. You'd better use it. You'd better enjoy it.

Nature's Orgasmic State

Life is about experiences. It's like music. You don't play a song to get to its end. You play it to experience it, to be in it, to feel it, to think about it, and be amazed along its way.

Some of us are born to this earth on a quest for discovery and ecstasy. A little hard to find perhaps, but a worthwhile pursuit nonetheless. But you can't live your life in full-time ecstasy. That would be like an orgasm that never quits. You need something as good, but tamer, more sustainable, something healthful and helpful. That something is the state of flow.

Flow is a state of being where self-consciousness falls away, irrelevant feelings and distracting thoughts disappear. You feel in balance. There is more clarity. You're more lucid. You're confident in your choices and actions. Fear vanishes as you move into more challenging endeavors. Activities become their own reward, and you know there are even more positive things to come. This is a state of being where you are in perfect vibratory resonance with nature's energy of conception and creation, nature's orgasm. This is flow.

In the flow state, you feel your true capability and strength, and your success is not questioned. Your ability to learn new things increases ten-fold. Your performance increases ten-fold. Relevant epiphanies emerge from your seemingly infinite mind as self-induced boundaries, criticisms, and your ego don't get in your way. You're so engrossed in your chosen activities that nothing else matters.

A flow state is triggered when you focus your attention on complex and challenging projects you enjoy that move you towards your embodied goals and targets, and you have a mastery of the skills needed to complete them well. Creativity, novelty, and unpredictability further enhance your engagement and deepens the flow state.

Being discriminating in favor of activities you desire, rejecting those that you don't, and avoiding distractions and interruptions, help bring about a state of flow and allows your passion and purpose to fuel it. Do it because you love it. Then, when you bring your focus and attention and intention, a natural synergy launches the perfect energy to run your show – flow.

When you're in flow, the brain produces a neurochemical cocktail of Dopamine, Serotonin, Norepinephrine, Anandamide, and Endorphins. It packs a wicked punch. You feel your best self, the self without all the baggage, self-doubt, and all the other negative shit. You feel bliss and a sense that you are in a zone of perfection.

Norepinephrine gets your brain and body ready for action by increasing alertness, focused attention, memory, and vigilance. Anandamide heightens your motivation, pleasure, and happiness. Dopamine engages your executive functions and turns on your fine-tuned motor-skills, pleasure centers, perseverance, and reward systems. Serotonin manages your mood, increases your memory processing, and improves your cognition. Endorphins work just like opioids, binding to the same receptors in the brain as opioids, blocking pain signals, and producing a feeling of euphoria. What's not to like?

Flow is engaged when our minds are stretched for a project which is new and challenging. Flow has no latency. The activity becomes its own reward, but there is even more to come. Flow is the cousin of ecstasy, but it can be perpetual. Flow is living in ecstasy without the continuous orgasm.

Experiencing flow in your life takes you to a new reality. In flow, you rise above the conflagration below. The worried and hurt self vanishes, and time is suspended. Flow enhances your autonomy and sovereignty, and you become a whiz kid -- a super-fast learner and alpha performer. Your pedestrian ego goes dormant. A rewiring takes place in your brain that quiets the scripted character you've created for yourself, and you are freer to express the expansive omnipotence of who you really are. You become your true self, beyond your self-image. You feel fully alive and aligned with nature's run. You're master of your destiny, and you know it.

In flow, you disassociate from the present moment, yet at the same time, you are fully present. You're less an observer and more a participant – fully engaged. Awareness, decisions, and actions merge. That's when you become superhuman, a true alpha-performer.

Deconstructing Chaos

Some people can't experience flow. They're connected to their devices and not to the natural creative energy around them. They're bombarded with disordered and disjointed information and misinformation and oscillations of a million random butterfly wings. Their minds try to make sense of the disparate range of chaotic inputs, but it's no use. They can't distinguish substantive signal from noise. Life's residue and deal sediment build up in their heads and soul; sludge that slows performance and blocks their connection to the creative energy, information, and intelligence of the quantum field. Psychic entropy befalls them. Their emotional debt becomes overdue. Their purpose and goals are unclear. Their intention and motivation are disengaged. They succumb to the bumps, threats, and tragedies that everyday life visits on them. Everything negative cuts deep. Creativity is gone. Stale thoughts replay over and over on an endless loop, and they're weakened.

The fix is to remove oneself from the pernicious environment and confines of the depthless material world that imposes that mess. The fix is to pull back, go to zero, refresh, reconnect, recharge, and relearn to enjoy still being alive. The fix is to go find a place to renew your connection with yourself and the singularity. Go find a place of solitude where you can be immersed in the world's orderly chaos. Go find a place in nature. Go off the grid. Go alone.

Some people don't like being alone. Sometimes I have to be. I need a way to clean out the sludge, jettison the waste, and reboot, re-center, and reconnect. I need a way to debrief, decompress, and deliberately look at the facts of my life and to plan. I have to get away, alone.

Solitude allows you time to ground your relationship with yourself and the universe. Go to zero and reflect and take pleasure in the moment when your self-identity is purely yours and not skewed by the reflections of others. I seek solitude in the forest and out on the rocks because that's when I see myself, my life, and the things most important, most clearly.

On personal getaways, I go to zero. Open issues resolve themselves. Tired ideas are released. New ideas come. Getting away from pressures and toxicity and immersing yourself in natural surroundings allows your neural pathways to relax, disengage, and realign. It affords you time to think with a different perspective. You gain a more thorough understanding of your projects and your plans infused with a new playfulness, creativity, strength, and maturity. You find new answers to old questions, new questions with new answers, or yet to be discovered answers.

The psychologist, Mihaly Csikszentmihalyi, who has researched "flow" more than anyone else, exclaimed, "If one reads the biographies of the physicists like Bohr, Heisenberg, Chandrashekhar, and Bethe, one gets the impression that without hikes in the mountains and the vision of night skies their science would not have amounted to much."

From the glacier cut mountains of British Columbia, the peaceful calm of Lake Como, the rugged peaks of the Colorado Rockies, to the crystal blue warmth of the Caribbean, the beauty and energy of these exceptional places are portals to inspiration and creativity at a core level. In the cities, you can see a handful of stars. In the mountains, you can see through to infinity. During the most challenging times in my life, I have found foundation and answers in nature. For me, that was so often the Colorado mountains.

Bill Gates does something like this in what he calls his "Think Week." He says he brings a stack of books and papers to read. You could do that, or bring your own writings, or better yet, bring nothing at all and go to zero and write something completely new yourself.

The type of place you choose, simple monastic asceticism, luxurious opulence, or bushwhacking in the wilderness, it makes little difference. What is essential is your undisturbed connection to the pure, honest energy of the natural world. Take a week. Take a day. I'll sometimes spend time, as an adjunct to a business trip, to be at a new coastline, a new forest, a different desert, even a quirky coffee place in a town, or part of town I've not been before where I can tap into the zen of a new place. But deep in the high-country is best for me.

There's a little grassy place next to a crystal mountain stream that flows through the bottom of a small valley. The entrance is hidden behind a tall stand of aspens that no motor of any sort can get to. There are no paths in or out. I'll bet the Ute knew about this place, but few others, I imagine. Undoubtedly the creek had been named by someone who had lost their way. The name speaks of desperation and defeat, but the place is anything but that. It's my connection to everything in the universe. It's more than hard to find, but I prefer it that way.

Puma Boy – Curious, Playful, Untamed, and Free

Mountain lions are patient hunters, stealthy, unflappable, the calmest killers around. Big cats, and this species goes by many names, panther, cougar, puma, mountain lion, are at the top of the food chain. They are apex predators, alpha killers.

They don't chase their prey; they lie in wait, they stalk, then pounce. Piercing the temporal bones of the skull of their prey is their favored method of closing the deal.

Big cats don't give a shit about what others think. They know their nature and pursue their path as nature intended. Young lion cubs learn their path and their nature through their quest for discovery and exploration. Lion cubs and children start out much the same.

Young children have an inherent natural inspiration that makes them want to explore and expand their knowledge. They are free of any self-imposed boundaries and move forward in unchartered territory to find new things and try new things. They are naturally in flow to see how they and their playful intentions interact with the universe, and then marvel at what they find and move on to the next adventure to do it all again.

Children naturally embrace their quest for discovery. They naturally explore. They don't fear failure. They're easily confident in their exploration. It's all about the journey. They jump right in, and they never give up. They're honest with themselves about their feelings, and they're honest with others. They're all about having fun, whether they are successful or not.

Their best play is unstructured – pure discovery.

Healthy children are curious, free to explore, and allow themselves to fail. Children see the good in the world around them and are enthusiastic about leaping into the unknown. If failure comes, they brush it off and move on to something new. Children are unhindered by the rules imposed by the world around them, and they impose none on themselves. They have no preconceived ideas of what to expect; they're explorers in search of something to learn. Their dreams are never dashed. They try again and again and again and again. The adult says, "failure is not an option," and it limits their thinking. The child says, "failure is not an option," and it opens their horizons because there is no failure after all. They allow their intuitiveness and wonder to seek new opportunities to win by unlocking their creativity, ambition, confidence, and motivation. There are no boundaries recognized by them. Children, those smart, unencumbered, little creatures, are born to have fun and learn. Anyone among us who is clinging to their own so-called wisdom as the only end-all-be-all answer has stopped learning and is on their way out.

The Design Challenge was a simple design competition to see who could build the tallest free-standing structure with 20 sticks of spaghetti, a length of string, a length of tape, and one marshmallow. More than 70

teams of four people each competed. They had 18 minutes to complete their structures. The average height achieved over all teams was 20 inches. Teams made up of all CEOs averaged 21 inches. Maybe they're a little bit smarter than the rest, you hope. Business school graduates made up the worst performing teams with structures averaging only 10 inches tall. Who made up the best performing teams? Kindergarteners. The children built structures 30 percent higher than the average, and structures 160 percent taller than business school students, all in the same 18 minutes. The answer as to why is simple.

While the adults started their process by making sure they understood the rules, jockeyed for power, status, and leadership positions within the groups, promoted their individual structure ideas to the groups, and organized and planned; the children just started building. The children made lots of attempts and created lots of failures and learned as they went along. The adults wanted to know "who is in charge," "what are the rules," and "what's the best plan," and they let the same cognitive biases that screw up their economic thinking interfere with learning about the relevant details of the challenge at hand – building the damn thing.

So, this is one of our paradoxes, moving from the preparedness of Sun Tzu to the wondrous exploration of a child. Some of my best deals came together when I was young, uncertain of my place in this world, and just starting to grow my skills. But I put myself out there and took risks. Starting my first company when I was as inexperienced as I was, or venturing into new territory without a proven quantitative business case for success, is why I was able to do those deals. I put myself out there and learned how to fly on the fly. I learned from those deals, and that knowledge has accumulated as I've learned from every deal. You don't need experience, expertise, a proven plan, or anyone's approval to start working your next big deal, or your next six big deals. If you don't start, you don't get the deal. The kids built the tallest tower of spaghetti through trial and error.

There was one taller tower, though. It was built by a group that had fully prepared before ever being confronted with the challenge. The group of architects and engineers built the tallest tower. That doesn't take away from the kindergarteners though; in fact, I'll bet some of those kids went on to build on their experience and became master architects and engineers. The point is, if you're inexperienced, don't let that hold you back. Use it to your advantage. If you're new in a focus, you might not beat the established pro first time, but you can beat everybody else, and you can put that pro in your sights. If your focus addresses a challenge so new that people have never been confronted by it before, experience may be more of a hindrance than a help. New questions give rise to new answers.

Every day, give yourself an hour of free discovery, unstructured mental play, so you can explore in the creative cloud of nature's chaos to see what there is for you to learn. It's like spending some time in the wilderness letting new energy and information flow to you. New questions, new answers, and amazing new solutions will emerge, all while having fun.

We just played, and we accomplished so much.

It's a myth that humans use only ten percent of their brains. Science has shown that we use 100 percent of our brains over the course of a day. Unfortunately, most squander the bulk of their mental capacity on useless things.

When you achieve the flow of a child's sense of discovery and wonder, have the patient determination and freedom of the mountain lion, you'll know that chasing after the things you want is not the answer to your fulfillment. Chasing after deals, people, money, or accolades is not the answer. The answer is knowing that you are already whole and perfect and that nothing external is needed to create the outcomes and success you want. Those external things, the money, the deals, the accolades, the relationships, all are the result of understanding your role in creative energy.

Do you believe you can accomplish anything? You can. Do you believe you can accomplish anything without effort? That's a fool's trap. Success and accomplishment are easy, but they're not without effort. Each person is rewarded not for virtue, but through virtue. Just as your body without your breath is dead, so too is your hope without your work is dead.

Are you making decisions and taking the actions that are aligned with what you want and what you want to be? Are your decisions and actions compelled by fear, or worse, lethargy, or are they strategic and help you hit your targets. Each of your actions is the flap of a butterfly's wing, creating ripples and waves that impact your life and the world around you. What tornados will they produce? You're building the algorithms. You're writing the code. You're writing your story. You're the one deploying it all in real-time. Is it going to take you where you want to go? Are you willing to make the right decisions to take you where you want to go?

When you do, you may sometimes feel like you're the one person facing off against the system, the one person facing off against the behemoths, a David against the giant Goliath. You might feel fear or overwhelmed by this, but all is not what you've been told it is. The common interpretation of the story of David and Goliath is flawed. It's not been understood. Your fears are baseless.

Goliath, like most giants you encounter, was protected by his usual armored garb, brass helmet, brass gloves, brass-scaled coat and breastplate, brass shin guards, and lawyers. David was offered a similar suit, but he refused to armor up before the fight. He knew he didn't need all that stuff. He didn't want it. David knew how to achieve his goals using his knowledge of energy and nature. He'd killed bully predators with his sling many times before while protecting his sheep. Not an insignificant feat with the tools available in those days, but he had practiced and was skilled. His use of creative energy had never failed him.

As he approached Goliath, David affirmed his chosen outcome to the giant, to the world, and to himself. "I will strike you down and give your dead body to the birds," he asserted. A single stone flies from David's whirling sling at a staggering velocity fueled by the energy unleashed by his mind and skill, hitting Goliath in the center of his forehead. Whack! The giant is stunned, gets dizzy and confused, and falls to the ground in a useless heap. David then takes Goliath's own sword and cuts off the giant's head. I'm sure David thought it wasn't all that eventful. He left the dead body for the birds as he said he would do.

The story of David and Goliath has come to signify the story of the underdog prevailing against all odds, but that wasn't what happened. Goliath may have been huge, protected with all kinds of armor and lawyers, but David knew how to use the tools and energy nature fashioned for him. Who was the underdog? It wasn't David. The crowds just saw the comparative size; they missed the more important dynamics. Who was smart? Who was in flow? Who was going to win?

When you embrace the skills and techniques that use the ever-present stream of creative energy, you are deadlier than any of your opponents; because, like David, you have all of nature's principles on your side, riding the wave of creation. Nothing can stop that. You can shirk the protective armor and relax and know that you will make no lasting mistakes because you're not imposing your will on the world. You're using nature as nature intended to accommodate your intentions and the forms you've impressed upon it.

21

HITMAN

"...as for me, I am tormented with an everlasting itch for things remote. I love to sail forbidden seas, and land on barbarous coasts."
-- Herman Melville

Negotiating is a form of arbitrage, arbitrage you create mentally from scratch. Cognitive biases and other decision-making disorders create deviations from the pure mean of rational judgment, and therein lies our opportunities. We identify and capture the gap of pricing delta created by the imprecision and aberrations in the minds of our opponents. It's fodder for our negotiating success, but you must have a willingness to kill. My work is a cerebral determination of markets and market participants, discovering the deltas, creating the gaps, and taking advantage. I learned to thrive on change, uncertainty, and chaos. It's not chaos to me; it's a river, and a fun and interesting ride.

The early wounds, the early failures, the friendly fire, all that shit and the winnings, too, were just the learnings and catalyst for creating Applied Influence. What stands in the way becomes the way. But it was more than just a way to a unified method for winning negotiations; it is the path to a full life experience, the Theory of Everything – if you choose to use it.

A Hitman wins on two vectors. One, by working within the system, not as the system intended, but as nature intended. And two, as a disrupter, by changing the system, but only if the system gets changed. They're not mutually exclusive; both can be pursued simultaneously. Both require your cognitive bench, personal congruity, self-governance, and forward-focused creativity. The self-control and patience needed for your clandestine activities and covert action can be daunting. Sometimes it seems crazy, but the freedom is worth it. Remember, though, nature is a harsh meritocracy. Expect nothing less.

Brains are the new brands. Nobody can count on anything produced under the guise of a big corporate logo to be leading-edge, cutting edge, inventive, transformative, mutative, creative, let alone amazing. There are some smart corporate execs out there, but even the smart ones are held back by an army of corporate zombie drones, laggards in the backwater of the backside of the bell curve -- ballast. The interesting stuff is created by the singular agent, the lone wolf, the puma, the Hitman. Corporate zombie drones are looking forward to the weekend. The Hitman is waiting for them to leave.

After developing Applied Influence, I looked out at the landscape to see what markets were ripe for me to enter, disrupt, and exploit – what would I unleash this new skill set on? Would it really boost the level of alpha performance as I expected? A new game, a clean slate, these are exciting things for me.

If Applied Influence worked as I predicted, I figured I could make a positive impact for hundreds, even thousands of companies amounting to billions or trillions of dollars to their bottom line. I figured that was a big fucking deal.

When your plans are bold and audacious, you might feel a twinge of insecurity about those plans or yourself. That's normal. But if you've done your homework and you know you're right, it doesn't matter if you feel a twinge. The target is all-important. Focus on that.

Fortune 500 Fixer

Decades ago, Walmart, and other big-box discount stores like it, had changed the consumers' psyche such that they always expected to get brand-named stuff at a "discount." The consumers decided they cared less about personal service; they wanted cheaper prices. Discount big-box stores became the rage, and virtually every retail sector rolled up into that model. Small shop stores in town closed everywhere. Big box stores were in vogue, and developers were more than happy to accommodate the demand and built thousands of power centers. New life was breathed into malls for "premium" goods and other specialty crap. "Lifestyle" centers were invented so people could have that "small-town feel" while shopping since they could no longer actually shop in town. Private equity bought into the big-box store bubble too, and with another level of debt added, helped fuel the demand for space and expansion. Publicly-traded real estate investment trusts (REITs) were created to help fund the construction and then to roll-up all these retail properties into massive portfolios. Vast moonscapes of land were graded, paved, and striped for parking. Motus Humanea got into their cars and ventured out to these centers to buy some more stuff to feed their souls. They didn't notice the lemming kill scattered along the edges of the out lots; their attention was focused on the fast-food bounty they'd find at the food court they could shovel into their mouths to keep their feelings in check. How could this not be paradise?

Well, it wasn't. Once Jeff Bezos and others like him decided to capitalize on the inherent laziness of humans and start delivering all their crap to their front doors, the shiny luster of the malls, power centers, lifestyle centers, outlet centers, and most all shopping centers began to fade. The bookstores, music stores, and video stores were the first to go, but soon most retail sectors were feeling the chill. Big box stores would attempt to off-load space and shrink their store footprints. It wasn't enough of a change to matter, so it didn't really matter. Their strategy changed from shrinking their store footprints to shrinking their national footprints, and stores started to close permanently. First, just the worst performers closed, then there were more worst performers, and they too were closed. Then more stores closed, and the bankruptcies came. Office supply, electronics, appliances, apparel, shoes, home décor, mattresses, toys, beauty, sporting goods, department stores of all kinds, you name it, no sector was spared. Dozens of clothing and so-called fashion companies came apart at the seams and unraveled. A real retail apocalypse unfolded. Add an economic recession to the mix, and you've got huge opportunities for those willing to sort through the wreckage.

I chose two target trajectories as part of my dominant strategy: first, represent viable national users to take over vacated box space for its intended use or the myriad of creative adaptive reuses; and second, represent national users with substantial existing property portfolios that would benefit from renegotiating their existing real estate contracts and leases. All my clients would benefit from the vulture value I could unlock with Applied Influence leveraging the markets, dramatically reducing their occupancy costs. What's not to like?

Usually, it's the C-suite and senior execs that invite me into their company because they're the ones that want change. Their middle managers tend to defend the status quo. I like running projects for people who are decisive and stand by their decisions. These often are people who have experience starting their own companies, and people who have invested their own money. People who think like entrepreneurs and wealthy individuals know what they want, and they don't waiver much. They don't feel like they have to lie to you or otherwise manipulate their relationships. If our thinking is aligned, then there are no questions about next steps, and I go make them happen. If they agree to my free reign and full autonomy, I'm good to go.

I contacted the senior execs at the firms I knew would benefit from my work and told them what I could do and why. The details of how I mostly kept to myself and locked down. Soon, I had several Fortune 500 clients asking for help, and I started scheduling my flights.

Landing in new places is like a new puzzle, a new game. Figuring out the people, the infrastructure, the commerce, the industry, the systems, the trends, the sentiment, the biases, and the market is just the start. Then there's the culture, beauty, filth, oddities, and food, always new food, and history of how the place came about. That's all before studying the sites. There's always the risk I won't be successful, I suppose. But that's not been a problem. That just makes me pay attention more. I relish in the adventure.

I'm reminded of a flight I took early on in this hunt. It was a beautiful spring day, an empty airplane, and I have a seat with a lot of room. A young woman sits down beside me and buckles up; long black hair, olive skin, 23, 24 maybe, beautiful. I'll often go an entire flight without speaking three words to the person next to me, but she introduced herself to me. "I'm Lakshmi," she said. "Of course you are," I thought, amused at what a fun and interesting place the universe is. It was serendipity. I'd just been reading about Lakshmi, the Hindu goddess of wealth and prosperity, while researching attitudes about affluence in different cultures. "I'm Steve," I said, smiling and interested to learn more.

Lakshmi was warm and engaging the entire trip, and we talked most of the way. We talked about her and cultures and history and India and the universe, and of course, wealth and prosperity. We talked about how the creation of wealth and prosperity needn't be limited to money, but include all forms of advantage, wellbeing, and good fortune, such as peace and patience, persistence and purity, health and enlightenment, courage, victory, beauty, and morality and ethics. We agreed that there was no reason to accept anything less.

We got off the plane, said goodbye, and she walked away, presumably to bless some other mortal. As I walked on, I had the feeling that this new program of mine was going to work out just fine. I had a confident calm that I would execute these projects as I intended if I kept my connection with nature and stayed open and accepting of those states of being Lakshmi espoused. It was a nice flight. The education, lasting.

The first flow of business from my new strategy occurred with the home improvement and construction industries. I consulted, ran brokers, partnered with brokers, and brokered deals myself. I investigated space, secured space, and built space. I'd see every option myself first, sometimes as many as 30 or 40 in a day. Sometimes multiple markets in a day. Sometimes I wouldn't know what town or what hotel I'd crash at for the night until late into the evening. I'd eat in the car. I'd eat in the room. I'd eat on the plane. Time in restaurants seemed like a waste, only to be savored if the food was worth it. It usually wasn't. I was a road warrior, a site cyborg (a little bionic and I don't have to sleep much), digitizing property data to be deconstructed and analyzed for my decision making and later dissemination. Similar to Google spiders that crawl the internet and grab each piece of information and tag it so it can be organized and called up, I'd use dozens of resources to do the same on my opponents, markets, and the landscapes I was operating in.

Real estate is a hands-on business, though. You can't know what you need to know just from databases. Information is not knowledge. You can get cold demographics and market data, and that's good, but you don't get to see the neglected building across the street and who's tagging what and why. You've got to be on the ground to see it, smell it, and know what type of cars go by, what's being sold in the sidewalk kiosks and by whom. Is the trade area thriving or dying, clean or filthy, open or closed? What are the sentiments of the people that make up the population, or those that only venture in during the day or night? Are they happy? Sad? Angry? Gauging the velocity of money and trends requires your objective presence, not a salesperson trying to make a buck.

I'd see all the target sites, stalking horse sites, and all alternative sites, often alone and often on weekends or nights, so I could spend time in each area uninterrupted to take it all in and strategize my parallel negotiations, my killer BANANAs.

Some rollouts were so fast I would sometimes pick up the CEO, COO, president, or real estate head at the airport late at night. We'd grab some food and water and then hit the streets touring trade areas and sites throughout the night and finishing up as the sun was coming up. I'd then drop him at his hotel or back at the airport to do it again in another city on another day. If I needed to schedule local brokers, contractors, bankers, or landlords in on those nocturnal tours, I would, and they would be there too.

We'd have weekly conference calls with the principals of the firms and heads of the relevant departments (operations, construction, legal, finance) and "go 'round the horn" discussing each of the 20, 50, or 100 sites we were focusing on that month. These were supported by digital site packs my firm prepared for each location, so the quality and format of the information was consistent across all markets. I protected my clients against the drivel and misinformation from those with misaligned agendas. My clients only got pure vetted data and tours I orchestrated.

I was constantly on the move. Sometimes I'd be on a plane and forget where I was coming from or headed to.

With the government work ebbing and the home improvement retailer rollouts well underway, a new set of projects came my way from the sports and health industries as a result of my selective outreach. Among them was a company with a national portfolio of hundreds of big-box retail facilities. Their in-house transaction people had been handling their own lease renewals up to this point with very little success. Mostly they just rolled over on their renewal options. If they didn't have an option, they'd try to negotiate some pittance off the landlord's new rent number. It was a sorry state of affairs.

Two of the senior execs in the company that had ultimate responsibility for their entire real estate portfolio wanted to bring me on board to shake things up and get some new results. They desperately wanted to reduce their occupancy costs as well as get cheap capital dollars to fund renovations and refurbishment because many of their sites were old and showing wear. The new competitors in the markets were coming out with new, highly-designed facilities with the latest technology, so these legacy players needed to upgrade their own facilities to compete. As we were discussing whether we were a good fit together or not, I told them of a $15,000,000.00 mortgage balloon payment that one of their landlords had coming due on one of the sites they needed to renegotiate -- awesome info, killer leverage. It was like they were seeing the morning sun for the very first time. "How did you know that?" they asked. I smiled. I started working on their deals immediately.

I created the project timelines and process and procedures. I ran demographics, pulled geodata, identified relevant transaction data, and pulled expenditure and demand money flows on all the sites, stalking horses, and alternate sites, and built dossiers on all the landlords. This was my state-of-the-art version of Sun Tzu's operation of "knowing the landscape." After conducting my in-market research, I built detailed market analyses for each site that included a summary of all my research and analysis as well as a target of occupancy costs for each site I thought I could and should achieve. I set a pricing target for each project and made my clients aware of what they were. I went out on a limb. I set the mark. The metrics tracked the success of my results compared to my clients' objectives, the prior contract obligations, and my targets.

After I finished the first five deals, I showed the results to the SVP in charge of real estate. The efficacy of Applied Influence was obvious. In high-priced communities from Marin County to Silicon Valley, I had captured savings for this client of 33%, 20%, 21%, 26%, and 35% on the first deals. Collectively, I had saved them over 27% off their obligations and secured well over a million dollars in debt-free capital improvement dollars. The landlord in the first transaction sent my client a half-million-dollar check within days of signing the contract, per the terms of the agreement. My client didn't know what to do with the money when it landed on his desk. I just had to laugh. I was just getting started. After seeing the success I had achieved for his company, the SVP wanted me to spearhead negotiations on all the sites in the portfolio.

I achieved close to a 30 percent savings on average for all the transactions I did for this client, not to mention the millions in debt-free capital improvement and tenant finish dollars. It all went straight to their bottom line. It was Applied Influence.

About this time, I made contact with one of the biggest holding companies in the world. They operated more than 20 retail brands and subsidiaries worldwide in more than a thousand locations. I had reached out to them via email with just a quick summary of the success I was having with my methods. They invited me to their HQ and soon contract and lease renegotiations got underway for big-box, outlet, showroom, and specialty stores across the U.S. Like most large companies, they had their own in-house real estate department, but the president wanted to move away from how business had been handled for years and bust up their own status quo. Again, I was imposed on a new real estate department, but it didn't take long for the people there to see the benefit.

We kicked off the relationship by identifying about 20 projects for occupancy cost reductions of their 1,500-site portfolio. These first sites stretched from the financial centers of New York, through the heavy industrial regions of the northeast and Midwest, including the Great

Lakes. Soon I was handling their contract renegotiations for sites throughout their portfolio from coast to coast, achieving a 100 percent success rate reducing occupancy costs. Savings on new deal terms were well over 20 percent and often exceeded 30 percent. The number and variety of retail projects continued to increase as I ran operations for corporately owned stores and distribution facilities, as well as franchised operations.

Rollout work stepped up as I scoured New England for sites to accommodate new big-box outlet stores and oversaw the writing of dozens of contracts all along the Eastern Seaboard. The national footprint was so dense for some of these companies, we had to avoid cannibalizing other owned stores and keep our distance from affiliate companies.

I stayed data-driven guided by granular demographics as well as trade area co-tenancies and money velocity. I could tell you how much money people in each specific trade area made and what they were spending it on, what existing sales were for almost any product line and the resulting gap, or pent up demand in each trade area for specific products. I could tell you the number of renters, or the number of owner-occupied homes, what the values were, and how much money they spent on home improvements and appliances. I could tell you how old or young the people that made up the population were, how many people had health club memberships and how many times they worked out every week and how much sports equipment they bought and how many cars they had. I could tell you how fast their internet connections were and to what extent they'd moved their purchasing online. I could tell you how many law degrees, engineering degrees, teachers, and scientists there were. I could tell you how many people spoke other languages and what they were. I ran regression analyses with more than fifty variables to determine which were most impactful for determining successful store locations. This was Motus Humanea and trade area markets deconstructed for all to see. Well, not all, just me and my clients.

Using Applied influence and data specific to each client industry, I continued to hit 100 percent of my client objectives for cost savings. More business came in.

I secured home improvement sites from the great northwest to South Miami and everywhere in between, from the deep south to the northern Rockies. The pipeline kept flowing.

I renegotiated discount big-box apparel store leases throughout the Appalachian region of the Eastern United States.

I handled the entire real estate portfolio for a specialty high-end kitchen design, equipment, and appliance company with showrooms in the wealthiest towns and trade areas from coast to coast, and the distribution facilities to support them.

I opened a headquarters facility and 24 new markets for a consumer broadband provider.

I oversaw a half-billion-dollar portfolio disposition made up of hundreds of specialized facilities across the U.S for a global energy company, maintaining an embedded crew to handle all the due diligence work.

I completed a 350-site lease valuation project to target sites for occupancy costs reductions for a national healthcare provider.

I completed a 325-market site-selection suitability analysis to locate the world headquarters for a communication services company and e-commerce platform, pitting the top contenders against one another based on education, cost of living, quality of living, economic development incentives, and state and local financial incentives.

From that first big telco deal I did in Denver, nothing gets government bureaucrats all abuzz like the sound of new job creation. It's like a drug for them, and they're all addicted, and they all want to take credit. I don't care. They can take the credit as long as I get my deal done on my terms, and that sometimes includes big incentives to my clients from the Fed, states, counties, and municipalities. Mix and match, it can be a cornucopia of goodies mostly in the form of free money. For these government types, there's no need to ask if growth is good. For them, it's always good. And money? No problem, it's not their money. It's the taxpayers' money, or rather, it was.

There are economic development incentives available for almost any project that's going to generate jobs or tax revenues or otherwise give the politicians a reason to blow their horns. You just have to ask for the incentives. Ask for them from every level of government, from city councils right through to the Feds, and be willing to sort through the proposals. And don't just accept what they offer, use that only as a starting point. These can be worth millions, billions -- tax abatements, tax credits, tax deferrals, subsidies, grants, relocation assistance, employment assistance, infrastructure incentives, utility rate adjustments, loans, loan guarantees, and loan bailouts, loans, loans, and more loans. Some governmental entities have discretionary funds to use for whatever purpose they want to make a deal. But that's not all. I haven't even gotten started. Special incentives are available for specific industries that various agencies deem desirable or deserving of help. Few are excluded. Most are included -- banks, energy (clean or dirty, all welcome), cars, aircraft (especially great if you're Boeing), agriculture, shipbuilding, food, bio-whatever, rural, urban, small business, defense, defense, defense, medical, fish, trade, hurricanes, homeland security, helium (say that last one sounding like a chipmunk), and of course diversity and the underemployed. It's free money.

These incentives aren't limited to U.S. companies. Big packages have gone to firms from all continents. The amazing thing is half the time the client companies don't even pursue the benefits offered or obtained for them.

Dealing with municipalities is a two-edged sword, though. They can get greedy. Take Berkley, for instance. Berkeley's an odd place, the People's Republic. It's kind of like Boulder in a lot of ways. Boulder is better. Berkeley is like Boulder's strung out older brother. Lots of healthy, young people milling around in a small-town cesspool of moldy old buildings with moldy old restaurants, old gray gum on the sidewalks, and syringes in the gutters.

The local government was pretty fond of their little town. It was a gold mine for them. They wanted more than a million and a half bucks mostly for municipal parking that didn't exist, and might not ever exist, so my client could put up a new 30,000 square foot building. I filed that idea in the trash can I labeled Graft. We never did the deal.

Regardless, you can't worry about those types of people or any of the setbacks you might experience, ever. I did scores, maybe hundreds, of projects that never came to fruition. But like the biggest scorers in basketball, football, or any sport, or any business for that matter, they also tend to have the biggest number of failed attempts. Do you want to hit some big success numbers? Go make lots of attempts and be willing to fail a lot, like the kids in the Design Challenge. You can have a lot of fun, and there are many great accomplishments for you to make if you just make the attempt.

The Skipper

I'm going to wrap this story up in Stamford, Connecticut, a short walk from the elevated MTA station where commuters travel to and from Grand Central in New York and points in between, and a short walk from the marina boat slips in Stamford Harbor, off the picturesque Long Island Sound, on a beautiful Spring day with deep blue skies and the sandpipers and oystercatchers flying about and enjoying their freedom. I was finishing the site selection for a new headquarters and specialty products commodity trading floor for an East Coast refiner owned by private equity.

At the same time, I was renegotiating a lease to secure a new term with better prices and great incentives for a large health facility in the Rocky Mountain West. The landlord was a private real estate investment company that, coincidentally, was also headquartered in Stamford. Stamford, CT, is a popular hedge fund haunt about an hour's ride north of New York City. You'd think the food would be better there given the residents' net worth, but it's actually pretty shitty, except on Bedford and Summer Streets in the summer months.

This landlord had leases with my client for several different facilities around the country. These guys owned properties in 26 states, and they were not particularly interested in talking with me about modifying the lease, let alone reducing rent and coughing up dollars for capital improvements. My client had an option to renew the lease at a much higher rate than what I thought was appropriate. The strategy of the landlord's rep was simply to not return phone calls and force my client to exercise their option at the excessive rate. Sound familiar?

As with all my transactions, I did extensive research on the landlord. I knew all about the company and the principals, what they owned, how they bought it, how they managed it, their vacancies and debt levels. I had previous dealings with this landlord having done a telco switch, colocation, and data center lease with them several years before.

The Rocky Mountain rep's title was "President," and he was "President" for some of the fund entities, but there was an organizational financial and executive structure above that. That is what was located in the Stamford offices near the marina. The location near the marina was convenient because the man who was really in charge, the Chairman and CEO, spent much of his time, at least during the summer months, out on his yacht on Long Island Sound. I'll call him "Skipper."

Since I wasn't getting much of a response to my calls or emails from the fund President, I set my sights on the people that held control over all the investments, the Skipper and his CFO. Since I was doing other work in Stamford and New York, I was on the east coast with some regularity. I started sending messages to the Skipper each time I was going to be in the area and suggest we meet. No response, although sometimes that would make the fund President stir a bit, but not for long. Since the Skipper spent so much time on his yacht, I offered to meet him on his boat. There was no response to that either. Too bad, it would have been nice. Regardless, I started walking into their Stamford offices unannounced and got to know the office staff there over several months. The Skipper was usually on his yacht. I can't blame him. It is beautiful there in the summer.

The turning point came when, one afternoon, I arrived at their Stamford office and the Skipper was also there. The Skipper wasn't happy that he was being put on the front line and having to negotiate or having the stress that came with it. He figured he had employees for that, and he wasn't happy that his employee, the fund President, was putting him in that position. I had totally screwed up the hierarchy that was supposed to have been followed. The Skipper instructed his office staff to get the fund President on the phone for me. They were happy to oblige.

The staff walked me into the office the fund President used when he was in Stamford and sat me down behind his desk, next to his phone. I then had a conversation with the fund President while I was sitting behind his own desk in Stamford, on his own phone, while he was on a cell phone stuck in traffic in Denver; and his boss, the Skipper, was in an office just thirty feet to my left. The picture was almost surreal. The fund President hadn't been calling me back, but now I'm sitting in his office, thirty feet from his boss, and he's being told by his boss to fix it with me. The Skipper wanted me off his back, and the way to do that was to have the fund President expedite a solution for me. Given the circumstances, he did. It didn't take long to put together terms that worked well for my client and me. He then set me up with the CFO to work through the contracts so no hiccups would occur.

I had ignored the hierarchy of authority I was supposed to follow and, in so doing, rearranged the pecking order. I had interrupted the habitual behavioral patterns of both the Skipper and the fund President which put them on unfamiliar ground, putting them a little off-balance, and allowing me to direct the course of action that followed.

I finished up the new headquarters and commodity trading floor for the refiner too. I like Stamford. I've had some okay meals there too. It was summer. But when I took the train back to New York, my mission was to have a meal at the Oyster Bar and Restaurant at Grand Central. It's a classic and well worth my time. Like Sarge's Deli in Murray Hill, worth my time.

22

A SECRET SOCIETY OF KILLERS

AND REDEMPTION

To live a life of fixer philosopher, to live a life full as the poet intended, to create a world to be embraced incessantly, to do this at all is not something that happens by itself. It's a fierce and furious roller-coaster love affair with life.

Here's a hard truth: There is nobility in attempting to stand alone and do something different. But nobody will celebrate you if you lose. The nobility of your attempt will be lost in the shadows. As I said, nature is a harsh meritocracy. Expect nothing less.

What does it mean to be a Hitman? Retired General and former Secretary of Defense, Jim Mattis, once said, "Be polite, be professional, but have a plan to kill everybody you meet." What I do isn't rocket science. I just mete out justice and remind the opposition that there are two sides to every transaction. In this time of wimp negotiators, it seems to have been forgotten. What I do is not barter; it is calculated outcomes achieved. I manage through the chaos while my opponents struggle with uncertainty.

Your life and work are dependent on your presence of mind and ability to maintain calm attentiveness. Maintain your self-possession. Transcend; fly above the conflagration below. You arrive at a place where you know that not only is everything possible, but that it is probable if you choose. But remember a deal is not a deal until it's done. It's also useful to know that a little deal takes as much time and effort as a big deal. So, pick your targets accordingly.

Not everyone considers making money a top priority, and that's okay. There's a lot of good that real negotiating can get done without a big income. Regardless, I always thought that if you can't make a million dollars doing it and make some positive change in the world, why bother?

Primary, secondary, and tertiary markets, I've been to most of them. When I was writing the first draft of the previous Hitman chapter, I started listing the over 300 cities, towns, and trade areas where I'd handled negotiations using Applied Influence, but I realized that wasn't important. That I was always successful is more important, but even that is not the most important takeaway. The most important takeaway is the freedom found when you realize anything is within your reach. I have been rich, and I have been poor. Rich feels better at the moment. But being poor has been the catalyst for new and more profound and lasting growth. Being broke is only temporary. Adversity breeds success. It helps you laser focus on the things you need to focus on to create a killer dominant strategy and then implement it.

So, now, what do you want? What will you do to get it?

There are defining moments in your life -- high-impact moments that change the course of your world. Sometimes you know real-time they're happening, sometimes only in hindsight. The night I made camp on the summit of the mountain after losing the Transit property, looked deep into the universe, and discovered the next morning new principles and truths to live by and inspire me that have lasted to this day. Sitting on the pier in Key West, watching the sun come up, knowing I was going to cut ties with the behemoth and be free to make my own way. Driving forbidden mountain trails during winter storms in the middle of the night and standing alone with nothing but wilderness, snow, and sky around me; wind and ice in my face, acknowledging the loneliness, but looking forward to the future. Learning the power and reach of what can be accomplished with skilled negotiations and the thought experiment that started it all. It became part of my quest. There are defining moments that build your character.

One of the most profound lessons I learned early on was the correlation between risk and achievement, that risk combined with ability led to achievement and rewards. The risk I was willing to take on building my first company led to my first big telco deal. The risk I was willing to take on leaving the behemoth and starting another new company from scratch led to the communication services rollouts. Risk is not without risk, though. You don't always win. My entry into enterprise software was a huge education, but expensive. But there is good in everything. Lasting friendships and partnerships were made then.

You learn the lessons of the past and your mistakes. You build value with that and know you have everything you need to succeed going forward. Everything is perfect. There is good in all things. Your strength, knowledge, and confidence are already present and naturally engage through Applied Influence and the Theory of Everything.

You learn the lessons of Sun Tzu for non-cooperative game dominion, specifically the calm need for cogent understanding and acceptance of the landscape and preparedness without distraction.

I had a class in college called Arguments. At the beginning of the semester, the professor tested all the students using an exam that purported to measure our personal rationality – how rational each one of us was. I thought it was a silly test because, to me, rationale is rational, and the irrational is not. A is A; A is not B. How obvious is that? In any event, when the professor announced the scores, she also announced that I had the highest score in the class, not only of that class, but the highest score she had ever seen. Not believing the first outcome, she had all the students retake the test with different questions -- same result. I guess I won that argument. A is A.

What I've learned since is this: Though logic can build you a path from A to B, imagination and creativity are what opens new worlds for you.

At the beginning of this book, I warned of the information hazard it might contain, the forbidden knowledge some call it. Sure. I hope it works for you. I expect you'll use it wisely and ethically. I expect if you've dabbled with it while reading the book, you've seen what it can do.

I started out as a frightened child, but that was a long time ago. Life is unfair, but I made unfair work for me. I leveraged my adversity into knowledge and skill. And with that, I founded an elite club, one that has no "official" members. But they're all smart -- all killers.

I'm a hitman. I'm an explorer. I'm a lover. I'd like to tell you I'm invincible, but that's not really the case. I'm a bit tired, and though I might have been bloodied a time or two, I've never given up. You can never give up. Never lose sight of your targets. If you experience dark times, and you will, use first principles first: one foot in front of the other, take one more breath, know this too will pass. You'll survive and be better for it. Do you feel a little off, a little disengaged? That prescient friend, Aristotle, said, "There was never a genius without a tincture of madness." Embrace it.

Being hyper-productive makes me feel good. My production means I'm alive. It means I'm on adventure. It's a game, a serious game, and the objective is to see how much fun you can have and how much you can learn. There's no cap on how much fun you can have or how much you can learn, or how much you can earn for that matter. The satisfaction and fun are in the flow of the journey. The melody is in the music, not at the end of the song. Well, in deal-making, it's there too.

Here's the bottom line. Maybe you've been around the block a few times, maybe around the world. Your carry-on luggage is sitting in the middle of the floor in your office half-full of dirty clothes from your last trip, and you're wearing some of the other half. You've got some bucks in the bank and some hard assets in your name that the rest of the world hasn't yet discovered their true value. They will soon. The lemmings will too. Pride is supposed to be the deadliest of the seven deadly sins, but I think that's bullshit. Taking a look at your life and feeling appreciation for what you've done and who you were and have become, is a good thing – it's a blessed fucking good thing.

So, what do you see when you look back? What do you want to see when you look back? That's what you're to build now.

Life is transient, episodic. You move through experiences from one chapter to the next, a series of installments and happenings, all leading to an eventual, inevitable end. Make no mistake about it, the "it" of life is the journey. There is nothing else. When my lifelong friend and accomplice, my brother from a different mother, Don, was dying, I prepared a meal for him, two-inch-thick ribeye cap steaks, salted and seared over an open flame. We ate together under a starry sky high in the Rockies among the aspen trees and the rocks. We told each other stories. We reminisced. We laughed together. Now he's no longer on this earth. Life is the ultimate gift. You can squander it, waste it, dismiss it as your personal pain, or you can cherish every moment and care for it as the most wondrous and perfect thing. So, what are you going to do with yours?

When you can embrace your own life as you would embrace a child you love, nurture it as you would nurture a child you love, forgive yourself for failings as you would forgive a child you love -- accept your life and allow it to unfold and fully express itself; nothing can be kept from you.

Living with supreme autonomy, sovereignty, freedom, and the knowledge that despite your faults and insecurities, you are willing to attempt to overcome any obstacle you choose knowing full well what failure might impose, but accepting that risk and embracing the dangers because to live means to live fully. You will experience failure, and you will feel pain. Like a love lost, some pain is worth it. But some pain is not, and that you need to shirk.

Nature is simple, yet infinitely complex. We make rational decisions based on the information we know, but it is impossible to know all the information that impacts any situation, that millionth butterfly wing. All systems are interconnected, all things are interconnected. Our success is predicated on accommodating the unpredictable, expecting the unexpected, making sense of the chaos. It requires an acceptance of risk of the unknowable and appreciation for the inevitable.

If you've ever jumped out of an airplane, you know what I mean. You may be confident the chute was rigged properly. You saw the plane airborne just a moment before, so that should be okay. You are confident gravity will work consistently as before, and you know what you have to do after you've left the plane and in freefall: checking your altimeter, deploying the chute, steering and landing. Simple. But consider the field of chaos you accept throughout the process, the thousands of parts on the plane, the attitude or mental fitness of the pilot, the components and integrity of your altimeter or the nylon of your chute, or a million other variables, that butterfly you couldn't imagine.

Life is a risk. You could be dead at any moment. Experience all the good you can find now.

I've been a runner much of my life. Races are always fun, and crossing the finish line always feels like an achievement. You get to look forward to the free treats and jerseys and the like for completing the run. 6Ks, half-marathons, and marathons all look about the same at the end of the race. The finish-line areas for marathoners are a little special because 26 miles can be brutal for any runner. The elite runners finish in about two hours. The race sponsors might give out medals to anyone who finishes in less than five hours. I got mine. But give some thought to the marathon runners who finish last. I've written a lot about alpha performance, but challenge your preconceptions for a moment. How was the performance of the runner who took 12 hours, or 18 hours, or more, the runner who left blood and waste and tears on the course but finished the race? Who is the elite human? What is real strength? Who is special, the two-hour runner coming in to cheering crowds, or the one who crossed the finish line alone and in the dark without even a dry bagel to mark the event?

So, what do you want to do? What is important to you? What are you in love with?

The highest values within us seek to manifest in form. Our values define what resonates with us, what and who we're attracted to -- music, art, and another of like mind and heart. This can't be denied. We seek to connect value for value; the higher the values, the stronger the connection. This is the nature of beauty. Our highest values direct our attention, and our intellect and wisdom form our appreciation for music, art, love, and all expressions of nature – for all things beautiful. Our capacity to love and our appreciation of beauty are irrevocably connected. Simplicity, elegance, and substance are things that can't be faked.

The person who seeks the highest and best for oneself also seeks the highest and best in others, and in all things, using the power and ability of their own mind to decide. Beauty is a natural and uninhibited flow of energy in a timeless expression of perfection.

Beauty inspires. It makes one dream of what can be and cultivates a gratitude for what is.

I wouldn't wish my early life on anybody, but I wouldn't change it now. I'm grateful for it because out of that shit, shot green new shoots that blossomed into a good life. Turd blossoms happen, and from that pile of shit came Applied Influence, The Theory of Everything.

I've always believed the power of mind and logic and reason was to be my salvation, the path to my redemption. That set me on a quest of discovery. That has been a journey through the material, metaphysical, mental, and more. How did I get here? This is how.

I've discovered that salvation and redemption weren't missing. They came with the hunt. No kongming lock necessary, already whole and solid. But in my quest, I discovered something more, ecstasy. The ecstasy is in freedom.

So, what are you going to do?

The Zeroth Point Launch

The Zeroth position denotes the zero point at the beginning of a series, sequence, path, direction, or launch. It is more meaningful and important than the first natural number in a series, or any subsequent number, because the subsequent numbers in the series are locked into that series, whereas zero, the zeroth position, has the potential to begin all series, any series. It is the potential of a ray and of rays in all directions. It is the center of a circle, from a two-dimensional perspective. It is the center of a sphere, from a three-dimensional perspective. It is the center of a glome, from a four-dimensional perspective. It is also the center of a hypersphere, from any perspective conceivable. Zero is infinite, pure potential, and that's where we start. And from a quantum field perspective, it's awash in zero-point energy. It's the start of something new.

So, what do you want to do?

Zero is everything, the beginning of your own personal big bang. Quantum mechanics shows us that nothing doesn't exist. There is always an energy that waits for your thoughts to engage it. The rate of expansion of the universe is increasing, that's a macro trend you don't want to short. Go long. Go big. Expanding your life is its natural resonance.

This is the end of the book, but it's really just the beginning. It's the beginning of something new for you.

At this moment, I'm in New York typing these final words to complete this book. I'm contemplating zero, this time the digit "0", and the completeness and infiniteness the character itself displays, the circle that never ends, a Mobius strip with infinite dimensions, nothing and everything at the same time. I close my eyes and take several long, slow breaths. I focus on my breathing and start visualizing the numbers as I count backward from 20; I'm going to zero, 19, 18, 17, I let the tension go. 16, 15 14, I start to feel a part of the singularity as any separateness or boundaries disappear. 13, 12, 11, 10, uncertainty leaves and is replaced with calm and confidence; 9, 8, 7, 6, 5. I can feel happiness and joy rising in me as I become part of the infinite. 4, 3, 2, and as I hit 1, I know I have access to all knowledge and wisdom and everything because it's all a part of me. And then I arrive at 0, the zeroth position, and for what feels like the first time, I feel an explosion of ecstasy, serenity, and unity with the cosmos. It's fascinating, awesome. I'm awed by the pure joy I feel for being alive and for the ones I love, and my enthusiasm for all the new good I will discover and produce in my life moving forward. I feel in perfect resonance with the song of my life, and I have so much gratitude. I'm ready to close this verse. I feel exhilarated. I'm ready to build something new and awesome and great. I'm ready to go exploring again and be challenged. I'm ready for the next big adventure in my life. I'm ready to win again. I stand on the edge of the abyss and I laugh.

THE END

Write me with your stories, questions, or if you want to connect with other killer negotiators: Steve@KillerNegotiator.com and venture into www.KillerNegotiator.com

Made in the USA
Columbia, SC
07 June 2021